THE SUFFERING OF THE AHL-UL-BAYT AND THEIR FOLLOWERS (SHI'A) THROUGHOUT HISTORY

(Illustrated Edition)

Compiled by

Sheikh Mateen J. Charbonneau

First Published in Washington, DC

April 2012

Re-Published

May 2023

© Copyright 2023 Joshua Charbonneau

www.mateenjc.com

Paperback: 407 pages
Publisher: Household Publictions
Date of publication: May 22nd, 2023
Language: English

Email: mateenjc.wordpress@gmail.com

Dua Faraj

O' Allah, bless Muhammad and the family of Muhammad. O' Allah, be for Your representative, the Hujjat (proof), son of Al-Hassan, Your blessings be on him and his forefathers, in this hour and in every hour, a guardian, a protector, a leader, a helper, a proof, and an eye until You make him live on the earth, in obedience (to You), and cause him to live in it for a long time. O' Allah, bless Muhammad and the family of Muhammad.

I dedicate the reward of this book to the leader of the women of the worlds Fatima Zahra (as) daughter of the Holy Prophet Muhammad (s)

About the Author	6
Preface	9
Ali (as) (as) Taken by Force to Pledge Allegiance	15
Fatima's House Set on Fire	15
Martyrdom of Fatima Zahra (as)	15
Bilal's protest and banishment to Syria	77
Ammar Yasir & Abdullah ibn Masud Beaten	89
Abu Dharr's Banishment to Syria	98
Cursing of Imam Ali (as) from the pulpits	157
The Battle of Jamal (The Camel)	167
The Battle of Siffin	184
The Martyrdom of Ammar Yasir	184
The Christian Monk who Testified to the Wilayat of Ali	184
Martyrdom of Malik Al-Ashtar	211
The Martyrdom of Mohammad ibn Abu Bakr	217
Assassination of Imam 'Ali (as) in Salat	220
Crucifixion of Maytham At-Tammar	230
Martyrdom of Hujr ibn Adi, His Son and Companions	242
Martyrdom of Qambar the servant of Ali	250
Martyrdom of Amr bin Humaq	252
Mass Murder & Torturing the Shia of Ali	260
Martyrdom of Imam Hassan (as) & His Burial Met with Arrows	272
Martyrdom of Zaid ibn Ali and His Son Yahya ibn Zaid	277

Martyrdom of Muslim ibn Aqil, His Sons and Hanee ibn Orwah 280

Tragedy of Karbala.. 299
    Hurr ibn Yazid ar -Riyahi 304
    Wahab ibn Abudullah Qalbi 309
    John bin Huwai the Freed Servant of Abu Dharr 313
    Habib ibn Mazaahir 315
    Ali Akbar 319
    The Youths of Karbala Qasim, Aun and Muhammad 328
    Abu Fadl Abbas ibn Ali 345
    The 6 month old Infant Son of Hussain (as), Ali Asghar 353
    Imam Hussain (as) 357

The Fate of the Women of Ahl ul Bayt after Karbala 364

Benefits of Ziyarat Imam Hussain (as) 389

Miscellaneous 404
    The Imprisonment of the Man from Damascus & Miracle of Imam Jawad 404
    The Murder of Nisa'i the Famous Sunni Author of one the Sahih Sitta 406

About the Author

Joshua Adam Charbonneau is an American Muslim. He was born in 1982 in Sumter, South Carolina. He is of French Canadian and American descent. He was born into a Christian family, and later chose to revert to Shi'a Islam at the age of 17, having studied both faiths. After reverting to Islam he chose the name Mateen which in Arabic means strong, firm and unshakable. His first language is English and he also learned Quranic Arabic. In 2008 at age 26 he moved to Washington, DC area and has been an active part of the Muslim community. In 2022 he moved to Turkey and is leading an English speaking community. Other activities include majalis, jumah services, weekly youth and adult classes in various communities throughout the United States (virtually) and Turkey.

- Converted to Shia Islam on July 2nd 1999 at the age of 17
- Learned Quranic Arabic in the year 2000
- Independently studied Islamic books full time from the year 1999-2007
- Filmed a documentary for al-Anwar Hussain TV entitled The Journey of the Spirit in 2011
- Started studying Islamic Seminary classes (Howza) in March 2013 at Imam Ali Center in Springfield, Virginia and also studied abroad in Najaf al-Ashraf and Karbala. He currently is continuing higher studies. His teachers include Sheikh Mustafa Akhound, Sheikh Mirza Abbas Shamsudin, Sheikh Saed Ali Kulayni, Sheikh Muhammad BagherNejad, Sayed Ibn Abbas Naqvi, Sheikh Mohammad Jafar Danesh, Sayed Baqir Imrani, Sayed Raad al-Alawi, Sayed Muhammad Baqir Shirazi, Sayed Muhammad Baqir Qazwini, Sayed Murtadha Modarresi, Sayed Mohsen Modarresi, Sayed Sajjad Modarresi, Sheikh Abul Hassan Yemaani, Sheikh Haani al-Hakim and Sayyid Anvar Sajadi.

- Authored several books entitled; The Suffering of the Ahl ul Bayt and their Followers (Shia) throughout History, Christians who defended and died for Prophet Muhammad and his Family (English, Spanish, French), Mystery of the Shia, A Study Guide for Logic, an extensive book of narrations entitled Prophetic Gems, A Commentary to the Faith of Shia Islam (Aqaed Imamiyya) of Allama Muzaffar, Recalling the Sacrifices of Karbala, Esteemed Women of Islam and 450 Questions and Answers About Shia Islam Answered.

- Founded a nonprofit organization to send free books to prisoners in March 2014 entitled; 2nd Chance Books has sent 23,000 Shia books inside the prisons throughout the country and has over 3,000 American Shia converts participating.

- Filmed a documentary for Ahlulbayt TV entitled Faith Behind Bars

- Achieved a certificate from Harvard University in Islamic Studies

- Had articles about my life published in magazines in America, Iran, China and Azerbaijan

- Was crowned with the turban from the hand of Sheikh Ahmad al-Haeri on the martyrdom of Muslim ibn Aqil (ra) / Day of Arafat in 2016

- Filmed an Autism Awareness workshop for Muslim communities

- 2017 started teaching online classes for Imam Sadiq Howza

- Was crowned with the turban from the respected and honorable marja' Ayatollah Sayed Muhammad Taqi Modaressi on the 3rd of Shabaan / the birth anniversary of Imam Sajjad (as) in the Holy city of Karbala, Iraq 2018

- Was certified at the 17th annual conference of Shia scholars of N. America and Canada for Mediation training by the Northern Virginia Mediation Service (NVMS)
- 2019 Faculty Member of John the Martyr Seminary of Karbala

Being crowned with the turban from the respected and honorable marja' Ayatollah Sayed Muhammad Taqi Modaressi on the 3rd of Shabaan / the birth anniversary of Imam Sajjad (as) in the Holy city of Karbala, Iraq.

Preface

In the name of Allah the Most Gracious the Most Merciful, may Allah shower His blessings on our beloved Prophet Muhammad (s) and his Purified Household. May Allah open our eyes and bestow on us the baseera (insight) to see the truth and an open heart to accept it. May Allah hasten the reappearance of our awaited savior, Imam Mahdi and allow us to be among his humble devoted followers. May we see the time when he will make apparent to everyone the true teachings of Islam as they were taught by his grandfather the Prophet of Allah (s) and not the Islam that was changed by the corrupt rulers and dictators to fit their desires. May Allah continue to bless Muhammad and the family of Muhammad (as) and may He remove His Mercy from those who bear enmity towards them.

إِنَّ الَّذِينَ فَتَنُوا الْمُؤْمِنِينَ وَالْمُؤْمِنَاتِ ثُمَّ لَمْ يَتُوبُوا فَلَهُمْ عَذَابُ جَهَنَّمَ وَلَهُمْ عَذَابُ الْحَرِيقِ

"Surely those who tormented the believing men and the believing women and then did not repent, theirs shall be the punishment of Hell, and theirs shall be the burning punishment."[1]

Imam Baqir (as) said *"Since the death of the Holy Prophet we Ahl ul bayt have been humiliated, made distant and have been deprived and killed and made to leave our home town and we felt frightened for our blood and the blood of our followers. The cheaters, through their lies, got nearer to the leaders, judges and governors in every city and our enemies told false and invalid traditions relating to their past leaders and quoted riwayah (narrations) that we had never told. They only wanted to humiliate us and wanted to accuse us of falsehood and wanted to get nearer to their leaders through lies. After the passing away of Hassan this became very common during the*

---
[1] Quran 85:10

time of Mu'awiya. At that time, in every city, Shias were killed, their hands and feet were cut off and they were hanged on accusations of their being near to us and talking about their love for us. Then after that adversities increased in numbers and strength, from the martyrdom of Hussain (as) until the time of ibn Ziyad. Then came Hajjaj and he killed them (Shia of Ali) for every doubt and accusation until it was said that this person (Shia) was Zindiq (atheist) and majusi (Zoroastrian) and Hajjaj liked it better that these words be used rather than say that they were Shia of Hussain, peace be upon him."[2]

نَتْلُوا۟ عَلَيْكَ مِن نَّبَإِ مُوسَىٰ وَفِرْعَوْنَ بِٱلْحَقِّ لِقَوْمٍ يُؤْمِنُونَ (٣) إِنَّ فِرْعَوْنَ عَلَا فِى ٱلْأَرْضِ وَجَعَلَ أَهْلَهَا شِيَعًا يَسْتَضْعِفُ طَآئِفَةً مِّنْهُمْ يُذَبِّحُ أَبْنَآءَهُمْ وَيَسْتَحْىِۦ نِسَآءَهُمْ إِنَّهُۥ كَانَ مِنَ ٱلْمُفْسِدِينَ (٤) وَنُرِيدُ أَن نَّمُنَّ عَلَى ٱلَّذِينَ ٱسْتُضْعِفُوا۟ فِى ٱلْأَرْضِ وَنَجْعَلَهُمْ أَئِمَّةً وَنَجْعَلَهُمُ ٱلْوَٰرِثِينَ (٥) وَنُمَكِّنَ لَهُمْ فِى ٱلْأَرْضِ وَنُرِىَ فِرْعَوْنَ وَهَٰمَٰنَ وَجُنُودَهُمَا مِنْهُم مَّا كَانُوا۟ يَحْذَرُونَ (٦)

"Lo! Pharaoh exalted himself in the earth and made its people castes. A tribe among them he oppressed, killing their sons and sparing their women. Lo! he was of those who work corruption. And We desired to show favour unto those who were oppressed in the earth, and to make them examples and to make them the inheritors, And to establish them in the earth, and to show Pharaoh and Haman and their hosts that which they feared from them."[3]

The oppressors you will read about in this book are even worse than Pharoah. I say this because even Pharoah had enough compassion to spare the women from among Musa's (as) followers but look and see how these oppressors treated Lady

---

[2] Kitab e Sulaym Ibn Qays Al-Hilali

[3] Quran 28:3-5

Fatima (as) the daughter of our beloved Prophet (s)!

يُرِيدُونَ لِيُطْفِـُٔوا۟ نُورَ ٱللَّهِ بِأَفْوَٰهِهِمْ وَٱللَّهُ مُتِمُّ نُورِهِۦ وَلَوْ كَرِهَ ٱلْكَٰفِرُونَ (٨)

"Intend they to put out the light of Allah with their mouths, but Allah will perfect his light though averse may be the disbelievers!"[4]

وَعَدَ ٱللَّهُ ٱلَّذِينَ ءَامَنُوا۟ مِنكُمْ وَعَمِلُوا۟ ٱلصَّٰلِحَٰتِ لَيَسْتَخْلِفَنَّهُمْ فِى ٱلْأَرْضِ كَمَا ٱسْتَخْلَفَ ٱلَّذِينَ مِن قَبْلِهِمْ وَلَيُمَكِّنَنَّ لَهُمْ دِينَهُمُ ٱلَّذِى ٱرْتَضَىٰ لَهُمْ وَلَيُبَدِّلَنَّهُم مِّنۢ بَعْدِ خَوْفِهِمْ أَمْنٗا يَعْبُدُونَنِى لَا يُشْرِكُونَ بِى شَيْـٔٗا وَمَن كَفَرَ بَعْدَ ذَٰلِكَ فَأُو۟لَٰٓئِكَ هُمُ ٱلْفَٰسِقُونَ (٥٥)

"Allah has promised, to those among you who believe and work righteous deeds, that He will, of a surety, grant them in the land, inheritance (of power), as He granted it to those before them; that He will establish in authority their religion - the one which He has chosen for them; and that He will change (their state), after the fear in which they (lived), to one of security and peace: 'They will worship Me (alone) and not associate aught with Me.'If any do reject Faith after this, they are rebellious and wicked."[5]

Then I was guided, author Muhammad al-Tijani al-Samawi writes of his discovery to the true path of Islam, that of adhering to the teachings of the Ahlulbayt. In his book he describes what the scholar As-Sayyid As-Sadr relates to him: "As-Sayyid As-Sadr said: It is inevitable that we pass through difficult times because the path of Ahl al-Bayt is a difficult one. A man once came to see the Prophet (s) and said to him, "O Messenger of Allah, I love you." He replied, "Then expect many tribulations." The man said, "I love your cousin Ali." He replied, "Then expect many enemies." The man said, "I love al-Hassan and al-Hussain." He replied, "Then get ready for poverty and

---

[4] Quran 61:8

[5] Quran 24:55

much affliction." What have we paid for the cause of justice for which Aba Abdillah al-Hussain (as) paid his life and the lives of his family's members and companions; and for which the Shi'a along the path of history have paid and are still paying up to the present day as a price for their allegiance to Ahl al-Bayt? My Brother, it is inevitable that we go through difficulties and give sacrifices for the cause of justice, and if Allah helped you in guiding one man to the right path, it is worth the whole world and what is within it."

Al-Tijani continues, "As-Sayyid as-Sadr also advised me against isolating ourselves and ordered me to get even closer to my Sunni brothers whenever they wanted to keep away from me, and to consider them innocent victims of distorted history and bad propaganda, because people are the enemy of what they do not know."[6]

This does not mean agree with their teachings, but rather not to shun them when they come to us. If we reject them when they come to us, make fun of them or are rude with them then how will they ever come towards Ahlul Bayt?

ٱدْعُ إِلَىٰ سَبِيلِ رَبِّكَ بِٱلْحِكْمَةِ وَٱلْمَوْعِظَةِ ٱلْحَسَنَةِۖ وَجَٰدِلْهُم بِٱلَّتِى هِىَ أَحْسَنُۚ إِنَّ رَبَّكَ هُوَ أَعْلَمُ بِمَن ضَلَّ عَن سَبِيلِهِۦۖ وَهُوَ أَعْلَمُ بِٱلْمُهْتَدِينَ (١٢٥)

"Invite to the way of thy Lord with wisdom and beautiful preaching; and argue with them in ways that are best and most gracious: for thy Lord knows, best who have strayed from His Path, and who receive guidance." [7]

Many Muslims have never even heard of the events that took place against the Ahlul Bayt. They were taught all their lives one way and that is all they have seen and the only way that

---

[6] Then I was guided by Dr. Muhammad Tijani

[7] Quran 16:125

they know. This book is written to teach the dear brothers and sisters what actually took place after the martyrdom of our Prophet. We cannot hold them accountable until we know that they are aware and then having known choose to reject Ahlul Bayt (as). Even the idol worshippers were given a chance to hear the truth and submit so why not give this chance to our fellow Muslim's?

وَإِنْ أَحَدٌ مِّنَ ٱلْمُشْرِكِينَ ٱسْتَجَارَكَ فَأَجِرْهُ حَتَّىٰ يَسْمَعَ كَلَٰمَ ٱللَّهِ ثُمَّ أَبْلِغْهُ مَأْمَنَهُۥ ذَٰلِكَ بِأَنَّهُمْ قَوْمٌ لَّا يَعْلَمُونَ (٦)

"And if anyone of the idolaters seeketh thy protection (O Muhammad), then protect him so that he may hear the Word of Allah, and afterward convey him to his place of safety. That is because they are a people who know not." [8]

I found that when researching what happened to the Ahl ul Bayt (as) and their followers that the accounts were spread throughout multiple books and not all present in one place, so I thought that it would be good to compile all these accounts into one place to make it easy on the reader. In this humble attempt I have compiled several excerpts about the life and struggles of the Ahl ul bayt (family of Muhammad) and their Shia (followers), and to inform the people about the oppressive events and incidents were inflicted upon the Ahl ul Bayt (family of Muhammad) and their Shia (followers). I have included all of the books that I referenced for this project so that you may study them and come to your own conclusion. I hope that you, my dear brother or sister, benefit from this work and that you grow closer to Allah, our beloved Prophet (s) and his Ahl ul Bayt (as), inshallah (God willing).

Mateen J. Charbonneau

---

[8] Quran 9:6

Note: The spellings of the names may differ, but that is because I kept the original spellings found in their respective sources.

The use of (s) after the Prophet's name is an abbreviation for peace be upon him and his family. The use of (as) after the names of Fatima (as) and the 12 Imams (as) is an abbreviation for peace be upon him/her in Arabic; Alayhi Salam. The use of (ATF) after the name of Imam Mahdi (ATF) is an abbreviation for may Allah hasten his reappearance. The use of (RA) is an abbreviation for May Allah be pleased with him/ her in Arabic; Radi-Allahu Anhu.

Imam Sadiq (as) said:

"Write and spread your knowledge among your brothers. If the end of your life approaches, leave your books as an inheritance for your sons, since there will come a time of sedition during which the people will only find comfort with their books.[9]

---

[9] Mishkat ul Anwar by Al Tabarsi Hadith#736

Ali (as) (as) Taken by Force to Pledge Allegiance

Fatima's House Set on Fire

Martyrdom of Fatima Zahra (as)

There are many hadith making it imperative on the umma to follow Ali. One of them is narrated by Ammar Yasir, which the ulema have recorded in their books[10]. They narrate a lengthy,

---

[10] Hafiz Abi Nu'aim Ispahani in Hilya; Muhammad Bin Talha Shafi'i in Matalibu's-Su'ul; Baladhuri in Ta'rikh; Sheikh Sulayman Balkhi Hanafi in Yanabiu'l-Mawadda, Chapter 43, from Hamwaini; Mir Seyyed Ali Hamadani Shafi'i in Mawaddatu'l-Qurba, Mawadda V; Dailami in Firdaus

detailed hadith that cannot be related here in full. It may be stated briefly that when people asked Abu Ayyub why he had gone to Ali (as) and had not sworn allegiance to Abu Bakr, he replied that one day he was sitting with the Prophet when Ammar Yasir came in and asked the Prophet (s) a question. In the course of his conversation, the Prophet said: *"O Ammar! If all the people go one way and Ali alone goes the other way, you should follow Ali. O Ammar! Ali will not allow you to diverge from the path of guidance and will not lead you to destruction, O Ammar! Obedience to Ali is obedience to me, and obedience to me is obedience to Allah."*

In light of these injunctions, and in light of Ali's opposition to Abu Bakr, shouldn't people have followed Ali (as)? Even if the Bani Hashim, Bani Umayya, distinguished companions, the intelligent ones of the nation, the Muhajirs, and Ansars had not been with him (and they were with him), people should have followed Ali. Yet after the martyrdom of the Prophet, we find that the people did quite the opposite!

Ali (as) and the Bani Hashim did not take the oath of allegiance immediately. Sunni historians have written that Ali (as) offered his allegiance after the demise of Fatima (as). It is reported by them[11] that Ali (as) offered his allegiance after Fatima's death. Some of the Sunni ulema believe that Fatima (as) died 75 days after the Prophet's death. Ibn Qutayba also holds the same view, but most of the historians claim that she died six months after the Prophet died.

It follows, therefore, that Ali's allegiance came sometime after 3 to 6 months of the Prophet's death. Mas'udi in his *Muruju's-sahab*, Volume I, page 414, says *"None of the Bani Hashim swore their allegiance to Abu Bakr until the death of Bibi Fatima."*

---

[11] Bukhari in his Sahih, Volume III, Chapter of Ghazawa Khaibar, page 37, and Muslim Bin Hujjaj, in his Sahih, Volume V, page 154,

Ibrahim Bin Sa'd Saqafi narrates from Zuhri that Ali (as) did not pay allegiance until six months after the Prophet's death, and the people did not have the courage to pressure him except after the death of Bibi Fatima (as). Ibn Abi'l-Hadid in *Sharhe Nahju'l-Balagha* relates the same fact.

In any case, the Sunni ulema insist that Ali's allegiance was not immediate but came only after some time had passed and then only when circumstances forced him to do so (which is not a true or valid allegiance).

'Aisha said: *"Ali did not offer allegiance to Abu Bakr for six months, and no one of the Bani Hashim offered allegiance until Ali did."*[12]

Zuhri said: *"Ali did not swear allegiance until six months after the Prophet's death."*[13]

Here are twelve proofs that Ali's allegiance was taken not willingly but forced.

(1) Abu Ja'far Baladhuri Ahmad Bin Yahya Bin Jabir Baghdadi, one of the reliable Sunni traditionists and historians, writes in his History that when Abu Bakr called Ali (as) to swear allegiance, Ali (as) refused. Abu Bakr sent Umar who went with a torch to set fire to Ali's house. Fatima (as) came to the door and said: *"O son of Khattab! Have you come to set my house on fire?"* He said: *"Yes, this is more effective than anything your father did."*

(2) Izzu'd-Din Ibn Abi'l-Hadid Mu'tazali, and Muhammad Bin Jarir Tabari, narrate that Umar went to the door of Ali's house with Usayd Bin Khuza'i, Salama Bin Aslam and a group of men. Umar then called out, *"Come out! Or else I'll set your house on*

---

[12] Ibn Abi'l-Hadid, in his Sharhe Nahju'l-Balagha, Volume II, page 18, narrates from Zuhri

[13] Ahmad Bin A'sam-e-Kufi Shafi'i in Futuh, and Abu Nasr Hamidi, in Jam'a Bainu's-Sahihain report from Nafiy, quoting from Zuhri

fire!"

(3) Ibn Khaziba reports in his *Kitab-e-Gharrar* from Zaid Bin Aslam, who said: *"I was one of those who went with Umar with torches to Fatima's door. When Ali and his men refused to offer allegiance, Umar said to Fatima, "Let whoever is inside come out. Otherwise, I will set the house on fire along with whoever is inside." Ali, Hassan, Hussain, Fatima, and a party of the Prophet's companions, and the Bani Hashim were inside. Fatima said: "Would you set my house on fire along with me and my sons?" He said: "Yes, by Allah, if they do not come out and pay allegiance to the caliph of the Prophet."*

(4) Ibn Abd Rabbih, one of the famous Sunni ulema, writes in his *Iqdu'l-Farid, Part III, page 63*, that Ali (as) and Abbas were sitting in Fatima's house. Abu Bakr told Umar: *"Go and bring these people. If they refuse to come, fight them." So, Umar came to Fatima's house with torches. Fatima came to the door of the house and said: "Have you come to burn our house?" He said: "Yes..." and so on.*

(5) Ibn Abi'l-Hadid Mu'tazali in his *Shahre Nahju'l-Balagha*, Volume I, page 134, quoting from Jauhari's *Kitab-e-Saqifa*, writes in detail about the affair of the Saqifa-e-Bani Sa'ad:

"The Bani Hashim and Ali were assembled in Ali's house. Zubair was also with them since he considered himself one of the Bani Hashim. Ali used to say, 'Zubair was always with us until his sons were grown up. They turned him against us.' Umar went to Fatima's house with a group of men. Usayd and Salma were also with him. Umar asked them to come out and swear allegiance. They refused. Zubair drew his sword and came out. Umar said: 'Get hold of this dog.' Salma Bin Aslam snatched the sword and threw it against the wall. Then they dragged Ali to Abu Bakr. Other Bani Hashim also followed him and were waiting to see what Ali would do. Ali was saying that he was the servant of Allah and the brother of the Holy Prophet. Nobody listened to him. They took him to Abu Bakr, who asked him to take the oath

of allegiance to him. Ali said: "I am the most deserving person for this position, and I will not pay allegiance to you. It is incumbent on you to pay allegiance to me. You took this right from the Ansar based on your relationship with the Prophet. I also, on the same ground, protest against you. So be just. If you fear Allah, accept my right, as the Ansar did yours. Otherwise, you should acknowledge that you are intentionally oppressing me.' Umar said: 'We will not leave you until you swear allegiance.' Ali said: 'You have conspired well together. Today you support him, so that tomorrow he may return the caliphate to you. I swear by Allah that I will not comply with your request and will not take the oath of allegiance (to Abu Bakr). He should pay allegiance to me.' Then he turned his face toward the people and said: 'O Muhajirs! Fear Allah. Do not take away the right of authority of Muhammad's family. That right has been ordained by Allah. Do not remove the rightful person from his place. By Allah, we Ahl ul Bayt have greater authority in this matter than you have. There is a man among you who has the knowledge of the Book of Allah (The Qur'an), the Sunna of the Prophet, and the laws of our Religion. I swear by Allah that we possess all these things. So do not follow yourselves lest you should stray from the truth.'" Ali returned home without offering allegiance and secluded himself in his house until Fatima died. Thereafter, he was forced to offer allegiance.

(6) Abu Muhammad Abdullah Bin Muslim Bin Qutayba Bin Umar Al-Bahili Dinawari, who was an ulema and an official Qazi of the city of Dinawar, writes in his famous *Ta'rikhu'l-Khulafate Raghibin wa Daulate Bani Umayya*, known as *Al-Imama wa's-Siyasa*, Volume I, page 13:

"When Abu Bakr learned that a group hostile to him had assembled in Ali's house, he sent Umar to them. When Umar shouted to Ali to come out and to swear allegiance to Abu Bakr, they all refused to come out. Umar collected wood and said 'I swear by Allah, Who has my life in His control, either you will come out, or I will set the house with all those in it on fire.' People said: 'O Abu Hafsa! Fatima is also present in the house.'

He said: 'Let her be there. I will set fire to the house.' So all of them came out and offered allegiance, except Ali, who said: 'I have taken a vow that until I have compiled the Qur'an, I will neither go out of the house nor will I put on full dress.' Umar did not accept this, but the plaintive lamentation of Fatima and the snubbing by others, forced him to go back to Abu Bakr. Umar urged him to force Ali to swear allegiance. Abu Bakr sent Qanfaz several times to summon Ali, but he was always disappointed. At last Umar, with a group of people went to the door of Fatima's house. When Fatima heard their voices, she cried out 'O my father, Prophet of Allah (s)! What tortures we are subjected to by the son of Khattab and the son of Abi Quhafa!' When the people heard Fatima's lamentation, some went back with their hearts broken, but Umar remained there with some others until finally they dragged Ali from the house. They took Ali to Abu Bakr, and told him to swear allegiance to him. Ali said: 'If I do not swear allegiance what will you do to me?' They said: 'We swear by Allah that we will break your neck.' Ali said: 'Will you kill the servant of Allah and the brother of His Prophet?' Umar said: 'You are not the brother of the Prophet of Allah (s).' While all this was going on, Abu Bakr kept silent. Umar then asked Abu Bakr whether he (Umar) was not following Abu Bakr's orders in this matter. Abu Bakr said that so long as Fatima was alive he would not force Ali to swear allegiance to him. Ali then managed to reach the grave of the Prophet, where, wailing and crying, he told the Prophet what Aaron had told his brother, Moses, as recorded in the Holy Qur'an: 'Son of my mother! Surely the people reckoned me weak and had well nigh slain me.' (7:150)

After narrating this affair in detail, Abu Muhammad Abdullah Bin Qutayba says that Ali did not swear allegiance and returned home. Later Abu Bakr and Umar went to Fatima's house to placate her and to seek her pardon. She said: "Allah be my witness that you two have offended me. In every prayer I curse you and will continue cursing you until I see my father and complain against you."

(7) Ahmad Bin Abdu'l-Aziz is an ulema. Ibn Abi'l-Hadid writes

about him in the following words: *"He was a man of learning, a traditionist, a great literary figure."* He writes in his *Kitab-e-Saqifa* and Ibn Abi'l-Hadid Mu'tazali also quotes from him in his *Sharhe Nahju'l-Balagha*, Volume I, page 9, on the authority of Abi'l-Aswad, who said:

"A group of the companions and prominent Muhajirin expressed their indignation at Abu Bakr's caliphate and asked why they were not consulted. Also, Ali and Zubair expressed their anger, refused to swear allegiance, and retired to Fatima's house. Fatima cried aloud and made solemn entreaties, but to no effect. They took away Ali's and Zubair's swords and hurled them against the wall, breaking them. Then they dragged them to the mosque to force them to swear allegiance."

(8) Jauhari reports from Salma Bin Abdu'r-Rahman that when Abu Bakr heard that Ali, Zubair, and a party of the Bani Hashim were assembled in Fatima's house, he sent Umar for them. Umar went to the door of Fatima's house and shouted, *"Come out, otherwise, I swear I will set your house on fire!"*

(9) Jauhari, according to Ibn Abi'l-Hadid in his *Sharhe Nahju'l-Balagha*, Volume II, page 19, narrates on the authority of Sha'bi:

"When Abu Bakr heard about the gathering of the Bani Hashim in Ali's house, he said to Umar: 'Both you and Khalid go and bring Ali and Zubair to me so that they can take the oath of allegiance.' So Umar entered Fatima's house and Khalid stayed outside. Umar said to Zubair 'What is this sword?' He replied, 'I have acquired it for allegiance to Ali.'

Omar snatched the sword and hurled it at the stone inside the house and broke it. Then he brought him out to Khalid. He came back into the house, where there were many people, including Miqdad, and all the Bani Hashim. Addressing Ali, he said: 'Get up! I'm taking you to Abu Bakr. You must pay allegiance to him.'

Ali refused. Umar dragged him to Khalid. Khalid and Umar forced him along the road which was packed to capacity with men who witnessed this scene. When Fatima saw Umar's behavior, she, along with many women of the Bani Hashim (who had come to console her), came out. They were lamenting and wailing with high-pitched cries. Fatima went to the mosque where she said to Abu Bakr: 'How soon have you sacked the Ahl ul Bayt of the Prophet of Allah (s). I swear by Allah, I will not talk with Umar until I see Allah.' Fatima showed her extreme disapproval of Abu Bakr and did not speak to him for the rest of her life."[14]

(10) Abu Walid Muhibu'd-Din Muhammad Bin Muhammad Bin Ash-Shahna Al-Hanafi (died 815 A.H.), one of the leading Sunni ulema writes in his *Rauzatu'l-Manazir Fi Khabaru'l-Awa'il wa'l-Awakhir*, in connection with the Saqifa affair: "Umar came to Ali's house prepared to set it on fire with all its inmates. Umar said: 'Enter into what the community has entered.'"

(11) Tabari, in his *Ta'rikh* Volume II, page 443, reports from Ziyad Bin Kalbi that: "Talha, Zubair, and some of the Muhajirin were at Ali's house. Umar Bin Khattab went there and demanded that they come out. If they did not, he said, he would set the house on fire."

(12) Ibn Shahna, in *Hashiyya-e-Kamil* of Ibn Athir, Volume XI, page 112, writes in connection with the Saqifa that: "Some of the Prophet's companions, and the Bani Hashim, Zubair, Atba Bin Abi Lahab, Khalid Bin Sa'id Bin As, Miqdad Bin Aswad Kindi, Salman Farsi, Abu Dharr Ghifari, Ammar Bin Yasir, Bara'a Bin Azib, and Ubai Bin Ka'b refused to swear allegiance to Abu Bakr. They assembled in Ali's house. Umar Bin Khattab went there intending to burn down the house. Fatima protested to him. Umar said: 'Enter where all others have entered.'"

Kitab-e-Isbatu'l-Wasiyya, compiled by Abi'l-Hassan Ali Bin Hussain Mas'udi, author of *Muruju'dh-Dhahab*. He wrote in great detail about the events of that day: "They surrounded Ali

---

[14] See Sahih Bukhari, Part V and VII

and burned the door of his house. They dragged him out of the house and pressed the best of the women, Fatima, between the door and the wall so forcefully that Muhsin, her unborn son, died of miscarriage."

The Shias have not concocted these things. What occurred has been preserved in the pages of history. The miscarriage is a fact.

You may also refer to *Sharhe Nahju'l-Balagha*, Volume III, page 351. Ibn Abi'l-Hadid wrote that he told his teacher, Abu Ja'far Naqib, that when the Prophet was told that Hubbar Bin Aswad had attacked his daughter Zainab's litter with a lance, because of which Zainab (as) suffered a miscarriage, the Prophet allowed him to be put to death.

Abu Ja'far said: *'Had the Prophet of Allah (s) been alive, he would have surely ordered the death penalty for him also who had frightened Fatima (as) so much that her child, Muhsin, died in miscarriage.'*

Two well known Sunni scholars, Bukhari and Muslim, write in their *Sahih* that Fatima (as) rejected Abu Bakr because she was angry. Because of her displeasure she did not talk to him for the rest of her life. When she died due to her injuries, her husband, Ali, buried her at night. He did not allow Abu Bakr to join her funeral and offer prayers for her.

Muhammad Bin Yusuf Ganji Shafi'i has recorded the same report in his *Kifaya*, ch.99. Also, Abu Muhammad Abdullah Bin Muslim Bin Qutayba Dinawari in his *Imama wa's-Siyasa*, p.14, writes that Fatima (as), while sick in bed, said to Abu Bakr and Umar: *"Let Allah and the angels be my witnesses that both of you have made me indignant. When I meet the Holy Prophet, I will certainly complain against you."* The same book also records: *"Fatima was indignant with Abu Bakr and refused to see him for the rest of her life."*

There is a well known hadith narrated by many Sunni

ulema[15] that the Holy Prophet of Allah (s) repeatedly said: *"Fatima is a part of my body, she is the light of my eyes, she is the fruit of my heart, she is my soul between my two sides. He who grieves Fatima grieves me; he who grieves me, grieves Allah; he who makes her angry, makes me angry; what pains Fatima pains me."*

Ibn Hajar Asqalani, in his *al-Isaba fi tamyiz as-Sahaba*, quotes from the *Sahih* of Bukhari and Muslim that the Holy Prophet of Allah (s) said: *"Fatima is a part of my body; what pains her, pains me; that which exalts her spiritual attainment exalts my spiritual attainment."*

It is reported[16] that the Holy Prophet said: *"Verily, Fatima, my daughter, is a part of my body; what makes her happy, makes me happy; what is painful to her is painful to me."*

Abu'l-Qasim Hussain Bin Muhammad (Raghib Ispahani) narrates in his *Mahadhiratu'l-Ubada*, vol.II, p. 204, that the Holy Prophet of Allah (s) said: *"Fatima is a part of my body; hence, he who enrages her, enrages me."*

The ulema[17] have reported that the Holy Prophet said to his daughter: *"O Fatima, verily, if you are angry, Allah is also angry; if you are happy, Allah is also happy."*

---

[15] like Imam Ahmad Bin Hanbal in Musnad; Sulayman Qanduzi in Yanabiu'l-Mawadda; Mir Seyyed Ali Hamadani in Mawaddatu'l-Qurba; Ibn Hajar in Sawa'iq, reporting from Tirmidhi, Hakim and others, with a slight difference in wording

[16] Muhammad Bin Talha Shafi'i in his Matalibu's-Su'ul; Hafiz Abu Nu'aim Ispahani in Hilyatu'l-Auliya, vol. II, p.40, and Imam Abdu'r-Rahman Nisa'i in his Khasa'isu'l-Alawi,

[17] Hafiz Abu Musa Bin Muthanna Basri (died 252 A.H.) in his Mu'ajam; Ibn Hajar Asqalani in Isaba, vol.IV, p.35; Abu Ya'la Musili in his Sunan; Tibrani in Mu'ajam; Hakim Nishapuri in Mustadrak, vol.VII, p. 154; Hafiz Abu Nu'aim Ispahani in Faza'ilu's-Sahaba; Hafiz Ibn Asakir in Ta'rikh-e-Shami; Sibt Ibn Jauzi in Tadhkira, p. 175; Muhibu'd-din Tabari in Dhakha'ir, p. 39, Ibn Hajar Makki in Sawa'iq, p. 105 and Abu Irfanu's-Subban in As'afu'r-Raghibin, p.171,

It is quoted[18] that the Holy Prophet said: *"Fatima is a part of my body, so whoever enrages Fatima, verily, enrages me."*

There are many such hadith recorded in Sunni authentic books, like *Sahih* of Bukhari; *Sahih* of Muslim; *Sunan* of Abu Dawud; Tirmidhi; *Musnad* of Imam Hanbal; *Sawa'iq-e-Ibn Hajar*; and Sheikh Sulayman Balkhi's *Yanabiu'l-Mawadda*.

These are but a sample of the many historical facts recorded by Sunni historians. This affair was so commonly known that the poets of old mentioned it. One of the Sunni poets, Hafiz Ibrahim of Egypt, says in a poem in praise of Umar: *"No other person but Abu Hafsa (father of Umar) could have the courage of addressing the chief of the Adnan Clan (Ali) and his comrades, saying: 'If you fail to pay allegiance, I will set your house on fire and will not leave any inmate of the house alive, even Fatima herself.'"*

First, the Prophets and their successors acted according to the will of Allah Almighty. Accordingly, we cannot raise any objection as to why they did not wage war, or why they adopted silence before the enemy, or why they suffered defeat.

If you study the historical facts regarding the lives of the Holy Prophets and their successors, you will find many similar instances of acquiescence. The Holy Qur'an has narrated some of those events. In the surah of *Qamar* (The Moon), the Holy Qur'an relates what the Prophet Noah said when his people rejected him: *"Verily, I am overcome (by these people), so give help." (54:11)*

In the sura of *Maryam*, the Qur'an tells us of the silence of Abraham when he sought his uncle Azar's help and received a disappointing reply: *"And I will withdraw from you and what you*

---

[18] Muhammad Bin Isma'il Bukhari in his Sahih, in the chapter Manaqib Qarabat-e-Rasulullah, p.71, quotes from Miswar Bin Makhrama

call upon besides Allah, and I will call upon my Lord." (19:48)

So, just as Abraham withdrew from the people when he did not receive support from his uncle Azar, Ali (as) also must have withdrawn from the people and gone into seclusion.

If you study the commentaries of both sects, you will find that his withdrawal from people was physical, not merely psychological. I recall that Imam Fakhru'd-din Razi says in his *Tafsir-e-Kabir*, vol.V, p.809: *"Isolation from something means keeping aloof from it. What Abraham meant was that he wanted to keep aloof from them, both from the physical and religious point of view."*

The chronicles report that after this rejection Abraham migrated from Babylon to Kuhistan in Fars and lived a solitary life in those mountainous surroundings for seven years. He then returned to Babylon and again publicly proclaimed Allah's message and broke the people's idols. At this the people flung him into the fire. Allah Almighty made the fire cool and safe for him, and so his Prophethood was firmly established. In the sura of *Qasas* (The Narratives), the story about Moses running away in fear of his life has been narrated in this way: *"So he went forth, fearing, waiting, (and) he said: My Lord, deliver me from the unjust people."(28:21)*

In the sura of *A'raf* (The Elevated Places), the Holy Qur'an tells us of Aaron's plight when Moses had left him in charge of the Bani Israel. The people immediately began to worship the golden calf and, because Aaron had no one to support him, he remained silent. The Qur'an says: *"And he (Moses) seized his brother by the head, dragging him towards him. He (Aaron) said: Son of my mother! Surely the people reckoned me weak and had well nigh slain me." (7:150)*

So according to the Holy Qur'an Aaron did not draw the sword against the people. He assumed silence when they adopted Samiri's Golden Calf as the object of worship because he (Aaron) recognized that he was outnumbered. Similarly, Ali (as), whom the Holy Prophet (s) pronounced to be the counterpart of Aaron (as we have discussed in detail earlier), was also perfectly justified in assuming patience and forbearance when he had been left alone. The Imam was forcibly brought to the mosque and an open sword was put on his head to force him to swear allegiance. Later he went to the tomb of the Holy Prophet and repeated the same words that Allah Almighty has related through the tongue of Aaron. Aaron had said to Moses: *"Surely the people had reckoned me weak and had well nigh slain me."*

The Prophet Muhammad's example regarding this point is of course most instructive. We should consider why he maintained complete silence for thirteen years in the face of hostile activities of the enemy in Mecca until finally he had to abandon his native city in the darkness of the night.

The great jurist, Wasiti Ibn Maghazili Shafi'i, and Khatib Khawarizmi report in their *Manaqib* that the Holy Prophet (s) said to Ali (as): *"The community has a strong grudge against you. Shortly after my death they will deceive you and reveal what they have in their hearts. I order you to be patient and control yourself at that time so that Allah may give you its reward and a good recompense."*

Secondly, Amiru'l-Mu'minin (as) never looked to himself but was always mindful of Allah. He was completely absorbed in (the way of) Allah. He resigned himself and his people to the will of Allah. Hence, his patience and forbearance in gaining his right were for Allah's sake so that there might not be discord among the Muslims and that people might not return to their previous infidelity.

When Fatima's property was taken from her, she came home, depressed and dismayed. She said to Ali (as): *"You have receded like a fetus. You have retired from the world like an accused person and have broken your hawk-like wings. Now the weak wings of a bird do not support you. This Ibn Qahafa (Abu Bakr) is forcibly snatching away from me my father's gift and my children's means of subsistence. In fact these people abused me with open ill will and railed at me."* She spoke for a long time.

The Imam listened to Fatima (as) until she was silent. Then he gave her a short reply which satisfied her. He said: *"O Fatima! In the matter of religion and preaching truth, I have never been inactive. Do you wish that this sacred religion remains secure and that your Holy father's name is called in mosques until eternity?"*

She said: *"Yes, that is my most ardent desire."*

Ali (as) said: *"Then you should be patient. Your father has given me instructions regarding this situation, and I know that I should be forbearing. Otherwise, I have such strength that I could subdue the enemy and take back your right from them. But you should know that in that case the religion would be destroyed. So, for the sake of Allah and for the security of Allah's religion, be patient. The recompense in the hereafter for you is better than your right which has been usurped."*

It was for this reason that Amiru'l-Mu'minin made patience his custom. He assumed forbearance and silence for the safety of Islam. In many of his sermons he has referred to this point.

It is reported[19] that when Talha and Zubair broke their allegiances and left for Basra, Ali (as) ordered the people to assemble in the mosque. Then after praising Allah Almighty he said: *"After the death of the Holy Prophet, we said that we were his Ahl ul Bayt, his successors, and the rightful people to receive his heritage. No one except us could claim the right of rulership after him. But a group of the hypocrites snatched away our Holy Prophet's rulership from us and entrusted it to those who were our opponents. By Allah, our hearts and eyes wept for it. By*

---

[19] Ibrahim Bin Muhammad Saqafi, who is one of the trustworthy ulema of the Sunni's, Ibn Abi'l-Hadid, and Ali Ibn Muhammad Hamadani

Allah, we were full of grief and indignation. I swear by Allah that if there were no fear that the Muslim community would be shattered, we would have overturned the caliphate. They occupied the seat of power until they reached their end. Now Allah has returned the caliphate to me. And these two men (Talha and Zubair) also swore allegiance to me. Now they have proceeded to Basra intending to cause dissension among the people."

Among the great scholars, Ibn Abi'l-Hadid and Kalbi, have reported that at the time of his setting out for Basra Ali (as) addressed the people. He said: *"When the Holy Prophet of Allah (s) died, the Quraish swooped down upon us and deprived us of the right which we deserved more than anyone else. So, I thought that it was better to adopt patience at that time, rather than allow the Muslims to disintegrate and their blood to be spilled, for they had embraced Islam only recently."*

Ali's silence and his abstaining from challenging the caliphate of Abu Bakr and Umar was not due to his concurrence with them. It was because he wanted to avoid causing bitter conflict among the people and because he wanted to save the religion from annihilation. So, after six months of silence and disapproval, then, as stated by sunni ulema, he offered allegiance and cooperated with them. In a letter sent to the people of Egypt through Malik Ashtar, he clearly writes that his silence was for the sake of preserving Islam.

The original text of Ali's letter, which Ibn Abi'l-Hadid has recorded in his *Sharh-e-Nahju'l-Balagha*, vol.IV, p.164, is as follows: *"Allah Almighty sent Muhammad as a witness of the Prophets to warn the people. So, when the Holy Prophet died the Muslims disputed among themselves as to who should succeed him. I swear by Allah that I never thought or believed, nor were there the least signs of it, that the people of Arabia would take away the right of succession from the Ahl ul Bayt and give it to others after him. It was unimaginable that after the death of the Holy Prophet, despite his clear decree, they would deprive me of that right.*

I was greatly distressed that the people ran to a certain person (Abu Bakr) and swore allegiance to him. So, I withdrew myself until I saw that a group of people diverged from Islam and intended to destroy Islam. Then I feared that if I did not help Islam and the Muslims, Islam would suffer such destruction as would be more painful to me than the snatching away of the caliphate. Of course, political power cannot last long. It must dissipate like the clouds. It was under these conditions that I had to rise, so that paganism would become weak, and Islam become firm." [20]

Aban ibn Abi Ayyash has narrated from Sulaym ibn Qays. He (Sulaym) heard from Salman Farsi, who said: *"After the Holy Prophet (s) passed away and people did what they did, Abu Bakr, Umar, Abu Ubaydah ibn Jarrah came to people and told the Ansar their argument. The Ansar told them the argument of Ali (as). They (Abu Bakr, Umar, and Abu Ubaydah) said: "O group of Ansar, the Quraysh are more deserving of the caliphate than you, because the Holy Prophet (s) was from Quraysh, and Muhajireen are better than you since Allah in His Book has spoken about them first and has given them merits. The Holy Prophet (s) has said: "Imam will be from Quraysh."*

Salman says: "I went to Ali (as) when he was giving the ritual bath to the Holy Prophet (s) since the Holy Prophet (s) has said that none other than Ali (as) must give him the ritual bath. When the Holy Prophet (s) said to Ali (as) that none other than him should give him the ritual bath, Ali (as) had asked: "O Prophet of Allah (s), who would help me in giving the bath?"

The Holy Prophet (s) had replied, "Archangel Jibra'eel will help." So, when giving the bath whenever Ali (as) wanted to turn any part of the Holy Prophets (s) body, the part would turn itself. After Ali (as) had completed giving the ritual bath, hunut

---

[20] Peshawar Nights by Sultanul Waizin Shirazi

and shroud, he let me in, and he also let Abu Dhar, Miqdad and Lady Fatima, Hassan (as) and Hussain (as) in. Ali (as) stood in front and we stood behind him and recited the prayer. And 'Aishah was in her room - she did not know anything. Allah had put a curtain over her eyes. After that ten people from Muhajireen and ten people from Ansar – they were coming in and praying and going out until such time that there was no one left from the Muhajireen and Ansar who had not prayed."

Salman said: "I told Ali (as), when he was giving the bath to the Holy Prophet (s) what the community had done and I told him Abu Bakr is at this time on the pulpit of the Holy Prophet (s) and people are not happy to pay allegiance with one hand, but they are paying allegiance with both hands, left and right."

Ali (as) replied: "O Salman, do you know who was the first to pay allegiance to him on the pulpit of the Holy Prophets (s)?"

Salman: "No, but I can say that I saw him in the shade of Bani Sa'eedah at the time when the Ansar were quarreling. The first one who paid allegiance was Mughirah ibn Sha'abah, after him Bashir ibn Sa'eed paid allegiance, then Abu Ubaydah Jarrah, then Umar ibn Khattab, then Saalim Mawla Abi Huzayifah and Ma'az ibn Jabal."

Ali (as) said: "I am not asking about these people, but do you know who was the first to pay allegiance when he first went on the pulpit?"

Salman said: "No, but I saw one very old man who supported himself with a stick and had a mark in between his two eyes; the mark was very dry. He went to the pulpit first of all and bowed and was crying and saying. "Praise is due to Allah who did not make me die until I saw you in this place. You stretch your hand." So, Abu Bakr stretched his hand and the old man paid allegiance.

Then the old man said: "This religion is like the religion of Adam." Then he got down from the pulpit and walked out of the Masjid."

At that time Ali (as) asked: "O Salman, do you know who this person was?"

Salman said: "No, but I did not like his talk - it was like he was pleased with the sad demise of the Holy Prophet (s)."

Ali (as) said: "This was Iblis - May Allah curse him. The Holy Prophet (s) had informed me that Iblis and his top companions were present when, by God's command, the Holy Prophet (s) had declared me caliph in Ghadir Khum, and the Holy Prophet (s) had informed people that I was Mawla (master) of everyone and he (the Prophet) had commanded people present that they should pass this message to those that were not present at Ghadir. So, the companions of Iblis came and told him: "This community is blessed and is infallible. Now you and we have no power to manipulate them since they have been told who is their refuge and who is their leader after their Prophet." At that time Iblis was saddened and he went away from there."

Ali (as) said: "After this I was informed by the Holy Prophet (s) when he said: "People will pay allegiance to Abu Bakr in the shade of Bani Sa'eedah, when they will quarrel through my right and authority. After that they will come to mosque and the first person that will pay allegiance to him on my pulpit will be Iblis who will come in the form of an old man and say so and so. After that he will go out and gather his companions, Shaytan and Iblis. They will all go into his prostration and say: Oh my Lord and my Almighty You are the One who made Adam come out of Heaven and said which community is it that which will not deviate after the death of their Prophet? Never - You thought that I will not be able to manipulate them (and I will have no ways) - Now how do you people find me with what I did with them when they left Allah's obedience and the command of their Prophet, and this is what

Allah has said: "And certainly the shaitan found true his conjecture concerning them, so they followed him, except a party of the believers". (Surah Saba 20)

Iblis made his thought a true action and people obeyed him except a few faithful ones."

Salman said: "When it was night, Ali (as) made Lady Fatima (as) ride and took hands of his sons Hassan (as) and Hussain (as) and went to each and every house of those Muhajireen and Ansar who were of Badr and reminded them of his rights called them to help him. But except 4 people nobody came forward to help. He asked the helpers to shave their heads and in the morning go to him with their weapons ready to help and pay allegiance to death. In the morning except 4, no one kept their promise."

So, I (Sulaym) asked: "Who were those 4?"

Salman replied: "Myself, Abu Dhar, Miqdad and Zubayr.

Then on the second night Ali (as) returned to all those who did not come and reminded them to fulfill their promise. They all said they would turn up the next morning but except us no one turned up. On the third night Ali (as) went again and again on the third day except us no one turned up.

When Ali (as) saw their treachery and disloyalty, he remained inside his house and started compiling the Quran, and did not come out of his house until the whole Quran was compiled. At that time verses were written in wood, skin and pieces.

After he had collected all the verses and wrote with his own hands in the manner the verses were revealed, with their meanings, and wrote those verses that were revealed to replace previous verses, and the verses that were those on which action was no longer required, then Abu Bakr sent people to his house to come out and pay allegiance to him. He (Ali) sent a message saying that he was busy, and he had taken an oath that except for prayers he will not wear a cloak until he has collected and compiled the Quran. So, for a few days they kept quiet. Ali (as) compiled and completed the whole Quran in one piece of cloth and came to people when they were with Abu Bakr in Masjide Nabawi. He very loudly said: "O people, since the passing away of the Holy Prophet (s) I was busy giving him the ritual bath, and compiling the Quran, until it has been collected in one piece of cloth. There is not any verse that Allah has revealed which is not in this compilation, and there is not a single verse that the Holy Prophet (s) did not make me read, and there is no verse of which the Holy Prophet (s) did not tell me the meaning."

Then Ali (as) said to those people: "So that you do not tell me surely we were heedless of this (Surah Araf 172)"

Then Ali (as) said to them: "So that on the Day of Judgment you do not say that I did not call you to help me and did not remind you of my right, and I did not call you to the Book of Allah from beginning to end."

Umar said: "You are calling us to you, but the Quran that we have is sufficient for us."

Then Ali (as) went home.

Umar told Abu Bakr: "Send somebody to Ali (as) to ask him to pay allegiance, since until such time he does not pay allegiance there is no value attached to the caliphate, and if he pays allegiance, we will give him amnesty."

Abu Bakr then sent a man to Ali (as) to say: "The caliph of the Prophet of Allah (s) is calling you." The man came and said this to Ali (as).

Ali (as) replied: "Glory be to Allah, how soon have you wrongly accused the Holy Prophet (s)! Abu Bakr knows it and those present near him also know it that Allah and His Prophet have not appointed any caliph except myself." The man returned and told Abu Bakr what Ali (as) had said.

Abu Bakr asked the man to return to Ali (as) and say:

"Amirul Mumineen, Abu Bakr, is calling you." The man returned to Ali (as) house and said what Abu Bakr had told him.

Ali (as) replied: *"Glory be to Allah, By God, it has not been long, when everything is forgotten. By God, he knows that this title is not appropriate for anyone except myself. The Holy Prophet (s) ordered him, and he was seventh in number who had saluted me saying Amirul Mumineen.*

So, Abu Bakr and his companion Umar, from the seven people asked him: "Is this an order from Allah and His Prophet?"

The Holy Prophet (s) said to both of them: "Yes, surely, this is true from Allah and His Prophet. No doubt, he is Amirul Mumineen (Leader of Believers), Sayyidul Muslimeen (Leader of Muslims), Sahibu Liwail (the standard bearer on the day of judgment), Ghuml Muhajileen (the one whose forehead shines). On the Day of Judgment Allah will make him sit on the path and he will make his friends go to Paradise and his enemies go to Hell."

The man returned to tell Abu Bakr what Ali (as) had told him. That day the man kept quiet.

At night Ali (as) made Lady Fatima (as) ride and held the hands of his two sons Hassan (as) and Hussain (as) and there was no companion of the Holy Prophets (s) left to whose house he did not go, and bearing Allah as his witness, told of his rights and called them to help him, but except for us four no one agreed. We shaved our heads and offered our help to him. Amongst us the one who had most intelligently helped him was Zubayr. When Ali (as) saw that people had left him and did not help him, and all of them had joined Abu Bakr and showed him respect and obeyed him, he stayed at home.

Umar asked Abu Bakr: *"What is it that has stopped you from sending somebody to Ali to ask him to pay allegiance because except him and those four, there was nobody left who*

35

had not paid allegiance?" Abu Bakr was a little softer at heart, kinder, cleverer, and more thoughtful. The other one was very short-tempered, hard-hearted and an oppressor.

Abu Bakr replied by asking whom he should send to Ali, to which Umar replied that he was sending Qunfuz, who was a very tough, short-tempered oppressor from Tulaqa[21], and was from the tribe of Adi ibn Ka'ab.

Abu Bakr sent him to Ali (as) and sent more men to help him. He went and requested permission from Ali (as). Ali (as) refused permission. The helpers of Qunfuz returned to Abu Bakr and Umar.

These two were sitting in the mosque with people gathered around them. They all told that Ali (as) did not give them permission. Umar told them to go back to Ali (as) and if he refuses, enter without permission. They went and asked permission. Lady Fatima (as) told them that she was not permitting them to enter. They returned, but Qunfuz, the cursed, remained. His companions told that Lady Fatima had said such and such, and she was not permitting them to enter.

Umar said angrily: "What do we have to do with women?"

Then Umar told those people who had gathered around him to collect wood. They all collected, and Umar himself lifted and went to the house of Ali (as), Lady Fatima (as) and their two sons, and arranged wood all around the house and then said in a voice loud enough to make Ali (as) and Lady Fatima (as) hear: "By God, O Ali, come out and pay allegiance to the caliph of the Holy Prophet of Allah (s), otherwise we will burn your house."

Lady Fatima (as) said: "O Umar, what do you have to do

---

[21] When Makkah was conquered the Holy Prophet (s) had released him -hence Tulaqa

with us?"

He replied: "Open the door, otherwise we will burn your house."

Lady Fatima (as) said: "O Umar, are you not afraid of Allah and are you entering our house?"

Umar refused to return. He asked fire to be brought and he set the door on fire, then he pushed it and entered.

Lady Fatima (as) came in front and screamed loudly: "O Father, O Prophet of Allah (s)!"

Umar raised his sword with the shield and hit her on the side. She screamed: "O Father" He then lifted a whip and hit her on the hand and she cried: "O Prophet of Allah (s), Abu Bakr and Umar behaved very badly after you."

Ali (as) rushed, held him by the neck and pushed him away and Umar fell down and hurt his neck and nose. Ali (as) intended to kill him. He remembered what the Holy Prophet (s) had said, and he said: "By Him, who gave Muhammad the status of Prophethood, O son of Sahak, if the Book from Allah had not been revealed and if the Holy Prophet (s) had not taken a promise from me before, then you would have known that you could have never entered my house."

Umar, complaining, sent somebody, and some people came and entered the house. Ali (as) went forward to lift his sword, so Qunfuz returned to Abu Bakr and Abu Bakr was frightened that Ali (as) with his sword, would go to him, since he knew Ali's bravery and determination.

Abu Bakr said to Qunfuz: "Return to Ali's house and if he comes out then fine, otherwise enter his house. If he refuses then set the house on fire."

Qunfuz, the cursed, returned and entered the house, without permission, with his companions. Ali (as) went forward to pick his sword – these people, who were so many went forward against him, got hold of him, raised their swords, arrested him and tied a rope in his neck.

Lady Fatima (as) came in between Ali (as) and those people near the door of the house, so Qunfuz hit her with a whip. When she passed away, the mark of the wound was still on her shoulder. May Allah curse Qunfuz and the one who sent him!

Then they pulled Ali (as) by force until they brought him to Abu Bakr. when Umar was standing with a sword behind Abu Bakr Khalid ibn Walid, Abu Ubaydah ibn Jarrah and Salim Mawla Abu Huzayfah, Mughirah ibn Sha'aba and others were sitting near Abu Bakr with weapons in their hands."

Sulaym says: "I asked Salman: "Did these people enter the house of Lady Fatima (as) without permission?"

He replied: "Yes, by God, when she did not even have a chaddor over her. So, she screamed: "O Father, O Prophet of Allah (s), Abu Bakr and Umar behaved so badly after you, while your eyes have not even closed in the grave" and she was saying this loudly."

Salman said: "I saw Abu Bakr and those sitting near him crying with tears and whoever was there was crying except Umar, Khadid ibn Walid, and Mughirah ibn Sha'aba. Umar was saying: "We have nothing to do with women and their opinion."

Salman said: "Ali (as) was taken to Abu Bakr and he was saying: "By God, if I had my sword in my hand, then you would see that you would have never reached this stage. By God, I do not consider myself bad in doing jihad with you. If I had even forty people, then I would disperse your community. May God curse that community who paid allegiance to me and then became disloyal."

When Abu Bakr saw Ali (as) he screamed and loudly said: "Release him."

Ali (as) said: "O Abu Bakr, how soon did you act against the Holy Prophet (s)! And with what rights and reasons you called people to pay you allegiance? Did you not pay allegiance to me (yesterday) by the command of Allah and His Prophet?"

Qunfuz the cursed, had hit Lady Fatima (as) with a whip when she came in between Ali (as) and the people and Umar had sent him saying: "If Fatima comes in between you and her husband, hit her." so Qunfuz, the cursed, forced her to take refuge behind the door and he pushed the door so her rib near the side got broken and she had a miscarriage. So she was continuously ill until she attained martyrdom in this.

Salman said: "When Ali (as) was taken to Abu Bakr, Umar very rudely told Ali (as): "Pay allegiance to Abu Bakr and leave your useless talks."

Ali (as) asked: "If I do not pay allegiance what will you people do?"

People said: "We will kill you with humiliation and degradation."

Ali (as) said: "That will mean that you killed Abdullah and the brother of Prophet of Allah (s)." Abu Bakr said: "As far as Abdullah is concerned it is correct, but we do not accept you the brother of the Prophet of Allah (s)."

Ali (as) said: "Do you deny that the Holy Prophet (s) had declared brotherhood between him and myself?"

Abu Bakr said: "Yes." Ali (as) repeated this thrice.

Then Ali (as) turned towards those people who had gathered around Abu Bakr and said: "O group of Muslims, Muhajireen and Ansar, I am asking you to swear By Allah that you have heard the Holy Prophet (s) say such and such in Gadhir Khum and say such and such in the Battle of Tabuk." He did not leave anything that the Holy Prophet (s) had said, until he reminded them of absolutely everything.

Everyone replied: "Indeed, Yes."

When Abu Bakr heard this, he got frightened that people might help Ali (as) to stop what was being done.

He quickly said: "What you have said is true and I have heard it with my own ears, I knew and my heart remembered it but I also heard after that the Holy Prophet (s) say: "We Ahl ul bayt are those whom Allah has chosen and gave us status and has chosen the hereafter against this world for us. And Allah has not decreed that Prophethood and caliphate be the same."

Ali (as) asked: "Is there any one among the companions of the Holy Prophet (s) who can be a witness to what you have said?"

Umar said: "The caliph of the Holy Prophet is saying truth. I have heard the Prophet of Allah saying this."

Abu Ubaydah, Salim Mawla Abu Huzayfah and Ma'az ibn Jabal said: "He has told the truth. We have heard it from the Prophet of Allah (s)."

Ali (as) said to him: "You have completed your cursed Sahifah which you agreed in Ka'abah (i.e if Muhammad is killed of dies you people will take away this chaliphate from Ahlulbayt)

Abu Bakr asked: "How did you know about this? We did not tell you."

Ali (as) said: "O Zubayr you, and Salman you, and Abu Dharr and Miqdad you - I am asking you for the sake of Allah and for the sake of Islam, did you not hear the Holy Prophet (s) say when you were listening: "This one and that one - until he counted upto five - they have made between them a written agreement and have vowed to keep it if I am killed or I die?"

They replied: "Indeed, yes we heard the Holy Prophet (s) say that to you. Yes, we heard that these people had made an agreement and vowed to keep it if he is killed of dies. They will overpower you and O' Ali; they will remove you from this caliphate."

Ali (as) said: "When the Holy Prophet (s) said this I asked: "O' Prophet of Allah (s) may my parents be sacrificed for you, when this happens what do you instruct me to do?"

Salman, Abu Dhar, Miqdad and Zubayr said: "He instructed you that if you find helpers then you fight against them and get your rights, if you do not get helpers then you pay allegiance and save your blood."

Ali (as) said: "By God, if those forty people who paid allegiance to me had been loyal to me then I would have fought against you in the way of Allah. But remember, By God, until the Day of Judgment your generation will not get it (caliphate). And what makes your talks a lie - which you have attributed to the Holy Prophet (s) is Allah's saying: "Or do they envy the people for what Allah has given them of His grace? But indeed We have given to Ibrahim's children the Book and Wisdom and We have given them a grand kingdom." (Surah Nisa: 54)

What is meant by Book here is Prophethood, wisdom is tradition and grand kingdom is caliphate and we are Ibrahim's children."

Miqdad stood up and said: "O Ali, what is your command for me? By God, if you command me, I will fight with this sword and if you command me I will stop."

Ali (as) replied: "O Miqdad, stop, and remember what promise the Holy Prophet (s) took from you and his will."

Then I stood up and said: "By Him in whose Hands is my life, if I knew that I will be able to remove any oppression and the religion of Allah will attain status, then I would put my sword on my neck and would fight at each and every step." Then, addressing people, I said: "What! Are you attacking the one who is the brother of the Prophet of Allah (s), his wasi, caliph of his community and the father of his sons? Then I am giving you good news that trouble will come to you and do not hope for any type of ease."

Abu Dharr stood up and said: "O that community, who after the death of its Prophet is puzzled, and whom Allah has stopped helping due to their sins, surely Allah says: "Surely Allah chose Adam and Nuh and the descendants of Ibrahim and the descendants of Imran above the nations. Offspring, one of the other, and Allah is Hearing, Knowing." (Surah Ale Imran: 33 & 34)

And the children of Muhammad are the descendants of Nuh and they are the children of Ibrahim from Ibrahim, and they are chosen ones from Isma'eel and they are the progeny of Prophet Muhammad (s) and are the household of Prophethood, are the place for Messengers and are those to whom angels descend and ascend. And they are like high skies and are like those mountains that are firm, and they are like that Ka'abah over which the veil hangs and are those springs which are clear and stars who guide people, and a tree like a blessed tree that produces light and its oil is blessed. And Muhammad (s) is the seal of Prophets and is the Leader of Bani-Adam and Ali is Wasi of Awsiya (successor of the successors) and Imam of Muttaqeen (pious) and is the leader of those whose forehead shines and he is the one who never tells a lie, the one who differentiates between truth and falsehood and is wasi of Muhammad (s), the inheritor of his knowledge, and has more rights than anyone over the faithful. Like Allah has said: "The Prophet has a greater claim on the faithful than they have on themselves, and his wives are (as) their mother; and the possessors of relationship have the better claim in the ordinance of Allah to inheritance, one with respect to another, that (other believers, and (than) those who have fled their homes), except that you do some good to your friends; this is written in the Book. (Surah

Ahzab: 6)

So, you also bring forward whom Allah has brought forward and put behind him whom Allah has left behind and give Wilayat (guardianship) and inheritance to the one to whom Allah has given."

Umar stood up and said to Abu Bakr who was sitting on the pulpit: "You are sitting on the pulpit and this man is sitting and is prepared for war - he is not getting up to pay you allegiance. Give us order to cut his neck off."

At this time Hassan (as) and Hussain (as) were standing and when they heard what Umar said they started crying. Ali (as) hugged both of them and told them: "Do not cry, By God, these people are not able to kill your father."

Umme Ayman, who had brought up the Holy Prophet (s) came forward and said: "O Abu Bakr, how soon have you all revealed your hypocrisy and jealousy!"

Umar gave order and she was removed from the mosque. He said: "What do we have to do with women?"

Buraydah Aslami stood up and said: "O Umar, are you attacking the brother and the father of the children of the Holy Prophet (s)? And you are that very person whose reputation in Quraysh is known to us. Are you two not the ones to whom the Holy Prophet (s) had told to go to Ali (as) and greet him saying 'Amirul Mumineen'? And you two had asked if this was in accordance with Allah and His Prophet's command, and the Prophet (s) had said YES.

Abu Bakr said: "Yes it was like that but the Prophet of Allah had after that said: "For us Prophethood and caliphate cannot be combined together."

Buraydah said: "The Holy Prophet (s) had not said that. By God I will not remain in a city in which you stay as Amir."

Umar gave order and he was beaten and thrown out of the mosque.

Then he (Umar) said: "O' ibn Abi Talib, stand up and pay allegiance."

Ali (as) asked: "If I do not do it then?" He said: "At that time we will cut your neck." Ali (as) said it three times. Then he without opening his palm, stretched his hand and Abu Bakr put his hand on his (Ali's) hand and was happy with that. Before allegiance Ali (as), when a rope was tied to his neck, said loudly: "Son of my mother! Surely the people reckoned me weak and had well nigh slain me." (Surah Araf: 150)

Zubayr was told to pay allegiance - he refused. Umar, Khalid ibn Walid and Mighirah ibn Sha'aba with a few people rushed to him, took away his sword from his hand, threw it on the floor and broke it, and held him by the neck.

Zubayr said, when Umar was on his chest: "O son of Sahhak, By God, if my sword was in my hand, then you would not have got away from me." He then paid allegiance.

Salman says: "Then they held me, and twisted my neck until it became like a piece of flesh, then took my hand and twisted it, and then forcefully I paid the allegiance. Then Abu Dharr and Miqdad also paid allegiance forcefully.

And among us there was nobody as outspoken as Zubayr because when he paid allegiance he said: "O son of Sahhak, By God, if these evil people who supported you were not present then you would not able to come to me, and my sword would be with me, because I know your cowardice and disgrace, but you have got a few evil people from whom you gained strength and are attaching."

Umar became very angry and said: "Are you talking about Sahhak?" Zubayr asked: "Sahhak who? And can you stop me talking about Sahhak when Sahhak was a prostitute. Do you *deny that? Was she not an Ethiopian servant of my grandfather Abdul Muttalib? Your granddfather Nufail committed adultery with her, so your father Khattab was born. After adultery that servant girl was given to your grandfather by Abdul Muttalib, then your father was born, so he was my father's servant who was born by adultery." Then Abu Bakr made peace between these two (Zubayr and Umar) and then both stopped quarrelling."*

Sulaym ibn Qays says: "I said to Salman: "O' Salman, you paid allegiance to Abu Bakr and you did not say anything?"

Salman replied: "After allegiance I said to all "Forever and forever may you be destroyed. Do you know what you have done to yourselves? You have done good and you did bad - it is good because you chose the tradition of those who passed away before- that is fighting and disuniting. And it is bad because you left the tradition of your Prophet until you removed caliphate from its mines and from him whose right it was."

Umar said: "O Salman, now that your companion has paid allegiance, and you have paid too, say what you like and do what you like, and your companion can say what he wants."

Salman said: "I said to Umar: "I have heard the Holy Prophet (s) say that until the day of judgment the sins of the entire community will be on you (Umar) and your companion whom you have paid allegiance and the punishment of that will be equal to the punishment of the entire community."

So, Umar said: "Say what you like. What! Have you not paid allegiance? And God has not made your eyes calm in a way that your companion gets caliphate."

Salman said he said: "I bear witness that I have read in various Books of Allah that you, with your names, ancestors and attributes, are one of the doors of Hell."

Umar said to me: "Say what you like Has Allah not

taken away the caliphate from the Ahlulbayt whom you had made your God, apart from Allah?"

So, I said to him: "I bear witness that I have heard from the Holy Prophet (s). He said it when I asked him about the verse: "But on that day shall no one chastise with (anything like) His chastisement. And no one shall bind with (anything like) his binding." (Surah Fajr: 25,26) He told me that it meant YOU (Umar)."

Umar said: "Shut up - May Allah make you die – O' servant, O the son of evil tongued."

Ali (as) said: "O' Salman I hold you by oath - keep quiet."

Salman said: "By God, if Ali (as) had not ordered me to keep quiet, I would have told him all that has been revealed relating to him, and I would have told him also all that I have heard from the Holy Prophet (s) concerning him and his companion."

When Umar saw that I was quiet, he told me "No doubt, you are very obedient to him and listen to what he says."

When Abu Dharr and Miqdad paid allegiance, they did not say anything.

Umar said: "O Salman, why did you not keep quiet like your two companions kept quiet? By God, you do not love Ahl ul bayt any more than these two and you do not respect their rights more than these two. You saw them pay allegiance quietly."

Abu Dharr said: "O Umar, are you taunting me about the love of Ale-Muhammad and the respect of their rights? May Allah curse, and he did curse those people who held enmity with them, accused them and took away their rights, and made people ride over their necks and reversed the community to their previous beliefs."

Umar said: "Amen – May Allah curse those who took their rights. By God, Ale-Muhammad are equal in this."

Abu Dharr said: "So why did you challenge Ansar through Ale-Muhammad and their rights?" Ali (as) said to Umar: "O' son of Sahhak, if we do not have any right in this, then is it yours and the son of a woman who eats flies (Abu Bakr)?"

Umar said: "O' Abul Hassan, now that you have paid allegiance, keep quiet because people were happy with my companion and were not happy with you - what is my fault in this?"

Ali (as) said: "But God and His Prophet are not happy with anyone except myself so you, your companion and those who obeyed you, and those who supported you, and good news be for you on Allah's anger with you, and His Punishment and His degradation of you. O' ibn Khattab, may evil befall you, if only you knew how you have erred! If you knew of what you have come out in what you have entered and what evil you have done for yourself and your companion!"

Abu Bakr said: "O' Umar, now that he has paid allegiance to us and we have been saved from any harm from him, leave him to say what he wants to say."

Ali (as) said: "Except one thing, I do not say anything. O' four people (Salman, Zubayr, Abu Dharr and Miqdad) I am reminding you I have heard the Holy Prophet (s) say: "No doubt, there will be one coffin of fire in which there will be twelve people - six from the beginning) and six from the end, that will be in a well which is in the bottom level of the Hell. And this coffin will be the one that will be locked. There will be a stone kept on the well. When Allah wishes the Hell fire to be lighted, He will remove that stone from the top of the well. At that time the Hell will set alight with the flames and heat of the well."

Ali (as) continued: "I asked the Holy Prophet (s), and

you were present, who are the ones from the beginning?

He (s) replied that from the beginning there will be Adam's son who killed his brother, and Pharaoh of Pharaohs, and the one who argued with the Prophet Ibrahim (as) concerning God and two people of Bani Israel who changed their Book and their Tradition - one of these two is the one that made Yahudi, a Yahudi, and the other made Nasrani a Nasrani. And the the sixth one is Iblis. And from the end is Dajjal, and these five who are Sahifah, and Kitab, and Jibt and Taghut, O my brother who made an agreement and contract of enmity towards you. And after me, they will overpower you. This one and this one, until he gave names and counted also."

Salman says he said: "You have told truth - we bear witness that we heard the Holy Prophet (s) say that."

Uthman said: "O' Abul Hassan, have you or your companions have any hadith concerning me?"

Ali (as) said: "Yes, why not? I have heard the Holy Prophet (s) saying that he has cursed you twice, and then he did not even repent when he cursed you."

Uthman got angry at that and said: "What do I have to do with you? You never leave me, neither during the time of the Prophet not after him."

Ali (as) said: "Yes, May Allah humiliate you."

Uthman said: "By God, I have heard the Holy Prophet (s) saying: "Zubayr will be killed when he becomes an apostate of Islam."

Salman says: "Ali (as) told me, and this was between him and myself: "Uthman has said truth, and this will be when after Uthman is killed. He will pay allegiance to me and then will break it and be killed an apostate."

Salman says: "Then Ali (as) said: "Except four, after the

Holy Prophet (s) everyone has become an apostate. After the Holy Prophet (s) people became like Haroon and those who followed him and like the cow and those who followed it." So Ali (as) is like Haroon and Atiq (Abu Bakr) like the cow, and Umar like Samiri."

I heard the Holy Prophet (s) saying: "No doubt, a community of my companions will come who will have a high status with me so that they pass the sirat (bridge on the day of judgment) and when they will see me and I will see them, they will recognize me, and I will recognize them. They will come very near to me. I will say: "O God, these are my companions, my companions." It will be said: "Do not you know what they did after you? Indeed, they reverted when you parted from them." I will say: "Go away and get destroyed."

And I have heard the Holy Prophet (s) say: "My community will choose the tradition of Bani Israel in exactly the same manner that one-foot falls on the other foot, one span equal to another span, one hand like the other, one distance like the other distance, until they enter a hole then these people will also enter that hole. Surely, Torah and the Quran were written by one Angel, on one skin, and with one pen, and all examples with tradition became like one." [22]

The Prophet turned towards his daughter and said: "You are the first one in my Ahl ul Bayt who will meet me, and you are the leader of the women of paradise. Soon after me, you will be oppressed and forced, and you will be beaten and your rib will be broken. May Allah curse your killer, and curse the one who ordered it and also curse those who became happy, and also curse those who help him and those who over power you, and curse the oppressor of your husband, and curse also those who oppress your children." [23]

---

[22] Kitab e Sulaym Ibn Qays Al-Hilali hadith #4

[23] Kitab e Sulaym Ibn Qays Al-Hilali hadith #61

فاطمة
لعن الله قاتلي

Confiscating the Property of Fadak from Ahl ul Bayt (as)

Fatima's Death and Burial Kept Secret

When the forts of Khaibar were conquered, the nobles, landlords, and prominent of Fadak came to the Holy Prophet. Fadak was an area in the valley of the Medina hills. It contained seven villages that extended as far as the seacoast. Many were very fertile and there were oases there. There was a peace treaty with the people stating that half of the whole of Fadak was to be in their possession and the other half would be the property of the Holy Prophet. This fact has been narrated by many traditionists and historians.[24]

When the Holy Prophet (s) returned to Medina, Gabriel revealed the following: *"And give to the near of kin his due and*

---

[24] Yaqut Hamawi, the author of Majimu'l-Buldan in his Futuhu'l-Buldan, vol. VI, p. 343; by Ahmad Bin Yahya Baladhuri Baghdadi (died 279 A.H.) in his Ta'rikh; Ibn Abi'l-Hadid Mu'tazali in his Sharh-e-Nahju'l- Balagha, (printed Egypt), vol. IV, p. 78, quoting from Abu Bakr Ahmad Bin Abdu'l-Aziz Jauhari; by Muhammad Bin Jarir Tabari in his Ta'rikh-e-Kabir, and by many other traditionists and historians.

(to) the needy and the wayfarer, and do not squander wastefully." (7:26)

The Holy Prophet (s) pondered the significance of this revelation. Gabriel appeared again and informed him that Allah had decreed: *"Let Fadak be given to Fatima."* The Holy Prophet (s) called Fatima (as) and said: *"Allah has commanded me to bestow Fadak as a gift to you."* So, he immediately gave possession of Fadak to Fatima (as).

The chief of the commentators[25] narrate that when the verse *"and give to the near of kin his due"* was revealed, the Holy Prophet of Allah (s) called Fatima (as) and bestowed the great Fadak upon her as a gift. Accordingly, so long as the Holy Prophet (s) lived, Fadak remained in Fatima's possession. That exalted lady leased the land; its revenue was collected in three installments. Out of this amount she took enough money for food for her and her children and distributed the rest to the poor people of Bani Hashim. After the demise of the Holy Prophet (s), the officers of the ruling caliph snatched this property from Fatima (as).

It is an admitted fact that the caliphs confiscated Fadak on the basis of the well-known hadith narrated by Abu Bakr, who declared that he had himself heard the Holy Prophet (s) say: *"We Prophets do not leave behind any legacy; whatever we leave as inheritance is charity"* (i.e., the property of umma).

First, it was not an inheritance, but a gift. Second, the purported hadith is unacceptable. First, whoever contrived this hadith uttered it without thinking about the words he used. If he had been careful about it, he would never have said: *"We*

---

[25] Ahmad Tha'labi in his Kashfu'l-Bayan; Jalalu'd-din Suyuti in his Tafsir, vol. IV, reporting from Hafiz Ibn Mardawiyya; the famous commentator Ahmad Bin Musa (died 352 A.H.) reporting from Abu Sa'id Khadiri and Hakim Abu'l-Qasim Haskani; Ibn Kathir; Imadu'd-din Isma'il; Ibn Umar Damishqi; Faqih-e-Shafi'i in his Ta'rikh, and Sheikh Sulayman Balkhi Hanafi in his Yanabiu'l-Mawadda, ch. 39, reporting from Tafsir-e-Tha'labi, Jam'u'l-Fawa'id and Uyunu'l-Akhbar

Prophets do not leave any inheritance," because he would have known that his lying would be exposed by the very wording of this concocted hadith. If he had used the words *"I have not left behind any legacy,"* his attempted hadith would have been more plausible. But when he used the plural *"We Prophets..."* we are obliged to investigate the truth of the hadith. Now based on this statement we refer to the Holy Qur'an for guidance. We find that there are several verses which tell us that the Prophets in fact did leave inheritances. This proves that this hadith is to be rejected outright.

Many ulema[26] of the sunni sect have narrated the speech of Fatima (as) before a large gathering of the Muslims. The opponents were stunned when they heard her reasoning and could not reply. Since they had no answer to give, they caused a disturbance.

One of the arguments of Fatima (as) rejecting the hadith was that, if the hadith were true, then why were there so many verses about the inheritances of the Prophets (as). She said: *"At one place the Holy Qur'an says, 'And Solomon was David's heir.'"(27:16)*

About the Prophet Zakariyya (as) the Holy Qur'an says: *"Therefore grant me from thyself an heir, who shall inherit of me and inherit (also) of the house of Jacob." (19,5-6)*

---

[26] In his Kitab-e-Saqifa the great scholar and traditionist, Abu Bakr Ahmad Bin Abdu'l-Aziz Jauhari, about whom Ibn Abi'l-Hadid says in his Sharh-e-Nahju'l-Balagha that he was one of the eminent ulema and traditionists of the Sunni's; Ibn Al-athir in his Nihaya; Mas'udi in Akhbaru'z-Zaman and in Ausat; Ibn Abi'l-Hadid in Sharh-e-Nahju'l-Balagha, vol. IV, p. 78, quoting from Abu Bakr Ahmad Jauhari's book Saqifa and Fadak in different ways and from a number of sources, some of which refer to the fifth Imam Muhammad Baqir through Siddiqi Sughra Zainab-e-Kubra and some of which refer to Abdullah Ibn Hassan on the authority of Siddiqi Kubra Fatima Zahra and on the authority of 'Aisha and also on the authority of Muhammad Bin Imran Marzabani, he from Zaid Bin Ali Bin Hussain; he from his father, and he from his father Imam Hussain; and he from his illustrious mother, Fatima Zahra; and many other ulema.

About Zakariyya's invocation the Holy Qur'an says: *"And Zakariyya, when he cried to his Lord: 'O my Lord, leave me not childless, though Thou art the best of inheritors.' So, we responded to him and gave him Yahya." (21: 89,90)*

After that she said: "O Son of Abu Qahafa! Is it there in the Book of Allah that you are an heir of your father, and I am deprived of my father's legacy? You have committed a great slander. Have you people deliberately abandoned the Book of Allah (the Holy Qur'an) and ignored it altogether? Am I not the descendant of the Holy Prophet? Why are you depriving me of my right? Why are all these verses of inheritance, which are intended for all people in general and for the Prophets in particular included in the Holy Qur'an? Is it not a fact that the verses of the Holy Qur'an shall remain unchanged until the Day of Judgment? Does not the Holy Qur'an say: 'And those who are akin are nearer one to another in the ordinance of Allah...' (8:75)" and: 'Allah enjoins you about your issue! The male shall have the equal of the shares of two females.' (4:12) and: 'Bequest is prescribed for you when one of you approaches death, if he leave wealth, that he bequeath unto parents and near relations in kindness. (This is) a duty for all those who ward off (evil).' Then why have I, in particular, been deprived of my father's legacy? Has Allah revealed some special verses to you, which exclude my father (from his right). Do you know the outward and inner meanings of the Holy Qur'an better than my father, Muhammad, and my cousin, Ali?"

When they were silenced by these arguments and true facts, they had no answer. They resorted to deception and abusive language.

She cried: "Today you have broken my heart. On the Day of Judgment, I will file a suit against you in the Divine Court of Justice and Allah Almighty will decide the case justly. Allah is the best judge. Muhammad is the master and lord; our and your promised time is the Day of Resurrection. That day the transgressor will be losers, and your repentance will do you no *good. For everything there is an appointed time and you will know before long who will be afflicted with scornful chastisement."*

Many scholars have recorded that when Fatima (as) finished pleading her case, Ali (as) began his remonstrance in the public gathering of Muslims in the mosque of Medina, turning towards Abu Bakr, he said: *"Why did you deprive Fatima of her father's legacy, though she was its owner and possessed it during the lifetime of her father?"*

Abu Bakr replied: *"Fadak is the booty of the Muslims. If Fatima produces complete evidence that it is her own property, I will certainly give it to her; otherwise, I will deprive her of it."*

The Imam said, *"Is it not a fact that when you pronounce a judgment about Muslims, in general, you pass quite a contradictory judgment concerning us?*

Hasn't the Holy Prophet said that the onus of proof lies on the plaintiff and that of defense on the defendant? You have rejected the judgment of the Holy Prophet and, contrary to religious law, you demand witnesses from Fatima who has been in possession of the property since the time of the Holy Prophet. Moreover, is the word of Fatima, who is one of the Ashab-e-Kisa (people of the mantle) and who is included in the verse of purity, not true?" If two persons were to give evidence that Fatima had committed some wrong, tell me how would you treat her?"

Abu Bakr said, *"I would inflict punishment on her as I would any other woman."*

The Imam (as) said, *"If you did this, you would be an infidel before Allah, because you would have rejected Allah's evidence about Fatima's purity. Allah says 'Verily, Verily, Allah intends but to keep off from you every kind of uncleanness, O you the People of the House, and purify you (with) a thorough purification.' Is this verse not revealed in our praise?"*

Abu Bakr said: *"Why not?"*

The Imam (as) said: *"Is it possible that Fatima, whose purity Allah has verified, would lay a false claim to a petty property? You reject the evidence of the purified one and accept the evidence of the Arab who urinates on the heel of his own foot!"*

After saying this the Imam returned to his home angry. His protest excited the people. Everyone said: *"Truth is with Ali and Fatima. By Allah, Ali speaks the truth. Why is the Holy Prophet's daughter treated so outrageously?"*

Ibn Abi'l-Hadid narrates that the people were deeply impressed by the protests of Ali (as) and Fatima (as) and began to cause a disturbance. Abu Bakr, who saw that the two Holy persons had already left the mosque went to the pulpit and said: *"O people! Why are you so disturbed? Why do you listen to everybody? Since I have rejected their evidence, they are talking nonsense. The fact is that he is a fox who is betrayed by his own tail. He creates all sorts of disturbances. He minimizes the importance of disturbances and incites the people to create agitation and uproar. He seeks help from the weak. He seeks assistance from women. He is like Ummu't-Tihal with whom people of her own house were fond of fornicating."*

Aren't these remarks outrageously abusive? Do they accord with praise, respect, love and sympathy, which the Holy Prophet (s) had said were due his family? How long will Sunni's remain absorbed in this misguided faith and fanaticism? For how long will they oppose the Shias and call them Rafidi's (rejectors) and infidels because they criticize the words and actions of people which are recorded in their own books?

Consider the matter justly. Was the insolence of the aged companion of the Prophet justified? The wicked and abusive language of Mu'awiya, Marwan, and Khalid was not as distressing as that which comes from the mouth of the man who is called the "companion of the cave." Respected reader! We were not present at that time. We hear the names of Ali, Abu Bakr, Umar, Uthman, Talha, Zubair, Mu'awiya, Marwan, Khalid, Abu Huraira, etc. We have neither friendship nor enmity with any of them. We see two things: first, those whom Allah and His Prophet loved and for whom respect, and loyalty was commanded. Second, we examine their deeds and utterances. Then we decide with a fair mind. We resist letting our preference for someone distort our judgment.

We aren't the only ones who are shocked at such behavior. Even the fair sunni ulema are amazed to learn it. Ibn Abi'l-Hadid writes in his *Sharh-e-Nahju'l- Balagha*, Vol.IV, p. 80, that the utterances of the Caliph filled him with astonishment. He asked his teacher Abu Yahya Naqib Ja'far Bin Yahya Bin Abi Zaidu'l-Basari to whom the caliph's words referred. He said that the statements were not indirect. The reference was explicit.

Ibn Hadid said: *"If they had been explicit, I would not have put the question."* Upon this he laughed and said: *"These things were said against Ali."* Ibn Hadid repeated the words in astonishment: *"Were all those words said against Ali?"* His teacher said: *"Yes, O son! This is what rulership means."*

Resorting to abusive language is the tactic of one who has no convincing reply. All this was done to Ali (as) about whom, as reported by all the sunni leading ulema in their reliable books, the Holy Prophet (s) said: *"Ali is with the truth and the truth is with Ali."*

In reference to both Ali (as) and Fatima (as), the Holy Prophet (s) said that their trouble was his own trouble. The Holy Prophet (s) said: *"He who troubles these two troubles me, and the one who troubles me troubles Allah."*

It is also written in all the sunni authentic books that the Holy Prophet (s) said, *"He who reviles Ali reviles me, who reviles me reviles Allah."*

Muhammad Bin Yusuf Ganji Shafi'i, in his *Kifayatu't-*

Talib, ch. 10, narrates a detailed hadith on the authority of Ibn Abbas, who told a section of the Syrians, who were cursing Ali (as) that he had heard the Holy Prophet (s) saying about Ali (as): *"He who abuses you abuses me, and he who abuses me abuses Allah, and he who abuses Allah will be thrown straight into Hell."*

After this hadith he quotes many other hadith from authentic sources all of which prove that those who abuse Ali (as) are infidels. Chapter 10 of his book is entitled: *"Concerning the Infidelity of One who Abuses Ali."* Also, Hakim in his *Mustadrak*, vol. III, p. 121, has quoted this same hadith. So, according to all these hadith, those who curse Ali (as), curse Allah and his Prophet (s). All of them (like Mu'awiya, the Bani Umayya, the Nasibi's, the Khariji's) are themselves cursed.

There is a second point which disproves the supposed hadith: *"We leave no inheritance..."* The Holy Prophet (s) said: *"I am the city of knowledge and Ali is its gate; and I am the house of wisdom and Ali is its door."*

Both sects accepted this. Certainly, one who was the gate of the Holy Prophet's knowledge understood all hadith and instructions of the Holy Prophet (s), particularly those concerned with the problems of inheritance. On them depends the welfare of the whole nation.

The Holy Prophet (s) also said: *"One who wishes to acquire knowledge should come to Ali's door."* If his knowledge had been incomplete, the Holy Prophet (s) would not have said that Ali (as) was the best judge in the whole community.

He said: *"Ali is the best of all among you in interpreting the laws."* This hadith is recorded in all the authentic books.

Would the Holy Prophet (s) proclaim the superiority of a man's mastery of the laws, if that man did not understand the problems of inheritance and the rights of the people? Part of the purpose of the Holy Prophet (s) was to secure social reform for the people in this world and peace and comfort for them in the hereafter. How could he make Ali the Commander of the Faithful (as) and yet not convey to him a tradition such as this, which affects the entire social order?

As I have already said earlier, the Holy Prophet (s) said: *"For every Prophet there is a vicegerent and heir; verily, Ali is my vicegerent and heir."*

If you say that their inheritance did not mean inheritance of wealth but that of knowledge (although it has been proven that they meant inheritance of wealth) my point of view becomes clearer. The heir of the Prophet's knowledge deserved the position of caliphate more than any one of those who were devoid of the Holy Prophet's knowledge.

Second, it has been proven that the Prophet (s) made Ali (as) his immediate successor and heir, according to the hadith narrated by Sunni ulema. Allah appointed him to this rank. Could the Prophet have neglected to tell his successor and heir?

Moreover, it is very strange that in resolving questions regarding religious laws Abu Bakr and Umar accepted Ali's decisions. The sunni ulema and historians have recorded the judgments pronounced by Ali (as) during the caliphate of Abu Bakr, Umar, and Uthman.

The Sunni's say it is very strange that we claim that the caliphs did not know the religious ordinances and that Ali (as) used to remind them. There is nothing strange about it. To know all the ordinances is very difficult. It would not be possible for a man to have such perfect knowledge unless he was the Prophet of Allah (s) or the 'Gate of Knowledge' of the Holy Prophet (s). The Sunni ulema have recorded these facts in their authentic books. I cite an example so that uninformed men may not think that we say these things to offend them.

The Sunni ulema[27] report the following incident: *"Umar wanted to stone a woman because she had given birth to a child after a six-month pregnancy. Ali said, 'Allah says in the Holy Qur'an that the time, from conception till the prescribed time of suckling, covers a period of thirty months. Since the suckling period is for two years, the period of pregnancy is six months. This means that a birth of a child is possible after a pregnancy of six months.' So, Umar set the woman free and said, 'If Ali had not been there, Umar would have perished.'"*

In the same chapter he quotes from Ahmad Bin Hanbal's *Manaqib*: *"When Umar faced a difficult problem and was unable to understand it, he relied upon Ali's understanding."*

Several such events took place during the caliphate of Abu Bakr and Uthman. When they became entangled in some difficulty, they called Ali (as) as the real arbiter. They themselves acted according to his decision.

Now you may wonder why they did not accept Ali's evidence in the case of Fadak. Now in that case they chose to follow their own desires and snatched away the right of Fatima (as).

The third argument to prove the falsity of this hadith is Caliph Abu Bakr's own statement and action. If the hadith were correct, whatever the Holy Prophet (s) had left would have been confiscated. The heirs would have had no right over anything left behind, but Abu Bakr gave Fatima's apartment to her and gave the apartments of the wives of the Holy Prophet (s), 'Aisha, Hafsa, and others to them as their heritage.

Besides this, if the hadith were correct and if Abu Bakr believed that it was the Holy Prophet's ordinance, then why, after

---

[27] Imam Ahmad Hanbal in his Musnad; Imamu'l-Haram Ahmad Bin Abdullah Shafi'i in his Dhakha'ir-e-Uqba; Ibn Abi'l-Hadid in his Sharh-e-Nahju'l-Balagha; and Sheikh Sulayman Hanafi in his Yanabiu'l-Mawadda, Ch.56, quoting from Ahmad Bin Abdullah; Ahmad Bin Hanbal, Qala'i; and Ibn Saman

confiscating Fadak (which he considered to be charity belonging to the Muslims) did he write a document that the property be returned to Fatima (as)? Later Umar intervened and destroyed the document.

Ibn Abi'l-Hadid in his *Sharh-e-Nahju'l-Balagha* and Ali Bin Burhanu'd-din Shafi'i in his *Ta'rikh Siratu'l-Halabiyya*, vol. III, p. 391, write that Abu Bakr was moved to tears by Fatima's impassioned speech. He wept because of Fatima's plight and subsequently wrote a document stating that the property be returned to her. But Umar destroyed the document.

It is however surprising that the same Umar, who during Abu Bakr's caliphate objected to the returning of Fadak, returned it to its heirs during his own caliphate. Similarly, the Amawid and Abbasid caliphs also returned it to the heirs of Fatima (as).

The well-known traditionist and historian of Medina, Allama Samhudi (died 911 A.H.), in his *Ta'rikhu'l-Medina* and Yaqut Bin Abdullah Rumi in his *Mu'ajamu'l-Buldan*, state that during his caliphate, Abu Bakr took possession of Fadak. Umar, during his reign, returned it to Ali (as) and Abbas. If Abu Bakr occupied it on the order of the Holy Prophet (s) and considered it the property of the Muslims, on what principle did Umar entrust the property of all the Muslims to a single individual?

Sometimes a witness is cleverer than the plaintiff for whom he gives evidence. The Caliph had no such idea. If the property had been returned for the expenses of the Muslims, it must have been so recorded in history. But all the prominent historians write that it was released in favor of Ali (as) and Abbas. Ali (as) accepted Fadak as its rightful heir, not as an individual Muslim. One Muslim may not possess the property of all the Muslims.

Perhaps the reference is to Umar Ibn Abdu'l-Aziz, but Ali (as) and Abbas were not alive during the time of Umar Bin Abdu'l-Aziz. That is a separate story. Allama Samhudi in his *Ta'rikhu'l-Medina* and Ibn Abi'l-Hadid in his *Sharh-e-Nahju'l-*

Balagha, vol. IV, p. 81, narrate from Abu Bakr Jauhari that when Umar Bin Abdu'l-Aziz occupied the seat of the caliphate, he wrote to his governor at Medina to return Fadak to the descendants of Fatima (as). Accordingly, he called Hassan Bin Hassanu'l-Mujtaba (and according to some reports he called Imam Ali Ibnu'l-Hussain) and returned Fadak to him.

Ibn Abi'l-Hadid writes about it in his *Sharh-e-Nahju'l-Balagha*, vol. IV, p.81, in the following words: "*This was the first property which was snatched away unjustly and then was given over to the descendants of Fatima by Umar Bin Abdu'l-Aziz.*"

It remained in their possession for a long time until Caliph Yazid Ibn Abdu'l-Malik usurped it again. Then the Bani Umayya occupied it. When the caliphate went to the Bani Abbas, the first Abbasid Caliph, Abdullah Saffa, entrusted Fadak to the descendants of Imam Hassan (as), who distributed its income, according to the rights of inheritance, to the descendants of Fatima (as).

When Mansur persecuted the descendants of Imam Hassan (as), he snatched away Fadak from them again. When his son, Mahdi, became the caliph, he returned it to them. When Musa bin Hadi became the caliph, he again usurped Fadak. When Mamunu'r-Rashid the Abbasid occupied the seat of the caliphate, he ordered Fadak to be released to the descendants of Ali.

Yaqut Hamawi quotes Mamun's order in his *Mu'ajamu'l-Buldan*. Mamun wrote to his governor at Medina: "*Verily, the Holy Prophet of Allah (s) bequeathed Fadak to his daughter, Fatima. This fact was established and commonly known to the descendants of the Holy Prophet.*"

The well known poet, Di'bal Khuza'i, was also present at this time. He recited some couplets, the first of which means: "*Today we are all happy and rejoicing. Mamun has returned Fadak to the Bani Hashim.*"

It has been proved by irrefutable arguments that Fadak had been given by the Holy Prophet (s) to Fatima (as). It was usurped without any justification. But later caliphs, on grounds of justice or for political considerations, returned it to the descendants of that oppressed lady.

If Fadak was bestowed upon her as a gift, why did she claim it as her heritage and not say anything about a gift? At first she claimed it as a gift. But when witnesses were required from the property's occupants, in contradiction to the injunction of the Holy Prophet of Islam, she produced witnesses. Their evidence was rejected. She was thereby forced to seek protection under the law of inheritance.

This fact is recorded not only in Shia books, but also in those written by Sunni prominent ulema[28] that at first Fatima (as) remonstrated with Abu Bakr that she owned Fadak and that the Holy Prophet of Allah (s) had given it to her. Since witnesses were not available, she was forced to claim her right according to the law of inheritance.

Also, the ulema[29] narrate that the first claim of Fatima (as) was that Fadak had been a gift. When her witnesses were rejected, she was much pained and said in anger that she would not talk to Abu Bakr and Umar again.

And so, it was...she never saw them again and did not speak to them. When the time of her demise approached, she specified in her will that none of these people was to take part in her funeral prayers. Her uncle, Abbas, offered the funeral prayers, and she was laid to rest at night. According to Shia

---

[28] It is recorded in Siratu'l-Halabiyya, p.39, compiled by Ali Bin Burhanu'd-din Halabi Shafi'i (died 1044 A.H.)

[29] Imam Fakhru'd-din Razi in his Tafsir-e-Kabir concerning the claim of Fatima; Yaqut Hamawi in his Mu'ajamu'l-Buldan; Ibn Abi'l-Hadid Mu'tazali in Sharh-e-Nahju'l-Balagha, vol. IV, p. 80, from Abu Bakr Jauhari and the fanatical Ibn Hajar in Sawa'iq-e-Muhriqa, p.21, under the heading Shuhubhat-e-Rafza, VII Shubha.

sources and according to the statements of the Imams, Ali (as) performed the funeral prayers.

Will you please tell me which religious ordinance demands witnesses from one who is in possession of the property? It has been proved that Fatima (as) was in possession of Fadak. As reported by all Sunni ulema, Abu Bakr's demanding witnesses from her was against religious law. Does our religious law not say that witnesses should be produced by the plaintiff and not by the holder of the property?

Second, nobody denies the general significance of the 'Verse of Evidence', but it also has a specific significance. What do you mean by its specific significance? The proof for this is the report recorded in the authentic books of hadith, regarding Khazima Ibn Thabit. He gave evidence in support of the Holy Prophet (s) in a case concerning the sale of a horse. An Arab had made a claim against the Holy Prophet (s) and his (Khazima's) single evidence was considered sufficient. The Holy Prophet (s) gave him the title of Dhu'sh-Shahadatain because he was regarded as being equal to two just witnesses. This example shows that the 'Verse of Evidence' allows for exceptions under some circumstances. When Khazima, an individual believer and companion from among the community, was made an exception to the verse, Ali (as) and Fatima (as) who were infallible according to the 'Verse of Purity' were in a better position to enjoy this exception. They were definitely free from all falsehood. To reject their evidence was to reject the evidence of Allah.

Fatima (as) claimed that her father bestowed Fadak upon her as a gift and that it was in her possession and control during the Holy Prophet's lifetime. She was asked to furnish witnesses. She produced Amiru'l-Mu'minin Ali Bin Abi Talib and Hassan and Hussain as her witnesses. But their evidence was rejected. Was this action not unjust? It is beyond comprehension how anybody could reject Ali's testimony. Allah Almighty says in the Holy Qur'an that we should be with Ali, that is, we should follow him. Zaid-e-Adl became the embodiment of truth because of his extreme truthfulness.

Similarly, Ali (as) was also called 'the truthful,' as Allah says: *"O you who believe! Be careful of (your duty to) Allah and be with the truthful ones." (9:119)* Truthful ones" refers to the Prophet Muhammad (s), Ali, and the Ahl ul Bayt (as).

Sunni prominent scholars have written in their books and commentaries that this verse was revealed in praise of Muhammad (s) and Ali (as). "The truthful ones" refers to these two Holy men, and according to some reports it means Ali (as); other reports say that it refers to the progeny of the Holy Prophet (s).

The Sunni ulema[30] narrate that the Holy Prophet (s) said: *"These truthful ones are Muhammad and Ali."*

It is related[31] that Ibn Abbas said: *"In this verse 'the truthful ones' are Muhammad and his Holy descendants."*

And they[32] write: *"With the truthful ones, that is, with Ali Bin Abi Talib."*

Allah says: *"And he who brings the truth, and he who accepts it as the truth - these are they that guard (against evil)." (39:33)*

---

[30] Imam Tha'labi in the commentary Kashfu'l-Bayan, Jalalu'd-din Suyuti reporting from Ibn Abbas in his Durru'l-Manthur, Hafiz Abu Sa'id Abdu'l-Malik Bin Muhammad Khargushi reporting from Asma'is in his Sharafu'l-Mustafa, and Hafiz Abu Nu'aim Ispahani in his Hilyatu'l-Auliya

[31] Sheikh Sulayman Hanafi in his Yanabiu'l-Mawadda, ch. 39, p.1191, reporting from Muwaffaq Bin Ahmad Khawarizmi, Hafiz Abu Nu'aim Ispahani, and Hamwaini relates on the authority of Ibn Abbas

[32] Sheikhu'l-Islam Ibrahim Bin Muhammad Hamwaini, one of the Sunni eminent scholars, in his Fara'idu's-Simtain, Muhammad Bin Yusuf Ganji Shafi'i in his Kifayatu't-Talib, ch. 62, and Muhadith Sham in his Ta'rikh, reporting from his sources.

The ulema narrate in their books[33] from Ibn Abbas: "*He who brings the truth' is Muhammad, and 'he who testifies to it' is Ali Bin Abi Talib.*"

Allah says in chapter of Hadid (Iron) of the Holy Qur'an: "*And (as for) those who believe in Allah and his apostles, these it is who are the truthful and the faithful ones in the sight of their Lord; they shall have their reward and their light.*" (57:19)

Imam Ahmad Ibn Hanbal in his *Musnad* and Hafiz Abu Nu'aim Ispahani in *Manazil Mina'l-Qur'an Fi Ali* narrate on the authority of Ibn Abbas that this Holy verse was revealed in praise of Ali (as) referring to him as being among the truthful ones.

In the Chapter Nisa Allah says: "*And whoever obeys Allah and the Apostle, these are with those upon whom Allah has bestowed favors from among the Prophets and the truthful and the martyrs and the good, and a goodly company are they.*" (4:69)

In this verse also the truthful ones refers to Ali. There are many hadith narrated by sunni ulema and ours, indicating that Ali (as) was the truthful one of the community and in fact the most exalted among the truthful ones.

Many of prominent ulema[34] have written in their books that the Holy Prophet (s) said: "*There are three great truthful*

---

[33] Jalalu'd-din Suyuti in Durru'l-Manthur, Hafiz Ibn Mardawiyya in Manaqib, Hafiz Abu Nu'aim in Hilyatu'l-Auliya, Muhammad Bin Yusuf Ganji Shafi'i in Kifayatu't-Talib, ch.62, and Ibn Asakir in his Ta'rikh, reporting from a selection of commentators, narrate the following on the authority of Ibn Abbas and Mujahid.

[34] The following have all recorded this hadith: Imam Fakhru'd-din Razi in his Tafsir Kabir; Imam Tha'labi in Kashfu'l-Bayan; Jalalu'd-din Suyuti in Durru'l-Manthur; Imam Ahmad Bin Hanbal in the Musnad; Ibn Shirwaih in Firdaus; Ibn Abi'l-Hadid in Sharh-e-Nahju'l-Balagha, vol. II, p.451; Ibn Maghazili Shafi'i in Manaqib; and Ibn Hajar Makki in Sawa'iq-e-Muhriqa (30th hadith out of the 40 hadith that he has commented on concerning the virtues of Ali) quoting from Bukhari, who reports from Ibn Abbas, with the exception of the last phrase.

ones: - Hizqil, the Believer of the people of Pharaoh; Habib Najjar of the Surah Yasin, and Ali Bin Abi Talib, who is superior to them all."

Also they[35] narrate that the Holy Prophet (s) said: *"There are three truthful ones: - Habib Najjar, the Believer of the people of the Chapter Yasin who said, 'O people! follow the Prophets;' Hizqil, the believer of the people of Pharaoh, who said, 'Do you kill a man who worships Allah?', and Ali Ibn Abi Talib, who is the most exalted of them all."*

Sunni's themselves prove with various hadith in conformity with the Holy Qur'an, that Ali (as) occupied the highest rank among the truthful ones and yet they call others as "siddiq" (truthful) although not a single verse has been reported about their being truthful.

Reader! Please be just. Was it proper to reject the evidence of the person whom Allah calls "siddiq" in the Qur'an, one whom we have been commanded to follow?

The Holy Prophet (s) said: *"Ali is always with truth and truth revolves round Ali."*

It is narrated[36] that the Holy Prophet (s) was heard

---

[35] Sheikh Sulayman Balkhi in his Yanabiu'l-Mawadda, ch. 42, quoting from the Musnad of Imam Hanbal; Abu Nu'aim Ibn Maghazili Shafi'i; the great orator Khawarizmi, quoting from Abu Laila and Abu Ayyub Ansari, in his Manaqib; Ibn Hajar in his Sawa'iq (and a host of others)

[36] Khatib Baghdadi in his Ta'rikh, vol. IV, p. 321, Hafiz Ibn Mardawiyya in Manaqib, Imam Ahmad Bin Hanbal in Masnad, Fakhru'd-din Razi in Tafsir-e-Kabir, vol.I, p. 111, Ibn Hajar Makki in Jam'u's-Saghir, vol.II, pp. 74,75, 140 and Sawa'iq-e-Muhriqa, ch.IX,Fasl 11, hadith 21, narrating from Umme Salma and Ibn Abbas also in Yanabiu'l-Mawadda, ch. 65, p. 185, taking from Jam'u's-Saghir of Jalalu'd-din Suyuti, in addition, in Ta'rikhu'l-Khulafa, p.116, Faizu'l-Qadir, vol. IV, p. 358, narrating from Ibn Abbas Manaqibu's-Sabi'in, p. 237, hadith 44 quoting from the author of Firdaus; Sawa'iq-e-Muhriqa, ch.59, Part 2, p. 238, narrating from Umme Salma and Muhammad Bin Yusuf Ganji Shafi'i in Kifayatu't-Talib, some of them narrating from Umme Salma, some from 'Aisha and some from Muhammad Bin Abu Bakr.

saying: *"Ali is with the Qur'an and the Qur'an is with Ali; there will never be a difference between the two, and the two will not separate from each other until they reach me at the pool of Kauthar."*

Some narrators have reported these words: *"The right is always with Ali, and Ali is always with the right. There will be no difference between the two, and the two will not be separate from each other."*

Ibn Hajar writes in *Sawa'iq-e-Muhriqa*, ch. 9, Part 2, p. 77, that the Holy Prophet (s) on his deathbed, said: *" I leave behind with you two things: The book of Allah and my progeny, my Ahl ul Bayt."* Then, holding Ali's hand, he raised it and said: *"This Ali is with the Qur'an, and the Qur'an is with Ali. The two will not separate from each other till they reach me at the pool of Kauthar. Then I will ask each of them about the matter of succession."*

Also, it is generally narrated that the Prophet (s) said: *"Ali is with the right and the right is always with Ali. They revolve around each other."*

Sibt Ibn Jauzi, in *Tadhkirat-e-Khawasu'l-Umma*, p.20, in connection with the 'Hadith of Ghadir', narrates that the Holy Prophet (s) said: *"Let the right move round Ali, in whatever direction he moves."* Sibt commenting on this says: *"This hadith proves that if there is any difference between Ali and any other companion, the right will certainly be with Ali."*

It is recorded in the books that have been mentioned and in other authentic books of Sunni's that the Holy Prophet (s) often said: *"He who obeys Ali verily obeys me, and he who obeys me verily obeys Allah. He who disobeys Ali verily disobeys me, and he who disobeys me verily disobeys Allah."*

Abu'l-Fath Muhammad Bin Abdu'l-Karim Shahrastani reports in his *Milal-wa-Nihal* that the Holy Prophet (s) said: *"The reality is that Ali is always on the right, and those who follow him are on the right."*

With all these explicit reports, which are recorded in authentic books, wasn't refusing to agree with Ali (as) the same as refusing to agree with the Holy Prophet (s)?

Also reported[37] on the authority of Salman Muhammadi, that the Holy Prophet (s) said: *"Fatima's love is useful to us in a hundred places, the easiest of them being Death, the Grave, the Mizan (the Balance), Sirat (the bridge) and the Questioning. So, if my daughter, Fatima, is pleased with somebody, I am also pleased with him. If I am pleased with somebody, Allah is also pleased with him. If my daughter, Fatima, is displeased with somebody, I am also displeased with him. If I am displeased with him, Allah is also displeased with him. Woe be to him who oppresses Fatima and her husband. Woe be to him who oppresses Ali and Fatima and their Shia's."*

I ask you what conclusion you draw in light of these authentic hadith and the hadith recorded by Bukhari and Muslim that Fatima (as) remained indignant with Abu Bakr and Umar until she died.

Someone may say the hadith of "indignation" means religious indignation and not ordinary worldly indignation. Her indignation regarding Abu Bakr and Umar, which is recorded in all reliable books, was not religious. That is, Fatima (as) did not feel angry with Abu Bakr and Umar because they violated any religious injunction. Of course, if anyone had aroused her religious indignation, he would have been subject to his Prophet's curse. But Fatima's anger resulted from a change in her condition, which every sensitive person feels when he fails to achieve his object. Since Fatima (as) had made a request for Fadak and the Caliph did not accept her claim, she was naturally affected by it and felt indignant at that time. But later this slight

---

[37] Parsa of Bukhara in his Faslu'l-Khitab; one by Imam Ahmad Bin Hanbal in Musnad and by Mir Seyyed Ali Hamadani Shafi'i in Mawadda XIII of Mawaddatu'l-Qurba.

displeasure disappeared from her mind, and she was satisfied with the decision of the Caliph. The proof of her satisfaction was her silence. And when Ali (as) took the reins of the caliphate, he did not for all his supreme authority, take back Fadak under his control. This, too, is proof that he was satisfied with the decision of the previous caliphs.

First, to say that Fatima's anger was not religious but worldly. You would have expressed this view without careful study. According to the principles of the Qur'anic verses and the hadith of the Holy Prophet (s), no perfect believer would ever show such an indignation, not to speak of Fatima (as), whose eminence is evident from the "Verse of Purity": "Verse of Mubahala" and the Sura Hal Ata of the Holy Qur'an. (76:1)

There are numerous hadith in all the authentic books that Fatima (as) occupied the highest rank of iman (belief) and that the Holy Prophet (s) had explicitly said about her: *"Verily, Allah has filled my daughter, Fatima, with belief from head to foot."*

Any believer, man or woman, whose special mark is to admit the truth, would never show any indignation when a judge issues a just order. Nor would such a believer cling to that anger and wrath till his death insisting in his will that none of those who were in any way connected with those orders should be allowed to join in his funeral prayers.

Moreover Fatima (as), about whose purity Allah Himself gives evidence, could never make a false claim, so that a judge might reject her claim.

Second, if Lady Fatima's indignation was merely "worldly indignation", or her disappointment in having her claim rejected, her anger should have subsided soon, particularly after the regret shown by those responsible for her anger. There should have been no grief in her heart. The Holy Prophet (s) said: *"One of the signs of a believer is that he does not naturally nurse any grudge based on carnal sentiments, against anybody."*

Also, the Holy Prophet (s) said: *"If a believer happens to commit a fault, the aggrieved believer does not feel antipathy towards him for more than three days."*

So, the pure and truthful Fatima Zahra (as), who was, according to the testimony of Allah Almighty, imbued with faith from head to foot, could never bear malice against anybody. And it is acknowledged by both sects that Fatima (as) left this world angry with Abu Bakr and Umar. So, it follows from this that Fatima's indignation was purely religious. When she saw that the order was passed against her in violation of the commands of Allah and her Holy father, she felt furious with religious displeasure and this was that anger, which incurred Allah's and His Prophet's wrath.

Third, Silence does not necessarily mean concurrence. Sometimes the oppressor's rigidity forces acquiescence.

Fatima (as) was not only grieved, but she left this world indignant. Both Bukhari and Muslim wrote: *"Fatima was indignant with Abu Bakr. She kept aloof from him and did not talk with him for the rest of her life."*

Fourth, Ali (as) did not, during the period of his caliphate, take possession of Fadak and return it to the descendants of Fatima (as), this indicated his acquiescence in the decision of the previous caliphs. Even here you would be mistaken. The Holy Imam was not free to act during the period of his caliphate so as to have stopped any innovation or restore any right. Whenever he intended to take such a step, there was immediate opposition.

If he had returned Fadak to the descendants of Fatima (as), his opponents, particularly Mu'awiya and his followers, would have claimed that Ali (as) acted against the practices adopted by Abu Bakr and Umar. Besides this, in order to pass such orders, authority and independence were necessary. But people had not allowed him such power. He could not introduce anything that would have violated the precepts and practices of the previous caliphs. Ali's powerlessness is evident from the following two examples.

Since the previous caliphs had removed the pulpit from its place where the Prophet (s) had placed it, the Imam intended to return it to its original place. But the people opposed him and would not tolerate anything contrary to the practice of Abu Bakr and Umar, even though it might be compatible with the practice of the Holy Prophet (s).

Similarly, when the Imam forbade the people to offer congregational tarawih prayers, they rose against him and claimed that Ali (as) wanted to change the way of Caliph Umar.

So how could Ali (as) restore Fadak to the descendants of Fatima (as)? If he had done so and said that it had been unjustly confiscated, the people would have cried that Ali Bin Abi Talib was inclined towards the world and was usurping the right of the Muslims for their own descendants. Hence, he thought it proper to be patient. Since the real claimant had left this world, he suspended his claim to it, so that when the last of the divinely guided Imams comes to restore rights to their just claimants, he will secure his right.

In such a state of affairs the silence of the Imam did not mean that he was satisfied with the decision. If he had considered the action of the previous caliphs just, he would not have argued his case before them. Also, he would not have expressed his anguish and displeasure and would not have invoked Allah to be the arbiter.

It is recorded in *Nahju'l-Balagha* that Ali (as) in a letter to the Governor of Basra, Uthman Bin Hunaif Ansari wrote: *"Among those things on which the sky casts its shadow was Fadak, which was in our possession. But a group showed niggardliness and the other side, Fatima, and her descendants withdrew from pursuing their claim. And the best Judge is Allah."*

If you say that Fatima (as) was satisfied with the decision in the last days of her life and pardoned those responsible for it. I am afraid you are mistaken here. As has been proved beyond doubt earlier through reliable hadith that oppressed Lady remained indignant until she died.

To prove my point of view I should like to submit the following report[38]: *"Umar asked Abu Bakr to go with him to visit Fatima. They had certainly enraged her."* (Some reports say that it was Abu Bakr, who asked Umar to go with him to visit Fatima (as). This seems more plausible.)

In short, both of them went together to the door of Fatima (as) but she did not allow them to visit her. When they asked Ali (as) to intervene, he remained silent, but he allowed them to go in. When they went in and saluted her, she turned her face to the wall.

Abu Bakr said: *'O part of the Prophet's liver, by Allah, I value the relationship of the Holy Prophet with you more than my relationship with my daughter, 'Aisha. Would that I had died soon after the Holy Prophet of Allah (s). I know your rank and position more than any one else. If I have deprived you of your right of heritage, it was really because of the Holy Prophet, whom I myself heard saying: 'We Prophets do not leave any heritage. What we leave is charity (for the Muslims).'*

Fatima (as) then said to Amiru'l-Mu'minin (as) that she would remind them of a hadith of the Holy Prophet (s) and ask them to say in the name of Allah if they had not heard the Holy Prophet (s) saying it: *'Fatima's pleasure is my pleasure, Fatima's indignation is my indignation. So, one who loves my daughter Fatima loves me; one who pleases Fatima, pleases me. One who offends Fatima, offends me.'*

---

[38] Abu Muhammad Abdullah Bin Muslim Bin Qutayba Dinawari (died 276 A.H.) in his *Ta'rikh-e-Khilafa'i'r-Rashidin*, known as *Al-Imama wa's-Siyasa*, vol. I, p. 14 and other Sunni ulema, like Ibn Abi'l-Hadid, write in their authentic books.

Both said: *'Yes we heard these words from the Holy Prophet of Allah (s).'*

Then Fatima (as) said: *'I call Allah and His Angels to witness that both of you have offended me and did not treat me justly. When I meet the Holy Prophet I will certainly complain to him of you both.'*

Abu Bakr, being troubled at these words, began to weep and said: *'I seek Allah's shelter from the Holy Prophet's anger.'*[39]

Fatima (as) began to weep and said: *'I swear by Allah that I will certainly call down curses upon you in all my prayers.'*

After hearing this, Abu Bakr went out, weeping. People gathered round him and consoled him. To them he said: *'Woe be to you. You are all happy, sitting with your wives comfortably, but I am in this wretched state. I do not need your allegiance. Rid me of it. By Allah, after what I have seen and heard from Fatima, I do not want any Muslim to suffer the burden of allegiance to me.'*

These reports, related by sunni notable ulema, show that the oppressed Fatima (as) remained indignant with Abu Bakr and Umar until the last hour of her life.

The clearest proof of Fatima's anger in this regard is that she made the following will to her husband, Amiru'l-Mu'minin Ali: *"None of those persons who have oppressed me and snatched away my right should be allowed to join my funeral. They are certainly my and the Holy Prophet's enemies. Do not allow any one of them or their associates to offer funeral prayers for me. Bury me at night when people are asleep."*

---

[39] If he were truly remorseful then he would have returned what he had taken from the Prophets household, which he did not. You cannot steal something and say I am sorry yet keep the item you stole. Did they return Fadak to Fatima (as)? Did they return the government rule back to Imam Ali (as)? No, they did not so this shows that they were not truly remorseful or trying to make things right.

Bukhari writes in his *Sahih* that Ali (as) complied with Lady Fatima's will and buried her at night quietly. People tried their best to find where Fatima (as) was buried, but they could not. It is unanimously accepted that Fatima (as) was, according to her will, buried at night. The Holy Prophet (s) left a single daughter to serve as his memory. The sunni ulema agree that he said: *"Fatima is a part of my body. She is my legacy and trust. Respect her as you respect me. Never do anything to incite her anger against you. If she is angry with you, I also will be angry with you."*

Mir Seyyed Ali Hamadani Faqih Shafi'i writes in his *Mawaddatu'l-Qurba* that the Holy Prophet (s) said: *"Those who grieve Fatima will be strictly dealt with by me on the Day of Judgment. Fatima's pleasure is my pleasure, and Fatima's anger is my anger. Woe be to him with whom Fatima is indignant."*

How tragic is it that for all these declarations, the Community not only ignored her but also snatched away her right and caused her so intense torment. Even while still a young woman, she declared: *"I was subjected to so many troubles that if days had been subjected to such troubles, they would have turned into nights."* [40]

What Amir al-mu'minin Ali (as) said on the occasion of the burial of Fatima while addressing the Holy Prophet (s) at his grave: *"O' Prophet of Allah (s), peace be upon you from me and from your daughter who has come to you and who has hastened to meet you. O' Prophet of Allah (s), my patience about your chosen (daughter) has been exhausted, and my power of endurance has weakened, except that I have ground for consolation in having endured the great hardship and heart-rending event of your separation. I laid you down in your grave when your last breath had passed (when your head was) between my neck and chest.*

---

[40] Peshawar Nights by Sultanul Waizin Shirazi

... *Verily we are Allah's and verily unto Him shall we return. (Qur'an 2:156)*

Now, the trust has been returned and what had been given has been taken back. As to my grief, it knows no bounds, and as to my nights, they will remain sleepless till Allah chooses for me the house in which you are now residing.

Certainly, your daughter would apprise you of the joining together of your ummah (people) for oppressing her. You ask her in detail and get all the news about the position. This has happened when a long time had not elapsed and your remembrance had not disappeared. My salam (salutation) be on you both, the salam of a grief stricken not a disgusted or hateful person; for if I go away it is not because I am weary (of you), and if I stay it is not due to lack of belief in what Allah has promised those who endure."[41]

---

[41] Nahjul Balagha sermon 201

Bilal's protest and banishment to Syria

Bilal of Africa was the first muezzin[42]. When Madina developed all the characteristics of a state, it also acquired a treasury, and the Prophet (s) appointed Bilal its officer in charge. He oversaw the *bayt ul maal* (Treasury) of the state of Madina. This made him the first treasurer of Islam. He made allocations of all funds. He was also responsible for distributing funds to the widows, orphans, the wayfayers and other poor people who had no means of supporting themselves.[43]

From the day the Holy Prophet (s) and other Muslims migrated to Madina Bilal used to call the the people to the mosque to gather them there i.e. at the time of prayers, mobilization of the army, or when there was a problem to be solved he used to say adhan and immediately the people poured into the mosque and formed a gathering.

All were familiar with the voice of Bilal and they always waited to hear his invigorating call that invited them to Allah and to good things.

However, when after the Holy Prophet (s), Abu Bakr attained to caliphate he decided to go to the mosque in that capacity and to stand in the Prophet's niche so that by this means he might strengthen the pillars of his government and contact the people directly. The first step for the formation of a gathering

---

[42] Person who calls to prayer

[43] A Restatement of the History of Islam and Muslims page 553

and the people coming to the mosque while the Prophet (s) was alive was the saying of the adhan by Bilal inviting them to the mosque. However, Bilal did not say adhan after the Holy Prophet's demise and was the most sensitive, the most natural and at the same time the most dangerous tactics that Bilal employed against the caliphate. From that point onwards Bilal did not participate in any official gatherings of theirs. The absence of Bilal, who held a delicate post, from the stage and the society, could make the people think about the problem of the day.

The supporters of the caliph thought that if Bilal said the adhan the hue and cry of the opponents of the caliph would die down and the people would come to the mosque, as they were accustomed to do on hearing the voice of Bilal. The saying of adhan by Bilal could draw a curtain on the intrigue of the administration of the caliphate and deceive the simple minded and common people.

With these thoughts in mind, they located Bilal after a good deal of search and asked him to say the adhan for the prayers.

Bilal had been trained in the lap of Islam for twenty-three years and had been directly concerned with the various events which formed the history of the new nation. He had recognized and accepted Islam with sincerity and had heard what the Holy Prophet (s) had said regarding the leader and leadership. Especially he was aware of the unambiguous remarks of the Holy Prophet (s) about the caliphate of Imam Ali (as) and knew that the ruling administration had come to power against the orders of Allah and the Holy Prophet (s). According to his belief only the commander of the faithful Imam Ali (as) was entitled attain the caliphate. In the circumstances it is evident as to what reply he was going to give to those who approached him.

The messengers of the caliph insisted very much but Bilal repeated the same reply every time and did not pay any heed to their words. By not saying the adhan Bilal wished to oblige the people to think about the matter and to remind themselves gradually of the time of the Holy Prophet (s) and the recommendations made by him with regard to Imam Ali (as) and to his Imamate. It was this reason that when people asked him as to why he did not say adhan he said in reply *"After the Holy Prophet of Islam I shall not say the adhan for another person."*

On the other hand, nonparticipation of the Commander of the Faithful Ali (as), Salman, Abu Zar, Zubayr, Bilal, Miqdad, Sohayb, etc. in the gatherings which were usually formed in the mosque strengthened Bilal's stand and became the cause of the people doubting the rightfulness and legality of the ruling body and even objecting to it.

The administration of the caliphate was scared and worried because of the stand taken by Bilal and tried to make him and other opponents surrender.

It was in this state of fear that the caliph sent some people formally to Bilal to make that "obstinate and inflexible black man" surrender to the caliphate at any costs by means of promises, threats, or allurement of money and position.

However, Bilal was not prepared to ignore the truth and "to do as the Romans do." He saw Islam personified in Imam Ali (as) and believed that even if the recommendation of the Holy Prophet (s) had not been there, no one except Imam Ali (as) was fit for the caliphate. He was convinced that true Islam was the same that was put forward by Imam Ali (as) and his friends though few in numbers. He, who had borne hardships and suffered torture for the same Islam, could not now see it as a plaything of material desires and of the administration of the caliphate. He, therefore, gave a clear-cut reply to the representatives of the caliph in these words: *"I shall not say the adhan for anyone except the person whom the Holy Prophet selected as his successor."*

At last Umar, who was a close friend of the caliph Abu

Bakr and was considered to be the most important factor for his selection as caliph and great supporter of his continuance in that office decided to discuss the matter with Bilal personally.

When Umar saw Bilal, he was thinking: *"Now I shall make him surrender and shall take him out of the fold of the opponents of the caliph."*

After salutation and exchange of compliments Umar said: *"O' Bilal! Why have you left us alone these days? I was very keen that you should be with us so that we could entrust you with some tasks. Why don't you come to the mosque? We expect you to say adhan and call the people to the mosque to offer prayers with the caliph of the Holy Prophet. I understand that you have said that you will no longer say adhan. Why so? Do you remember that this very Abu Bakr delivered you from the servantry of and persecution by your cruel master? Is it proper that you should abandon him now and should not say adhan for him?"*

Bilal began recollecting the past events of history like persecution and the period of his banishment and homelessness, his migration to Madina, military engagements with the infidels and the polytheists, conquest of Makkah and the passing away of the Holy Prophet (s). He said to Umar: *"How happy were the days when the Holy Prophet was among us and invited the people to Allah and justice. And how hard, dark and calamitous these days are! With what conditions are we confronted?"*

Bilal turned the conversation to the matter under discussion and while tears were flowing down his cheeks he continued to say: *"Let us see whether Abu Bakr purchased me for the sake of Allah and set me free for the sake of Allah, or he had some other motive. If he did all of this for the sake of Allah, he does not enjoy any right on me and if he did not act for the sake of Allah, I am still his servant and under his control, but I am free in the matter of faith. And as I have already said I am not going to say adhan for any other person after the Holy*

Prophet. Furthermore, I am going to swear allegiance only to that person whose allegiance is my responsibility. I accept only that person as Caliph who has been nominated by the Holy Prophet as his successor. And then I say to you if Abu Bakr had not purchased me and set me free on that day and I would have died in that condition, because I was then certainly a true believer and would have gone to paradise. But in the present circumstances when you want me to participate in this matter, I do not know whether I am destined to go to paradise or hell and whether or not I can preserve my faith."

Umar was very much annoyed on hearing these words and cast on Bilal a harsh angry look full of scorn. After a few moments he got up and went away much agitated.

All the plans of the administration of the caliphate for making Bilal surrender were frustrated and it could not cause the slightest damage to his firm determination. He persevered fearlessly, did not listen to the promises made with him, remained undaunted in the face of threats, and did not surrender. In view of the stand taken by Bilal and the sensitiveness that had been created in the society owing to his refusing to take the oath of allegiance to Abu Bakr the administration of the caliphate drew its last plan to punish him. As it was feared that some people might join him and trouble might increase, one of those present suggested that it would be better if Bilal was exiled from Madina to a place distant from the capital so that by this means the hue and cry might come to an end and the people might forget him.

However, the advisors of the caliph said: *"If we exile him openly, we shall be blamed more. It is possible that Imam Ali may object to it. In that event our action will produce a result contrary to that desired by us. It will, therefore, be better if he is subjected to threats and torture so that he may be compelled to leave Madina of his own free will."*

This scheme was approved by the majority vote and

accordingly Bilal was tortured during day and night and subjected to threats of death. At last, he received a message on these lines: *"Either you should swear allegiance to Abu Bakr and say adhan or quit Madina."*

Some historians have written thus: Umar said to Bilal: *"Now that you do not say adhan you should not remain in Madina so that you may not become the cause of corruption of others."* And he subjected Bilal to pressure.

Thus, the spokesman of the movement of Islam was placed in a strange predicament. On the one hand it was difficult for him to forsake the city of the Prophet (s) and on the other hand it had also become impossible for him to stay there. He pondered as to whether he should stay on in Madina or resist the pressure.

After all, how could he abandon Madina the tomb of the Holy Prophet (s) his master, as it was the city of his friend with many remembrances? However, he was obliged to prefer going away from there so that possibly he might persuade the people more to think about the current and unsatisfactory affairs and, they might resort to objection, criticism, and occasionally disobedience, and possibly the usurped right might return to its owner. This had to be done because there was no other remedy. If he had stayed on in Madina it would have been necessary for him to agree with the rulers, and he would have to explain the existing situation and his own stand. If he had stayed on, he would have to confirm the actions of the government and this was impossible for Bilal, because in his opinion these actions were unjust. He decided to go to Syria and got ready for the banishment come what might. Before deciding to leave Madina Bilal had consulted the family of the Holy Prophet (s). When he got ready to depart, he first of all went to see and say farewell to Imam Ali.

This meeting took place in a very disturbing atmosphere and the Imam was much moved. Tears were rolling on the cheeks of Bilal like pearls and perhaps he was saying *'If I had the option I would not at all have gone away from you and the tomb of the Holy Prophet. I hope that I shall return.'* Then he visited the tomb of the Holy Prophet (s) in a state of extreme sadness and kept weeping for a long time.

He said: *"O' honorable Prophet of Islam! You yourself are aware of how sad days we are passing and what a strong blow has been struck on the body of your religion. O' Prophet of Allah (s)! I have in fact been compelled as a consequence of the ever-increasing pressure of the administration of the caliphate to go away from your city to Syria."*

At the time of dawn of that night Bilal departed from Madina and proceeded to Syria.

At last, after surmounting various difficulties faced by him on the way between Madina and Damascus, Bilal completed the journey. When he came near Damascus he stopped for a moment and stared at the city with surprise and said to himself: *"What a dull and sad city it is! It appears that death has cast its shadow everywhere. O' Lord! How can I live here? I have been thinking that the journey has come to an end, and I can take rest for a while, but now I have become more tired and sad. O'Lord! What should I do? I ought to put up with their condition and remain patient while I am away from my master Imam Ali and his faithful companions. When I have borne all these inconveniences how can I live here as I did in the past?"*

Bilal proceeded to the gate of the city with a very heavy heart and located a place for himself after a good deal of wandering and searching.

Bilal was pleased and satisfied because he had been able to withstand the oppression and strength of the powerful persons and to speak the truth. He thanked Allah and prided himself on his own existence on seeing that his very being was dangerous for the rulers and they feared even his silence.

Bilal resided in Damascus for some time. Though he himself was in Damascus, his soul was in Madina. He was continuously thinking about some solution of the problem. At last, he lost patience and decided to return to Madina so that he might see the family of the Prophet and his honorable Imam once again. He also thought the political condition of the government would not consider his return to be expedient, and it was possible that they might restrain him. However, as he had taken a decision, he said to himself: *"I shall perform this journey even though it may cost me my life."*

Bilal left Damascus with great courage and enthusiasm and special attattchment to the Prophet's family. The path which seemed to be long at the time of his starting the journey was covered soon. He reached near Madina and saw the quiet spectacle of the city. He saw the walls of the Holy Prophet's Mosque from a distance and recollected the sweet memories of the past. He sighed and tears began to flow from his eyes.

After his arrival in the city Bilal went immediately to the tomb of the Holy Prophet (s). The spies also saw Bilal and thought of arresting him. However, they did not consider it expedient to do so, but went to the authorities and reported the arrival of Bilal to them. The authorities were scared and worried on hearing this news. On the other hand, this news reached Lady Fatema Zahra the beloved daughter of the Holy Prophet (s) and in the meantime, Bilal came to know that she was not in good health. The news distressed him, and he began humming by the side of the tomb of the Holy Prophet (s): *"O' Prophet of Allah (s)! After you the world has become dark and Imamate has been converted into caliphate and people who are not fit for this position have usurped it. O' Prophet of Allah (s)! I have come to know that your daughter is not in good health. O' Prophet of Allah (s)! Your successor Ali is staying at home. By means of his silence he is preserving the exaltation of Islam and the unity of the Muslims. O' Prophet of Allah (s)! I have just returned from my journey to Syria. I had been exiled there……….."*

Then due to acute disturbance of mind Bilal fell on the ground and became unconscious.

After the demise of the Holy Prophet (s) his only daughter Fatima who dearly felt the separation of her beloved father, gradually became ill. And when she heard that Bilal had returned to Madina she expressed the desire that he should say adhan once again.

Time for noon prayers approached. The muezzin of the Holy Prophet (s) went on the roof of the mosque and began to say adhan with his loud voice as he had been doing in the recent past. He said *Allahu Akbar!"*

On hearing the voice of Bilal, the first muezzin of the Holy Prophet (s) the people of Madina came out of their houses and proceeded to the mosque. All of them wondered as to how Bilal was saying adhan again after the death of the Holy Prophet (s). A few moments later a larger number of people gathered in the mosque and Bilal continued to say adhan.

When Bilal pronounced Takbir loudly and Lady Fatima heard it in her house she was reminded of the glorious and sweet days of her father's time. She sighed and began to weep. Her children also joined her in weeping.

When Bilal said *"Ashhadu an laa ilaha illAllah"* (I bear witness that there is no God but Allah) Lady Fatima wept more bitterly. However, when the adhan reached the delicate stage, she lost her sense owing to intense grief. Bilal was, therefore, advised to stop saying adhan at once, because the life of Lady Fatima Zahra was in danger.

The people who gathered near the mosque, in the streets, on the roads and in whose eyes a particular enthusiasm and fervor was rolling suddenly came to themselves when Bilal's adhan was cut off and wondered as to why this had happened.

Of course, Bilal said his last adhan with his entire self

and with his faith in the Holy Prophet (s) and love for his school.

Bilal, who was no longer keen to live owing to the pressure of hardships, got ready to play an enlightening and informative role among the people with his political activities. He mobilized the people against the people of authorities in government by means of discussions and fiery speeches in such a way that the people began to raise objections and shouted harsh slogans of protest against the government, and it was feared that they might cause disturbances. The agents of government, therefore, poured into the mosques arrested Bilal and exiled him to Syria once again.

After his second exile Bilal was not permitted even to take permission from the Holy Prophet's sacred tomb because the officials kept a watch over him everywhere and he himself realized the position very well. Hence, he turned his face to the tomb of the Holy Prophet (s) and opened out his heart for quite some time after offering him salutations.

Bilal arrived in Damascus and was much grieved on account of the conditions that had been created for him. He prayed for Islam and the Muslims day and night and felt very sad when he saw in danger the pains taken by the Holy Prophet (s) for many years.

Indeed, Bilal was living in Damascus under extreme pressure by the government. It was very rare that anyone might be able to see him and at all times he lived alone. The matters had come to such a pass that he now greatly suffered on account of lonliness.

Bilal was born like this, lived like this and eventually ascended the alter of love. It was an ascension that took him to the highest peak of glory and martyrdom. Now he is in the great world with a world of greatness. All his friends were shedding tears on his martyrdom. It was Bilal the black servant who made history and rolled up the old aristocratic order of the age of ignorance and began to shine as an eternal face that will serve as an example in the annals of history of mankind. He has really made himself immortal. He has become a paragon of piety and purity.

The people were endeavouring much to glorify and attend his funeral. All those who were participating in the ceremonies of his burial were weeping bitterly. Damascus was one of the important bases of Umayyad imperialism and the theatre of appearance of the usurped caliphate of the unlawful heirs of the Islamic revolution. Still, despite the savage and tyrannical rule of Bani Umayyah, a large number of people attended his funeral. In other cities of the Islamic territories and especially in Madina the people were very much grieved and saddened. They mourned Bilal's death for a long period. Bilal was one of those few people who defended the truth till the last moment of their lives. He preached true Islam. Neither the tortures of different kinds weakened his firm determination, nor was he allured, nor terrified by threats, nor did he swear allegiance to an undeserving person, nor did he sacrifice Islam and reality for the sake of expediency, worldliness, name, and wealth.

After leading a life of freedom and self-sacrifice in the path of Islam, Bilal passed away in such circumstances that he possessed no material thing. Noble-minded Muslims buried his dead body in the graveyard named Saghir situated in Damascus and mourned his death for some days. His grave is a place of pilgrimage of the Muslims and freedom loving people of the world from that time until today. It is the grave from which lessons of freedom, reality, sincerity, self-sacrifice, and steadfastness are learnt and which teaches us as to how a person should live and how he should die.

All the Muslim historians, to whichever sect they belong, while mentioning the close and faithful companions of the great leader of Islam have named Bilal as one of them and have placed him in the the category of those who were near him. Thus, it is observed that in consequence of Islam and enforcement of its commands and valuable teachings Bilal, who was not more than a servant before the dawn of Islam, secured such a high status that he was reckoned to be one of those people who were the sincerest, the most devoted, and the most proximate companions of the Holy Prophet (s).

So long as Bilal was alive, he endeavored for the advancement of Islam and was sincerely devoted to the family of the Holy Prophet (s) till the last moment of his life.[44]

---

[44] Bilal of Africa by Hussain Malika Ashtiyani pages 100-111

Ammar Yasir & Abdullah ibn Masud Beaten

Moreover, Uthman beat the companions who objected to his oppression. Among them was Abdullah Bin Mas'ud[45], who was a Hafiz[46], Qari[47], treasurer of the public treasury, a scribe who recorded the revealed verses, and one of the chief companions of the Holy Prophet (s). Abu Bakr and Umar, both of whom used to take counsel from him, held him in high esteem.

Ibn Khaldun in his History commented that Caliph Umar insisted that Abdullah remain with him because he possessed complete knowledge of the Holy Qur'an and because the Prophet (s) spoke highly of him. Ibn Abi'l-Hadid and others have written the same thing.

Sunni ulema agree that when Uthman intended to compile the Holy Qur'an, he obtained all the copies from the scribes. He demanded the copy of the Holy Qur'an from Abdullah Bin Mas'ud also. Abdullah did not give it to him. Uthman himself went to his house and took the copy of the Holy Qur'an from him by force. Later, when Abdullah learned that, like other copies of the Holy Qur'an, his copy had been burnt, he was much aggrieved.

In social and religious gatherings, he narrated the condemnatory hadith that he knew about Uthman. When this news reached Uthman, he had Ibn Mas'ud so severely beaten by his servants that his teeth were broken, and he was confined to bed. After three days he succumbed to his injuries.

---

[45] Abdullah ibn Mas'ud was not a Shia, but it would benefit to know his story to expose the cruelty and injustice of Uthman.

[46] A person who memorized the whole Quran

[47] Qur'an reciter

Ibn Abi'l-Hadid writes in detail[48] about these facts and goes on to say that Uthman went to see the ailing Abdullah. They talked together for some time. Uthman said, *"O Abdu'r-Rahman! Pray to Allah for my forgiveness."*

Abdullah said, *"I pray to Allah to take my right from you"* (that is, that justice be done).

When Abu Dharr, a close companion of the Holy Prophet (s), was banished to Rabza, Abdullah went to see him off. For this Abdullah was given forty lashes. So, Abdullah insisted to Ammar Yasir that Uthman not be allowed to offer Abdullah's funeral prayers. Ammar Yasir agreed, and after Abdullah's death, he offered the funeral prayers along with a group of the companions. When Uthman learned of the funeral arrangement, he came to Abdullah's grave and asked Ammar why he had said the funeral prayers. He replied that he was constrained to do it because Abdullah had willed it.

Abdullah ibn Masood was one of the principal companions of the Prophet (s). As noted, before, he was the first man who read Qur'an in Kaaba in the presence of the leaders of the Quraysh and was beaten up by them for doing so. He was one of the most knowledgeable men in Medina. He spent much time in the company of the Prophet (s) and had more familiarity with his practices and precedents than most of the other companions. It was for this reason that Umar had asked him to be always with him. There were many occasions when Umar did not know how the Prophet (s) had solved a problem or had taken a decision in some matter. On such occasions, he consulted Abdullah ibn Masood, and acted upon his advice. In his later years, Umar had appointed him treasurer of Kufa.

Abdullah ibn Masood was the treasurer of Kufa when Saad bin Abi Waqqas was its governor. Uthman dismissed Saad

---

[48] In Volume I, pages 67 and 226 of *Sharh Nahju'l-Balagha* (printed in Egypt) under "Ta'n VI,"

and made Walid bin Aqaba the new governor. Walid took a loan from the treasury. When the stipulated time had passed, and the loan was not returned, Ibn Masood asked him to pay it. He informed Uthman about it. Uthman wrote to him: *"You are my treasurer. Do not demand the loan from Walid."* Ibn Masood resented this. He threw away the keys of the treasury and stayed at home. From that time, Abdullah ibn Masood became a critic of Uthman's fiscal and political policies.

Walid wrote to Uthman about him, and the latter asked him (Walid) to send him (Ibn Masood) to Medina. Ibn Masood arrived in Medina and went into the Mosque. When he entered the Mosque, Uthman was reading the sermon. When Uthman saw him entering the Mosque, he said: *"A foul and despicable beast is coming toward you."*

Ibn Masood said: *"That is not so. I am the companion and friend of the Apostle of God. I fought at Badr, and I am a Companion of the Tree."*

'Aisha also heard in her chamber what Uthman had said, and she cried out: *"Is this the kind of language you use for a companion of the Apostle of God?!"*

Uthman ordered Abdullah ibn Masood to get out of the Mosque of the Prophet (s). Uthman's servants threw him out of the Mosque, and down on the ground breaking his ribs.

Ali (as) rose to upbraid Uthman and said: *"You have hurt a friend of the Apostle merely at a report from Walid. You know that Walid is a liar."* He then carried Ibn Masood to his home.

Uthman was not satisfied with what he had done. After breaking the ribs of Abdullah ibn Masood, he stopped payment of his pension, and forbade him to leave Medina. Ibn Masood wished to go to Syria and to take part in the campaigns, but Uthman repeated what he had heard Marwan saying: *"He has created enough trouble in Kufa; do not let him do the same in*

Syria."[49]

As noted, before, Abdullah ibn Masood had made his own collection of the verses of Qur'an, and he had arranged them in chronological order. But Uthman had appointed his favorite, Zayd bin Thabit, to collect and to arrange the verses of Qur'an. He did not "recognize" the collection of Ibn Masood and ordered him to surrender his copy. Abdullah ibn Masood refused to do so whereupon the servants of Uthman broke into his house, and forcibly seized the copy of Qur'an from him. This copy was burned at Uthman's orders.

Uthman used the powers of state in dealing with men like Abu Dharr el-Ghiffari, Ammar ibn Yasir and Abdullah ibn Masood because they refused to compromise with their principles. All three of them had to pay a penalty for this refusal but they gladly paid it.

Uthman, however, also tangled with some of those men who were not too finicky about such things as principles. Among them was Abdur Rahman bin Auf and Amr bin Aas. Both were directly responsible for his accession to the throne.[50]

Abu Dharr having returned to Medina from Syria was busy in his preachings when one more heart-rending incident came to pass and that was the burning of the Holy Qur'an. He was already grieved to see that the Islamic State was being ruined. The wealth of Muslim ummah was being spent on relatives and kinsmen of the Caliph. The door of the Public Treasury was completely closed to the needy, the poor, the orphans, and the widows, but it was wide open to the descendants of Umayyah. The poor people were starving while the relatives of the Caliph were purchasing houses, gardens, and lands. All of a sudden, he got the news that the Caliph got

---

[49] (p. 160) *(al- Fitna-tul-Kubra {The Great Upheaval}, published in Cairo in 1959)*

[50] A Restatement of the History of Islam and Muslims by Sayed A A Razwy

different copies of the Qur'an collected from a far and wide, and put them to flames. Therefore, this important incident became the target of his preaching. The historian Abul Fida writes that this happened in 30 A.H.[51]

The historian Ya'qubi writes in his book that Uthman collected the Qur'an and arranged it in such a way that he placed big surahs (chapters) together and the small surahs together separately, and sending for copies from all sides, got them washed with hot water and vinegar and set fire to them. As a result of it no Qur'an was left except the copy belonging to Ibn Mas'ud which was with him in Kufa. When Abdullah Ibn 'Amir, the Governor of Kufa, asked Ibn Mas'ud for his copy he refused to give it. At this news Uthman wrote to 'Amir to arrest Ibn Mas'ud and send him to Medina. When Ibn Mas'ud came and entered the masjid, Uthman was busy delivering his speech. Seeing Ibn Mas'ud he said, *"An ugly and ill-natured animal has come."* Ibn Mas'ud also strongly retorted in response. Hearing it Uthman ordered people to beat him. So, the people beat him and dragged him in such a way that two of his ribs got fractured.

It is written in the Persian translation of *Tarikh A'tham Kufi*[52] that Uthman tore off the Qur'an and got it burnt. The same is given in the book *"Successors of Muhammad."*[53]

According to *"Najatul Mu'minin"* by Mulla Mohsin Kashmiri, Uthman got the ribs of Ibn Mas'ud fractured and snatching his Qur'an got it burnt.

According to *Rauzatul Ahbab* vol. 2, p. 229[54], Uthman ordered, *"My Qur'an must be given currency in my domain and*

---

[51] (Tarikh Abul Fida, vol. 2, p. 100, printed in Amritsar, 1901 A.D.)

[52] Printed in Bombay vide page 147 line 8

[53] W. Irving p.160 printed in London, 1850 A.D.

[54] Printed Lucknow

the remaining Qur'ans should be burnt." Accordingly, all the remaining copies of Qur'an were got burnt.

According to other sources[55], Uthman sent word to Hafsah, the wife of the Holy Prophet (s), to send him the Scriptures so that he might copy them out and then return them to her. Hafsah sent those Scriptures which were with her and Uthman appointed Zayd bin Thabit, Abdullah bin Zubayr, Sa'id bin 'As, Abdul Rahman bin Harith to collect and copy the Scriptures, and asked all the three men of the Quraysh to write the Qur'an in the colloquy of Quraysh in case there arose some difference on some point in it, because the Qur'an had been revealed in their language. They did accordingly till the Scripture was copied out and Uthman returned the Scriptures to Hafsah as promised and sent one newly prepared copy to her. Now only the copy of the Qur'an prepared by Uthman remained in existence and all the other copies were got burnt.

According to *Fathul Bari* of Ibn Hajar 'Asqalani vol. 4, p. 226, Uthman sent back the Qur'an of Hafsah but Marwan snatched it forcibly from her and burnt it.[56] Uthman got all the copies of the Qur'an burnt except his own and got Abdullah Ibn Mas'ud beaten so much that he developed the disease of hernia. Then he sent him to prison where he died.

According to *Tuhfah Ithna ' Ashariyah* of Abdul Aziz, Ubayy bin Ka'b gave his Qur'an to Uthman, and he escaped beating. That Qur'an was also burnt.[57]

Another example of Uthman's cruelty was his beating of Ammar Yasir. Ulema of both sects relate that when Umayyad

---

[55] Tarikh al-Qur'an by Abdul Qadir Makki, p. 36 printed Jeddah 1365 A.H. Sahih Bukhari vol. 6, p. 26 printed Bombay, Mishkit Sharif printed Dehli, p. 150, and Tafsir Itqan Suyuti, printed Ahmadi, vol. 1, p. 84;

[56] According to Tarikh Khamis p. 270, Isti'ab p. 373 and Sawa'iq Muhriqah p. 68

[57] The great companion of the Prophet Abu Dharr chapter 18

oppression increased, some companions of the Prophet (s) wrote to Uthman, asking him to relent. They said that if he continued to assist his cruel Umayyad Governors, he would not only be harming Islam, but he would himself be subjected to serious consequences. They asked Ammar Yasir to deliver the petition since Uthman himself had acknowledged Ammar's virtue. They had often heard Uthman say that the Prophet (s) said that faith was blended with the flesh and blood of Ammar.

So, Ammar took the letter to Uthman. When he arrived, Uthman asked him, *"Do you have business with me?"*

He replied: *"I have no business of a personal nature. But a group of the Prophet's Companions has written in this letter some suggestions and advice for your welfare. They have sent them to you through me."*

After reading a few lines, Uthman threw the letter down. Ammar said: *"It was not good of you. A letter from the companions of the Holy Prophet of Allah (s) deserves respect. Why did you throw it on the ground? It would be proper for you to have read it and replied to it?"*

"You are lying!" Uthman shouted. Then he ordered his servants to beat him, and Uthman himself kicked him in the stomach. He fell, unconscious; his relatives came and took him to the house of Umm Salma (one of the Prophet's wives). From noon until midnight he remained unconscious. The tribes of Hudhail and Bani Makhzun turned against Uthman because of his cruelty to Abdullah Bin Mas'ud and Ammar Yasir. [58]

Ammar ibn Yasser was also one of the earliest converts to Islam. As noted, before, the pagans in Makkah tortured his mother and father to death. They were the first and the second martyrs of Islam, and this is a distinction that no one in all Islam can share with them. Like Abu Dharr el-Ghiffari, Ammar was

---

[58] Peshawar Nights by Sultanul Waizin Shirazi

also one of the few favorites of Muhammad, the Apostle of God, who once said: *"Ammar is the embodiment of all Iman (Faith)."*

Just like Abu Dharr el-Ghiffari and a few others, Ammar also was not very popular with the brokers of economic and political power of his time, and a head-on collision between him and them was inevitable.

Ammar migrated first to Abyssinia, and then to Medina. He was the first Muslim to build a Mosque. He built it in Makkah itself, and he prayed in it. And he built, with others, the Mosque of the Prophet (in Medina). While other Muslims carried one brick at a time, he carried two. He also dug, with others, the trench at the siege of Medina. He was covered with dust. The Apostle of God himself removed dust from his head and face.

When Ammar heard the news of the death of Abu Dharr el-Ghiffari, he mourned for him. Uthman interpreted his lamentations (for Abu Dharr) as a reproach to himself. He was highly incensed, and ordered him also to leave Medina, and to go to Rabza (in exile). When Ammar got ready to leave Medina, the Banu Makhzoom whose client he was, were infuriated. Ali (as) was also displeased. He went to see Uthman, reproved him for banishing Abu Dharr, and told him not to do the same to Ammar. Uthman said to him: *"You are no better than Ammar, and you too deserve to be banished from Medina."* Ali (as) answered: *"Go ahead and do that."* Then the other Muhajireen intervened and told Uthman that he could not banish everyone with whom he happened to be displeased.

On one occasion, Uthman had taken a piece of jewelry from the treasury for his own family. Among those men who raised objection to this act, was Ammar ibn Yasir. Uthman was beside himself with rage. *"How do you dare to question me?"* he roared. He then ordered his servants to seize him. They seized him, and Uthman beat him up brutally until he lost consciousness. He was taken from the mosque in that state to the house of Umm Salma, the widow of the Prophet (s). Ammar was unconscious the rest of the day. When he regained consciousness at last, he rose, took ablutions, offered his prayers, and said: *"Thank Allah, it's not the first time that I have been tortured for speaking the truth."* (the first time when Ammar was tortured for upholding the truth of Islam, he was in Makkah. In those days, it was Abu Jahl who tortured him).

On another occasion, some companions of the Prophet (s) drafted a letter of advice to Uthman, and they requested Ammar to present it to him. When Ammar presented the letter to Uthman, he again lost his temper. Once again, he ordered his servants to knock him down. They knocked him down, and Uthman kicked him in his groin, and beat him up until he fainted."[59] [60]

---

[59] *(al- Fitna-tul-Kubra {The Great Upheaval}, published in Cairo in 1959*

[60] A Restatement of History of Islam and Muslims by Sayed Ali Asgher Razwy

Abu Dharr's Banishment to Syria

Uthman was also cruel to Jandab bin Junada, known as Abu Dharr Ghifari, one of the intimate companions of the Holy Prophet (s) and a learned man. Great traditionists and historians of both sects have reported that this ninety-year-old man was unjustly exiled from place to place with utmost ignominy - from Medina to Syria, to Medina again, and then from Medina to the desert of Rabza. He rode on a naked camel accompanied by his only daughter. He died in Rabza in penury and neglect. Sunni prominent ulema and historians, and many others[61] have recorded Uthman's cruelty. It has been widely reported how he mistreated the pure-hearted Abu Dharr, the loved one of the Holy Prophet (s), and how Abdullah Bin Mas'ud, the hafiz (memorizer of Quran) and recorder of revelation, who was given forty lashes because he bid farewell to Abu Dharr Ghifari. Insulting treatment was likewise shown to Ali (as) for the same reason.

---

[61] Including, Ibn Sa'd, in his Tabaqat, Volume IV, page 168; Bukhari in Sahih, Kitab-e-Zakat; Ibn Abi'l-Hadid in his Sharhe Nahju'l-Balagha, Volume I, page 240 and Volume II, pages 375-87, Yaqubi in his History, Volume II, page 148; Abu'l-Hassan Ali Bin Hussain Mas'udi, the famous traditionist and historian of the fourth century in his Muruju'dh-Dhahab, Volume I, page 438.

The Holy Prophet (s) himself testified to Abu Dharr's veracity. Also, Sunni ulema have written that the Prophet (s) said: *"Abu Dharr among my people is like Jesus among the Bani Isra'il in truthfulness, devotion, and piety."*

Muhammad Bin Sa'd, one of the high-ranking ulema and traditionists of the Suni sect on the basis of several authorities[62] have related that the Holy Prophet (s) said: *"The earth has not borne nor has the sky covered, a man more truthful than Abu Dharr."*

If the Holy Prophet (s) confirms the truthfulness of a man, we can be certain that that man spoke the truth. Nor does Allah call that person his loved one who is a liar. If there were a single instance of Abu Dharr telling lies, the early ulema of the Sunni sect would have recorded it, as they have concerning Abu Huraira and others.

The Prophet (s) testified to his righteousness and also predicted his torture. Hafiz Abu Nu'aim Isfahani narrates[63] from his own sources that Abu Dharr said that he was standing before the Prophet (s) when the latter said to him: *"'You are a pious man; soon after me you will suffer a calamity.' I asked: 'In the way of Allah?' He said, 'Yes in the way of Allah!' I said: 'I welcome Allah's command!'"*

Surely the suffering the venerable companion Abu Dharr endured in the desert by the order of Mu'awiya, Uthman, and their Bani Umayya was the same calamity predicted by the Holy

---

[62] In Tabaqat, Volume IV, pages 167, 168; Ibn Abdu'l-Birr in Isti'ab, Volume I, Chapter of Jundab, page 84; Tirmidhi in Sahih, Volume II, page 221; Hakim in Mustadrak, Volume III, page 342; ibn Hajar in Isaba, Volume III, page 622 Muttaqi Hindi in Kanzu'l-Ummal, Volume VI, page 169; Imam Ahmad bin Hanbal in Musnad, Volume II, page 163 and 175; Ibn Abi'l-Hadid in Sharhe Nahju'l-Balagha, Volume I, page 241; from Mahidi; Hafiz Abu Nu'aim Isfahani in Hilyatu'l-Auliya and the author of Lisanu'l-Arab

[63] In his *Hilyatu'l-Auliya*, Volume I, page 162

Prophet (s).

I really wonder at the Sunni's self-contradictory statements. On the one hand they narrate the hadith from the Prophet (s) that *"All my companions are like stars; if you follow any one of them, you will be rescued."* On the other hand, when one of the most venerable companions of the Holy Prophet (s) is tortured and dies in misery, they defend the offender! They should either disprove the statements of their own ulema or admit that the attributes mentioned in the verse under consideration do not relate to those who brutalized the revered companions of the Holy Prophet (s). Sunni's say Abu Dharr chose to go to Rabza of his own free will. Such statements reflect attempts of their fanatical ulema to conceal the misdeeds of their elders. Abu Dharr's forced banishment to Rabza is commonly acknowledged.

As an example, I will confine myself to quoting one narration[64], Abu Dharr was asked about his journey to Rabza. Abu Dharr said that he was forcibly exiled and sent to the wilderness. He continued: *"The Holy Prophet informed me about this. One day I fell asleep in the mosque. The Prophet came and asked me why I was sleeping in the mosque. I said that I fell asleep inadvertently. He asked me what I would do if I were banished from Medina. I said I would go to the Holy land of Syria. He asked me what I would do if I were banished from there, too. I said I would come back to the mosque. He again asked me what I would do if I were turned out from here also. I said I would draw the sword and fight. He asked me if he should tell me something which would be to my benefit. When I said 'Yes,' he said to me: 'Go to whatever place they take you.' So I listened to what he said, and I obeyed him. After this Abu Dharr said, 'By Allah, when Uthman will go before Allah, he will stand*

---

[64] Which has been recorded by Imam Ahmad Bin Hanbal in Musnad, Volume V page 156, Ibn Abi'l-Hadid in Sharhe Nahju'l-Balagha, Volume I, page 241, and Waqidi in his History from Abu'l-Aswad Du'ili.

a sinner regarding my case.'" [65]

It was reported to Uthman that Abu Dharr el-Ghiffari had spoken before the Muslims in the Mosque as follows: *"I am Abu Dharr el-Ghiffari, companion of Muhammad, the Last Messenger of God. Allah has elevated Adam, Noah and the children of Abraham and Imran over and above the rest of mankind. Muhammad has inherited the legacy of all these Prophets. He combines in his person all their qualities, attributes and achievements. And Muhammad's successor is Ali ibn Abi Talib. O' Muslims, who are bewildered today, if after the death of your Prophet, you had put him (Ali) ahead of others, as Allah put him ahead of others, and if you had put those men behind whom Allah has put behind, and if you had left authority and power at its source, i.e., in the house of your Prophet, then you would have received the blessings of Allah. There would not have been any one poor or destitute. Nor any two men would have disagreed on the interpretation of the Message of Allah, and everyone would have carried out his duties toward Him, and toward the other members of the community, as was done in the times of His Messenger himself. You would have found guidance and enlightenment at its fountainhead, i.e., in the house of Muhammad. But you allowed the authority and the power of the house of your Prophet to be usurped, and now you are paying the penalty."*

The informers also told Uthman that Abu Dharr was drawing attention of the Muslims to his (Uthman's) deviations from the practices of the Prophet (s) as well as from the practices of Abu Bakr and Umar.

Uthman ordered Abu Dharr to leave Medina, and to go to Syria and to live there. In Syria, Mu'awiya had consolidated his position, and he had cultivated a secular instead of an Islamic lifestyle. Abu Dharr witnessed many foul and un-Islamic

---

[65] Peshawar Nights by Sultanul Waizin Shirazi

practices at the court of Syria. He noticed that the gold and silver of the province was being squandered in Damascus on the luxuries of the nobles while there were many Muslims who were starving. Mu'awiya soon learned that Abu Dharr was no less irrepressible in Damascus than he was in Medina. Abu Dharr recited those verses of Qur'an in which the hoarders of wealth are denounced. He was blunt in his criticism and spoke the truth regardless of cost to himself. Mu'awiya had built a palace for himself.

Abu Dharr said to him: *"If you built this palace out of the funds which belong to the Muslims, then you have betrayed a trust; and if you built it from your personal wealth, then you have been guilty of extravagance and vanity."*

Abu Dharr told Mu'awiya and the Syrian nobles that they would be branded in hell with the gold and the silver that they were hoarding.

At last, Mu'awiya's patience reached the breaking point, and he wrote to Uthman:

"I fear that Abu Dharr may incite the people to rebellion. If you do not want rebellion in the country, then you should recall him to Medina immediately."

Uthman agreed. Mu'awiya mounted Abu Dharr on a camel without a *howdah* (saddle), and he ordered the camel-driver to travel non-stop to Medina. Abu Dharr arrived in Medina half-dead with wounds, exhaustion, and exposure.

But even in this state, Abu Dharr could not acquiesce in falsehood, injustice, exploitation, and disobedience to the commandments of God. The love of truth and justice burned in his heart like a flame. If any case of embezzlement came to his attention, he denounced it, and castigated its authors publicly. At last Uthman could take it no more. He summoned Abu Dharr to his court and the following exchange took place between them:

Uthman: I will banish you from Medina.

Abu Dharr: Will you banish me from the city of the Prophet?

Uthman: Yes.

Abu Dharr: Will you send me to Kufa?

Uthman: No.

Abu Dharr: Will you send me to Basra?

Uthman: No.

Abu Dharr: Where else can you send me then?

Uthman: Which is the place that you dislike most?

Abu Dharr: Rabza.

Uthman: That's where I will send you.

Uthman kept his word, and banished Abu Dharr el-Ghiffari to Rabza. He also issued orders that no one should talk with him or walk with him. But Ali (as) came to see him, and to talk and walk with him. With Ali (as) were his own sons, the sons of Aqeel ibn Abi Talib, and his nephew, Abdullah ibn Jafar.

It was a heart-breaking scene. Ali (as) was parting company with his bosom friend, and the friend and beloved of Muhammad Mustafa (s). His own heart was full of sadness, but he tried to comfort his friend with the following words: *"O Abu Dharr, you were angry with these people because they deviated from the course charted by Allah. Therefore, Allah Himself will recompense you. They are afraid of you because they think you might deprive them of their gold and silver. But if you were also like them, they would have become your friends."*[66]

---

[66] A Restatement of History of Islam and Muslims by Sayed Ali Asgher Razwy

"O' Abu Dharr! You showed anger in the name of Allah therefore have hope in Him for whom you became angry. The people were afraid of you in the matter of their (pleasure of this) world while you feared them for your faith. Then leave to them that for which they are afraid of you and get away from them taking away what you fear them about. How needy are they for what you dissuade them from and how heedless are you towards what they are denying you. You will shortly know who the gainer is tomorrow (on the Day of Judgment) and who is more enviable. Even if these skies and earth were closed to some individual and he feared Allah, then Allah would open them for him. Only rightfulness should attract you while wrongfulness should detract you. If you had accepted their worldly attractions, they would have loved you and if you had shared in it they would have given you asylum."[67]

Then Hussain (as), the younger grandson of Muhammad Mustafa (s), turned his misty eyes toward the beloved of his grandfather, now going into exile, and said: "O my uncle, Allah will change even a time like this. Your enemies have 'saved' their worldly interests from you but you have saved your Hereafter from them. What they have saved is utterly worthless but what you have saved, is something that will last forever."

Ali (as) and his companions walked in silence with Abu Dharr, and when time came to part, the latter said: "O poeple of the House of Muhammad! May Allah bless you. Whenever I see you, recollection comes to me of my friend and beloved, Muhammad, the Apostle and beloved of Allah."

Abu Dharr, his wife and his servant, were banished to Rabza in the desert, and sometime later, he died there. His wife and servant covered his face, turned it toward the Kaaba, and sat by the roadside not knowing what to do. Presently, they saw some riders coming from the direction of Iraq. These riders were

---

[67] Nahjul Balagha sermon 130

Abdullah ibn Masood, an old friend of Muhammad (s), and some other travelers. They were going to Medina. When they saw Abu Dharr's widow, they halted and asked her who she was and what she was doing in that desolate place.

Abu Dharr's servant told them who they were and informed them that the body of Abu Dharr was lying unburied as the ground was rocky and they were unable to dig a grave.

Abdullah ibn Masood burst into tears and lamented the death of his own friend, and the friend of the Apostle of God.

Abdullah ibn Masood and his companions dug a grave, arranged a simple funeral, said prayers, and buried Abu Dharr el-Ghiffari.

Burayda b. Sufyan al-Aslami from Muhammad b. Kaaba al-Qurazi from Abdullah b. Masood told me that when Uthman exiled Abu Dharr to Rabza, and his appointed time came, there was no one with him except his wife and a servant. He instructed them to wash his body and to drape it in a shroud, and lay him on the surface of the road, and tell the first caravan that passed who he was and ask them to help in burying him. When he died, they did this. Abdullah b. Masood arrived with some other men from Iraq on pilgrimage when they saw the bier on the roadside. The servant rose and said, *"This is Abu Dharr, the Apostle's friend. Help us to bury him."* Abdullah b. Masood broke out into loud weeping and said: *"The Apostle was right; you walked alone, and you died alone, and you will be raised alone."* Then he and his companions dismounted from their camels and buried him, and he told them his story and what the Apostle (s) had said on the road to Tabuk.[68]

Abu Dharr was one of the earliest converts to Islam, and he was one of those who were loved and admired by the Prophet (s) himself. The Prophet (s) used to say: *"The blue sky never held*

---

[68] *The Life of Muhammad*

its canopy over a man who was more truthful than Abu Dharr."

Abu Dharr learned that Uthman gave a lot of money to Marwan bin al-Hakam; and he gave to his brother, Harith bin al-Hakam 300,000 dirhems; and he gave to Zayd bin Thabit Ansari 100,000 dirhems. Abu Dharr criticized all this, and he told the hoarders how they would be burned in hell. He read the verse of Quran: *"Give tidings of torture to those who hoard gold and silver and do not spend their wealth for the sake of Allah"* (9:34).

Marwan bin al-Hakam informed Uthman what Abu Dharr was reading. Uthman sent his servant to Abu Dharr and forbade him to read the Qur'anic verse in question. Abu Dharr said: *"Does Uthman forbid me to read the Book of Allah, and to forget His commandments? If I have to choose between the pleasure of Allah and the pleasure of Uthman, I shall certainly choose the pleasure of Allah."*

Abu Dharr was persistent in his criticism of the hoarders of wealth, and he called upon the Muslims not to be spendthrifts.[69]

Abu Dharr struggled against the merchandising school of politics. In Islam, his voice was the first one that rose in protest against religious and political totalitarianism, and economic exploitation, and his was also the first voice to rise in defense of the Muslim "under-dog." His voice was stifled but his ideals could not be stifled. He lifted his ideals out of Al-Qur'an al-Majid. Any attempt to stifle his ideals is an attempt to stifle Al-Qur'an al-Majid.

Abu Dharr's voice was the voice of the Conscience of Islam, and his platform was the Rights of Man. May God bless him to all eternity.[70]

---

[69] *al- Fitna-tul-Kubra {The Great Upheaval}, published in Cairo in 1959 p.163*

[70] A Restatement of History of Islam and Muslims by Sayed Ali Asgher Razwy

Abdul Hamid of Egypt and Allamah Abdullah Subaiti write that Abu Dharr stayed in Medina after the death of Umar. He saw that Uthman was favourably inclined towards Bani Umayyah whose influence had grown deep into the Islamic State which had assumed the magnificence of a kingdom. People indulged in pomp and show and led highly luxurious lives. They had become fond of the worldly gains. He saw that most of the companions were totally changed. Zubayr, Talha and Abdul Rahman bin Auf (having reconciled with the government) had purchased lands and houses. Sa'd bin Abi Waqqas had agates fixed in his palace, had raised it very high, broadened the courtyard and made turrets on it. Therefore, Abu Dharr stood up and came out openly. He was not to be deterred by any commander or caliph. He started inviting people to austerity and attacking Uthman in his speeches.

One day he came to know that Uthman had given the fifth part of the tribute from Africa to Marwan bin Hakam, 300,000 dirhams to Harith bin al 'As, 100,000 dirhams to Zayd bin Thabit, immeasurable wealth from the booties of Africa to his foster brother, Abdullah bin Ali Sarah and the land of Fadak to Marwan which had been snatched from Fatima, the daughter of the Holy Prophet (s). He started to recite this verse in the masjid: *"Announce a painful torture to those who amass gold and silver and do not spend them in the way of Allah"*. (Surah Taubah, 9: 34)

Marwan came to know that Abu Dharr attacked him and Uthman, he complained to Uthman, who ordered his servant to call Abu Dharr to him. Abu Dharr went to him. At sight of him Uthman said: *"Abu Dharr! Desist from what I am hearing, otherwise you will not find anybody more inimical to you than I!"*

Abu Dharr said, *"O Commander! What have you heard about me?"*

Uthman said, *"I have come to know that you instigate*

people against me."

Abu Dharr asked, *"How is it?"*

Uthman said, *"You recite the verse, "Announce a painful torture………" in the masjid.*

Abu Dharr said, *"O Commander! Do you stop me from reciting the Book of Allah and from disclosing the shortcomings of those who have abandoned the commands of Allah! By Allah, I cannot offend Allah for the sake of Uthman. The displeasure of Uthman is better for me than the displeasure of Allah."*

Hearing this Uthman frowned at Abu Dharr but could not decide how to refute the charge. Therefore, he did not say anything and kept quiet for some time. Abu Dharr rose and went away from there, with a firm determination to criticise those who worked against the commands of Allah more than ever. Abu Dharr attacked Uthman more frequently. So, he got very angry and waited for an opportunity to exile Abu Dharr. One day he got the chance and availed himself of it.

According to Ibn Wazih the author of *'Tarikh Ya'qubi'* people informed Uthman that Abu Dharr Ghifari taunted him in the masjid and had delivered a speech at the gate of the masjid thus: *"O people! He who knows me knows me, but let him, who does not recognize me know that I am Abu Dharr Ghifari. My name is Jundab bin Junadah Rabazi. Allah elevated Adam, Nuh, the progeny of Ibrahim and the children of Imran, out of the people of the world. The Prophet Muhammad (s) is the heir to Adam's knowledge and to all virtues which had distinguished the Prophets, and Ali ibn Abi Talib is the successor of the Prophet and heir to his knowledge.*

O bewildered people! If after your Prophet you had preferred one whom Allah has preferred, and had put him last whom Allah has placed last, and had confined the governance and inheritance among the Ahlul Bayt, you would have got countless blessings from above your heads and from under your feet, and no friend of Allah would have been poor and destitute, and no part of the Divine obligations would have been lost, and no two persons would have disputed about the Divine command simply because they would have found the information about that commandment in the Divine Book and the tradition of the Prophet, according to the Ahlul Bayt of their Prophet. But since you have wilfully done what you should not have done, you must suffer the punishment for your wrongdoing, and it will not be long before those who have wronged will know to whom they will return."

It is also recorded in the same book of history that Uthman was also informed that he had made changes in the Sunnah (tradition) of the Holy Prophet (s) and the traditions of Abu Bakr and Umar on the foundation of which the edifice of his Caliphate was raised, and that Abu Dharr placed that complaint before the public.

On hearing these things Uthman sent Abu Dharr to Mu'awiya, Governor of Syria. According to *Tarikh Abul Fida*, this thing happened in 30 AH.

Scholars say that as Abu Dharr continuously criticized Uthman's actions that violated the religious laws, Uthman imposed severe restrictions on him. It was his directive that nobody should talk to Abu Dharr or go near him or sit with him. Public meetings were held again and again to proclaim this order.

According to the version of Allamah Majlisi and Allamah Subaiti, Ahnaf bin Qays often used to come to the masjid and sit there. One day he prayed to Allah: *"O Lord! Replace my unsociability with love and my loneliness with company and grant me such a worthy companion as has no peer"*.

After finishing this prayer, he saw a man sitting and worshipping in a corner of the masjid. He rose from his seat, approached him, and sat down by his side. Then he said to him, *"Who are you gentleman and what is your name?"*

He answered, *"Jundab bin Junadah."*

On hearing this he said, *"Allah is great, Allah is great!"*

Abu Dharr said, *"Why did you recite Takbir?"*

He answered, *"When I entered the masjid today, I prayed to Allah to grant me the best companion. He fulfilled my wish very soon and granted me the honor of meeting with you."*

Abu Dharr said, *"I owe it to Allah, more than you, to glorify Him because I was adjudged to be a suitable companion. O Man! Listen to me. The Holy Prophet has told me that you and I will be on a very high place and will remain there till all are free from reckoning. O servant of Allah! Get away from me or you will face some trouble".*

He asked, *"How is that friend?"*

Abu Dharr replied, *"Uthman bin Affan has forbidden people to sit with me and has ordered that whosoever meets me, talks to me and sits with me, will be punished."*[71]

In short, Uthman became disgusted with Abu Dharr's truthfulness. He carried on his work despite the restrictions and Uthman got regular information about it. At last, being tired of Abu Dharr he decided to send him to Syria.

Historians say that being tired of Abu Dharr's cry of truthfulness Uthman subjected him to every kind of repression in Medina. It was his order that no one should talk to him, and none should sit with him. He was forced to keep his mouth shut, but his truthful cries also persisted. When he gave a speech in the masjid of the Prophet (s) his words reached the ears of the

---

[71] *Hayatul Qulub*, by Allamah Majlisi vol. 2. and *Abu Dharr al-Ghifari*, by Allamah Subaiti

people. As he spoke on matters that were enjoined by Allah and His Prophet (s) his speech moved the hearts of the common people. People grew disgusted with the wrongdoings and anti-Islamic activities of Uthman. Therefore, he deemed it politically expedient to turn him out of the city. With this end in view, he decided to send him to Syria. Uthman perhaps thought that as Mu'awiya was the Governor of Syria and the most cunning man, Abu Dharr could be completely paralysed there. Accordingly, Uthman forced Abu Dharr to leave for Syria.

Abu Dharr left his hearth and home with his family and reached Syria. His arrival in Syria confirmed the prediction of the Prophet (s), which the latter had once made to Abu Dharr during their conversation. According to the exhortation of the Prophet (s) he showed patience and accepted his exile silently.[72]

Abu Dharr was already tired of and disgusted with the anti-Islamic ways of Uthman, but when he reached Syria and saw the behaviour of Mu'awiya that was ruining Islam he was extremely astonished and said to himself that the entire administrative set-up was out of order. He was compelled to think on account of the style of life of Mu'awiya that Islam as presented by the Prophet (s) was not only becoming weak but extinct. In view of these things his natural emotions were excited. Sincerity and frankness impelled him to raise a cry of truth. As he was extremely brave, he never hesitated to tell the truth. So, without thinking that Mu'awiya was the king of the day, he began to perform his Islamic duties and opened his mouth to prevent Mu'awiya from doing anti-religious deeds and told him clearly that his modus operandi was as anti-Islamic as that of Uthman bin 'Affan. Allamah Subaiti writes that Uthman's exiling Abu Dharr from Medina to Syria is a positive proof of the fact that Uthman diverted the critical attitude of Abu Dharr from

---

[72] al-Ghadir Allamah Amini, vol. 8, p. 302

himself to Mu'awiya.[73]

The historian Balazari, Allamah Majlisi, Allamah Subaiti and Allamah Amini write that when Abu Dharr reached Syria, Mu'awiya was getting his palace *al-Khizra* constructed. Thousands of labourers were working there. One day Mu'awiya was looking at it with pride. Abu Dharr saw him, went near him, and said, *"O Mu'awiya! If this palace is being built with the Public Treasury, it is a breach of trust and if it is done with your money, it is extravagance."*

Hearing this Mu'awiya kept quiet turned his face from his side and made no answer. Abu Dharr went away and reached the masjid. He took his seat there. Some people complained to Abu Dharr against Mu'awiya saying that they got nothing out of the gifts although a year had passed. Abu Dharr inclined his head forward and then he stood up. People looked at him. He said: *"By Allah, such innovations have gained currency these days as are not to be found in the Holy Qur'an or the Hadith. By Allah, I see that the truth is being effaced and untruth is becoming stronger. Truthful people are being falsified and the sinners are being given preference over the virtuous. O aristocrats! O Mu'awiya and his governors! Sympathize with the poor. Let those who amass gold and silver and do not spend in the way of Allah, know that their foreheads, sides, and backs will be branded with fire. O' the hoarders of wealth! Don't you know that when a man dies everything separates from him. Only three things remain for him, lasting charity, useful knowledge, and a virtuous son, who prays for him."*

People heard his lecture, the oppressed poor gathered round him, and the rich began to fear him. When Habib bin Muslimah Fahri saw a crowd of people near Abu Dharr, he said, *"It is a great nuisance!"* He immediately went to Mu'awiya and said to him, *"O Mu'awiya! Abu Dharr will totally upset the*

---

[73] Abu Dharr al-Ghifari

Syrian administration. If you need Syrians, you should nip this nuisance in the bud."

Mu'awiya thought to himself: *"Should I deal with him strictly or leniently? The fire will flare up further by strictness. Should I complain to Uthman? But what will Uthman say? He will say that I could not improve even one man out of my subjects. Hence, it is better to turn him out of Syria."*

It has been a common practice to suppress with an iron hand the truthful statements of the godly people on account of their bitterness. How could the worldly people remain silent after hearing the speeches of Abu Dharr whose religious fervour had become quite natural with him, and then how could a person like Mu'awiya, who considered the biggest personality lower to him in his vanity of power and cunningness, act upon the advice of Abu Dharr and how could he tolerate his bitter remarks? Abu Dharr in exhorting tone used to recite the Qur'anic verse: *"Give them the sad tidings of the severest punishment to those, who amass gold and silver and do not give them in charity",* and it was usual with him that he used to recite this verse against Mu'awiya in most of the streets, and on the roads of Syria. When he recited it the poor and the needy surrounded him and often, they complained to him of the pleasure seeking of the rich governors and of their own poverty. Mu'awiya used to get the information of his preaching activities regularly. At last, he imposed severe restrictions upon him and inflicted tortures on him from all sides. When even this much did not work he threatened Abu Dharr with death.

When Abu Dharr heard the threat of death he said, *"The dynasty of Umayyah threatens me with poverty and death. I wish to tell them that poverty is more desirable to me than richness, and I like to be under the ground rather than to be above it. I am neither cowed down by the threatening of death, nor by death itself."*

Allamah Majlisi writes on the authority of Shaykh Mufid

what the Syrians said about the great sermons of Abu Dharr: When Uthman exiled Abu Dharr from Medina and sent him to Syria, he took his residence in our midst, and started a series of speeches, which stirred us quite a lot. He used to begin his speech with the praise of Allah and the Prophet and then said: *"Love for the progeny of the Prophet is obligatory on all. One who is without love for them will not even smell the fragrance of Heaven"*. He then added, *"O people! Listen to me. I used to honor my covenants before acknowledging Islam, during the days of ignorance, before the revelations of the Qur'an and before the appointment of the Prophet. I told the truth, treated my neighbours with sympathy, considered hospitality my duty, was generous to the poor, and let them share my riches with me. When, afterwards, Allah revealed His Book and appointed His Prophet, I inquired about the matters and came to know that the same manners and customs that were ours were also contained in the exhortations of the Prophet. O people! It is most befitting for the Muslims to adopt good morals. It is true that the Muslims acted according to the precepts of Islam, but my friends! The behaviour of the Muslims was good for a short time. Then it so happened that the tyrants showed such evil deeds, as we had not seen before. These people destroyed the traditions of the Prophet, introduced innovations, and contradicted the person who told the truth, joined a group of wicked people, and forsook them who were pious and worthy. O Allah! Take my soul if You have for me better things with You than those which are in this world, before I distort your faith or change the tradition of Your Prophet. O people! Be attached to the worship of Allah and desist from sins".*

Then he described the merits of Ahl ul Bayt which he had heard from the Prophet (s) and advised people to stick with the Ahl ul Bayt.

The Syrians say that they listened to his speeches intently and a great crowd of people gathered round him when he delivered a sermon, till Mu'awiya informed Uthman of these happenings, consequently he called Abu Dharr to Medina.

As Abu Dharr had greatly vexed Mu'awiya through his religious lectures, he, in order to silence him somehow, took courage to send him a bag of money because he could not think of any other means to do it.

Scholars and historians say that Mu'awiya in order to silence Abu Dharr despatched a bag of three hundred gold dinars to him through his special envoy. Seeing this he said, "Tell Mu'awiya that I need no money from him and returned the bag.[74]

Abu Dharr had seen with his own eyes after the death of the Prophet (s) all those tragic events which the progeny of the Prophet (s) were forced to face.

Anyway, troubles surrounded Abu Dharr from all sides. Great tortures afflicted him at the hands of Bani Umayyah. Oppressions were let loose on him. But he did not show any weakness and did not refrain from his preaching activities. He now started more serious attacks.

Abdullah Subaiti, Abdul Hamid Misri and Manazir Ahsan Gilani say that Abu Dharr kept on performing the duty of preaching regularly and giving warning of painful chastisement to the hoarders. At last, Mu'awiya began to think of plans to save himself from his biting remarks and, to frustrate his mission. He concluded, however, that there could be a chance of freedom from the attacks if hoarding is proved with those who speak against it. Therefore, he hit upon a plan, and got convinced that it would surely hit the target.

Ibn Athir, after mentioning the Qur'anic verses, writes that when Abu Dharr could not be silenced in anyway, Mu'awiya sent somebody with a thousand dinars to Abu Dharr at night. Abu Dharr took the money and distributed it among the needy before dawn and did not keep even a single coin, for himself.

---

[74] al-Ishtiraki az-Zahid, Tarikh Balazari, al-Ghadir, vol 8, p 293

Mu'awiya, after the morning prayer, called the man who had taken the gold coins to Abu Dharr; ordered him to go to Abu Dharr and tell him in a feigned anxiety, *"O Abu Dharr! Save me from the torture of Mu'awiya. Mu'awiya had sent those gold coins to somebody else, and I have delivered them to you by sheer mistake."*

The messenger of Mu'awiya went to him and told him exactly in the same manner what Mu'awiya had taught him. Abu Dharr said, *"O son! Tell Mu'awiya that the money sent by him was distributed among the needy before the day dawned. I have none of the coins at this moment with me, and if he has a mind to take them back he should give me three days time, during which I will provide them to him from somewhere."*

That man repeated the same thing to Mu'awiya who said, *"Undoubtedly Abu Dharr does himself what he asks others to do."*[75]

Abdullah Subaiti, after quoting this incident writes in a philosophical passage that Abu Dharr was a personality of a very lofty character. Bani Umayyah showed great short sightedness in understanding him. That is why they felt the need of such a political swindling. Abdul Hamid Misri writes after this incident: *"Mu'awiya understood that Abu Dharr was true to his words. He spent all the dinars in one night. Mu'awiya failed to achieve his purpose. He showed leniency to Abu Dharr but to no avail. Then he used violence against him but to no effect. In the end, he wanted to purchase him for three hundred dinars, but could not succeed."*[76]

Abu Dharr was busy preaching in Syria when the time of Hajj arrived. He sought the permission of Uthman and expressed his wish to go out of Syria to pilgrimage and to stay at the shrine

---

[75] Tarikh Kamil, vol. 3, p. 24, Tafsir Ibn Kathir, part 10, p. 54

[76] Abu Dharr al-Ghifari

of the Holy Prophet (s) for a few days. Uthman sent him the letter of permission from Medina and Abu Dharr went for Hajj. He performed Hajj and he went to Medina. He stayed near the grave of the Prophet (s) for a few days and then came back to Syria.

On his return from Hajj again he restarted his preaching activity. On one side he was using his full force in exhortations and on the other side innumerable applications of the rich people were reaching Mu'awiya to seal Abu Dharr's lips. The main theme of these applications was that people recited on the roads and streets the verse of the Qur'an in which there is a warning for the moneyed people being branded with the heated gold and silver, thus creating difficulty in their passage to Syria. Because of it Mu'awiya got it proclaimed that nobody was allowed to be in the company of Abu Dharr or sit with him.[77]

When Abu Dharr got the news of this social boycott, he himself began to ask people not to come to him or sit with him. This was because he thought that if somebody came to him, he would be subjected to torture by the government. But as he could not help preaching, he himself reached the place where some people had gathered and began to perform his duty.

According to Ibn Khaldun when a group of people went to see him after this order of social boycott, Abu Dharr himself asked them to leave and remain away from him.[78]

It appears from Balazari's report that those people who had contacts with Abu Dharr and listened to his speeches were more severely dealt with than Abu Dharr himself.[79]

How courageous Abu Dharr was! He did not tolerate any

---

[77] Tabaqaat Ibn Sa'd, p. 176

[78] Tarikh Ibn Khaldun, p. 27

[79] Tarikh Balazari, vol. 5 p. 65)

severity to those who used to visit him and did not want them to suffer any inconvenience. But so far as his personal sentiments were concerned, he insisted on expressing them with full faith and fervour. He never bothered about any gain and loss in the way of Allah.

Abu Dharr was a truthful man. He used to admonish others fearlessly to do lawful acts. Mu'awiya was a worldly man. Abu Dharr very often used to direct him to do what is good till people began to feel ashamed of the residents of Syria. One day Mu'awiya said to Abu Dharr, *"You are not so virtuous as to direct me to do good deeds before the public."*

Hearing this Abu Dharr said, *"Be quiet! Shame on you!"*

In short, when Mu'awiya could not mend his ways and could not suppress Abu Dharr's tongue, he decided to banish him from Syria. Consequently, he resolved to send him to Jabal al-'Amul. Subaiti says that when Abu Dharr called the people there towards Ahlul Bayt they readily accepted the invitation! As the area was quite extensive his call did not remain confined only within the internal limits of Jabal al-'Amul but reached the adjoining areas as well.

It is obvious that Mu'awiya had sent Abu Dharr from Syria to Jabal al-'Amul only because he thought that his preaching activities among those strangers would come to a stand-still, but when he came to know that Abu Dharr with his fiery speech had made the people in Jabal al-'Amul inclined towards the truth, he called him back to Syria immediately. Allamah Subaiti writes that Abu Dharr made the people devotees of Ahlul Bayt through his preachings and laid the foundations of two masjids there one at Sirfand which is situated near the riverbank between Sur and Sayda and the second in Mes situated at Haulah. [80]

---

[80] Abu Dharr al-Ghifari

Abu Dharr restarted his work on his arrival in Syria. He used to sit at the Gate of Damascus, after the morning prayers, and when he saw the line of camels laden with the government owned goods he called in a loud voice: *"People! This line of camels that is coming is not laden with goods but with fire. Accursed be the people, who direct others to do good but do not do good themselves, and woe be to those who prohibit others from evils but commit them themselves."*[81]

Then he rose from there and went to the gate of Mu'awiya's palace and made the same speech. This had become his routine and he used to do it regularly. At last, Mu'awiya got him arrested.

Abu Dharr had in view the tradition, which has been quoted by Khatib al-Baghdadi and Ahmad bin Hanbal. According to this tradition the Holy Prophet (s) said to his companions: *"O my companions! Listen attentively. After me the rulers (of my ummah) will be like the aristocrats. To them there will be no difference between justice and injustice and between truth and falsehood. But, whosoever goes to them to justify their falsehood, and supports them in their injustice, will have no connection with me, and will not reach me at the Cistern of Kauthar and the man who has no connection with them, does not justify their falsity, and does not support them in their injustice, will be from me and I will be from him, and he will reach me at the Cistern of Kauthar."*[82]

Every sensible man can understand that under the circumstances Abu Dharr could not care about any power. His conduct; apart from being natural and innate, was the result of the Holy Prophet's teaching. There is not a single instance recorded in the authentic histories to show that in his lifetime Abu Dharr had ever hesitated to tell the truth.

---

[81] Tarikh Ya'qubi, vol. 2 p. 148 and al-Ghadir, vol. 8, p. 299

[82] Tarikh al-Khatib al-Baghdadi, vol. 2, and vol. 5, Musnad Ahmad bin Hanbal vol. 1

Jalam bin Jandal Ghifari, the Governor of Qinsarin says: "Once, during the Caliphate of Uthman when I was the Governor of Qinsarin I, went to Mu'awiya, the Governor of Syria on some business. Suddenly I heard that somebody was shouting at the gate of the palace and was saying loudly: The line of camels coming to you is laden with the Hell-fire. May Allah curse those who ask others to do good but do not do it themselves. May Allah curse those who prohibit others from evil but commit them themselves.

At that time, I saw that the face of Mu'awiyah changed, colour on account of anger. He asked me if I recognized the man, who was crying. I answered in the negative. Then Mu'awiya said, this is Jandab bin Janadah Ghifari. He comes to the gate of our palace daily and repeats the same words that you heard just now. Then he ordered him to be killed.

Suddenly I saw that Yaqudunah brought Abu Dharr dragging and made him stand in front. Mu'awiya said to him, "O the enemy of Allah and His Prophet! You come daily to us and repeat such words. I would have surely got you killed if I could kill any companion of the Prophet without Uthman's permission. Now I will get his permission regarding you."

I wanted to see Abu Dharr because he was from our tribe. When I looked at him, I saw he was tawny-coloured, lean and tall. His beard was not thick, and his back was bent on account of old age.

Abu Dharr said in answer to Mu'awiya: "I am not an enemy of Allah and His Prophet, but you are the enemy of Allah and His Prophet, and your father was also an enemy of Allah and His Prophet. You people professed Islam for self interest but remained infidels at heart. The Prophet of Islam cursed you twice and damned you so that you may never be satiated. I have heard from the Prophet of Allah (s) that his ummah should remain on guard against the mischief of the man with big eyes and wide gullet, who is never satiated with food although he eats *too much, when he becomes the ruler of his ummah.*

Hearing this Mu'awiya said, "I am not that man spoken of by the Messenger of Allah". Abu Dharr said, "O Mu'awiya! It is no use denying that you are definitely the same man and listen! The Prophet has informed me that by that man he meant you and you alone. O Mu'awiya! One day when you were passing in front of the Prophet, I heard him say: O Allah! Damn him, and do not fill his stomach except with dust. O Mu'awiya! I have heard him also say that Mu'awiya's flank is in Hell-fire." Hearing this Mu'awiya laughed shamefully, ordered him to be arrested, sent him to prison and wrote to Uthman about the whole affair."[83]

Having sent Abu Dharr to prison, Mu'awiya in his letter to Uthman complained against Abu Dharr which meant that he should be called back from Syria. Accordingly, Uthman called him from Syria to Medina.

A camel rider started with Mu'awiya's letter and presented it before Uthman at Medina. As soon as Uthman received the letter, he at once wrote back to Mu'awiya: *"Your letter to hand; I came to know what you wrote about Abu Dharr. As soon as you receive this letter send Abu Dharr to Medina on the back of a rash camel with a hard-hearted rider who keeps the camel running day and night in order to send Abu Dharr to sleep so that he forgets to speak of you and me both."*

On receipt of this letter Mu'awiya sent for Abu Dharr and made him ride on the bare back of a mischievous camel with a cruel rider. He told the rider to keep the camel running day and night and not to let him stop at any place till he reaches Medina. Abu Dharr was tall and lean and by that time had become so old that all the hair of his head and beard had grown grey. Besides this he had grown very weak. There was no cloth or saddle on the back of the camel. The guide gave him merciless treatment.

---

[83] *Hayat al-Qulub*, vol. 2, p. 1043, *al-Ghadir*, vol. 8, p. 299, as quoted from *Tarikh Ya'qubi*

Because of all these troubles and injuries Abu Dharr's thighs were wounded and ruptured, and he felt great pain and exhaustion.

Historians agree that Abu Dharr was sent from Syria all alone. His family was not with him. Most probably he was not allowed to go home and take his family with him. He must have been called from the prison and directly despatched to Medina.

According to Allamah Majlisi and Allamah Subaiti when Abu Dharr was to leave for Medina and the Muslims got the news of his departure, they came to him and asked him where he was going. Abu Dharr replied, *"Uthman has called me to Medina. I am going from here at his call. O Muslims! Uthman being offended with me had sent me here towards you. Now I am again called to Medina. I know that this time I have been called for torture. But it is essential for me to go, anyhow. Listen! Relations between Uthman and me will remain like this. You should not feel sorry and worried in this respect."*

When Abu Dharr was leaving, people accompanied him to bid farewell to him till they reached Dair Maran outside the city. There he offered his prayers in congregation. Then he delivered an address, whose translation is given here from *Hayatul Qulub*: *"O people! I bequest a thing which is useful to you."* After that he asked them to thank Allah. All said, "All praises are for Allah". Then he bore testimony to the Oneness of Allah and the Prophethood of Muhammad and all followed suit. Then he said, "I acknowledge the Resurrection of the Day of Judgment, and the existence of Heaven and Hell. I believe in what the Prophet brought from Allah and I call you as witness to this belief of mine". All said, "We are witness to what you have said", After that he said, "Whosoever of you will die with this belief will be given the glad tidings of Allah's mercy and generosity, provided that he is not the helper of the sinners, supporter of the actions of oppressors, and accomplice of the tyrants. O' group of people! Fury and indignation should also be a part of your prayers and fasting when you see that people on *earth sin against Allah. Do not please your leaders with things which are the cause of Allah's wrath. If those people introduce such things in the Divine faith the reality of which you do not know, leave them, and bring their guilt to the limelight, even if they torture you and turn you out of their company, deprive you of their gifts, and banish you from the cities, so that Allah may be pleased with you. Certainly, Allah is most Glorious and Elevated. It is not proper to enrage Him to please His creations. May Allah forgive you and me. I now leave you to Allah and wish that peace and mercy of Allah be upon you."*

All said in reply, *"O Abu Dharr! O companion of the Messenger of Allah! May Allah keep you safe and bestow His blessings upon you! Would you not like us take you again back to our city and support you in the face of enemies"*. Abu Dharr said, *"May Allah send mercy on you! Now you may go back. Certainly, I am more forbearing than you in calamities. Never be scattered and worried, and do not have differences among you."*

Historians say that when Abu Dharr reached Medina, leaving his family behind in Syria, extremely tired and exhausted he was presented before the king of the time, Caliph Uthman. At that time there were many people present in the court. As soon as Caliph Uthman saw Abu Dharr, he started reviling him without having any regard for his honor in the eyes of the Holy Prophet (s).

It appears from the statements of the historians that Uthman said whatever came to his mind in that state of fury and rage. He even said, *"It is you who have committed improper acts."*

Abu Dharr said, *"I did nothing except that I gave you an advice and you took it ill and sent me away from you. Then I advised Mu'awiya. He also did not like it and turned me out."*

Uthman said, *"You are a liar. You are nursing sedition in your mind. You want to provoke Syria against me."*

Abu Dharr said, *"O Uthman! Only follow Abu Bakr and Umar and nobody will say anything against you."*

Uthman said, *"What does it matter if I follow them or not. May your mother die!"*

Abu Dharr said, *"By Allah, you cannot accuse me of anything except that I direct people to do good and prevent them from doing unlawful acts."*

At this Uthman was filled with rage and said, *"O courtiers! Advise me as to what I should do with this old liar. Should I punish him with flogging, send him to prison, get him killed, or exile him. He has created dissensions in the Muslim society."*

Having heard this Ali, who was present there, said, *"O Uthman! I advise you like the believer of the nation of Firaun to leave him to himself. If he is a liar he will get the recompense for it, and if he is truthful you will certainly be a sufferer. Allah does not guide him who is extravagant and liar."*

At this there arose an altercation between Uthman and Ali.[84]

Muhammad bin Ali bin A'tham Kufi, writes in this connection: Ali (as) said to Caliph Uthman, *"Do not give him (Abu Dharr) any trouble. If he is a liar he will suffer its consequences, and if he is truthful, that what he says will come to light."*

Uthman did not approve of this talk of Ali. Angrily he said to Ali, *"Dust in your mouth!"*

Ali (as) also repeated the same words. Then Ali (as) said, *"O Uthman! What is all this you are doing? What an injustice are you committing! It is not proper for you to utter such words*

---

[84] Tabaqat Ibn Sa'd al-Waqidi, died 230 A.H. vol. 4, p.168

about Abu Dharr who is the friend of the Prophet of Allah (s), on the basis of some unknown things that Mu'awiya has said. Are you not aware of the opposition, oppression, sedition and corruption of Mu'awiya?"

On hearing this Caliph Uthman kept quiet.[85]

Sayyid Nurullah Shustari writes that as soon as Abu Dharr saw Caliph Uthman before himself he used to recite the Qur'anic verse: *"Fear the day when the Fire of Hell will blaze up and their foreheads will be branded"*, by which he meant to say, *"O Uthman! It is wrong that you do not give to the poor the riches you hoard but give to your kinsmen if you ever give. The day is not far off when your flanks and foreheads will be branded in Hell."*[86]

According to Tabari once Ali (as) addressed Uthman and said, *"You have given up following your predecessors, and now you simply concentrate upon the Children of Umayyah and your own kinsfolk. You have completely ignored the poor. This is not right at all. From where have you got the right of unlawful distribution of the property of Muslims?"*

Uthman grew angry at this talk of Ali (as) and retorted, *"Those who went before us did wrong to their relatives. I don't want to do that. I am giving to my poor relatives whatever I can"* Ali said, *"Are they only rightful people whom you give thousand of dirhams from the Public Treasury of the Muslims? Is there no other poor man?"*[87]

---

[85] Tarikh A'tham Kufi and Majalisul Mu'minin

[86] Majalisul Mu'minin, p. 94

[87] Tarikh Tabari, vol. 4, p. 534 and Iqdul Farid, vol. 2, p. 272

Historians[88] narrates this incident thus: *"When Abu Dharr was presented in the court of Uthman he said to Abu Dharr, "I am informed that you have told the people the hadith of the Prophet that when the number of males of Bani Umayyah rises to full thirty, they will consider the cities of Allah as their booty and the servants of Allah their own servants and maids, and they will adopt the religion of Allah as a fraud."*

Abu Dharr said, "Yes, I have heard the Prophet say so."

Uthman asked the audience of the court, "Have you heard the Prophet say so?"

They said, "No."

Then he called Ali and said, "O Abul Hassan! Do you certify this hadith?"

Ali said, "Yes."

Uthman said, "What is the proof of the authenticity of this hadith?"

Ali replied, "The Holy Prophet's statement that there is no speaker, under the sky and upon the earth, who is more truthful than Abu Dharr."

Abu Dharr had stayed in Medina only for a few days after this incident when Uthman sent word to him, saying "By Allah, you will certainly be banished from Medina."[89]

Allamah Majlisi writes that after his return from Syria Abu Dharr was taken ill. One day he entered the court with the support of his staff. He had just arrived there when the

---

[88] Such as Abul Hassan Ali bin Hussain bin Ali al-Mas'udi (died 346 A.H.), Ahmad bin Abi Ya'qub and Ishaq bin Ja'far bin Wahhab bin Wazeh Ya'qubi (died 278 A.H.), and Muhammad bin Sa'd al-Zahri al-Basri, Katib al-Abbasi al-Waqidi (died 230 A.H.)

[89] Murujuz Zahab al-Mas'udi, vol. 1, p. 438 and Tarikh Ya'qubi, vol. 2, p. 148

functionaries of the government appeared in the court with 100,000 dirhams, which they had realized from the different parts of the State. As soon as Abu Dharr saw it, he said, *"O' Uthman! Whose property is this?"*

He replied, *"Of the Muslims."*

He asked, *"How long will it remain stored and not reach the Muslims?"*

The Caliph said, *"This money will lie with me till 100,000 dirhams more are received, because they have brought this wealth for me. Hence, I am waiting for more, so that I may give it to anybody I like and spend it where I deem proper."*

Abu Dharr said, *"Which are more, four dinars or 100,000 dirhams?"*

Uthman said, *"100,000 dirhams are more."*

Hearing this Abu Dharr said: *"O Uthman! Do you not remember that when you and I went to the Prophet late one night and seeing him sad asked him the reason for his sadness he did not even talk to us on account of the intensity of his grief. Then when we went to him next morning and seeing him happy and smiling asked him why he was so sad the last night and why he was happy that morning he said, "Last night after the distribution of the property of the Muslims only four dinars remained with me; so I was perturbed but I have now given them to the rightful person. Therefore, I am now happy."*

It is an established fact that Abu Dharr had seen the Holy Prophet (s) and his Ahlul Bayt from very close quarters and remained in very intimate company with them. He had seen very carefully every aspect of their life and had learnt much from it. He has seen with his own eyes not once but several times that the Holy Prophet (s) was lying hungry in the masjid and his children also were hungry at home.[90]

Abu Dharr had also seen Ali ibn Abi Talib working on wages wearing coarse clothes. He had seen patches of date leaves in the mantle of the daughter of the Prophet (s). He had also heard Ali (as) exhorting to his African maid servant Fizzah: *"O Fizzah! We, the Ahlul Bayt have not been created for the world or worldly gains. Instead, we have been created for the worship of Allah and the propagation of Allah's message, Islam. It is our duty to boost up the morality of man, to kindle the light of the Unity of Allah in the hearts of the people and to provide the ways and means for their well-being."*

Abu Dharr had also seen that Ali (as) ate the dried barley bread and kept the bag of his barley flour sealed so that nobody could mix ghee with it.[91]

He had also seen that Ali (as) used to take bags of flour on his back to the houses of the poor widows and orphans.

He had also seen Ali (as) saying to the world: *"O World! Go and deceive others. I have divorced you."*

He had also witnessed with his eyes that the progeny of Muhammad used to take food along with their servants and servants at the same dining-cloth.

He remembered well that once when four dirhams were left over after the Prophet (s) had distributed the money that was with him and this amount could not reach the deserving person, he felt very much grieved. He still recollected these words of the Prophet (s) addressed to him, *"O Abu Dharr! Even if I have gold equal to the Mount Uhud I do not like the least of it to be left over with me."*

---

[90] Ali'imun Nubuwwah, al-Mawardi, p.146, printed Egypt

[91] Allamah Kashif al-Ghita, The Shia -Origin and Faith, ISP 1982

Under these circumstances how could it be possible for Abu Dharr to observe silence when Islam was metamorphosed and the teachings of the guardians of Islam were being neglected? As soon as the Holy Prophet (s) died everything was changed. Injustice and tyranny were rampant, forced allegiance was demanded, the house of the Ahlul Bayt burnt, and the door was felled upon Fatima, the daughter of the Holy Prophet (s).[92]

Ali (as) was tied by the neck with a rope and the great companions lived in the seclusion of their homes. Being forced by circumstances Abu Dharr observed patience for some time. At last, he left Medina for Syria and settled there. After some time when he came back to Medina, he saw that worldliness of the rulers was at its height. Royal pomp and show had taken the place of the moderate life observed by the Holy Prophet (s). Favouritism and nepotism were the order of the day, and honesty and piety were the things of the past. The wealth of the Public Treasury was being squandered away. The wealth of Muslims was being used for personal needs. Every relative and well wisher of the Caliph had become a millionaire. Capitalism had expanded. There was an abundance of wealth. Nobody bothered about zakat. Nobody thought of helping the poor. Nobody cared for orphans and widows.

Seeing innumerable things of this kind, Abu Dharr tried to admonish the Caliph Uthman for the protection of Islamic ummah and Islamic State, and advised him as much as he could, but the Caliph did not pay heed to him. At last, in view of the promise that he had given to the Holy Prophet (s) and with that intensity of faith that Allah had preserved in his heart he came out on the scene and started publicizing the shortcomings of Uthman. In this connection he also censured hoarding of wealth and capitalism and initiated his speech with those Qur'anic verses which criticize the hoarding of wealth.

---

[92] al-Milal wan Nahl vol. 1, p. 25 printed in Bombay

As Abu Dharr could not tolerate that the wealth of the public property be spent only upon the Caliph's relatives, and the orphans and widows die of starvation, he accelerated his preaching, and consequently he had to go from place to place. He was exiled again and again sometimes he was banished from Medina and sent to Syria and sometimes he was forced to lead his life in a deserted place like Rabzah.

Historians say that Abu Dharr delivered his speeches on specific topics, in the masjid, outside the masjid, in the bazars, on the thoroughfares, on the streets, and at every place where he got an opportunity to do so. He did not fear his assassination because the Prophet of Allah (s) had told him that nobody would be able to kill him or turn him from his faith, nor did he fear reproaches because he had sworn allegiance to the Holy Prophet (s) on this point. He was dead-sure that whatever he did was in conformity with the wish of Allah and His Prophet (s). That is why he was busy all the time in discharging his duty with great courage and fervour.

On one side Abu Dharr's preaching grew intensive and on the other side Uthman was out of his beat with his self-indicating conscience in the mirror of his character. He consulted Marwan to know by which device Abu Dharr was to be silenced and how his criticism of Uthman's character, and his opposition to the hoarding of wealth could be stopped.

Marwan said, *"There is only one device to achieve that end, that is, some money should be sent to Abu Dharr. He may perhaps accept it and keep quiet."* Uthman heard this reply of Marwan and became silent. The reason of his silence was that he knew Abu Dharr's nature. He knew very well that Abu Dharr had no greed for money. But Marwan insisted and got the permission. He called two men, gave them a purse of two hundred dinars and said, *"Take it to Abu Dharr at night and tell him that Uthman had wished him well and asked him to take the purse and spend it on his needs."*

Those men came to Abu Dharr at night with the purse. He was, at that time, busy offering prayer in the masjid. Perhaps he was staying in the masjid of the Prophet (s) at that time because Uthman had forcibly called him from Syria while his family was still there.

Looking at the visitors Abu Dharr asked them who they were and why they had come? Presenting the purse to him they said, *"Caliph Uthman has sent you his regards and has asked you to accept these two hundred dinars for your expenses."*[93]

Abu Dharr said, *"Has he given an equal amount to any other Muslim as well?"*

They replied, *"No, to no one else. This is the Caliph's generosity towards you alone. Please accept it."*

Abu Dharr said, *"I am also one of the Muslims. When the Caliph has not given anything to any other Muslim, I alone cannot accept it. I do not need it when the other poor Muslims have been ignored. Go, take it back and tell him that only a little wheat is enough for me. I am earning my livelihood. What should I do with these dinars?"*[94]

Marwan had formed an utterly wrong opinion of Abu Dharr. He was under the impression that just as other seekers of the world did not care for faith and belief for the sake of wealth, Abu Dharr would also do the same. He did not know that Abu Dharr was on a much higher level as compared to the seekers of the world.

Anyway, those who had brought the purse of gold to Abu Dharr went back to Uthman and told him what Abu Dharr had said. Uthman said to Marwan, *"I already knew that Abu Dharr*

---

[93] Kashkol Bahai

[94] Abu Dharr Ghifari, p.126 and Hayatul Qulub vol. 2, p. 1039

would not accept the money."

Abu Dharr remained busy preaching as usual. Whatever he said was not in opposition to any particular person. Rather, he wanted the people not to forget Allah on account of hoarding of money but to strengthen the principles of Islam by sympathizing with the poor. Abu Dharr could not tolerate the wealth of the Public Treasury being spent on the undeserving persons freely while the needy starved. He could not even tolerate the tearing and burning of the Qur'an. He could not help criticizing those guilty of such heinous crimes. He had the commands of Allah and His Prophet (s) before him. He had the principles of Islam in view. He wanted the Muslim rulers to tread the path of Islam.

In short, on one side Abu Dharr was busy discharging his duty of preaching, and on the other side, Uthman was anxious how to gag him. To achieve this end, he tried to devise every kind of plan but could not succeed. At last, he ordered through a general proclamation, *"Nobody should sit with Abu Dharr, nor talk to him."*[95]

The order of the ruler had to be carried out unconditionally. As soon as this proclamation was made people gave up contact with him and ceased talking with him. People fled from wherever Abu Dharr passed lest it should be reported to the Caliph that they had met Abu Dharr. Nobody listened to him, nor attended to him. But what a brave man Abu Dharr was. He never cared for these things. He was convinced that whatever he was doing was in consonance with the Will of Allah. Therefore, he was completely satisfied with what he was doing and no restriction on his speech could succeed.

Subaiti says that in spite of the proclamation Abu Dharr continued exhorting the people as usual, so much so, that in Medina the descendants of Umayyah who were the supporters of Uthman, got tired of him and complained to Uthman, that Abu

---

[95] al-Mas'udi

Dharr had not given up his sermons as yet. He has tired us out. For Allah's sake devise some other means". Hearing this Uthman ordered Abu Dharr to be presented in his court.

Under orders from Uthman people caught Abu Dharr and brought him to the court. Uthman said, "*O Abu Dharr! I have warned you in every way, but you do not take my advice. What has happened to you?*"

Abu Dharr replied, "*Curse be on you, O Uthman! Is your mode of conduct similar to that of the Holy Prophet, or similar to that of Abu Bakr bin Quhafa and Umar bin Khattab? You are doing with us what the tyrants do.*"

Uthman said, "*I do not know anything. Get out of my city.*"

Abu Dharr: *I also do not want to stay near you. All right, tell me where should I go?*

Uthman: *Go wherever you like but be off from here.*

Abu Dharr: *May I go to Syria?*

Uthman: *No, I have got you dragged from there. You have made Syria offended with me. How can I send you there again?*

Abu Dharr: *Then, May I go to Iraq?*

Uthman: *No, you want to go where people criticize their rulers.*

Abu Dharr: *Should I go to Egypt, then?*

Uthman: *No.*

Abu Dharr: *Should I go to Kufa?*

Uthman: *No.*

Abu Dharr: *Where should I go then? Should I go to Mecca?*

Uthman: *No.*

Abu Dharr: *O Uthman! You stop me from going to the House of Allah! What does it matter to you if I go there and worship Allah till death?*

Uthman: *No, by Allah, never.*

Abu Dharr: *Then you should tell me where I should move away. Should I go out to the forest?*

Uthman: *No.*

Abu Dharr: *Then should I go back to my pre-Islamic days and take my residence in Najd. After all, tell me some place where I should go to.*

Uthman: *O Abu Dharr! You should tell me which place you like most.*

Abu Dharr: *Medina, or Mecca, or (according to Jahiz) Jerusalem.*

Uthman: *You cannot live here at any cost. Now you should tell me the place you dislike most.*

Abu Dharr: *Rabzah.*

Uthman: *Well, I order you to leave for Rabzah. Hearing this Abu Dharr said, Allah is Great! The Holy Prophet had truly said that all this was to happen.*

Uthman: *What had the Prophet said?*

Abu Dharr: *He had said that I would be banished from Medina, would be stopped from going to Mecca and would be forced to take my residence at the worst place Rabzah where I would die and would be buried by a group of Iraqis going to*

134

Hijaz.

Hearing this Caliph Uthman, according to A'tham Kufi, said *"Get up and go to Rabzah. Stay there and do not go anywhere."*

According *Dam'ah Sakibah* vol. 1, p. 194, he was tortured with severe injury. Then the Caliph ordered Marwan to send him to Rabzah on the bare back of a camel without a saddle, and to announce that nobody should go to see him off.[96]

It cannot be denied that exile is tantamount to assassination. Those who are banished from their homelands prefer assassination to exile. Events speak for themselves that those who were turned out of their homelands always wept bitterly. Patriotism is a gift of nature. Traditions have called it a part of faith. Prophet Yusuf used to weep for his homeland sitting on the royal throne of Egypt.

Not to speak of other Prophets, let us think of the life events of Prophet Muhammad (s). He was forced to migrate from Mecca to Medina. But whenever he remembered Mecca or saw some inhabitant of that city, his eyes were filled with tears. Alas! Abu Dharr was being driven out of his hometown. Imagine how he must have been feeling especially when he was leaving the tomb of the Prophet (s). But it could not be helped because he was forcibly sent into exile according to the established practice of Caliph Uthman, who expelled from his hometown every person with whom he got offended. According to the historian Tabari it was the practice of Uthman that he separated from the people the person, with whom he was displeased, and he used to say that no punishment was more severe than that.[97]

---

[96] Murujuz Zahab-Mas'udi, vol. 1, p. 438, Tarikh Ya'qubi, vol. 2, p. 148, Tabaqat Ibn Sa'd, vol. 4, p. 168. Hayatul Qulub, vol. 2, p. 1033. Majalisul Muminin p. 94, Tarikh A'tham Kufi, p. 131, Kitab al-Sufiyania, Abu Uthman Jahiz.

[97] Tarikhut Tabari, vol. 4, p. 527

Orders had been issued for the exile of Abu Dharr and also to the effect that nobody was to accompany him or talk to him or see him off or visit him. Abdullah ibn Abbas says that when Abu Dharr was turned out of Medina to Rabzah it was announced under orders from Uthman that nobody was to talk to Abu Dharr or to come out in order to see him off.[98]

This was the order that paralysed the people and confined them to their houses. Nobody could have courage to come out of his house to see off an esteemed companion of the Holy Prophet (s) like Abu Dharr except Imam Ali, Hassan, Hussain, Aqil, Abdullah bin Ja'far, Abdullah ibn Abbas and Miqdad bin al-Aswad.

Though the companions of the Holy Prophet (s) could not speak out their thoughts against Uthman's orders for Abu Dharr's exile, yet they became extremely perturbed. Not only those companions, who were present there, got perturbed but also those who were not in Medina but who heard the news of his banishment became restless. For example, Abdullah ibn Mas'ud who was in Kufa and likewise the people who belonged to his tribe became extremely agitated.

Allamah Subaiti says that the companions of the Prophet (s) expressed their indignation at the exile of Abu Dharr to Rabzah. According to *Mustadrak of Hakim* when Abu Darda heard the news of his banishment he exclaimed, *"Inna lillahe wa inna illaihe raji'un"* (*We are for Allah and we will return to Him*). He repeated it ten times.

When Abdullah ibn Mas'ud heard this news in Kufa he became restless and he addressed a gathering of people in the masjid of Kufa, *"O people! Have you heard this verse?" "Still, it is you who kill your own people, turning some of them out of their homes."* He objected to the Caliph by reciting this verse.

---

[98] Saqifah, Ahmad bin Abdul Aziz Jauhari, Murujuz Zahab, vol.1, p. 438, Sharh Ibn Abil Hadid

Walid, the Governor of Kufa reported this incident to Caliph Uthman. The Caliph wrote him back to send Ibn Mas'ud to him. When Abdullah ibn Mas'ud reached Medina Uthman was busy delivering his address. Seeing him Uthman ordered his servant Aswad to beat him. He dragged him out of the masjid and there throwing him down on the ground he gave him a sound thrashing, confined him in his house and stopped his pension for life.[99]

In short, on Uthman's order Marwan brought a camel without a. saddle and was about to send him off when suddenly Ali, Hassan, Hussain, Aqil, Ammar, Abdullah ibn Ja'far, Miqdad bin al-Aswad and Abdullah ibn Abbas came out and said, *"O the accursed Marwan! Stop. Don't seat him on the camel yet. We have to say good-bye to him."*

Ali (as) said, *"O Abu Dharr! Don't worry. People got scared of you because of their greed for the world, and you did not fear them on account of your faith till the time came when they exiled you. Abu Dharr! Every kind of trouble comes to him who is pious, but remember that Allah devises wonderful means of deliverance for the pious. Nothing can give you of consolation except the "truth". The "truth" will be your companion in loneliness. I know that you can get alarmed only by untruth and that cannot come near you."*

Then Imam Ali (as) asked his sons to bid farewell to their uncle. After hearing this Imam Hassan (as) said, *"O my dearest uncle Abu Dharr! May Allah have mercy on you. We are seeing what is being done to you. Our hearts are burning. Don't be worried. Allah is your guide and only Him you should have before you. O uncle! Have patience at this calamity till you reach my grandfather, while he is happy with you."*

Then Imam Hussain (as) said, *"O my uncle! You need not worry as Allah has power over everything. He can remove every*

---

[99] Abu Dharr Ghifari, p. 146, Musnad Ahmad bin Hanbal, vol.5, p 197

trouble in which you are involved. His Glory is wonderful. O uncle! People have made your life miserable. Of course, you don't care. Let the world separate from you, sooner or later. I pray to Allah for giving you support and patience. O uncle! Nothing is better than forbearance. Have trust in Allah. He is the disposer of your affairs."

Ammar said in great anger, *"May Allah not sympathize with him who has put you to great trouble and may he not give rest to him, who has made you restless. O Abu Dharr, by Allah, if you had welcomed the world of the world- seekers, they would not have turned you out, and if you had approved of their conduct, they would have befriended you. When you stood firm to your faith, the seekers of the world grew weary of you. Don't be worried as Allah is with you. These are the unfortunate worldly-minded people who sustain the greatest loss."* Similarly, other people also spoke and consoled Abu Dharr in different words.

After hearing these speeches Abu Dharr burst into tears and said, *"O the blessed members of the Holy Prophet's Family! When I saw you, I remembered the Holy Prophet and blessing surrounded me. O my revered ones! You alone were the means of solace to me in Medina. Whenever I saw you, I got the satisfaction of my heart and peace of mind. O my elders! Just as I was a burden to Uthman in Hijaz, I was the burden to Mu'awiyah in Syria. He did not like to send me to Basrah or Egypt, because he has his foster brother Abdullah ibn Sarah as the Governor of Egypt, and the son of his maternal aunt, Abdullah ibn 'Amir as the Governor of Basrah. He has now sent me to a place which is a desert where I do not have any supporter other than Allah. By Allah, I know Allah alone is my helper and for Him alone I will not care for any wilderness."*

According to Allamah Subaiti, after this Abu Dharr, who had grown old and weak, raised his hands towards the sky and said, *"O Allah! Be witness that I am friend of the Ahlul Bayt and will always be their friend for your sake as well as for the sake of the hereafter, even if I am cut to pieces in my love for them."*

After that Ali (as) said, *"O Abu Dharr! May Allah have mercy on you. We very well know that the cause of your being driven from place to place is only your love for us, the descendants of the Holy Prophet."*

Abu Dharr knew that love for the Ahlul Bayt (as) is the foundation of Islam. According to Jazairi, Imam Ja'far al-Sadiq (as) has quoted the Holy Prophet (s) as saying: *"Just as everything has its foundation, the foundation of Islam is the love for us, the Ahlul Bayt."*[100]

Anyway, when these great personages returned to Medina after having seen off Abu Dharr sorrowfully, Uthman got highly displeased with them.

A'tham Kufi writes: *"Abu Dharr started for Rabzah and Ali and other companions came back. The Caliph sent for Ali and asked him why he had gone out of Medina to bid farewell to Abu Dharr and why he had taken a group of the companions with him, in defiance of his orders. Ali asked him if it was incumbent upon him to carry out the orders of Uthman even if they conflicted with the obedience to Allah and the truth. He, then, swore by the name of Allah that he would never do it."*[101]

Abu Dharr was passing his days at Rabzah in utter solitude and loneliness. There was nobody to look after him too to inquire about his condition. He had no means of solace. Had his family been with him he would not have felt his loneliness so painful. They were still in Syria and Abu Dharr was driven out of Syria to Medina and then banished to Rabzah.

Abdul Hamid Jaudatus Sihar writes that when Mu'awiya came to know that Uthman had exiled Abu Dharr he sent his wife (with others) to Rabzah. When Abu Dharr's wife came out

---

[100] Anwar No'maniah

[101] Tarikh A'tham Kufi, p. 131, printed Dehli

of her house she had only a bag with her. Mu'awiya said to the people, *"Look at the belongings of the preacher of austerity."*

At this Abu Dharr's wife said, *"It contains a few coins and not dirhams or dinars and those too, only to suffice for the expenses."* When the wife reached Rabzah she saw that Abu Dharr had constructed a masjid there.

Various historians have mentioned the construction of a masjid by Abu Dharr at Rabzah. We find its mention in the books of Tabari, Ibn Athir and Ibn Khaldun. In the Arabic copy of Tabari there is a sentence that *"Abu Dharr had drawn a line of a masjid there and at that place he used to offer his prayers"*, just as today also people collect some earth in a jungle and name it a masjid. It was not a proper masjid, nor was it possible for him to construct a masjid like the one of today. According to Abdul Hamid during the days of Hajj when people passed through Rabzah they offered prayers in the masjid of Abu Dharr. This means that, that was not a populated place. If there had been a population there it would have been mentioned in some book of history that the people of that place offered prayers in that masjid, just as a mention is found of the pilgrims offering their prayers in it.

Allamah Subaiti writes that Abu Dharr was in a state of loneliness and was passing his days in such a condition at Rabzah that no human being could be seen there, except an occasional wayfarer who sometimes passed that way. There was not a place where he could take refuge. There was a tree under which he lived. There was no arrangement for his food. There were poisonous grasses all around, and they caused his and his wife's death."[102]

After that the author adds that the reason to send Abu Dharr to such a place was only to stop his speeches, so that nobody could hear him, since he had a charm in his tongue.

---

[102] Abu Dharr al-Ghifari, p.165, printed Najaf, 1364 A.H.

Whenever he spoke, he spoke the truth, which shook the foundations of the government.

In short, Abu Dharr was leading his life at Rabzah with his family in extremely straitened circumstances. There was no sympathizer there. But those honest men who had loved and reverence for him in their hearts used to go to see him. According to the historian Waqidi, Abul Aswad Duayli says: *"I wished with all my heart to visit Abu Dharr and ask him why he was turned out. Therefore, I went to him at Rabzah and asked him if he had come out of Medina of his own free will or he had been forcibly expelled."*

He said, *"Brother! How do i tell you that when I was sent to Syria, I thought that I had gone to a place which was an important place of the Muslims. I was happy there but I was not allowed to stay there and was called back to Medina. When I reached there I consoled myself with the idea that was the place to which I had migrated and where I had received the honor of companionship of the Holy Prophet. But, alas, I was turned out of that place also and now I am where you see"*. After that he said, *"O Abul Aswad! Listen to me. I was sleeping in the Prophet's masjid one day. By chance the Holy Prophet came in. He woke me up and said, "O Abu Dharr! Why are you sleeping in the masjid?"*

Abu Dharr: The sleep overwhelmed me and suddenly I went to sleep.

The Prophet (s): Tell me what you will do when you are turned out of this masjid?

Abu Dharr: I will go to Syria then, because signs of Islam are found there. It is also a place of Jihad.

The Prophet (s): What will you do when you are turned out of that place also?

Abu Dharr: I will draw my sword at that time and will

behead the man who turns me out.

The Prophet (s): I give a far better advice to you.

Abu Dharr: What is that advice?

The Prophet (s): You should let yourself be dragged when you are dragged, and that you should accept what is told to you and should not fight.

O Abul Aswad! According to the Prophet's advice I listened to them and accepted what they said. I still listen to them to accept what they say. By Allah, He will take revenge on Uthman for what he has done to me, and he will be proved the worst sinner in my case when he reaches in the court of Allah."[103]

The narrators of this authentic tradition are highly reliable and trustworthy as written by Allamah Amini in his book *al-Ghadir*: Somebody asked Abu Dharr during his stay at Rabzah, "O Abu Dharr! Do you have any wealth?" He said, "My wealth is my deeds". He also said, "By wealth I mean the wordly wealth and I want to know if you have any wordly wealth or not". Abu Dharr said, "I never spent a day or a night with treasure or the wordly wealth with me. I have heard from the Holy Prophet that the treasure of man is his grave i.e. the wealth of the world is nothing, but the conduct of man must be good, because this will be of use at every place especially in the grave. The wealth of the world remains in the world, and the good conduct benefits you in the Hereafter."[104]

---

[103] Sharh Ibn Abil Hadid, vol. 1, p. 241, Murujuz Zahab Mus'udi, vol. 1, p. 238, Tarikh Ya'qubi, vol. 2, p. 148, Mustadrak Hakim, vol. 3, p. 343, Hulyah Abu Na'im, vol. 1, p. 162, Tabaqatul Kubra Ibn Sa'd, vol. 1, p. 166, Musnad Ahmad, vol. 5, p. 156 and p. 180, Sunan Abi Daud, vol. 2, p. 282, Fatahul Bari, vol. 3, p. 213, Umdatul Qari Sharh Sahih Bukhari, vol. 4, p. 291

[104] Hayatul Qulub, vol. 2, p. 1046

Allamah Majlisi quoting Shaykh Mufid narrates from Abu Amamah Bahili that Abu Dharr after reaching Rabzah wrote his tragic experiences to Huzayfah bin al-Yaman, the companion of the Holy Prophet (s) who was probably at Kufa. In that letter he has given some pieces of advice and described his troubles and hardships. He writes:

In the name of Allah, the Beneficent, the Merciful

My dear Huzayfah,

I write to you to fear Allah in such a way that your crying exceeds limits. O brother! Renounce the world for the sake of Allah. Keep yourself awake the whole night in the worship of Allah and give your body and soul to hardship in the way of Allah. These are the useful practices. O brother! It is necessary for a man, who knows that the person with whom Allah is displeased will have to remain in Hell; to turn away from the worldly comforts, keep awake all the night for Him and suffer hardship in the way of Allah. O brother! It is essential for the man, who knows that the pleasure of Allah is a message to live in Heaven, to try constantly to seek His pleasure in order to get deliverance and success. O brother! One should not mind the separation of his family for the pleasure of Allah. Only the pleasure of Allah is the security of Heaven. If Allah is pleased all our affairs will be accomplished and the Hereafter will be agreeable. But if Allah is displeased it is difficult for us to have a happy end. O my brother! A person, who wishes to be in the company of the Prophets and saints in the Heaven, should mould his life as I have done, and should act upon what I have mentioned above. O Huzayfah! You are one of those people to whom I feel pleasure to tell of my pains and sufferings. In fact I console myself by telling you what befalls or has befallen me.

O Huzayfah! I have seen the tyranny of the tyrants with my own eyes and have heard their offensive words with my own ears. Hence, I was compelled to express my views on those disgusting talks and to tell them that whatever was being done was absolutely wrong. I did accordingly, and consequently those unjust people deprived me of every kind of privilege. They expelled me from city to city and drove me from place to place and they separated me from my brothers and kinsmen. O Huzayfah! They wreaked havoc upon me and worst of all they deprived me even from visiting the shrine of the Prophet.

O Huzayfah! I am putting before you my sufferings, but I am afraid lest this expression of mine should turn into a complaint against Allah. Huzayfah! I admit that whatever decision my Lord and Creator takes in my case is right. I bow my head before His command. May my life be sacrificed in His way. I am desirous of His pleasure. I am writing all this to you so that you may pray to Allah for me as well as for the devoted Muslims.

Peace be on you".

Abu Dharr

It is not known how Abu Dharr sent this letter to Huzayfah bin al-Yamin. When Huzayfah read this letter, his eyes were filled with tears. He recalled the traditions of the Holy Prophet (s) concerning Abu Dharr. What moved him most was Abu Dharr's exile and loneliness. He picked up the pen with extreme anguish and wrote a reply to this letter.

In the name of Allah, the Beneficent, the Merciful.

My dear Abu Dharr,

I received your letter and came to know your affairs. You have scared me of my return on the Day of Judgment and have persuaded me to do certain things, for the improvement and betterment of myself.

O brother! You have always been a well wisher of mine as well as of all the Muslims and have been sympathetic and kind to all. You were always anxious for the welfare of all. You always showed the people the path of virtue and forbade them to *do the evil. Of course, guidance is the exclusive right of Allah. He gives deliverance to whom He likes, and deliverance depends upon His pleasure. I pray to Allah for His general forgiveness and widespread blessing for myself, for the chosen and the common men and for all the people of this ummah I have come to know of those surprising facts, which you have mentioned in your letter, that is, your banishment from your hometown, your abandonment in a strange land without friends and supporters, and your having been thrown away from your house.*

O Abu Dharr! The news of your sufferings has broken my heart into pieces and the sufferings that you are experiencing now are extremely saddening. But I am sorry to say that I cannot do anything from here. Would that I had purchased your calamities for all my money. By Allah, had it been possible I would have sacrificed all that I have for you. O Abu Dharr! Alas! You are in troubles, and I cannot do anything. By Allah if it had been possible for me to share your troubles, I would have certainly done it. How painful it is that I cannot meet you.

It is difficult to reach you. If these cruel people, make me equal partner with you in your troubles I am willing to take upon myself your hardships. But, alas, it cannot be this way.

O Abu Dharr! Do not be worried. Allah is your supporter. He is seeing all these matters. Brother! It is necessary for both of us, you, and I, to invoke Allah and request Him for the bestowal of good reward and for deliverance from punishment for us. O Brother! The time is approaching near when you and I will be called in the presence of Allah and shall be leaving soon.

O brother! Do not be worried at the troubles you have been facing and do not be alarmed. Pray to Allah to grant you, its recompense.

O brother! I consider death is far better for us than to live here. Now it is necessary for us to leave this transient world, because soon disturbances will come in succession one after the other. *These disturbances will go on mounting and will crush up the virtuous people of the world. Swords will be unsheathed in these disturbances and death will surround men from all sides. Whosoever raises his head in these disturbances will certainly be killed. No tribe of all the tribes of the towns and the deserts of Arabia will remain unaffected. At that time the cruellest will be considered the most revered one, and the most pious one will be looked down upon. May Allah save us from the evils of that time.*

O Abu Dharr, I pray for you all the time. May Allah keep us under His mercy and protect us from haughtiness in worship. He is a great disposer of our affairs. We always expect His generosity.

Peace be upon you".

Huzayfah[105]

Scholars say that Abu Dharr was spending his days with his family at Rabzah when suddenly his son Zar fell sick. There was no physician in that deserted place to approach for treatment except trust in Allah. At last, the disease aggravated till the time of his death approached. The distressed mother took up his head from the sand and put it on her knee. The son breathed his last. The mother and sister started bewailing, Abu Dharr was deeply shocked, but his trust in Allah consoled him. He controlled himself and didn't weep. As it was a desert there were no arrangements for funeral. History does not tell us at this point how Abu Dharr buried his son, but it is known from an authentic source what he did after burial and how he expressed his feelings in words. Muhaddith Ya'qub Kulayni writes: "*When Abu Dharr's son Zar died Abu Dharr put his hand on Zar's grave and said, "O my son! May Allah have mercy on you. You were a very able son of mine. You have died while I am happy with you. You should know that, by Allah, I did not suffer any loss by your death, and I do not need anybody except Allah. O son! If there*

---

[105] Shifa 'us Sudur, Abu Dharr al-Ghifari p. 105 Al-Fusul by Murtaza Alamul Huda

had been no consideration for the horror after death, I would have been happy to wish to replace you in the grave. But now to my mourning your death has kept you off mourning (for me). By Allah, I did not weep on your death but what you have suffered makes me weep. Would that I had known what was asked of you and what you said in reply. O Allah! I have excused my rights which he owed to me. O my nourisher! I pray you to excuse whatever rights he owed to you. My Lord! You are more forgiving than I."[106]

Shaykh Abbas Qummi writes in his book *'Safinatul Bihar'* vol. 1 p. 483 that the words uttered by Abu Dharr on the grave of his son Zar were also uttered by Imam Ja'far Sadiq (as) on the grave of his son Isma'il.

Abu Dharr had not yet forgotten the death of his young son when his wife also left him forever. According to Allamah Abdul Hamid Abu Dharr and his family members were passing their days in such a condition that they had no proper arrangement for food except that they got a little piece of meat now and then out of the camel slaughtered for the government officials.[107] They generally used to eat grass or other such things in those days. One day Abu Dharr's wife ate some poisonous grass by which she contracted a fatal disease and died.[108] Abu Dharr also fell sick.

After the death of his wife Abu Dharr felt lonelier. He had only a daughter with him. When the people residing around Rabzah came to know of Abu Dharr's sickness some of them came to see him. According to the statement of Abu Dharr's daughter they said to him. *"O Abu Dharr! What are you suffering from and what do you complain of?"*

---

[106] Usul al-Kafi

[107] Tabari, vol. 5, p. 67

[108] Hayatul Qulub, vol. 2, p. 1049

Abu Dharr replied, *"I have complaint against my sins."*

They said, *"Do you desire something?"*

He said, *"Yes I desire to have Allah's mercy."*

They said, *"If you like we can call a physician."*

He said, *"Allah is the Absolute Physician. The diseases as well as the remedy are in His power. I don't stand in need of a physician."*[109] He was certain of his death.

Majlisi, on the authority of Sayyid Ibn Taus, quotes Mu'awiya bin Tha'labah as saying: *"When Abu Dharr's condition deteriorated at Rabzah and we got its information we left Medina for Rabzah to see him. After inquiring about his condition we desired him to make his will. He said that he had expressed his will, whatever it was, before the Commander of the Faithful.*

We asked, "By the Commander of the Faithful do you mean Caliph Uthman?"

He said, "Never! By the Commander of the Faithful is meant one who is the rightful Commander of the Faithful. O Ibn Tha'labah! Listen to me! Abu Turab, (The Father of the Earth) Ali is he who is the blossom of the earth. He is a divine scholar of this ummah. Listen! You will see many abominable things in the world after his death'.

I said, "O Abu Dharr! We see that you make friends with those whom the Holy Prophet loved."

Now we want to say something about the place Rabzah where Abu Dharr was confined, and he was not allowed to go out of its bounds.

Scholars and historians agree that Rabzah is situated at

---

[109] Hayatul Qulub

three miles from Medina near Zate Araq on the way to Hijaz and at that time it was not more than desolate wilderness. Shaykh Muhammad' Abdoh writes in the footnote on page 17 of vol. 2, of *Nahjul Balaghah* that Rabzah is a place near Medina where the grave of Abu Dharr lies. Ibn Abil Hadid says that Abu Dharr's exile to Rabzah was one of the causes that led to the revolt of the Muslims against Uthman.

There is no doubt that Abu Dharr achieved the highest rank of faithfulness. He kept in view till the last moments of his life that he had promised to the Prophet (s) to speak the truth and not to mind any reproach for the sake of truth. Shah Walyullah Dehlavi writes that it was the practice of the Prophet (s) that he took oath of allegiance of different kinds from different people i.e. to go on Jihad, to renounce innovation, to establish the Islamic laws, and to speak the truth.[110]

The oath that he had taken from Abu Dharr was that of speaking the truth. Abu Dharr acted according to the oath of allegiance after fully knowing its implications, and why should he have not acted so, when he had the conviction, which admitted of no doubt, that whatever he was doing was in absolute conformity with the Will of Allah and the intentions of the Holy Prophet (s).[111] In this respect he never cared for the mightiness of the government nor was he scared of his getting into troubles. He tolerated every kind of oppression and bore every kind of discomfort but did not stop from speaking the truth, till he was twice sent into exile. His last exile was without a parallel.

He lay confined in a desolate desert. To say nothing of a house for shelter, he had to stay under the shade of a tree, without any arrangement for food and without a place to reside, rest or sleep in. But with his lofty courage and determination Abu Dharr bore with cheerfulness all the hardships for the

---

[110] Shifa'ul 'alil

[111] Futuhatul Makkiyah Ibn Arabi, chapter 269).

pleasure of Allah. His wife and young son having died, the time had now approached when he was waiting for his own departure in that desolate place with his only young daughter with him.

Alas! The last day of Abu Dharr's life approached in that desolate place. He was in prayers and his daughter was restless and anxious in view of her father's condition and approaching end. There was no man, not even an animal in sight. The moment was near for the angel of death to come, for the humanity to cry, and for the daughter to be deprived of her fathers love. She had not only seen but was still observing the helplessness of her father for whose love she became emotional again and again.

We here reproduce the tragic story of Abu Dharr's death as related by his daughter, in the light of Majlisi's writing. She says: *"We were passing our days with untold sufferings in the wilderness. It so happened one day that we could not get anything to eat. We kept on searching round the jungle but could not find anything. My ailing father said to me, "Daughter! Why are you so much worried today?" I said, "Dad! I am extremely hungry and weakness has overtaken you also on account of intense hunger. I have tried my utmost to get something to eat but could not find anything so that I might feel honored before you".* Abu Dharr said, *"Do not be worried. Allah is the great disposer of our affairs".* I said, *"Dad! This is correct but there is nothing in sight for the fulfillment of our needs.* He said, *"Daughter! Hold me by the shoulder and take me to such and such direction. Perhaps we may find something there".* I held him by the hand and started in the direction he had asked me to go. On the way my father asked me to make him sit on the ground. I seated him on the hot sand. He gathered some sand and lay down with his head upon it.

As soon as he lay down on the ground, his eyes began to revolve, and he got into the agony of death. Seeing this I started crying hoarsely. Then keeping control over himself he said, "Why do you cry, daughter?" I said, "What else shall I do, then father?" It is a desert and not a single man is seen here. I do not *have a shroud for you and there is no gravedigger here. What will I do if you breathe your last in this desolate place?*

He wept at my helplessness and said, "My daughter! Don't be worried. That friend of mine in whose love and in whose children's love I tolerated all these hardships had informed me of this event in advance. Listen! O my dear daughter! He had told before a group of his companions at the Battle of Tabuk that one of them would die in a desert and a party of companions would go for his funeral and burial. Now, none of them is alive except me. All of them have died in populated places. Only I am left over and in a desolate wilderness. I have never seen such a desert land where I am lying in the agony of death. My sweet daughter! When I die cover me with my cloak and sit down on the way leading to Iraq. A party of believers will pass by that way. Tell them that Abu Dharr, the companion of the Prophet, has breathed his last. Hence please arrange his burial".

He was talking to me when the angel of death looked at his face. When my father looked at him his face flushed and he said, "O the angel of death! Where have you been uptil now? I have been waiting for you. O my friend! You have come in the hour of my great need. O the angel of death! May that man, who is not happy to see you never get deliverance. For Allah's sake take me soon to the most Merciful Allah so that I may be relieved of the hardships of the world".

After that, he addressed Allah and said, "O my Nourisher! I swear by Your Being, and You know that I speak the truth that I never abominated death and always wished to meet You".

After that the sweat of death appeared on the forehead of my father and looking at me, he turned his face away from the world forever. We are for Allah and to Him we shall return".

The daughter of Abu Dharr continued, "When my father died, I ran crying to that path which led to Iraq. I was sitting there waiting for the coming party. Suddenly it occurred to me that the dead body of my father was lying alone. So, I ran up to the dead body. Again, I came back to the side of the path lest the party should pass by, and I might not inform it. Thus, I came and went several times.

Now suddenly I saw some people coming on camels. When they drew near, I went towards them with tears in my eyes and said to them, "O companions of the Prophet! A companion of the Prophet has died". They asked me who he was. I replied, "My father, Abu Dharr Ghifari".

As soon as they heard it, they got down from the camels and accompanied me weeping. When they reached the place, they cried and were very much shocked at his sad demise and busied themselves with his funeral rites.

The historian A'tham Kufi states that the party, which was going to Iraq comprised Ahnaf bin Qays Tamim, Sa'sa'ah bin Sauhan al 'Abdi, Kharijah bin Salat Tamimi, Abdullah ibn Muslimah Tamimi, Hilal bin Malik Nazle, Jarir bin Abdullah Bajali, Malik bin Ashtar bin Harith etc. These people at once washed Abu Dharr and arranged for his shrouding. After the burial Malik bin Ashtar standing by the side of the grave delivered a speech that referred to Abu Dharr's affairs and a supplication about him. After the praise of the Almighty Allah, he said:

"O Allah! Abu Dharr was a companion of Your Prophet and a believer in Your Books and Your Prophets. He fought very bravely in Your way, remained steadfast to Your Islamic laws and never changed or distorted any of Your commands."

"O my Lord! Seeing some contraventions of the Book and the tradition he raised his voice and drew the attention of those responsible for the ummah towards making improvements, because of which they tortured him, drove him from place to place, humiliated him, turned him out of the country of your dear Prophet and put him to extreme hardships. At last, he breathed

his last in a state of utter loneliness in a deserted place."

"O Allah! Grant Abu Dharr a big portion of those heavenly blessings which You have promised for the believers and take revenge on one who has banished him from Medina and give him full deserved punishment."

Malik Ashtar prayed for Abu Dharr in his speech and all those who were present there said *"Amin"* (May it be so).

Anyway, when they had finished with the funeral ceremonies, it was evening and they stayed there overnight. They set off the next morning."[112] After Abu Dharr's burial these people left Rabzah but his daughter stayed there according to his will. After some days Caliph Uthman called her and sent her home.[113]

Abu Dharr's daughter was however still near her father's grave at Rabzah with a mind to stay there for a few days more when one night she saw Abu Dharr in her dream sitting and reciting the Holy Qur'an.

She said, *"Dad! What happened to you, and to what extent have you been blessed by the Merciful Allah?"*

He said, *"O my daughter! Allah has bestowed on me limitless favour, has given me every comfort and granted me everything. I am very happy with His generosity. It is your duty to be busy in the worship of Allah as usual, and not to let any kind of pride and haughtiness come to you."*[114]

Scholars and historians are unanimous that he died on 8th Zilhajjah, 32 A.H. at Rabzah. His age at the time of his death

---

[112] Tarikh Kamil, vol. 3, Izalatul Khulfa vol. 1, Tarikh Tabari, vol. 4

[113] Tarikh Tabari vol. 4 p. 527

[114] Hayatul Qulub, vol. 2

was eighty-five years.

Having suffered continuous oppressions, constant tortures, and hardships of the successive exiles at the hands of the worldly-minded men, Abu Dharr left this transient world at Rabzah, but the story of his love for Allah is still living and will last for ever. History is replete with examples; truthfulness and his straightforward and honest speeches are resounding in the hearts of the believers. He is still alive through his character even after his death; and he will remain immortal through the principles he held so dear.

The world knows that he died in the way of Allah. He suffered troubles and hardships in support of truth and in establishing and propagating the principles of Islam in the Islamic Government. But it is a pity that the tyrant does not repent of his tyranny. We reproduce this incident here in the word of the translator of the "History" written by Muhammad bin Ali bin A'tham Kufi, a historian of the 3rd century hijri. He writes:

"When the news of Abu Dharr's death reached Uthman, Ammar bin Yasir was present there. Ammar said, "May Allah have His Mercy upon Abu Dharr. Allah! Bear witness that we pray for mercy for him with all our heart and soul. O Allah! forgive him".

As soon as the Caliph heard it he lost his temper and said, "O fool!" You will meet the same fate. Listen to me! I don't feel ashamed on account of the exile of Abu Dharr and his death in the wilderness".

Ammar said, "By Allah, this will not be my end".

Hearing this, the Caliph ordered his courtiers, "Push him out, banish him from Medina and send him to the same place where Abu Dharr had been sent. Let him also lead the same life and don't let him come to Medina as long as I am alive".

Ammar said, "By Allah! I prefer the vicinity of wolves and dogs to my stay near you". After that he rose from there and came back to his house.

When the Caliph decided to send Ammar to Rabzah and the news reached the tribe of Bani Makhzum they flew into a rage. They said among themselves that Uthman had crossed the bounds of decency. After that they held a council and thought that it would be better if before taking any step this matter is settled by compromise. With this aim in view, they came to Ali.

Ali (as) asked them, "Why have all of you come at this time?"

They said, "A serious problem is facing us; the Caliph has decided to banish Ammar from Medina to Rabzah. Be kind enough to go to the Caliph and persuade him in suitable words to leave Ammar alone and not to banish him from the city otherwise such a disturbance will stir as would hardly be quelled".

Imam Ali listened to them, consoled them and asked them not to make haste. He told them, "I'll go to the Caliph and will try to settle the matter. I am sure it will be settled amicably. I am fully conscious of the situation. I'll bring him round to your viewpoint.

After this Ali went to Caliph Uthman and said, "O Uthman! You are too hasty in some matters and ignore the suggestions of friends and advisors. Once you turned Abu Dharr out of Medina. He was a very virtuous Muslim, a dignified companion of the Prophet of Allah (s) and the best of immigrants. You sent him to Rabzah where the poor fellow died in solitude. On account of this incident, the Muslims have turned all the more against you. Now I hear that you have decided to banish Ammar as well from the city. This is not a good thing. Have fear of Allah and desist from banishing Ammar from Medina. For Allah's sake don't give such troubles to the companions of the Prophet and let them live in peace."

Hearing this Uthman angrily said to Ali. "You should be the first to be banished from the city because it is you who are ruining Ammar and others".

Hearing these indecent words Ali said, "O Uthman! How dare you think like this about me? You will not be able to do it even if you wish it, and if you doubt my words just try. Then you will realize the actual state of affairs and will come to know whom you are facing. And now you say that I am ruining Ammar and others. By Allah all this disorder is from your side. I don't see any fault with them. You are committing such acts as are against the religion and decency. People cannot tolerate them, and are turning against you, and you cannot tolerate these things. You feel offended with everyone and then you cause them trouble. This attitude is far from the ways of the elders". After that he rose from there and went out.

When the people of Bani Makkzum came to Ali, to know what the Caliph had told him in their case, Ali said, "Tell Ammar to remain indoors and not to come out. Allah will save him from the evil designs. The Caliph also came to know of this conversation through somebody and he gave up the idea of exiling Ammar.[115]

---

[115] The Great Companion of the Prophet: Abu Dharr

Cursing of Imam Ali (as) from the pulpits

Mu'awiya and 'Amr al-Aas were "companions" and yet they fought against the successor of the Holy Prophet (s) and cursed and abused Ali (as) at public meetings and even in the addresses given after Friday prayers. They did so despite the fact, as reported by prominent ulema of the Sunni sect in their authentic books, that the Holy Prophet (s) had repeatedly said, *"He who abuses or curses Ali, abuses me. He who abuses me, abuses Allah."* The learned Taftazani has elaborately dealt with this topic in his *Sharhe Maqasid*. He writes that since the companions were inimical to one another, some of them had deviated from the right path. Some of them, on account of envy and worldly aspirations, perpetrated all kinds of cruelty. It is evident that most of the companions who were not infallible committed heinous acts but some ulema, because they favored them, have tried to cover up their faults.

In reference to both Ali (as) and Fatima (as), the Holy Prophet (s) said that their trouble was his own trouble. The Holy Prophet (s) said: *"He who troubles these two troubles me, and the one who troubles me troubles Allah."It is also written in all the authentic books that the Holy Prophet (s) said, "He who reviles Ali reviles me, who reviles me reviles Allah."*

Muhammad Bin Yusuf Ganji Shafi'i, in his *Kifayatu't-Talib*, ch. 10, narrates a detailed hadith on the authority of Ibn Abbas, who told a section of the Syrians, who were cursing Ali (as) that he had heard the Holy Prophet (s) saying about Ali: *"He who abuses you abuses me, and he who abuses me abuses Allah, and he who abuses Allah will be thrown straight into Hell."*

After this hadith he quotes many other ahadith from authentic sources all of which prove that those who abuse Ali (as) are infidels. Chapter 10 of his book is entitled: *"Concerning the Infidelity of One Who Abuses Ali."*[116] So according to all these hadith, those who curse Ali, curse Allah and his Prophet. All of them (like Mu'awiya, the Bani Umayya, the Nasibi's, the Khariji's) are themselves cursed.

Among the many clear proofs that Mu'awiya was an infidel and deserved damnation was his public rejection of the Commander of the Faithful and his ordering the people to recite imprecations against the Imam in their qunut's (supplication in daily prayers). Both Sunni's and we acknowledge this fact. Even the historians of other nations have recorded that this vile practice was openly pursued and that many people were put to death because they did not utter the curses. This outrage was discontinued by the Umayya Caliph, Umar bin Abdu'l-Aziz.

Obviously, one who curses the brother of the Holy Prophet (s), the husband of Fatima (as), the Commander of the Faithful, Ali Bin Abi Talib, and who orders others to do it is definitely damned. This fact has been recorded by all the Sunni

---

[116] Also Hakim in his Mustadrak, vol. III, p. 121, has quoted this same hadith

ulema in their authentic books and they[117] have, in slightly different words, reported that the Prophet (s) said: "*One who reviles Ali, really reviles me; who reviles me, really reviles Allah.*"

Dailami in his *Firdaus*, Sulayman Hanafi in *Yanabiu'l-Mawadda* have reported that the Prophet (s) said: "*One who gives pain to Ali, really gives pain to me, and the curse of Allah is upon him who causes pain to me.*"

Ibn Hajar Makki in his *Sawa'iq* narrates a hadith concerning the consequence to one who curses against any of the progeny of the Prophet (s). He reports that the Prophet (s) said: "*If anyone curses my Ahl ul Bayt, there is nothing for him but exclusion from Islam. If anyone injures me concerning my Ahl ul Bayt, may Allah's curse be upon him.*"

Therefore, Mu'awiya was certainly cursed. As reported by Ibn Athir in his *Kamil*, Mu'awiya used to curse Ali, the grandsons of the Holy Prophet (s), Hassan and Hussain and also Abbas and Malik Ashtar in the qunut of his daily prayers.

Imam Ahmad Ibn Hanbal reports in his *Musnad* from a number of sources that the Holy Prophet (s) of Allah (s) said: "*If anyone injures Ali he shall be treated as a Jew or Christian on the Day of Judgment.*"

Certainly, you must know that it is one of the tenets of Islam that to call Allah and the Holy Prophet (s) by ill names

---

[117] For instance, Imam Ahmad Bin Hanbal in his Musnad, Imam Abu Abdu'r-Rahman Nisa'i in his Khasa'isu'l-Alawi, Imam Tha'labi and Imam Fakhru'd-in Razi in their Tafsir (commentary), Ibn Abi'l-Hadid in his Sharh-e-Nahju'l-Balagha, Muhammad Bin Yusuf Ganji Shafi'i in his Kifayatu't-Talib, Sibt Ibn Jauzi in his Tadhkira, Sulayman Balkhi Hanafi in Yanabiu'l-Mawadda, Mir Seyyed Ali Hamadani in his Mawaddatu'l-Qurba, Dailami in his Firdaus, Muslim Bin Hajjaj in his Sahih, Muhammad Bin Talha Shafi'i in his Matalibu's-Su'ul, Ibn Sabbagh Maliki in his Fusulu'l-Muhimma, Hakim in his Mustadrak, Khatib Khawarizmi in his Manaqib, Abraham Hamwaini in his Fara'id, Ibn Maghazili Shafi'i in his Manaqib, Imamu'l-haram in his Dhakha'iru'l-Uquba, Ibn Hajar in his Sawa'iq, and other prominent ulema.

leads to infidelity. Muhammad Bin Ganji Shafi'i in his *Kifayatu't-Talib*, part X, reports that once Abdullah Ibn Abbas and Sa'id ibn Jabir saw on the brink of Zamzam a group of Syrians railing at Ali. They went to them and said: *"Who among you was abusing the Holy Prophet of Allah (s)?"*

They replied: *"None of us was abusing the Holy Prophet of Allah (s)."*

Then they said: *"Well, who among you was abusing Ali?"*

They said: *"Yes, we have been abusing Ali."*

Then Abdullah and Sa'id said: *"You should bear witness that we heard the Holy Prophet saying to Ali, 'One who abuses you really abuses me; one who abuses me, really abuses Allah. If someone abuses Allah, He will throw him headlong into the fire of Hell."*[118]

M. Shibli, the dean of India's Sunni historians of Islam, writes in his famous biography of Prophet Muhammad (s), *Sira-tun-Nabi*[119]: "Among all those extraneous forces which affect and influence the writing of history, none is more powerful than the government. But it will always be a source of pride for the Muslims that their pen was never subdued by the sword. Work on the compilation and collation of *Hadith* was begun in the times of the Banu Umayya. For full 90 years, from Sind in India (Indo-Pakistan) to Asia Minor and Andalusia in Spain, Ali (as) and the children of Fatima (as) were cursed from every pulpit in every mosque after every Friday sermon. Thousands and thousands of *hadith* glorifying Mu'awiya, were manufactured, and were put into circulation. In the times of the Abbasis, *hadith* were invented foretelling the birth and the excellence of each (Abbasi) khalifa by name. But what was the result of all this

---

[118] Peshawar Nights

[119] Volume I, 4th printing, published by the Maarif Printing Press, Azamgarh, U.P., India, in 1976

stupendous effort? The traditionalists (the collectors of the statements of the Prophet (s)) declared publicly at the same time (during the caliphates of the Umayyads and the Abbasis) that all these *hadith* were spurious, and they rejected them.

For the compilation of *hadith*, Mu'awiya had given the following orders:

1. All the traditions of the Prophet (s) in praise of Ali (as) or upholding his superiority in any way, should be suppressed.

2. Any man narrating the virtues of Ali (as) or quoting the *hadith* of the Prophet (s) in this regard, would do so at his own risk. His subsidies and stipends would be withheld from him. His house and other property would be confiscated. His testimony as a witness would not be accepted in the courts, and he would be ostracized by other Muslims.

3. On the other hand, every conceivable virtue should be attributed to Abu Bakr, Umar, Uthman, and of course, to Mu'awiya himself. People should be encouraged to make up "*hadith*" of the Prophet (s) in praise of these four men and their friends. Whoever invents such *hadith*, would become a favorite at the royal court, and would receive rich rewards in rank or cash or estates etc.

Concurrently with the founding of his "cottage industry" for manufacturing "*hadith*" of the Prophet (s), Mu'awiya also set up a "brain laundry" for the Muslims. He instituted the practice of cursing & denouncing the memory of Ali (as) and his children from the pulpit in every mosque in his empire so that the Muslim children were born, they grew up, and they died hearing curses upon Ali, and not knowing who he was. Whole generations lived and died in ignorance. Falsehoods were put into circulation by the government on a scale so vast that they became the staple of their lives. Mu'awiya and his successors kept their "brain laundries" just as busy as their "cottage industry."

Mu'awiya mobilized every means for waging propaganda

war against Ali (as) and the Banu Hashim. The momentum of the blitz he launched against them, has lasted down to our own times. He waged his war from the mosques. The prayer-leaders in them were paid to put weird and fantastic interpretations upon the verses of Qur'an in an attempt to show Ali (as) at a disadvantage. They tried to convince the rank-and-file Muslims that it would be in their interest "in both worlds" if they supported Mu'awiya against Ali (as) and the Banu Hashim.

Incumbents have the advantage of the media and educational arms of the state, and they control through subsidies the religious establishment itself.[120]

It must now be clear to the reader that the history of Islam was written under the direction of the party that held all the instruments of power in its hands. It must also be obvious to him that much of the historical material was "laundered" at the "brain laundries" established by Mu'awiya before it got into his hands. Mu'awiya was a most consummate master of the art of propaganda.

The full effects of propaganda have not yet become plain, yet it is already obvious that whole nations can be indoctrinated with wrong opinions and evil moral standards. Few, if any, minds are strong enough to resist the ideas constantly projected at them.[121]

If any hadith of the Prophet (s) of Islam was complimentary to Ali, Mu'awiya placed its narration under proscription. This proscription was not lifted when he died in 680. It was not lifted even when his dynasty, the Umayyads, perished in 750, and it was not lifted even through the long centuries of the caliphate of the Abbasi's.

---

[120] *Islam and Development, p. 16, 1980*

[121] *The Course of Empire - The Arabs and Their Successors, 1965*

The Abbasi's exterminated the Umayyads but they shared with them their animosity to Ali (as) and to the children of Muhammad. In this matter, the aims, and interests of the governments of Saqifa, the Umayyads, and the Abbasis converged; there was ideological compatibility among them all.

The Umayyads and the Abbasi's did their utmost to suppress the facts of history. Many of their khalifas had forbidden their subjects to say or to write anything about Ali (as) except falsehoods. Truth was under a siege and falsehood was rampant in their dominions. And yet, Truth asserted itself.

"Truth has (now) arrived, and falsehood perished: For falsehood is (by its nature) bound to perish." (Qur'an. Chapter 17; verse 81)

True statements were volunteered by sources which, in most cases, were inimical to Ali. Even his most rabid enemies like the Umayyads and the Kharjis, conceded the sublimity of his character. As noted before M. Shibli, the Indian historian, pointed out that the Shia Muslims did not write any history. Whatever history we have, has, therefore, come down to us from the non-Shia or the anti-Shia sources. It has come down to us from the archives of the governments of Saqifa, the Umayyads and the Abbasis. The story of the glorious deeds of Ali ibn Abi Talib, like the radiance of Truth itself, has filtered out of those archives.

Muslim, in his *Sahih*, wrote in a chapter entitled, *"The virtues of Ali ibn Abi Talib"*, the following: Muawiah ordered his governors everywhere to take the curse [of Ali ibn Abi Talib] as tradition, and that all the speakers must include it in their speeches. When some of the Companions protested very strongly against such a rule, Muawiah ordered their killing and burning. Among the famous Companions who were killed at the order of Muawiah were Hijr ibn Adi al-Kindi and his followers because they protested and refused to curse Ali, and some of them were buried alive.

Abu al-Aala al-Mawdudi wrote in his book *Caliphate and Kingdom:* Abu al-Hassan al-Basri said: Muawiah had four features, and if he had only one of them, it would have been considered a great sin:

1. Making decisions without consulting the Companions, who were the light of virtues.

2. Designating his son as his successor. His son was a drunkard, corrupt and wore silk.

3. He claimed Ziyad [as his son], and the Messenger of Allah said, "There is offspring for the honorable woman, but there is nothing for the whore."

4. His killing of Hijr and his followers. Woe unto him from Hijr and the followers of Hijr.[122]

There were some good Companions who used to dash out of the mosque immediately after the prayers so that they did not have to listen to the speeches that always ended with the cursing of Ali. For that reason, the Umayyads changed the tradition of the Messenger of Allah. They put the speech before the prayers, so that people listened to it against their will. What kind of Companions were these people! They were not afraid of changing the tradition of the Messenger of Allah, or even the laws of Allah, to reach their wicked and low objectives and to satisfy their sinister desires. They cursed a man whom Allah had kept cleansed and purified and made it obligatory for people to pray for him in the same way as they prayed for His Messenger. Furthermore, Allah and His Messenger made it obligatory for people to love him, and the Prophet (s) said, *"Loving Ali is believing, and hating him is hypocrisy."*[123]

The author of *Then I Was Guided,* Dr. Muhammad Tijani

---

[122] al Khilafah wa al Mulk, Syed Abul A'la Maududi, p 106

[123] Sahih, Muslim, vol 1 p 61

says in his book: *"I asked al-Sayyid al-Sadr about Imam Ali (as) and why they testify for him in the Adhan [the call for prayers] that he is "Waliy Allah" [the friend of Allah]. He answered me in the following way:*

The Commander of the Believers, Ali, may Allah's blessings be upon him, was one of those servants of Allah whom He chose and honored by giving them the responsibilities of the Message after His Prophet. These servants are the trustees of the Prophet (s), since each Prophet has a trustee, and Ali ibn Abi Talib is the trustee of Muhammad (s).

We favour him above all the Companions of the Prophet (s) because Allah and the Prophet favoured him, and we have many proofs of that, some of them are deduced through logical reasoning, others are found in the Qur'an and al-Sunnah [the Tradition of the Prophet Muhammad (s)], and these proofs cannot be suspect, because they have been scrutinized, and proven right, by our own learned people (who wrote many books about the subject) and those of the Sunni Madhahibs. The Umayyad regime worked very hard to cover this truth and fought Imam Ali and his sons, whom they killed. They even ordered people, sometimes by force, to curse him, so his followers - may Allah bless them all started to testify for him as being the friend of Allah. No Muslim would curse the friend of Allah in defiance of the oppressive authorities, so that the glory was to Allah, and to His Messenger and to all the believers. It also became an historical landmark across the generations so that they know the just cause of Ali and the wrongdoing of his enemies. Thus, our learned people continued to testify that Ali is the friend of Allah in their calls to prayer, as something that is commendable. There are many commendable things in the religious rites as well as in ordinary mundane dealings, and the Muslim will be rewarded for doing them, but not punished for leaving them aside. For example, it is commendable for the Muslim to say after al-Shahadah [i.e. to testify that there is no God but Allah, and that Muhammad (s) is His messenger]: And I will testify that Heaven is true and Hell is true, and that Allah will resurrect people from their graves.

Mu'awiya had made it compulsory to curse Ali and Ahl al-Bayt. This continued for sixty years until Umar ibn Abdul Aziz stopped it. Some historians inform us that the Umayyads themselves plotted to kill Umar ibn Abdul Aziz, and he was one of them, because he killed the Sunnah, which was the cursing of Ali ibn Abi Talib."[124]

---

[124] Then I Was Guided by Dr. Muhammad Tijani

The Battle of Jamal (The Camel)

Dr. Muhammad Tijani says in his book *Ask Those Who Know:* "The one who researches 'Aisha's position against 'Ali, the Commander of the Faithful finds a strange, surprising thing. There is no explanation for it except her envy and enmity to the household of the Prophet (s). History has recorded her incomparable hatred and malice towards Imam 'Ali. She reached the point where she was not even able to utter his name, not able to stand the sight of him. When she heard that the people had paid allegiance to him for the Caliphate after the murder of 'Uthman, she said: *"I wished that the skies had become like the earth before 'Ali had attained it."* She exerted every effort into causing problems for him, leading troops against him to wage a war of insurrection, and when the news of his death reached her, she prostrated in thanks to Allah.

Like me, are you not surprised at the *Ahl al-sunna wa'l-Jama'a* who report in their *Sahih's* that the Prophet of Allah (s)

(s) said: *"O 'Ali! none but a true believer loves you, and none but a hypocrite hates you."* Then they also report in their *Sahih's*, *Musnad's* and history books that 'Aisha hated Imam 'Ali (as) so much that she could not mention his name. Is this not a testimony from them regarding the nature of the woman? Just as al-Bukhari has reported in his *Sahih* that the Prophet of Allah (s) said: *"Fatima is a part of me. Whoever angers her angers me, and whoever angers me angers Allah."* Then al-Bukhari himself relates that Fatima (as) died whilst she was angry with Abu Bakr, not speaking to him to the time she died.

Are these traditions not [enough] testimony from them that Allah and His Prophet are both angry at Abu Bakr? This is what all intelligent people understand. I always say, therefore, that the truth will surface, no matter how much the falsifiers try to hide it, no matter how much the helpers of the Umayyads try to misrepresent and fabricate it. For the proof of Allah is evident upon His servants from the day of the revelation of the Qur'an until the final hour [of reckoning]. Praise be to Allah, the Lord of all the worlds.

Imam Ahmad reports that Abu Bakr once came to the Prophet of Allah (s) and sought permission to enter. Before he went in, he heard 'Aisha's voice raised, saying to the Prophet (s): *"By Allah! I surely know that 'Ali is dearer to you than me and my father"*, she repeated this twice or three times".

'Aisha's hatred for Imam 'Ali (as) was so much that she always tried to distance him from the Prophet (s) whenever she could find the means to do so. The Mu'tazili ibn Abi al-Hadid, in his commentary on the *Nahj al-Balagha* said the Prophet of Allah (s) beckoned to 'Ali (as) to come close. He came close until he sat between him and 'Aisha, and he and the Prophet (s) were clung together. She said to him: *"Can you not find a seat for this one except [on] my thigh?"*

He also narrated that one day the Prophet of Allah (s) was walking with Imam 'Ali (as) and the conversation became prolonged. 'Aisha approached as she was walking from behind until she came between them saying: *"What is it between you two that you are taking so long?"* Upon this the Prophet of Allah (s) became angry.

It is also reported that she once came upon the Prophet (s) whilst he was conversing quietly with 'Ali. She screamed and said: *"What is it with you and me, O son of Abu Talib? I have [just] one day with the Prophet of Allah (s)"*. Thereupon the Prophet (s) became angry.

How often did she anger the Prophet (s) with her conduct, which arose due to her intense jealousy and furious nature and her offensive words? Would the Prophet (s) be pleased with any believing man or woman whose heart was filled with hatred and malice towards his cousin, the leader of his progeny, he of whom he said: *"He loves Allah and His Prophet, and Allah and His Prophet love him."*

He also said about him: *"Whoever loves 'Ali has loved me, and whoever hates 'Ali has hated me."*

Allah, Glory be to Him, ordered the wives of the Prophet to remain in their houses and not to go out from them, displaying their ornaments. He also ordered them to read the Qur'an, to undertake the prayer, to pay *zakat* and to obey Allah and His Apostle (s). All the wives of the Prophet of Allah (s) obeyed the injunctions of Allah, and the commands of His Prophet (s), who forbade and warned them before he died: *"Which one of you will ride the camel and have the dogs of al-Haw'ab bark at her?"* All of them [obeyed] with the exception of 'Aisha. She disobeyed all his orders and scoffed at all the warnings.

Historians relate that Hafsa bint 'Umar wanted to go with her (for the battle of the Camel), but her brother, 'Abd Allah reproached her and recited the [aforementioned] verse to her. Hafsa then cancelled her plans. 'Aisha, however, rode the camel and the dogs of al-Haw'ab barked at her. Taha Hussain says in his book *"The Great Sedition"* (*al-Fitna al-Kubra*): "On her route, 'Aisha passed by some water and some dogs barked at her. She asked about the water and was told that it was al-Haw'ab. She was greatly shocked and said: *"Take me back! Take me back! I have heard the Prophet of Allah (s) saying while he was with his wives: 'Which one of you will the dogs of al-Haw'ab bark at'"?* 'Abd Allah b. Zubayr came, having been instructed to pacify her, bringing fifty men from the Banu 'Amir who falsely swore that the water was not that of al-Haw'ab."

I believe that this narration was fabricated during the time of the Banu Umayyah to reduce the severity of A'isha's disobedience, thinking that A'isha would be exonerated after her nephew, 'Abd Allah b. al-Zubayr, deceived her, coming with fifty men who swore by God and gave false testimony that the water was not that of al-Haw'ab. It is truly a foolish joke; they wanted to delude, through such reports, those of shallow perception and to convince them that 'Aisha was fooled because, when she passed the water and heard the barking of the dogs, and enquired about the water, it was said that they were at al-Haw'ab. She was distressed and said: *"Take me back! Take me back!"* Do the people who forged this narration search for an excuse for 'Aisha's disobedience of the order of Allah, and what was revealed in the Qur'an regarding the incumbency for her to stay in her house? Or do they seek for an excuse for her disobedience to the order of the Prophet of Allah (s) to stay within her house and the prohibition of riding a camel before arriving at the well of al-Haw'ab, the watering place of the barking dogs? Do they find an excuse for A'isha, after she rejected the advice of Umm Salama?

Historians have recorded the incident in which she said to her: *"Do you remember the day the Prophet of Allah (s) proceeded and we were with him and he turned left from [a place called] Qadid and sat alone with 'Ali and whispered to him for a long time? You wanted to force yourself on them; I tried to prevent you, but you disobeyed me and intruded. It wasn't long before you returned in tears. I asked: 'What happened to you?' And you replied: 'I approached them, and they were in conversation, so I said to Ali: 'I get with the Prophet (s) one day out of nine, so can you not, O son of Abu Talib, leave me with him on my day?' The Messenger of Allah came towards me, and he was red with anger, and said: 'Go back! By Allah, none except those who have abandoned faith can hate him'. I returned repentant and sad.'" 'Aisha said: "Yes, I remember that."*

Umm Salama continued: *"I will also remind you too that you and I were with the Prophet (s) and he said to us: 'Which one of you will be the rider of the trained camel, at whom the dogs of Haw'ab will bark, and she will have deviated from the right path?' We said: 'We seek refuge from Allah and His Prophet from that'. He touched your back and said: 'Don't be that one, O Humayra'".* 'Aisha said: "I remember that."

Umm Salama said: *"Do you not remember that day when your father came with 'Umar, so we put on our veils. They came in and spoke about what they wanted to, until they said: 'O Prophet of Allah (s) we do not know how long you will be with us. If only you were to tell us who will succeed you as Caliph over us, so that there will be after you a place we can turn to'. He said to them: 'As for me, I have seen his position [infront of you]. Were I to do this, you would all fall into disunity as the Israelites dispersed from Aaron'. They remained quiet and left. After they had departed, we came out to the Prophet (s) and you said to him, as you were more forthcoming with him than all of us: 'O Messenger of Allah who did you appoint as Caliph over them?' He said: 'The wearer of the mended shoe'. We went out and we saw it was 'Ali. You said: 'O Prophet (s), I do not see anyone apart from 'Ali'. He replied: 'He is the one'".* 'Aisha said: *"Yes, I remember that."*

Umm Salama said to her: *"So then, 'Aisha, how can you go ahead after this"?* She replied: *"I venture forth to reconcile the people".* Umm Salama sought to prevent her from the uprising, using strong words, saying: *"The pillars of Islam, if they lean, are not set erect by women; and if they crack, are not joined by women. The praiseworthy things for women are lowering their gazes and protecting their chastity. What would you say if the Messenger of Allah (s) appeared before you in one of these deserts and finds you driving your camel from one watering place to another? By Allah, if I were to embark upon this journey of yours, then it was said to me: 'Enter paradise' I would be ashamed to face Muhammad after having thrown off the veils he has placed upon me".*

Just as 'Aisha did not accept the advice of many sincere companions, al-Tabari in his history related that: Jariya b. Quddama al-Sa'di said to her: *'O mother of the believers, by Allah, the murder of 'Uthman is less despicable than you going out on this accursed camel from your house and bearing arms. Allah has imposed on you the veil and sanctity. You have destroyed your cover and defiled your respect. Surely, whoever sees your uprising sees your destruction. If you come to us obeying, then go back to your house. If you have come to us in coercion, then seek the help of the people."*

Historians have recorded that she was the general leader, supervising, separating [people] and issuing commands. Even when Zubayr and Talha argued as to who should lead the prayer, and when both wanted to lead, 'Aisha intervened and removed them both and ordered 'Abd Allah b. Zubayr, her nephew, to lead the people in prayer. She would dispatch messengers with letters which she sent to several regions, requesting their assistance against 'Ali b. Abi Talib (as) and urging them with the *jahili* zeal (the days of ignorance). She even recruited twenty thousand or more rabble and greedy Arabs to fight and depose the Commander of the Faithful (as).

Her urging resulted in zealous discord, where large numbers of people were killed in the name of defending and aiding the mother of the believers. The historians say that when the companions of 'Aisha came to 'Uthman b. Hanif, the governor of Basra, they took him along with seventy of his officers who oversaw the public treasury as prisoners. They brought them to 'Aisha who ordered that they be put to death.

They were slaughtered as sheep are slaughtered. It is [even] reported there were 400 men in all and that they were the first Muslims whose heads were cut off whilst they were patient.

Al-Sha'bi reported from Muslim b. Abi Bakra from his father: *"When Talha and Zubayr reached Basra, I put on my sword as I wanted to help them. I visited 'Aisha, she was ordering, prohibiting; she was in command. I remembered a hadith from the Prophet of Allah (s) which I used to hear him say: 'A community which has its affairs administered by a woman will never succeed'. I [therefore] withdrew from them and left them."*

Al-Bukhari has reported from Abi Bakra: *"Allah benefited me by a word during the days of the [battle of the] Camel. For when the Prophet (s) (s) heard that the Persians had made the daughter of Chosroes their Queen, he said: 'The people that have their affairs administered by a woman will never succeed."*

One of the things that makes us laugh and weep at one time is that 'Aisha went out of her residence in disobedience to Allah and His Prophet (s) and then ordered the companions to remain in their houses. This is surely a strange thing. How, dear Lord, could this occur? The Mu'tazili Ibn Abi'l-Hadid, in the commentary on the *Nahj al-Balagha,* reported, along with historians, that 'Aisha sent a letter when she was in Basra to Zayd b. Sawhan al-'Abdi in which she said to him: *"From 'Aisha, daughter of Abu Bakr, the truthful one, wife of the Prophet (s). To her devoted son, Zayd b. Sawhan. Remain at home and make the people abandon the son of Abu Talib. I hope to hear what I would love from you, since you are the most trustworthy of my family...*

Wasalaam."

This righteous man replied to her thus: *"From Zayd b. Sawhan to 'Aisha bint Abi Bakr: Allah issued a commandment to you and He also issued a commandment to us. He ordered you to remain in your residence, and He ordered us to fight. Your letter has come to me instructing me to do contrary to what Allah has ordered me to do, [You have asked me] to do what Allah has ordered you to do and that you do what Allah has asked me to do. Your order to me is [something] that I cannot obey, therefore there is no reply [necessary] to your letter."*

From this, it becomes clear to us that 'Aisha was not content with leading the army of the Camel, but rather, she craved for absolute control over the believers in all the corners of the land. In all matters, she would command Talha and al-Zubayr, who had been nominated for the Caliphate by 'Umar. Due to this, she made it lawful for herself to correspond with the chiefs of the tribes and with the governors, enticing them and seeking their help.

Due to this, she attained the status and fame among the Banu Umayyads, to the point where she became the source of reverence for all of them, and [she became one] whose power and rebuke they all feared. If the heroes and men, famous for their courage, abandon and flee from the lines of battle [when] facing 'Ali b. Abi Talib and would not stand in front of him, she stood, inciting, screaming, and arousing [the people].

The mind is perplexed at all of this, the historians are bewildered, for they knew her stance in the smaller battle of the Camel before the arrival of Imam 'Ali (as), and in the greater battle of the Camel after the arrival of Imam 'Ali (as). [They all know that] he summoned her to the book of Allah and that she refused, obstinately insisting on the battle. There is no explanation [for this], unless we understand the depth and extent of the envy and hatred that A'isha felt towards the Prophets progeny (as), who were devoted to Allah and his Messenger (s).

The Prophet (s) sensed the depth and danger of the schemes that revolved around him from all sides. No doubt he knew the influence and discord women could generate on the men, as he also knew that their plot was great enough to almost move mountains. He knew specifically that his wife, 'Aisha, was the instigator of the dangerous role because of the hatred and rancour that she felt towards his successor 'Ali (as) in particular and his family in general. How could he not know, when he lived observing her role and her enmity towards them? He sometimes got angry; sometimes his face would change colour and he would try to placate her at all times, informing her that one who loved 'Ali (as) loved Allah, and the one who hated 'Ali (as) was a hypocrite, whom Allah hated. Unfortunately, those *hadiths* do not permeate the depth of those souls which never accept the truth to be true, unless it be for her ('Aisha's) benefit, and they do not recognize anything to be correct unless it comes from her.

As a result, the Prophet of Allah (s) was patient when he realized that she was the test that Allah had sent to the *umma*, to examine it as He had tested the previous nations. *"Do the people think that they will be left alone when they say: 'We believe' and they will not be tested"* (Quran 29:2)?

The Prophet of Allah (s) warned the *umma* against her on several occasions. He even stood one day and pointed towards her house saying: *"From there is the mischief, from there is the mischief from where the horns of the devil will rise."*

Al-Bukhari has reported in his *Sahih*, in *"The Book Concerning the Houses of the Wives of the Prophet (s)"*, on the authority of Nafi' b. 'Abd Allah who said: *"The Prophet (s) stood up, addressing [the people] and pointed towards the residence of 'Aisha and said three times: 'From there is mischief from where the horns of the devil will arise."*

Muslim has also related in his *Sahih* from Ikrima b. 'Ammar from Salim from Ibn 'Umar who said: *"The Prophet of Allah (s) emerged from the house of 'Aisha and said: 'The pivot of disbelief is from here, where the horns of Satan will rise."*

Al-Bukhari also reported: *"When Talha, al-Zubayr and 'Aisha travelled to Basra, 'Ali sent 'Ammar b. Yasir and al-Hassan b. 'Ali who met us in Kufa. They ascended the pulpit, with al-Hassan ascending to the top while 'Ammar was standing below al-Hassan. We gathered towards him. I heard 'Ammar say: "Aisha has journeyed to Basra and, by Allah, she is the wife of your Prophet (s) in this life and in the hereafter; but Allah, the most blessed and exalted, is now testing you [to see] whom you obey, Him or her'".*

Allah is the Greatest. This *hadith* also indicates that obedience to her is disobedience to Allah, and to oppose and disobey her is to obey Allah. We can also note in the *hadith*, that the Umayyad narrators have added the phrase *"and the hereafter"* when saying *"She is the wife of your Prophet in this life and the hereafter"* so that they may lead the masses into thinking that Allah has forgiven her every sin she committed, and allowed her to enter His heaven, and her husband is His beloved Prophet of Allah (s). Otherwise, how did 'Ammar know that she will be his wife in the hereafter? This is another trick that the falsifiers of *hadith* narrators resorted to during the time of the Banu Umayyad. When they found that a *hadith* was widespread amongst the people, and there was no way to deny or refute it, they decided to add a paragraph or words, or to change some phrases to dampen the impact or to make it lose its intended meaning. Just as they did with the *hadith*: "I am the city *of knowledge and 'Ali is its gate"*, they added: *"and Abu Bakr is its foundation, 'Umar its walls and 'Uthman its roof."*

This trick is not hidden to the objective researchers who refute these additions that, most of the time, indicate the lack of intelligence of the falsifiers and their lack of wisdom and light of the Prophetic traditions. For they can observe the saying that Abu Bakr is its foundation means the knowledge of the Prophet (s) is derived from the knowledge of Abu Bakr, and this is disbelief. Likewise, the statement 'Umar is its walls means 'Umar prevents people from entering the city, i.e., prevents them from getting to the knowledge. The saying 'Uthman is it's roof is necessarily absurd since there is no city which has a roof, this is impossible. The researchers note too that 'Ammar swore by Allah that 'Aisha is the wife of the Prophet (s) in this world and in the hereafter. This is a shot in the dark. How could 'Ammar take an oath about something he did not know? Did he have a verse from the book of God? Or was it a covenant promised to him by the Prophet (s)?

So, we are now left with the true *hadith,* i.e., that 'Aisha travelled to Basra, and that she is the wife of your Prophet, but Allah is testing you through her to know whether you obey Him or her.

All praise is due to the Lord of the Worlds, who has given us intelligence through which we can differentiate between the truth and falsehood and has made clear to us the [right] path and then tested us by several things so that they can bear witness on the day of judgment. [125]

Aisha attacks Basra killing hundreds of Muslims even inside the mosque

Ali's governor in Basra was Uthman ibn Hunaif Ansari, the same companion of the Prophet whom Umar had appointed the Financial Commissioner of Iraq. When he learned that the army of 'Aisha, Talha and Zubayr was in the environs of Basra, he sent one of the friends of Ali – Abul Aswad ad-Du'ali – to see them and to find out the reasons why they came. Abul Aswad called on 'Aisha, and the following exchange took place between them.

Abul Aswad: O mother of believers, what is your purpose in coming to Basra with an army?

'Aisha: I came to seek vengeance for the murder of Uthman who was killed in his own house even though he had not committed any sin.

Abul Aswad: Whoever killed Uthman, is not in Basra.

---

[125] Ask Those Who Know by Dr. Muhammad Tijani

'Aisha: Yes, I know. But to get vengeance, I need the cooperation and the support of the people of Basra.

Abul Aswad: I hope you have not forgotten that the Messenger of God had ordered you to stay at home. In any case, it is not your business to meddle in politics and war. It is most unworthy of a widow of the Prophet to leave his home, and to fight against the Muslims.

'Aisha: Will any Muslim dare to fight against me?

'Aisha believed that if she went into the battlefield at the head of her army, the soldiers of the enemy host, upon seeing her confronting them, would either come over to her side, or would abandon the battle, and desert their master.

Abul Aswad next went to see Talha and Zubayr and asked them what their intentions were in coming to Basra in battle array.

Talha and Zubayr: We want vengeance from Ali for the murder of Uthman.

Abul Aswad: Ali did not murder Uthman nor did he have any share in his murder, and you know it.

Talha and Zubayr: If he did not, then why is he protecting the murderers?

Abul Aswad: Does this mean that you have broken the pledge of loyalty which you gave to Ali?

Talha and Zubayr: The pledge was taken from us on the point of sword. It was, therefore, invalid.

Abul Aswad could see that the rebel leaders were obsessed with war, and that further parleys with them were useless. He therefore, returned to Basra, and reported to Uthman ibn Hunaif what 'Aisha, Talha and Zubayr had told him.

The rebel leaders had made no secret of their intentions, but Uthman ibn Hunaif did not have a strong army, and knew that he could not defend the city against them. Therefore, when they appeared at the city gates, he opened negotiations with them. The two parties agreed that until the arrival of Ali, the rebels would not do anything to disturb the existing arrangement, and Uthman ibn Hunaif would continue to act as governor of Basra.

But hardly two days had passed when the rebel leaders violated the truce. Their army attacked the city at night, and took it by storm, and once it was within its walls, it appeared to go berserk. The soldiers spread into the city and killed 600 Muslims including 40 in the Great Mosque itself.

Talha and Zubayr forced their way into the governor's house where they captured Uthman ibn Hunaif and killed those who tried to defend him. They wanted to kill him also, but he told them that if they killed him, then his brother, Sehl ibn Hunaif, who was the governor of Medina, would kill all their relatives living in that city, in reprisal. They, therefore, had to curb their urge to kill the venerable friend of Muhammad. But they beat him up, plucked out all the hair on his head, his eyebrows and his beard, and drove him out of Basra. He managed, somehow, to reach the camp of his master, and staggered into his presence, more dead than alive!

Ali (as) was deeply aggrieved to see Uthman ibn Hunaif in the state in which Talha and Zubayr had sent him. He could hardly recognize him. He tried to comfort the old friend of Muhammad Mustafa with his tears.

The rebel army was now in possession of the city of Basra. It had succeeded in realizing its first aim. Its leaders expelled all friends and supporters of Uthman ibn Hunaif from the city if they did not kill them.

Murder of Muslim ibn Abdullah & Talha

Ali (as), however, still hesitated to fight, and decided to make one more attempt to rescue peace. He sent a young man, one Muslim ibn Abdullah who was noted for his piety, with a copy of the Qur'an, to appeal to the enemy to submit the dispute to the Judgment of God, and to uphold peace in the name of the sanctity of Muslim blood.

Standing in front of the enemy host at close range, Muslim ibn Abdullah opened the Qur'an, and said: *"I will read a passage from the Book of God so that you will know what are His commandments and prohibitions."* His speech, however, was interrupted by the archers of the enemy who shot arrows at the copy of the Qur'an he was reading. While he was trying to protect the copy of the Qur'an, one of the servants of 'Aisha crept up toward him, attacked him and killed him.

The body of Muslim ibn Abdullah was brought before Ali (as) and was placed on the ground. Ali (as) was lamenting his death when another body, that of one of his warriors who was shot and killed with arrows by the army of Basra, was brought before him. He tried to remove the arrows from the body, but he had not removed many when more bodies of his soldiers, riddled with arrows, arrived and were stacked before him in full view of the two armies. The rebels were practicing archery at Ali's army.

Tabari says in his *History*, (vol. III, p. 522) that when Ali (as) saw these bodies in front of him, he said: "Now it is lawful to fight against them."

Then Ali (as) lifted his hands toward heaven and prayed:*"O Lord! Be Thou a Witness that I have left nothing undone to preserve peace among Muslims. Now there is no choice left for me but to allow my army to defend itself from unprovoked attacks. We are Thy humble servants. Bestow Thy Grace and Thy Mercy upon us. Grant us victory over the enemy but if it is Thy pleasure to grant it to him, then grant us the crown of martyrdom."*

Ali (as) concluded his prayer, and then turning toward his

troops, addressed them thus just before giving them the signal to fight: *"O Muslims! Do not be the first to strike at your adversary; let your adversary be the first to strike at you. Once he does, then you must defend yourselves. If God gives you victory over your enemies, then remember that they are also Muslims. Therefore, do not kill the wounded among them. If they run from the field, do not pursue them, and let them save their lives. If you capture prisoners, do not kill them. Do not mutilate the dead, and do not rob them of their armor or weapons or other valuables which you may find on their persons. Do not plunder their camp, and do not molest their women even if they use foul and abusive language against you or your leaders. But above all things, do not be unmindful, at any time, of the presence of your Creator in your life. You are in His sight every moment."*

The two armies then charged at each other. The rebels had already lost Zubayr, one of their two generals, through desertion. The other general, Talha, was also destined to meet a fate like Zubayr's. Abul Fida, the historian, says that Marwan asked his servant to cover him so that he would not be seen. When the servant covered him, he strung an arrow to his bow, aimed it at Talha, and said to his servant: *"I saw this man (Talha) during the days when Uthman was besieged in his house. He was inciting and urging the crowd to enter the house, and to kill him. But today he wants vengeance for his blood. How touching! He truly loved Uthman. Here, I will give him a reward for that love. He richly deserves a reward. After all, such love must not go unrewarded."*

Marwan released the arrow. It was a fatal shot that caught Talha in the thigh, and he limped to his death in the rear of the army.

In the battle of the Camel, Talha was on his horse beside 'Aisha when Marwan shot an arrow at him which transfixed his leg. Then Marwan said: *"By God, now I will not have to search for the man who murdered Uthman."*[126]

Conclusion

'Aisha has the reputation of being highly knowledgeable in matters of religion, and she was also a *muhaditha*, i.e., a narrator of the traditions of the Prophet (s). Being so knowledgeable, is it possible that she did not know that she had no right to seek vengeance for Uthman's blood? Vengeance seeking is the business of the injured party, and imposing penalty upon the offenders is the duty of the government. 'Aisha was neither related to Uthman in any way nor she was a representative of the government of the Muslims. And yet she challenged the lawful government in the name of vengeance and pushed an immense number of Muslims into the flames of war. Her obsession with war made thousands of children orphans, and thousands of women widows.

A certain woman, one Umm Aufa al-Abdiyya, once asked 'Aisha: *"O mother of believers, what is your opinion about a woman who kills her own child?"* 'Aisha said that such a woman would be thrown into hell. Umm Aufa further asked: *"What will happen to a woman who killed more than 20,000 of her children at one time and one place?"* 'Aisha was incensed at the insinuation, and yelled scram at Umm Aufa.[127]

Some members of 'Aisha's own family wished she had never led armies and fought battles. On one occasion, she sent a messenger to her nephew, Ibn Abil-Ateeq, asking him to send his mule to her for riding. When her nephew received the message, he said to the messenger: *"Tell the mother of believers that by God, we have not washed the stains of the blood shed in the battle of the camel yet. Does she now want to start a battle of the*

---

[126] *Tabaqat,* vol. III, p. 223

[127] *Iqd-ul-Farid,* vol. III, p. 108

mule?"[128]

Ibn Abil Ateeq's remark was prompted in jest. But in 669 the day actually came when 'Aisha rode a mule in another "campaign." When the coffin of Imam Hassan (as) was brought to the mausoleum of his grandfather, Muhammad Mustafa, for burial, Marwan bin al-Hakam and other members of the Banu Ummaya appeared on the scene, in battledores. They were going to prevent the Banu Hashim from burying Imam Hassan (as) beside his grandfather. The Umayyads were not alone; 'Aisha, the mother of believers, came with them, riding a mule!

'Aisha may have lost the battle in Basra but she "won" the "battle" in Medina. Hassan (as) could not be buried with his grandfather because of her and Umayyad opposition, and he was buried in the cemetery of Jannat-ul-Baqi.

There is no way to rationalize the roles 'Aisha, Talha and Zubayr played after the death of Uthman. The fact that they were famous personalities in the history of the Muslims, does not change or affect the roles they played. An error does not become less reprehensible because some important person committed it. An error remains an error regardless of who committed it.

The wives of the Prophet were especially expected to be discreet in everything they said or did. After all, they had to be models before the *umma* of exemplary deportment and decorum. A lapse from excellence may be condoned in the wives of the commoners but not in them. Addressing them, Qur'an says: *"O consorts of the Prophet! If any of you were guilty of evident unseemly conduct, the punishment would be doubled to her, and that is easy for God. "(Chapter 33; verse 30)*[129]

---

[128] *Baladhuri in Ansab al-Ashraf, vol. I, page 431*

[129] A Restatement of History of Islam and Muslims by Sayed Ali Asgher Razwy

The Battle of Siffin

The Martyrdom of Ammar Yasir

The Christian Monk who Testified to the Wilayat of Ali

Mu'awiya accused Ali (as) of the murder of Uthman, but there was not even one person throughout the world of Islam of that day who might confirm this charge.

Those who considered Ali (as) innocent of this accusation had no doubt that Mu'awiya himself was an accomplice in the murder of Uthman, because, notwithstanding the fact that he could save Uthman he refrained from doing so. Moreover, Uthman had sons who were his heirs and the guardians of his blood. Mu'awiya stole a march on them and assumed this title himself. And even if he had taken a step in this behalf in the capacity of an agent it may be said that he would have made a mistake, because the proper way for solving such problems is to approach the law court and not to resort to rebellion and revolt.

Besides this Mu'awiya claimed that he had not taken an oath of allegiance to Ali (as), as had been done by Talha and Zubayr and it was not, therefore, incumbent upon him to obey the new Caliph.

Anyhow these stages were the outcome of some historical factors that proved to be more beneficial for the Umayyad party spirit as compared with the Hashimite justice. Furthermore, the historical events that manifested themselves during the period of the third Caliph were the most effective factors which according to the exigencies of the time proved harmful to Ali (as). Ali (as) had all these matters in view, and none knew better than he that during this interval, as demanded by the circumstances, the only way of overcoming the difficulties and the last means to arrive at a final solution was soothing covetousness and returning to the revival of party spirit and purchase of consciences! But Imam Ali (as) was a man who said: *"I am not going to seek help from the deviated seducers or to make them the means of success."* He made this position clearly known to Mughira who contacted him and suggested that Mu'awiya might be allowed to retain Damascus.

Imam Ali (as) gave the same reply to Mu'awiya when he asked him to entrust the government of Damascus and Cairo to him so that he (Mu 'awiya) might take oath of allegiance to him. Ali (as) rejected his request. He adopted this attitude because he considered himself under obligation to enforce Islamic principles and at the same time the path of solving the political problems in the way his contemporary politicians and those of later ages reflected upon was closed before him and he was not neglectful of it.

However, he was on his guard against treachery, deceit and bargaining and as his conduct was peculiar to himself, he did not pay attention to the political behaviour and policies of others. For this reason and considering the rule and principle which he had in view he did not agree to allow Mu'awiya to retain Syria and as a matter of principle his action regarding Mu'awiya was based on the same rule and principle according to which he had rejected Mu'awiya's request previously and had said: "I am not going to seek help from the seducers".

He also knew very well that the observance of this rule and principle was not compatible with the spirit of his time and following this policy would create the greatest difficulties for him. Nevertheless, the only factor and cause which made him persevere and consider the exigencies of time to be insignificant was that, he wished that there should be Ali (as) and not Mu'awiya.

Imam Ali (as) was struggling to safeguard and enforce this principle and rule and not to attain to rulership and kingdom. He did not desire a transient victory but wished to achieve a permanent and enternal victory. The clearest proof of the correctness of this claim and of his careful attention towards these things is that he said to some of his companions who were showing much humiliation before him: *"I know with which factor and means I should make you obey me. However, I tell you that I am not the man who would spoil and corrupt his faith so that your material desires may be fulfilled."*

Yes, the crux of the matter is that Ali (as) was campaigning against immorality, mischief, indecency, and corruption and in this struggle which he had undertaken against moral vices and to uproot indecency and uncleanness from the souls of the people, he did not exempt even those of his friends and kinsmen in whose nature this ailment had penetrated. In short in this campaign friends and enemies were equal in his eyes and in the circumstances, it is evident that for Mu'awiya, who was drowned in intellectual and practical evils, there was no place in this organization and he was a man who could not succeed by any other way except evil.

However, the object of dwelling at length on this subject

is that the genius and intelligence which has been attributed to Mu'awiya, and his extraordinary efficiency and competence about which much has been said, is all exaggeration and idle talk. In fact, the entire success of this man was indebted to those very fictitious qualities mixed with mischief and evil and such successes and victories as are the consequences of such vicious practices.

Another important point in this connection is that the apparent successes of Mu'awiya certainly sprang from the perseverance and steadfastness of Ali (as) in protecting the principles and elements of truth. It is evident that persons who were after wordly gains and pleasures and could not achieve their ends by associating with Ali (as) naturally turned to Mu'awiya to secure their goals.

Incidentally this aspect of the matter should also be made clear that the atmosphere preceding the rulership of Ali (as) had distracted the people from true Islamic principles and matters had taken such a turn, that it was said: *"Only that person who is dominant and powerful has a right to live, and predominance and victory can only be gained under the shadow of accumulation of wealth, hoarding, seizing an opportunity, enlargement of influence and acquisition of the objects of desire."*

It is apparent that if, in these circumstances, Ali (as) had resorted to diplomacy, he could have very easily eliminated the gains made by his opponents. And it is also evident that it was easier for Ali (as) to overcome Mu'awiya with the same weapon of politics then to subdue those who had broken the covenant.

The revolt of Mu'awiya during those days was not very important in the light of the true Islamic criteria. The real danger arose from the causes and effects of the prevailing atmosphere and the danger of resistance and perseverance in seeking absolute truth was the greatest of all.

However, despite all these conditions and circumstances

it must be admitted that the most important factors were perseverance, resistance and steadfastness in protecting and supporting absolute truth and ignoring the suggestions of those who asked Imam Ali (as) to resort to compromises and flattery.

Anyhow during the days when Ali (as) was staying in Kufa the condition of Mu'awiya and his activities which seemed languid and weak to every reflective and sensible person appeared all the more worthless and unimportant to Ali. Notwithstanding this, however, Ali (as) did not ignore the elements which had been created by the circumstances and events to the benefit of Mu'awiya which had prepared favourable environments for strenghtening his position. The matters had taken such a turn that Mu'awiya had begun coveting the office of the Caliphate and nurtured this fancy in his mind that he might be nominated for it. However, Ali, while being fully cognizant of this situation, remained steadfast and well composed. At the same time he could not only read clearly in the horizon of the coming events the evil results of the preliminaries of future campaigns, but he also afforded liberty of action to the enemy with perfect calmness, so that he might have a clear and well-founded ground for jihad against Mu'awiya, and the responsibility for the war which the agitators were going to start should be on the oppressive deviated persons, just as the responsibility for the previous war fell on the covetous breakers of the covenant and that for the future war was to fall on the Khawarij.

During the time when Ali (as) was in Kufa letters were exchanged between him and Mu'awiya, Ali (as) consulted his companions about current affairs and apprised them of the developments. His companions suggested that they might spend that year in Kufa and wait, but Ammar, Ashtar, Adyy bin Hatim (famous for his generosity) and Shurayh bin Hani opposed this view.

Ammar said: *"O Commander of the faithful! We have taken oath of allegiance to you and find none, who may rise against you. Previously there were persons who rose to fight against you, but the Almighty Allah routed them and helped you in accordance with the verse: "Whoever retaliates in the same manner as he was made to suffer and then is oppressed again, Allah will certainly help him." (Surah al-Haj, 22:60)*

And as clearly stated by Him in another verse: "Whoever breaks the covenant breaks it to his own detriment," (Surah al-Fath, 48: 10), those who broke the covenant received punishment for their conduct.

Another point is that during those days Kufa supported us and Basra was opposed to us. One group from amongst us was rewarded and the other was excused.

At present, however, we are involved in an irremediable trouble in Syria and a person, who has revolted, will not submit unless he is killed or defeated. In the circumstances we should forestall him. I would, therefore, request you to issue orders for mobilization."

Ashtar and others who were of the same opinion supported Ammar's view. Soon afterwards Ali (as) received news of the mobilization of Mu'awiya's forces, and it became certain that Mu'awiya was on the war path and was preparing to attack. The Commander of the Faithful, therefore, equipped an army consisting of 190,000 warriors and proceeded to Siffin at the head of this army. In this army as well the Commander of the cavalry was Ammar. The result of the first encounter of the two parties was that Mu'awiya obtained control of the waterway and did not allow Ali (as) and his forces to use it.[130]

Another instance of Ali's compassion was his treatment of Mu'awiya in the Battle of Siffin. Mu'awiya's soldiers had sealed off the Euphrates River. When Ali's army found that their expected supply of water had been intercepted, Ali (as) sent a

---

[130] Ammar Yasir- A Companion of the Prophet by Sadruddin Sharafuddin al-Amili

message to Mu'awiya saying that Mu'awiya should not seal off access to the water. Mu'awiya replied that he would deny them use of the water.

Ali (as) sent Malik Ashtar with a unit of cavalry. He pushed back Mu'awiya's army and secured access to the Euphrates. The companions said, *"O Ali! Let us retaliate and deny them water, so that the enemy may die of thirst and the battle will be over."*

Ali (as) said: *"No! By Allah, I will not retaliate by following their example. Let their troops have access to the Euphrates."* [131]

Before the brave and distinguished warriors of Badr and the Muhajirs and the Ansar and the soldiers of Muzar and Rabi'a and the chiefs of Yemen and Iraq could commence fighting and achieve any result from it, Ashtar, in order to achieve victory, put forward suggestions which obliged Mu'awiya and his minister to resort to cold war by discussion, debate, oration, lecturing and sending letters. These were the prerequisites for such a war. It is evident that the superiority of the supporters of Ali (as) in this cold war was as much established in the minds of the enemies as their superiority in the matter of swordsmanship.

If there were Mu'awiya, 'Amr al-Aas and his son Abdullah in that party, there were on this side, besides Imam Ali, great orators like Abdullah bin Abbas, Ammar Yasir, Malik Ashtar, Ash'ath bin Qays (although a hypocrite), Ahnaf bin Qays, Uthman bin Hunayf, Sa'sa'a bin Sohan, Adyy bin Hatim and hundreds of others from amongst the Muhajirs and the Ansar of Badr, all of whom possessed intelligence, insight, sagacity and experience and were very eloquent, whereas the persons in the opposite row did not possess these qualities.

Mu'awiya and his minister 'Amr al-Aas were persons

---

[131] Peshawar Nights by Sultanul Waizin Shirazi

who were extreme opportunists. They had gained experiences regarding the conduct of Ali (as) in the Battle of Basra to utilize them at the opportune time. They had now acquired an opportunity and wanted to profit from those experiences. Hence, to strengthen the morale of the Syrian soldiers and to dodge military action they resorted to stratagems. To achieve this end, they decided to defame the outstanding leaders and distinguished personalities of Iraq and to make them appear despised and degraded in the eyes of the Syrians.

Amr al-Aaswho had previously carried on correspondence with some Iraqi hypocrites like Ash'ath now began to lecture to the Syrians and endeavoured to delude and seduce them.

As soon as the sound of the speech of Amr reached the ears of Ammar he got up to put an end to this cold war. Despite his old age and feebleness, he raised his thunderous voice that was sustained by resolution and determination and said: *"O servants of Allah! Rise and hurry up towards these people who want to avenge the murder of a tyrant. Some benevolent and righteous persons who were opponents of cruelty and oppression and supporters of justice and goodness rose and killed that man. Now these people have risen and want to avenge the murder of such a person upon us. These persons who claim to be the avengers of his murder are of a type that if their worldly ambitions are achieved and Islam is destroyed, they will not mind it. Such persons asked us: "Why did you kill him?" We replied. "On account of the unlawful things he did." They said: "He didn't do anything unlawful."*

Do you know why they said all this? It was because he ensured their worldly gains. These are the people who plundered his existence and will not worry even if the mountains are demolished. I swear by Allah that they don't want to avenge the murder (of Uthman}. They relish and have become fond of worldly gains. They think that if the righteous person assumes the reins of government, he will restrain their unlawful profits and unlimited greed. These people have no previous record in Islam so that they should be worthy of rulership, but they have deceived their followers and told them: "Our chief and leader was killed unjustly." They said this in order to acquire the rulership and power. As you see and know this claim is nothing except deceit and fraud. And if they had not practised this fraud none would have taken oath of allegiance to them.

O Lord! If You help us it will not be Your first help because You have granted us victories earlier. And if Your Will is that they should assume rulership then put in store for them the result of their illegal acts whereby they have subjected the people to tyranny and torture."

When Ammar concluded his speech and enlightened the minds of the hearers in all respects he ordered his standard bearer, Hashim Marqal, to advance, and said: "*May my parents be your ransom! Advance and attack these Syrians and break up their rows*".

Ammar himself also went forward and reached in the centre of the opposing army near Amr al-Aas. Addressing 'Amr he said: "*O 'Amr! You have sold your faith for the sake of Egypt. Woe be to you! What mischiefs and evils have you roused against Islam!*"

Then Ammar began praying to Allah in the presence of the Syrians and said: "*O Lord! You know that if I realize that Your Will is that I should throw myself in this river I shall do so. O Lord! If I realize that You desire that I should thrust the point of my sword into my belly and bend myself, so that the sword may come out of my back, I shall do so.*

O Lord! You know that I have acquired what You have taught me and I know it very well that today no pious act is better than that I should perform jihad against these people who have violated human rights, and if I come to know that in the present circumstances there is an act which is liked by You more, I shall perform it."

As soon as 'Amr heard these words of Ammar he left the battlefield and hid himself. The Syrian army also trembled more on hearing Ammar speak than they trembled for the fear of his sword, though all of them knew well that a rebellious group would kill Ammar. The importance and the danger of the presence of Ammar was not unknown to Mu'awiya, and he was afraid of what was going to happen, he expressed his anxiety every now and then in various ways.

Ammar attacked valiantly and his standard bearer Hashim Marqil and his companions fell upon the Umayyad army like a furious storm and pushed it back.

At this moment Ammar remembered Abdullah bin 'Amr al-Aas (who in the beginning appeared to be a devout person and hesitated to support Mu'awiya but later joined his army saying that he was a follower of his father and not of Mu'awiya) and called out from the battlefield with a loud voice: *"O Abdullah! Have you sold your faith for the world?"*

Abdullah replied: *"It is not so. The fact is that I have risen to avenge the murder of Uthman."*

Ammar said: *"It is not at all so. I bear witness to the fact that you do not do anything for the sake of Allah. You should know that if you are not killed today, you will be killed tomorrow. Ponder carefully. When Allah gives recompense according to the intentions of the people, let me know what your intention is?"*

Ammar uttered these words and commenced his attack. This attack by Ammar was the commencement of an extensive battle during which the most severe and the most intense scenes of war were witnessed continuously for three days and nights. The third night of this battle is known as 'Lailatul Harir'.

In the afternoon of the day of the battle Ammar called back his soldiers from the front for rest. When his soldiers were resting the people were saying to one another: *"The enemy will* be immune this night from the blows of the swords of Ammar's soldiers."

Ammar was hearing these words and sharpening his sword and stimulating and equipping with arms his standard bearer and brave officer Marqil. Soon afterwards he ordered Marqil to attack and himself got ahead of the army. Then he said aloud: *"Who wants to proceed to Paradise? Paradise is under the shadow of the swords and the arrows. Today I shall meet my friends. Today I shall meet the Holy Prophet Muhammad (s) and his party."*

Ammar was moving ahead and other warriors were moving behind him, and all were advancing. The sun was about to set and the only light that could be seen in the extensive horizon was the lustre of the sword and the sparks of the blows. Once again Ammar decided to take rest and it was the moment when the last rays of the sun were shining on the stream of blood and its crimson rays were being reflected on all sides. At that moment, before Ammar could take rest, his eyes fell on 'Amr who was carrying Mu'awiya's standard on his shoulder. Ammar was reminded of something and shook his sword. Then he struck his hand on the back of his standard bearer and said: *"O Marqil! I swear by Him under whose control my life is that even if these people are in a position to annihilate us by dealing successive blows no weakness will take place in my faith, because we are right and they are following the wrong path. O Marqil! The standard which' Amr al-Aas is carrying on his shoulder is the same against which I have fought in the company of the Holy Prophet (s) and it is the fourth time that I am campaigning against it."*

Then he made an attack and said to Hashim 'Utba (Marqil): *"O son! Advance! Advance! May my parents be your ransom!"*

During this terrible fighting Ammar did not rest even for a moment. He fought on and persuaded his soldiers to do the same and ordered them to attack. He continued attacking the enemy like deadly lightening till the third day of the battle arrived on that day the fighting reached its climax and continued unabated. For the self-sacrificing warriors who accompanied Ammar it was immaterial whether they killed or were killed. Ammar, the old man, who was ninety-four years of age, was fasting and despite this he made deadly attacks on the enemy and pushed his standard bearer Hashim forward.

Hashim insisted upon him to hand over the command and responsibility for attack to him and to take rest for sometime to get rid of the fatigue caused by fasting but Ammar shouted at him and said: *"O son! May my parents be your ransom! Advance!"*

Anyhow, as a result of the severe and continuous attacks by Ammar, the cavalry of the Syrian forces fled. In this combat Zul Kala' Humyari, who was the commander of the Syrian army wavered and lost the power of resistance in the row which was the target of Ammar's attack. When the news of Zul Kala's hesitation and fear reached Mu'awiya he summoned him and deceived him with the assistance of his minister 'Amr al-Aas, and two persons took oath that what Zul Kala had heard about Ammar and had reported was true (i.e. the prophecy of the Holy Prophet (s) that a rebellious group will kill Ammar) but Ammar would at last leave his own army and would join the army of Mu'awiya and 'Amr. Hence, Zul Kala' had no alternative and must partake in fighting. They also assured him that eventually, when the dust of the war had settled, he would see that Ammar had arrived in his (Zul Kala's) row. Incidentally they also told him that if the prediction made by them did not come out to be true, he would be entitled to continue to remain hesitant in the future wars, and that he would have ample time for this.

On the third day the battle came to an end and Ammar, as steadfast as ever, remained busy in fighting like a champion. When the sun was about to set, and the night called *Lailatul Harir* arrived Ammar asked for water to break his fast.

A vessel containing milk was brought for him. Before drinking milk, he smiled and it might be said that his soul shone with that smile. In an ecstatic and happy condition, he said: *"My friend, the Prophet (s) told me: "Your last food in the world will be a gulp of milk mixed with water."*

Ammar drank the milk and then made an attack along with his military column and hastened towards Paradise which was embodied and perceptible in his eyes. There he saw the Holy Prophet (s) receiving him as he used to receive him previously in this world.

There is a great probability that Mu'awiya had fixed a big prize for the 'head of Ammar' so that he might be relieved of the embarrassment caused by the grinding argument which existed in the minds of the army personnel, just as he had ordered that all should guard the head of Zul Kala, lest he should receive any injury, and he had also promised awards for the safety of Zul Kala'.

Anyhow if Zul Kala' had remained alive after Ammar he would have created a great difficulty for Mu'awiya, and he could not satisfy him by any means. And the most important thing was that the tribe of Zul Kala' and the number of its members exceeded that of all other tribes.

In any case Ammar, while he had no guardsman to protect him drove forward dauntlessly like a lion and on having reached the battlefield said with a loud voice: *"Is there any combatant here?"*

At that moment a mounted soldier belonging to the tribe of 'Sakasak' came to fight against Ammar and was killed at his hands. Another horseman from amongst the Humyaris came in the field and he, too, was killed by Ammar. And all others who came thereafter met with the same fate.

Abul Ghadiya Juhani who had been on the track of Ammar since the days of Uthman, came near him. At this moment the cuirass of Ammar had fallen aside from his thigh. This man availed of the opportunity and gave a blow on the thigh of Ammar. Two other mounted men attacked Ammar simultaneously and put an end to his life.

Anyhow one of the particular pieces of good luck of Bani Umayya was the coincidence that at the moment when Ammar was killed Zul Kala' was also killed.

Ammar's martyrdom was a sorrowful event for the members of both the armies. One of the effects of this tragedy was that the defensive movement of Mu'awiya's army came to a standstill and the sound of the epic verses recited by the army of Ali (as) reached the sky. Before Ammar was killed there were, in both the armies, persons who entertained doubts in their minds, but after he was martyred truth became evident to them.

As a result of this tragedy anxiety and agitation prevailed in the minds that ended in the retreat of the Syrian army. Mu'awiya and 'Amr were then compelled to deceive their own army by means of misinterpretation and, in order to remain immune, delude and deceive their opponents in another manner.

However, if during these critical moments fate had not predominated, history would have adopted a course other than that which it did owing to the hypocrisy and discord of Ash'ath bin Qays.

When Abul Ghadiya killed Ammar, voices rose from both the camps saying: *"O Abul Ghadiya! Woe be to you! It was you who killed Abul Yaqzan (the pious man)! May Allah kill you!"*

Muhammad bin Muntashir said to Abul Ghadiya: *"O Abul Ghadiya! On the Day of Judgment your enemy will be a mighty enemy with a strong hand."* The only reaction of Abul Ghadiya was that he laughed and went his way.

Hana, a servant of Umar bin Khattab says thus about

himself: *"In the beginning I was with Mu'awiya and his companions used to say: "Allah forbid! In no circumstances shall we kill Ammar, because if we kill Ammar then, as it is said, we too shall be regarded as a rebellious group. On the day the Battle of Siffin ended I was walking about amongst those who had been killed. Suddenly I saw that Ammar Yasir had been killed. I went to 'Amr al-Aas and saw him resting on his throne. I asked him: "What have you heard about Ammar Yasir?"*

'Amr said: *"I heard the Holy Prophet (s) saying: A rebellious group will kill Ammar".*

I said: *"I swear by Allah that Ammar has been killed. What do you say now?"*

'Amr said: *"It is a false claim."*

I said: *"I have seen with my own eyes that Ammar has been killed."*

Amr said: *"Let's go and see. Show me his dead body."*

I took 'Amr al-Aas up to the dead body of Ammar. On seeing the corpse of Ammar the colour of the face of 'Amr al-Aas changed. Then he turned his face and began walking and said: "Ammar has been killed by the person who brought him in the battlefield!"

Khuzayma bin Thabit was a witness to the Battles of Camel and Siffin. He did not draw his sword in either of these battles and remained neutral. However, after Ammar was killed, he said: *"I have now become convinced of the rebellion and deviation of the Syrians."* Then Khuzayma partook in the battle and fought till he was killed.

Each of the two horsemen who had assisted Abul Ghadiya in killing Ammar were trying to take from Mu'awiya the prize which had been fixed for the head of Ammar. 'Amr al-Aas said to both: *"You two are fighting for the Fire of Hell and nothing else! I have heard the Prophet (s) saying: "One who kills Ammar and one who takes his clothes off his body will both go to Hell!"*

Mu'awiya interrupted Amr al-Aas and said in a reproachful tone: *"What you are saying is a dangerous jest. These two persons are fighting on our side and you are telling them that both of them will go to Hell!"*

Amr said: *"I swear by Allah that this is a fact, and you also know it. I wish that I had died twenty years earlier than today."*

When Abdullah bin 'Amr was returning from Siffin along with his father and Mu'awiya, he turned to his father and said: *"Father! I heard the Holy Prophet saying to Ammar: "A rebellious group will kill you."*

After hearing these words 'Amr turned to Mu'awiya with a peculiar malice and said: *"Do you hear what this boy is saying?"*

Mu'awiya said: *"Have we killed him? This is not at all the position. I hope people, who brought him into the battlefield have killed him."*

Then the two sly persons laughed.

One day 'Amr al-Aas said to his companions who had gathered round him: *"I wish that when the Holy Prophet breathed his last he might not have hated anyone, so that Allah might not send any person to Hell!"*

His companions said: *"What we felt was that the Prophet loved you and appointed you to governorship."*

'Amr said: *"Allah knows better whether he loved me or was kind to me just by way of affability. However, I observed that he loved a particular man."*

'Amr was asked: *"Who was that man?"*

He replied: *"He was Ammar Yasir."*

Then he was asked: *"Was he the same man whom you killed in the Battle of Siffin?"*

'Amr replied: *"Yes, by Allah! We killed him."*

Anyhow, after Ammar was killed the Syrians were leaving their own standard and were scattering, and as they did not wish to be styled the rebellious group they were mixing with the people of Iraq. It was at this juncture that 'Amr al-Aas endeavoured to test the intelligence and insight of his 'king' in respect of this difficulty and in the meantime to strengthen what he had injected in the minds of the Syrians regarding Ammar and to confirm the constancy of their power of insight. Mu'awiya turned his face from his minister and went to his army, stood at the head of the row and said to them: *"I am going to speak to you about the most sensitive matter of the day. This is the most important of all the topics and it concerns the Hadith regarding the rebellious group which is being passed on from one mouth to another.*

It should be known that the Hadith relating to the rebellious group is to our advantage and not detrimental to us. All of you should come to your senses and ponder carefully over the Hadith of the Holy Prophet. No doubt the 'rebel' stings us and we have become subjected to reproof. Well, let it be so! But it should be asked: "Are we not the same rebellious group who have risen to avenge the murder of Uthman and have been touched on account of that man having been oppressed? Yes, we are a rebellious group in this sense."

The hearers heard this bombastic logic of Mu'awiya and were convinced. The Syrians then departed with a light heart and a tranquil conscience.

'Amr al-Aas laughed and appreciated Mu'awiya's skill.

Ammar's martyrdom created a tumult in the Iraqi camp and the echo of this tumult draws a most vivid picture of the condition and position of Imam Ali (as). It is not necessary for us to discuss this point.

As soon as the news of Ammar's martyrdom reached Ali (as) he began weeping. Then he looked at those present round him and said: *"How long did you wish Ammar to live?"*

It might be said that the Commander of the Faithful wanted to ask: *"How long did you wish Islam to live?"*

Then he stood up and went towards the corpses of those who had been killed and reached by the side of the dead body of Ammar. At that moment he expressed grief over the martyrdom of Ammar in these splendid words: *"Any Muslim who doesn't consider the event of Ammar's being killed to be great, and doesn't treat it to be a painful tragedy, won't be recognized to be adult and mature. May Allah bless Ammar on the day on which he embraced Islam, the day on which he was killed and the day on which he will rise from earth once again! I saw Ammar at such a position that if the companions of the Holy Prophet were reckoned to be four he was the fourth and if they were five he was the fifth and none of the companions of the Prophet doubted this. Paradise has become essential for Ammar and his entitlement to Paradise did not depend on one or two instances."*

It has been said: *"Ammar is righteous and truth is with him. To whichever side Ammar turns truth turns along with him. One who kills Ammar will go to Hell."*

Anyhow, Ali (as) ordered that the funerals of Ammar and his standard-bearer and aide-de-camp Hashim Marqil might be placed side by side. He then offered prayers for both without, bathing their bodies and thereafter they were buried in Siffin in 37 A.H.[132]

---

[132] Ammar Yasir- A Companion of the Prophet by Sadruddin Sharafuddin al-Amili

When the Commander of the Faithful, (as), headed toward Siffin, a terrible thirst came on his followers. The water with them had been used up. They began to search for water to right and left but they did not find any trace of it. The Commander of the faithful, (as), turned off the main road with them and went a little way. A hermitage appeared before them in the middle of the desert. He went with them towards it. When he reached its courtyard, he ordered those (with him) to call for its occupant to come before them. They called him and he came.

The Commander of the Faithful, (as), asked him: *"Is this residence of yours near water, which will quench the thirst of these people?"*

"There is more than six miles between me and water. There is no water nearer than that to me. If it was not for the fact that I am brought enough water for each month to sustain me, I would be destroyed by thirst, he answered."

"Did you hear what the monk said?" the Commander of the Faithful, (as), asked.

"Yes," they answered. *"Order us to go to the place which he indicated. Perhaps we will reach water while we still have strength."*

"There is no need for you to do that," the Commander of the Faithful, (as), told them.

He turned the neck of his mule in the direction of the qibla (i.e. towards Mecca) and he directed them to a place near the hermitage. *"Uncover the ground in this place,"* he ordered them.

A group of them went straight to the place and uncovered it with iron shovels. A great shiny rock appeared. They said: *"Commander of the Faithful, here is a great rock on which the shovels are useless."*

"This rock is over water," he told them. *"If it moves from its position, you will find the water."*

They struggled to remove it. All the people gathered and tried to move it, but they could find no way to do that. It was too difficult for them. When he, (as), saw that they had gathered and striven to remove the rock, but it was too difficult for them, he put his leg over his saddle until it reached the ground. Then he rolled up his sleeves. He put his fingers under the side of the rock, and he moved it. He removed it with his hand and pushed it many yards away. When it had moved from its position, the white (glitter) of water appeared before them. They hurried to it and drank from it. It was the sweetest, coldest, and purest water that they had ever drank from on their journey. *"Get supplies and quench your thirst,"* he told them.

They did that. Then he went to the rock and took it with his hand and put it back where it had been. He ordered that its traces be removed with earth. The hermit had been watching from on top of his hermitage. When he realized what had happened, he called out: *"People, help me down, help me down."*

They helped him to get down. He stood in front of the Commander of the faithful, (as) and said: *"Are you a Prophet sent (by God)?"*

"No," he replied.

"(Then are you) an angel who is close to God?" he asked.

"No," was the answer.

"Then who are you?" asked (the hermit).

"I am the testamentary trustee of the Apostle of God, Muhammad b. 'Abd Allah, the seal of the Prophets, may God bless him and his family," he replied.

"Stretch out your hand," said the hermit, *"so that I may submit to God, the Blessed and Exalted, at your hands."*

The Commander of the Faithful, (as), stretched out his hand and told him: *"Make the twofold testimony."*

He said: *"I testify that there is no god but God alone without any partner. I testify that Muhammad is His servant and His Apostle. I testify that you are the testamentary trustee of the Apostle of God, the one with most right among the people to authority after him."*

The Commander of the Faithful, (as), made him understand the conditions of being a Muslim and then asked him: *"What is it that has prompted you to enter Islam after your long residence in this hermitage in opposition to it?"*

"I will tell you, Commander of the Faithful," he said. *"This hermitage was built to seek out the one who would remove that rock and then water would come from underneath it. Scholars before me died and they did not attain that (knowledge) but God, the Mighty and High, has provided me with it. We find in one of our books and a prose writer of our scholars that in this land there is a spring with a rock over it. No one knows its place except a Prophet or the testamentary trustee of a Prophet. He must be a friend of God who calls (men) to truth, whose sign is the knowledge of the place of this rock and his ability to remove it. When I saw you do that, I realized what we had been waiting for. The object of desire had been attained. Today I am a Muslim (converted) at your hands, a believer in your right and your servant."*

When he heard that, the Commander of the Faithful, (as), wept until his beard became moist with tears. He said: *"Praise be to God, by Whom I have not been forgotten. Praise be to God in Whose books I have been mentioned."* Then he summoned the people and told them: *"Listen to what your brother Muslim says."*

They listened to his words. Then they gave much praise to God and thanks for the blessing that he had bestowed upon them in giving them knowledge of the right of the Commander of the Faithful, (as). Then they went on and the hermit went before him amid a group of his followers until he met the Syrians. The hermit was among a group of those who were martyred there. He, peace be upon him, carried out the prayer over him. He buried him and sought much forgiveness for him. Whenever he was mentioned, ('Ali) would say: *"That was my servant."*

In this report there are (several) kinds of miracles. One of them is knowledge of the unknown, a second is the strength by which normal human capabilities were transcended, and (another) is the distinction (of him) from other men through the confirmation of the message about him in the first Books of God. This is validated by the words of God, the Exalted: That is their example in the Torah and their example in the Gospels.

Al-Sayyid Isma'il b. Muhammad al-Himyari speaks of the same thing in his glorious golden ode: *"During his journey he went by night after the evening prayer to Karbala' in a procession until he came to one who devoted himself to God on a piece of raised ground. He made his camp on inhospitable land. O wilderness, it is not (a place) where he meets a living soul other than the wild animals and the balding white-haired man (i.e.'Ali).*

He approaches and cries out at it. (The Holy man) looks down as he stands, like the defender (looks down) over his bow from a watchtower.

Is there water that can be attained near the position which you have settled at. He answers: There is nothing to drink, except at a distance of six miles and the water I have with me (here) between the sandy hill and the vast desert.

He turns the reins towards the flat ground. He uncovers a smooth rock that shines like golden leaf-paste for camels.

He says: Turn it around. If you turn it around, you will see. You; will not see if it is not turned around.

They came together to remove it. It is impossible for them. It is a difficult impossible task that cannot be performed.

When it had weakened them he stretched a hand towards it and when the conqueror comes it is conquered.

It was as if it was a ball of fallen cotton in a skein, which he pushed in a playground.

He gave them sweet delicious water to drink from under it, which was better than the most delicious, the sweetest.

Then when they had all drank, he put it back and went away. Its position is left alone. It cannot be approached."

Ibn Maymun added these words concerning that: *"The signs for the monk were a miraculous secret there and he believed in the noble born testamentary trustee of authority (wasi).*

He died a martyr, truthful in his (statement of) support, most noble of monks who have become fearful (of God).

I mean that the son of Fatima is the testamentary trustee of authority. Whoever declares (their belief in) his outstanding merit and his (illustrious) actions does not lie.

He is a man both of whose sides are (descended) from Shem, without any father from Ham, nor a father of a father.

He is one who does not flee and in battle only the striking of his sword dyed red (with blood) can be seen."[133]

Some of Imam Ali's words about the Battle of Siffin

During the battle of Siffin Amir al-Mu'minin (as) heard some of his men abusing the Syrians, then he said: *"I dislike you*

---

[133] Kitab Al-Irshad by Shaykh Al-Mufid

starting to abuse them, but if you describe their deeds and recount their situations that would be a better mode of speaking and a more convincing way of arguing. Instead of abusing them you should say, "O' Allah! save our blood and their blood, produce reconciliation between us and them, and lead them out of their misguidance so that he who is ignorant of the truth may know it, and he who inclines towards rebellion and revolt may turn away from it."[134]

When in Siffin the men of Mu`awiyah overpowered the men of Amir al-Mu'minin (as) and occupied the bank of River Euphrates and prevented them from taking its water, Amir al-Mu'minin (as) said: *"They are asking you morsels of battle. So, either you remain in ignominy and the lowest position or drench your swords with blood and quench your thirst with water. Real death is in the life of subjugation while real life is in dying as subjugators. Beware, Mu`awiyah is leading a small group of insurgents and has kept them in dark about the true facts with the result that they have made their bosoms the targets of death."*

Amir al-Mu'minin (as) had not reached Siffin when Mu`awiyah posted forty thousand men on the bank of the river to close the way to the watering place, so that none except the Syrians could take the water. When Amir al-mu'mimin's force alighted there, they found that there was no watering place except this one for them to take water. If there was one, it was difficult to reach there by crossing high hillocks. Amir al-mu'minin sent Sa`sa`ah ibn Suhan al-`Abdi to Mu`awiyah with the request to raise the control over water. Mu`awiyah refused. On this side Amir al-Mu'minin's army was troubled by thirst. When Amir al-mu'minin noticed this position he said, *"Get up and secure water by dint of sword."*

Consequently, these thirsty persons drew their swords out of sheaths, put arrows in their bows and dispersing Mu`awiyah's

---

[134] Nahjul Balagha sermon 206

men went right down into the river and then hit these guards away and occupied the watering place themselves.

Now, Amir al-Mu'minin's men also desired that just as Mu`awiyah had put restriction on water by occupation of the watering place, the same treatment should be accorded to him, and his men and no Syrian should be allowed water and everyone of them should be made to die of thirst. But Amir al-Mu'minin (as) said, *"Do you want to take the same brutal step which these Syrians had taken? Never prevent anyone from water. Whoever wants to drink, may drink and whoever wants to take away may take away."* Consequently, despite occupation of the River by Amir al-Mu'minin's army no one was prevented from the water, and everyone was given full liberty to take water.[135]

When Imam Ali (as) sent an expedition of 3,000 soldiers under Ma'qil bin Qays Riyahi against the Syrians, he issued the following instructions: *"Always keep the fear of Allah in your mind. Remember that you have to meet Him one day (let the fear of Allah guide you in all your activities against man) and your end will be towards Him and towards none else.*

Do not fight against anybody unless he wishes to fight against you. During winters travel in the mornings and give your army a rest in the afternoons. Do rush through journeys (unless absolutely necessary). Travel by easy stages, and do not tire out your army during the journey. Do not travel during the early part of the evening because Allah has meant this to be time for rest and comfort and not for march and exertion, make use of these hours to give rest to your body and mind.

When you have rested then begin your march with trust and faith in Allah in the early hours of the morning.

When you face your enemy, stand in the midst of your

---

[135] Nahjul Balagha sermon 52

army, never alone. Do not be over-anxious to fight and do not behave as if you craving for a combat or aspiring for an encounter, but at the same time do not try to avoid your enemy or to evade an engagement as if you are afraid or nervous. Keep my orders in mind and act accordingly until you get further instructions. Do not let the hatred and enmity of your opponents force you to a combat, do not begin a battle even if the enemy so desires unless you have explored every avenue of amity and good-will and have exhausted all the chances of a peaceful settlement."[136]

At Siffin Imam Ali (as) gave the following instructions to his soldiers before the battle: *"Do not take the initiative in fighting, let them begin it. It is because by the Favour of Allah you are on the side of truth and justice. Leave them until they begin their hostilities and then you are at liberty to take to fighting. Their keenness to begin a battle will be another proof of your sincere belief in the orders of Allah.*

If Allah favors you with success and inflicts defeat to the enemy, then do not attack those who have surrendered, do not injure the disabled and weak, do not assault the wounded, do not excite women and do not make them angry with rude behavior even if they use harsh and insulting words against your commander and officers because they are physically and mentally weak and get excited easily and frightened quickly. During the days of the Holy Prophet (s) we had strict orders not to touch, molest or insult women though they were unbelievers. Even in pre-Islamic days it was the custom that if a man struck a woman even with a stick or a stone, the revenge had to be taken by his sons and descendants."[137]

A letter sent by Imam Ali (as) to the people of various provinces, giving them the causes of the Battle of Siffin: *"The*

---

[136] Nahjul Balagha letter 12

[137] Nahjul Balagha letter 14

thing began in this way: We and the Syrians were facing each other while we had common faith in one Allah, in the same Prophet (s) and on the same principles and canons of religion. So far as faith in Allah and the Holy Prophet (s) was concerned we never wanted them (the Syrians) to believe in anything over and above or other than what they believed in and they did not want us to change our faith. Both of us were united on these principles. The point of contention between us was the question of the murder of Uthman. It had created the split. They wanted to lay the murder at my door while I am actually innocent of it.

I advised them that this problem cannot be solved by excitement. Let the excitement subside, let us cool down; let us do away with sedition and revolt; let the country settle down into a peaceful atmosphere and when once a stable regime is formed and the right authority is accepted, then let this question be dealt with on the principles of equity and justice because only then the authority will have power enough to find the criminals and to bring them to justice. They refused to accept my advice and said that they wanted to decide the issue on the point of the sword.

When they thus rejected my proposal of peace and kept on rattling threats, then naturally the battle, which was furious and bloody, started. When they saw defeat facing them across the battlefield, when many of them were killed, and many more wounded, then they went down on their knees and proposed the same thing, which I had proposed before the bloodshed had begun. I accepted their proposal so that their desire might be fulfilled, my intentions of accepting the principles of truth and justice and acting according to these principles might become clear and they might have no cause to complain against me. Now whoever adheres firmly to the promises made will be the one whose salvation will be saved by Allah and one who will try to go back upon the promises made, will fall deeper and deeper into heresy, error, and loss. His eyes will be closed to realities and truth in this world, and he will be punished in the next world."[138]

---

[138] Nahjul Balagha letter 58

Martyrdom of Malik Al-Ashtar

Ali's governor in Egypt was Muhammad ibn Abu Bakr. In 658 (38 A.H.) Mu'awiya sent Amr bin Aas with an army of 6000 warriors to conquer Egypt for him. Muhammad requested Ali (as) to send him aid to defend Egypt. Ali (as) realized that the only man who could save Egypt from the clutches of Mu'awiya and Amr bin Aas, was Malik ibn Ashter. He, therefore, sent him (Malik) as the new governor of Egypt, and recalled Muhammad ibn Abu Bakr to Kufa, but neither Malik nor Muhammad ever reached their destinations. Malik left Kufa to take charge of Egypt. But Mu'awiya's agents, disguised as innkeepers, were waiting to "greet" him at the frontier. They administered poison to him in his drink, and he died from its effect.[139]

Malik was Mu'awiya's nemesis. The agent who had administered poison to Malik, immediately reported his "exploit"

---

[139] Abul Fida

to Mu'awiya, and he (Mu'awiya) couldn't believe his own good fortune. In an ecstasy of delight, he exclaimed: "Today Ali has lost his second arm." By killing Ammar ibn Yasir, in the battle of Siffin, Mu'awiya had cut Ali's one arm; and now by killing Malik, he had cut his (Ali's) other arm also. After the death of Malik, Ali had lost both arms. Mu'awiya had "cut" Ali's arm with the aid of his secret but powerful weapon – poison!

Poison "dissolved" Mu'awiya's nemesis and freed him from fear for all time.

In those years Amr bin al-Aas reconquered Egypt for the Omayyads, eliminating through poison, Malik al-Ashter whom Ali (as) had dispatched there as governor.[140]

To Ali, the death of Malik was a staggering blow. If ever there was a man in Arabia who was a one-man army, it was Malik. His presence inspired confidence in his own army, and his name struck terror in the hearts of his enemies. The Arabs never produced a more formidable swordsman than him. By dint of grit and ability, he propelled himself to the top of the tree. It is one of the tragedies of the history of the Muslims that his career was cut short in the prime of life. He was brave, resolute, intelligent, chivalrous and faithful. There were many men who, until the death of Ammar ibn Yasir, were undecided if they should or should not fight on Ali's side. It was only after the fulfillment of the prediction of the Apostle of God that Ammar would be killed by the people of iniquity, that they were convinced that justice and truth were on Ali's side. But Malik never had such hang-ups. He knew that Ali (as) and Truth were inseparable, and he was most consistent in his devotion and support to him.

Malik ibn Ashter died at a time when Ali (as) needed him most, and there was no one who could take his place.

The shock to Ali, of the death of friends like Ammar ibn

---

[140] Francesco Gabrieli *The Arabs, A Compact History*, p. 69, 1963

Yasir and Malik ibn Ashter, was devastating but he was sustained by his Faith. He considered each new shock, each new sorrow, and each new misfortune, a new test of his faith, and it remained unshaken. His faith in the mercy of his Creator was greater than anything that could ever befall him, and he never surrendered to despair.

Malik was truly extraordinary. He was the consummate military professional, dedicated, dignified, and supremely competent and self-confident. He was a king among men.

A more remarkable man than him in his bold and salient individuality, and sharply marked light and shadow, is nowhere to be seen in Arabian history. Propaganda has made the names of some other men more well-known than his, but he remains incomparable. He was the Phoenix of Islam.

Perhaps it is impossible to pay Malik ibn Ashter a tribute greater than the one paid to him by his own master, Ali ibn Abi Talib. In the battle of Layla-tul-Harir, Ali (as) placed his hands on the shoulders of Malik and said: *"You have served me with the same distinction and devotion with which I served my master, Muhammad, the blessed Apostle of God."*[141]

When news of the assassination of Muhammad b. Abi Bakr, may Allah be pleased with him, reached Amirul Momineen (as) he wrote to Malik b. al-Harith al-Ashtar, may Allah bless him with mercy, who was then residing at Nasibayn. (He wrote): *"You are surely among those from whom I seek help to keep the banner of Islam high and to crush the haughtiness of the disobedient and to fortify the threatened borderline. I had appointed Muhammad b. Abi Bakr, may Allah bless him with mercy, to govern Egypt, but the rebels attacked him and as he was inexperienced about warfare, he was martyred - may Allah bless him with mercy. Now, come over to me so that we may look into the matter concerning Egypt, and appoint in your place a*

---

[141] The Restatement of the History of Islam and Muslims by Sayed Razwy

reliable, sane person from your companions." Then Malik - may Allah be pleased with him, appointed Shabib b. Amir al-Azadi to succeed him, and preceded till he arrived to meet Amirul Momineen, peace be upon him. Then he (i.e. Ali) explained to him the situation in Egypt and informed him about its people.

Then he said: "There is no one for this assignment except you, so be ready to go. And if there is anything, about which I have not guided you, you will depend upon your judgment and seek assistance from Allah for your intention. (In your dealing with them), mix severity and harshness with tenderness and gentleness, and be friendly for as long as friendliness serves the purpose. And be resolute when there is no alternative to severity."

He said: *Then Malik al-Ashtar - may Allah be pleased with him, rose and prepared for his journey to Egypt. And Ali, peace be upon him, sent a letter to the people of Egypt, before (Malik) arrived there:*

"In the name of Allah, Most Merciful, Most Benevolent, I praise Allah, none to be worshipped but He; and beseech Allah to bless His Prophet, Muhammad and his progeny. Surely, I have sent unto you a servant from the servants of Allah, who does not sleep in the days of fear and does not recoil from the enemy fearing any disaster. He is from the strongest among His servants and the noblest; and to the transgressors, more threatening than the burning fire. And from ignorance and blemish, he is the farthest. He is Malik b. al-Harith al-Ashtar, neither a cutting tooth nor a blunted edge. He is patient amid threats, calm and composed at the time of war. He has an original judgment and an agreeable patience. So, listen to him and obey him. If he commands you to march forth, march and if commands you to halt, halt for he does not advance or halt except by my order. I have sent him to you in spite of my need for him, for the sake of your welfare and because of my deep concern about your adversaries. May Allah guard and protect you with guidance and keep you steadfast with Taqwa. May He *bless us and you with what He likes and loves. May peace and mercy of Allah and His Blessing be upon you."*

When Malik al-Ashtar completed his preparations for journey to Egypt, the spies of Mu'awiya from Iraq wrote to inform him. He was very much distressed because he had his eyes set on Egypt. He knew that he would lose Egypt if al-Ashtar arrived there and to him al-Ashtar was a more powerful person than the son of Abu Bakr. So, he contacted a chief who paid the revenue at a place called al-Qulzum, informing him that Ali (as) has appointed al-Ashtar to govern Egypt and if you got rid of him on my behalf, I shall gift away the revenue to you for as long as you live, so plan to kill him in every way possible.

Then Mu'awiya collected the people of Syria and said: *"Verily, Ali has sent al-Ashtar to Egypt. Come and let us pray to Allah that He may relieve us of him."* Then he prayed, and so did the people with him.

Al-Ashtar travelled on till he came to al-Qulzum. The chief received him and greeted him and then said: *"I am among those who is liable to pay the revenue. And you and your companions have a right upon all that grows on my land. So be my guest and allow me to serve you and your companions and let your animals freely graze on my land, and I will count it from my liability."*

So, al-Ashtar became his guest, and he served him (al-Ashtar) and his companions for all their needs. And he brought to them food, including some honey, which had poison. When al-Ashtar drank from that honey, it killed him, and he died because of that.

Mu'awiya got the news, so he collected the people of Syria and said: *"Happy tidings for you! Allah, Most High, has answered your prayers; has relieved you of him and has killed him."* They rejoiced.

When the news of Ashtar's death assailed Amirul

Mo'mineen (as) he sighed and grieved, saying: *"What an excellent man Malik was! Had he been a mountain, he would have been its firm rock, and had he been from stone, he would have been solid. By Allah, some men in the world will be placated by his death; but it behaves for the mourners to mourn over him.*

We are for Allah and unto Him shall we return; and all praise to Allah, the Lord of all Universe. I shall seek reward from you for this sacrifice, for surely, his death is among the greatest worldly calamities. May Allah bless Malik with mercy; no doubt, he faithfully dispersed his charge and completed the appointed term (of life) and met his Creator; while we have reconciled ourselves to forbear every adversity after being bereaved of the Prophet, peace be upon him and his progeny, for that was the greatest calamity."[142]

---

[142] Al-Amali by Sheikh Al-Mufid 9th session Hadith 4

The Martyrdom of Mohammad ibn Abu Bakr

Muhammad ibn Abi Bakr was brought up by the Commander of the Faithful and was one of the staunchest friends of the Ahl ul Bayt.

Addressing this illustrious family, he says: *"O descendants of Fatima! You are a place of safety for my guardian and me. It is through you that on the Day of Judgment, the significance of my good actions will be greater. Since my love for you is sincere, I do not mind if somebody barks near me."*

Although he was the son of the first caliph, Abu Bakr, and the brother of 'Aisha, he was not called Khalu'l-Mu'minin (like Mu'awiya was). He was abused and deprived of his father's legacy!

When Amr Bin al-Aas and Mu'awiya Bin Khadij conquered Egypt, the supply of water was cut off to Muhammad Bin Abu Bakr. When he had nearly died of thirst, he was killed. He was then enclosed in the skin of an ass and the bundle was thrown into a fire. When Mu'awiya learned of this, he was very pleased.[143]

Amr bin Aas entered Egypt without any opposition, and when he encountered Muhammad ibn Abu Bakr, he easily defeated him. Muhammad had no army, and he tried to fight with a handful of soldiers. The Syrians captured him and tortured him to death. Amr occupied Egypt, and it became a part of Mu'awiya's dominions.

Ali (as) loved Muhammad ibn Abu Bakr as his own son. His death was another terrible shock he had to endure. He prayed for him and invoked God's blessings and mercy upon his noble

---
[143] Peshawar Nights by Sultanul Waizin Shirazi

soul.[144]

Hearing these facts, the Sunni's do not question why these damned people treated Abu Bakr's son, Khalu'l-Mu'minin Muhammad Bin Abu Bakr, so cruelly, but when Mu'awiya is cursed they immediately become angry?! So, you see the opposition to the progeny of the Holy Prophet (s) and it continues today.

Since Muhammad Bin Abi Bakr was one of the friends of the descendants of the Holy Prophet (s), the Sunni's neither call him Khalu'l-Mu'minin nor regret his murder. Since Mu'awiya was the bitterest enemy of the Ahl ul Bayt of the Holy Prophet (s), they call him Khalu'l-Mu'minin. May Allah save us from such fanatical perversity!

Allah says: *"And whoever kills a believer intentionally, his punishment is Hell; he shall abide in it, and Allah will send His wrath on him and curse him and prepare for him a painful chastisement."*[145]

This Holy verse explicitly says that if a man kills a single believer intentionally, he deserves Allah's curse and his abode is in Hell. Wasn't Mu'awiya associated with the murder of believers?

Would you hesitate to call Mu'awiya accursed? Is it not a fact that in the Battle of Siffin the great companion of the Holy Prophet (s), Ammar Yasir, was martyred by Mu'awiya's order? All the prominent ulema say with one accord that the Holy Prophet (s) said to Ammar Yasir: *"It will not be long before you will be killed by a rebellious and misguided group."*

Have you any doubt that thousands of devout believers were killed by Mu'awiya's subordinates? Wasn't the pure and

---

[144] The Restatement of the History of Islam and Muslims by Sayed Razwy

[145] *Quran 4:93*

valiant warrior, Malik Ashtar, poisoned by Mu'awiya's order? Can you deny that Mu'awiya's chief officials, Amr al-Aas and Mu'awiya Bin Khadij, brutally martyred the Commander of the Faithful's governor, the pious Muhammad Bin Abi Bakr? Not content with that, they put his body into the carcass of a donkey and set it on fire. If I were to give you the details about the believers killed by Mu'awiya and his officials, it would require not one night, but several.[146]

---

[146] Peshawar Nights by Sultanul Waizin Shirazi

Assassination of Imam 'Ali (as) in Salat

Mu'awiya, the governor of Syria, had been steadily escalating violence against the dominions of Ali. Some of his inroads reached Ain-at-Tamar and Anbar, only 170 miles north of Kufa. The men of Kufa were so unwilling to fight against the Syrians that Ali (as) found it impossible to take effective punitive action. Mu'awiya himself led a raid right across the Jazira from Raqqa to Mosul and met no resistance anywhere. At last, Ali (as) declared in the mosque of Kufa that he would leave the city with the few of his faithful followers in an attempt to halt the Syrian aggression against Iraq, even if it cost him his life. This threat awakened the citizens of Kufa to the specter of being left leaderless if Ali (as) was killed fighting against the Syrians. They were stung into action, and they began to mobilize for defense.

The battle of Siffin had been the first trial of strength between Ali (as) and Mu'awiya. Militarily, the battle had been a near-victory for Ali, but politically, it had become a stalemate. After some time, it began to appear that Ali (as) would take up the challenge of Mu'awiya. But just then Ali (as) was assassinated in the mosque of Kufa, and the second trial of strength never took place.

According to the historical accounts some of which are quite plausible, three Kharji's met in Kufa (some say in Makkah) to hatch a conspiracy. Each of them volunteered to kill each of the three leading political figures of the Dar-ul-Islam – Ali,

Mu'awiya and Amr bin al-Aas. By killing them, it is alleged, they hoped to put an end to civil wars in Islam, and to restore peace to the Muslim community.

One of the three conspirators was a certain Abdur Rahman bin Muljam. He stayed in Kufa to kill Ali, and the other two went to Syria and Egypt to kill Mu'awiya and Amr al-Aas. The plans of the would-be assassins of Mu'awiya and Amr bin al-Aas, according to the stories in circulation, went awry, and they were captured and were executed.

The Kharji's had been defeated at Nehrwan, and most of them had perished in the battle but a few had escaped. Abdur Rahman bin Muljam was one of those who had escaped. He was consumed with the desire to kill Ali (as) and was in quest of an opportunity to do so. By a coincidence, he met a Kharji woman, one Qattama, whose father and brothers had also been killed in Nehrwan, and she too had nursed an undying hatred of Ali.

Abdur Rahman fell in love with Qattama, and proposed marriage to her. She told him that the price of her hand was the head of Ali ibn Abi Talib. This only strengthened Abdur Rahman in his resolution. He promised his lover the moon if she asked for it, but she said that nothing was of interest to her if she could not get the head of Ali ibn Abi Talib!

Abdur Rahman bin Muljam carefully worked out his plans to kill Ali. A few other trusted Kharjis also volunteered their services to him, and together they rehearsed the assassination. Abdur Rahman bin Muljam took one extra precaution – he put his sword in deadly poison, and let it soak in it for three days.

On the morning of the 19th of Ramadan of the year 40 A.H., Ali (as) came into the Great Mosque of Kufa and called *Adhan* (the call to prayer). He took his place in the alcove and moments later the worshippers began to arrive. They stood behind him in serried ranks, and the prayer began. Standing in the front row, with other worshippers, were Abdur Rahman bin Muljam and his confederates. They were watching Ali's movements. In the folds of their cloaks, they were carrying swords burnished to a high sheen and soaked in poison.

Just when Ali (as) touched the ground with his forehead for *sajda*, Abdur Rahman bin Muljam stepped out of his row, and crept into the alcove. And just when Ali (as) lifted his head from the ground, ibn Muljam struck the fatal blow at his forehead with such deadly force that it split open.

Blood squirted from Ali's forehead in several streams, and he exclaimed: *"By the Lord of the Kaaba, I am successful!"*

The members of the congregation realized what had happened, and as soon as they concluded the prayer, they surrounded him. His sons, Hassan (as) and Hussain (as), carried him to his house. A physician came, and tried to dress the ghastly wound but could not stop the bleeding. The blow of the sword was fatal anyway, but the poison from its blade was also spreading rapidly in his body. The Arab historians say that it was the second time that Ali (as) was wounded in the forehead, the first time being when, in the battle of the Trench fought in 627, the sword of Amr bin Abd Wudd cut through his shield and helmet and struck it. His forehead still bore the scar left by the sword of Amr.

This is the account left by the Arab historians of the assassination of Ali, and the vast majority of the Muslims have accepted it as authentic. Though this account has the authority of "consensus" of the historians behind it, its authenticity, nevertheless, is suspect on the grounds of "circumstantial evidence." There are too many "coincidences" in it.

No one questions the fact that it was Ibn Muljam who killed Ali. But was it his own idea to kill him? It is quite probable that someone else who used subliminal techniques for doing so planted the idea in his mind. Ibn Muljam didn't know that he was only a cat's paw, and he went ahead and killed Ali.

At this time no one in Dar-ul-Islam was more interested in the assassination of Ali (as) than Mu'awiya. The plot to kill Ali, the skill displayed in its execution, and its success, show the touch of consummate subtlety and a high degree of professionalism that were characteristic of Mu'awiya alone, whereas Ibn Muljam was nothing more than a bumpkin. Mu'awiya employed the same "skill" in removing from the scene, real or fancied threats to his own security and power, on numerous other occasions in later times, with the same results.

Mu'awiya's spies had informed him that Ali (as) was preparing for the invasion of Syria. In the battle of Siffin, Mu'awiya had not responded to chivalrous treatment by Ali. This time, therefore, Ali (as) had decided, not to fight a lingering action but a swift one that would quell Mu'awiya's rebellion and would restore peace to the embattled empire of the Muslims. Mu'awiya also knew that Ali (as) had, this time, both the ability and the resolution, to bring the conflict to a speedy and successful conclusion. His only hope, therefore, for his safety in future, as in the past, lay in the succor that he could get from his old and trusted "allies" – treachery and intrigue. He, therefore, mobilized them, and they didn't disappoint him.

Mu'awiya made the act of the assassination of Ali (as)

look spontaneous and convincing by making himself and his crony, Amr bin Aas, the potential and intended "victims" of the conspiracy and fanaticism of the Kharji anarchists. But both "escaped" assassination by a rare "stroke of good luck." One of them "fell ill" on the day he was to be "assassinated," and did not go into the mosque; the other did not fall ill but went into the mosque wearing his armor under his cloak. He was "attacked" by his "assassin" but was "saved" by his armor. "Falling ill" would have been an indiscreet act and would have exposed both "victims." In this manner, "illness" and the armor "saved" both Mu'awiya and Amr bin Aas from the daggers of their Kharji assassins, but Ali (as) was not so "lucky." He did not fall ill, and he did not put on his armor when entering the mosque. In the mosque, Ibn Muljam was awaiting him with a sword soaked in poison. When Ali (as) rose from *sajda,* he struck at his forehead, and cleft it. The blow proved to be fatal.

Most of the Arab historians wrote histories that were "inspired" by Mu'awiya and his successors. He was of course free to inject any account into those histories. He, therefore, managed to save himself and Amr bin al-Aas from the indictment of history, and it was Ibn Muljam alone who went down in history books as the real and the only villain of the crime.

By a coincidence, the assassination of Ali (as) took place on the eve of his invasion of Syria.

Though the Kharji anarchists had aimed their daggers at all three of the leading political figures of the Muslim world, viz., Ali, Mu'awiya and Amr bin Aas, by a coincidence, the latter two escaped the attempts on their lives, and Ali (as) alone was killed.

By still another coincidence, the two men who escaped, i.e., Mu'awiya and Amr al-Aas, were intimate friends of each other, and both of them were – coincidence again – the mortal enemies of the third, i.e., Ali, who was the only one to be killed.

There are too many mysterious coincidences that saved the lives of Mu'awiya and Amr bin al-Aas but took the life of Ali (as).

Ali (as) spent the time still left to him in prayer and devotions; in dictating his will; in giving instructions to his sons, ministers and generals regarding the conduct of the government; and in urging them all never to forget the old, the sick, the poor, the widows and the orphans at any time.

Ali (as) declared that his elder son, Hassan (as), would succeed him as the head of the Kingdom of Heaven on Earth, and as the sovereign of all Muslims.

Though Ali (as) was steadily weakening from the loss of blood and from the action of poison, all his faculties were sharp and clear right to the last moment. To all those people who came to see him, he said that they ought to be aware, always, of the presence of their Creator in their lives, to love Him, to serve Him, and to serve His Creation.

The poison had done its work, and on the morning of the 21st of Ramadan of 40 A.H., Ali ibn Abi Talib (as) left this world to go into the presence of his Creator whom he had loved and served all his life. He was "God-intoxicated." His greatest ambition in life was to wait upon his Creator, every moment of his existence, and he realized it, and this is the meaning of his exclamation in the alcove of the mosque when he felt the edge of the sword at his forehead: *"By the Lord of the Kaaba, I am successful."*

Hassan (as) and Hussain (as) washed the body of their father, draped it in a shroud, offered the funeral prayers for it, and then buried it silently at midnight at Najaf Ashraf, at some distance from Kufa. No markings were placed on the grave, and the gravesite was kept a secret, as desired by Ali (as) himself.

Ali, Islam's greatest saint, hero, statesman, philosopher, and martyr, had left this world, and the world was not to find a man sublime like him to all eternity.

Many among the Muslims were the mourners of Ali's death but none mourned him more dolorously than the Dhimmis (the Jews, the Christians, and the Magians). They were utterly heart broken. And when the sick, the disabled, the cripples, the orphans and the widows in the empire heard that he had died, they felt that their world had collapsed. He had been a father to them all. He had taken them all by the hand. He had taken them all into his prayers. Many among them did not know until after his death that it was he who had fed them and had taken care of them. He had taken all mankind into his grasp.

Whereas Ali (as) was always accessible to the poor and the weak, his own greatest anxiety and fear were lest any of them be inaccessible to him. It was only in his dominion that the Dhimmi's[147], the powerless and the defenseless enjoyed complete security. No one could terrorize them or exploit them. With his death, their security was gone forever!

It is a truism that exercise of power cannot be combined with saintly purity, since once a man assumes responsibility for public affairs, the moral simplicities within which it is just possible, with luck, to be able to lead a private life, are soon hideously complicated to an extent that precludes all clear distinctions between right and wrong. This truism, however, has its own exception – in Ali. He upheld principle, in public life as in private, regardless of cost. He invariably put the right thing ahead of the smart thing, regardless of cost. The source of the principles that guided his private and public life was Al-Qur'an al-Majid as it was also the source of his political philosophy.

Ali (as) has many critics and enemies, but they cannot point out a single instance when he deviated from a principle. They cannot point out any conflict between his thought and speech on the one hand, or between his speech and deed on the

---

[147] Non-Muslims living under Muslim government

other. He was consistently consistent in thought, speech, and action.

Ali (as) represented the ultimate triumph of character and ideology. He was a rare combination of love of God, devotion to duty, strength tempered with tenderness, symmetry of disposition, and inflexible integrity. His greatest legacy to the world of Islam will remain forever his sublime character.[148]

If 'Aisha repented of her revolt against Amiru'l-Mu'minin (as) why did she perform a prostration of thanks when she heard the news of the Holy Imam's martyrdom? Abu'l-Faraj Ispahani, writing about the Imam in his *Maqatilu't-Talibin*, says: *"When 'Aisha heard the news of the martyrdom of Amiru'l-Mu'minin Ali, she offered a prostration (of thanks)."* Later however, she asked the informant who had killed Ali. She was told that it was Abdu'r-Rahman Ibn Muljim of the Bani Murad clan. Instantly she recited the following couplet: *"If Ali is away from me, the news of his death was brought by a servant, who may not have dust in his mouth."*

Zainab, daughter of Umme Salma, was present at that time. She asked 'Aisha if it was proper for her to express her jubilation and utter such words about Ali. It was a bad thing. 'Aisha replied that she was not in her senses and that she uttered those words through forgetfulness. She said: *"If such a thing appears in me again and I repeat those things, you may remind me, so that I may refrain from doing that."* These facts clearly show that 'Aisha did not repent later in life.

In view of the misdeeds of this accursed dynasty, the body of the Commander of the Faithful, Ali (as) was buried during the night, and no trace of his grave was left. The grave remained virtually unknown until the days of Caliph Harun ar-Rashid.

---

[148] The Restatement of the History of Islam and Muslims by Sayed Razwy

One day Harun went hunting in the locality of Najaf, where deer lived in large numbers. When the hounds chased the deer, they took refuge on the mound of Najaf, small hill which the hounds would not ascend. Several times, when the hounds retreated, the deer would come down, but when the hounds again leapt at them, the deer took refuge on the mound. Understanding that there was a reason for the hounds' behavior, Harun sent his men to inquire in Najaf. They brought an old man to him, and the caliph asked about the secret of why the hounds did not climb up on the mound.

The old man replied that he knew the secret, but that he was afraid to disclose it. The caliph guaranteed him safety, and the man told him: *"Once I came here with my father, who went on the mound and offered prayers there. When I asked him what was there, he said that they had come there with Imam Ja'far Sadiq for a visit. The Imam had said that this was the sacred grave of his revered grandfather, the Commander of the Faithful, Ali, and that it would shortly become known."*

At the caliph's behest that place was dug up, and the signs of a grave became apparent along with a tablet with an inscription in Syriac, meaning: *"In the name of Allah, the Beneficent, the Merciful. This grave has been prepared by the Prophet Noah for Ali, the Vicegerent of Muhammad, 700 years before the Deluge."*

Caliph Harun paid respects to the place and ordered the restoration of the earth. He then performed two rak'ats of prayer. He wept much and laid himself on the grave. Thereafter, on his orders, the whole matter was disclosed to Imam Musa Kadhem (as) at Medina. The Imam confirmed that the grave of his revered grandfather, Commander of the Faithful, Ali (as), was at that place. Harun then decreed that a stone building be erected over Commander of the Faithful's sacred grave, which came to be known as Hajar Haruni, "The stone structure built by Harun." In due course, the news spread, and Muslims visited the Holy place.[149]

---

[149] Peshawar Nights by Sultanul Waizin Shirazi

Crucifixion of Maytham At-Tammar

Maytham was born at Nahrawan near Kufa. He was from Persia. A woman from Bani Asad bought him. One day, Imam Ali (as) bought and gave him his freedom.

Maytham lived a simple life. He sold dates in the market of Kufa. Two things grew in his heart: faith in Islam and love for Imam Ali (as). Imam Ali (as) taught him that Islam was the only way to freedom. He (as) liked Maytham because he was a good man. The Imam went to Maytham's shop and taught him about Islam.

Imam Ali (as) bought Maytham from a woman belonged to Bani Asad. The Imam asked Maytham: *"What's your name?"*

"Salim," He answered.

The Imam said: *"Allah Apostle (s) has told me that the Persians call you Maytham."*[150]

Imam Ali bought Maytham as a servant and then freed him. He asked him what his name was; *"Salim"*, he said: *"But I heard the Prophet (s) saying that your true name was Maytham."*[151]

Maytham was astonished because no one knew his real name. So, he said: *"Allah and His Apostle are truthful."*[152]

Maytham said: *"He was correct, and you are also correct. My true name is Maytham."*

Imam Ali (as) said: *"Then stay with the name mentioned by the Holy Prophet (s) and give up the other name."*

Imam Ali (as) bought and freed him, but he put a bond of love around his neck so that he remained with him up to the last moment of his life. Even death could not break this bond.[153]

Whoever goes to the desert at night will see the sky full of stars. His heart will be afraid of Allah. Imam Ali (as) went to the desert at night to say his prayers. He took a friend of his to that desert to teach him a lesson about Islam.

Sometimes, Imam Ali (as) took Maytham to the desert. He told him about future matters. The Imam had learnt future matters from our Master Muhammad (s).

Maytham listened to Imam Ali's words. When the Imam said his prayers Maytham said them behind him. He listened

---

[150] Maytham At-Tammar by Kamal Syyed

[151] Master & Mastership by Allama Murtaza Mutahhari

[152] Maytham At-Tammar by Kamal Syyed

[153] Master & Mastership by Allama Murtaza Mutahhari

with awe to the Imam's prayers.

Maytham was brilliant. He got his knowledge from Imam Ali. One day he said to Abdullah bin Abbas, the nation's scholar: *"Ask me whatever you want about the Qur'an explanation. I've learnt everything from Imam Ali."* So, bin Abbas sat before Maytham to learn lessons about the Qur'an explanation.[154]

Maytham was a wonderful man. With his remarkable ability he gradually secured an honorable position among the companions of Imam Ali (as). He became aware of the realities and could understand their fine distinctions. He had great love for Imam Ali. He was as fond of him as a thirsty plant is of rain. He took his inspiration from Imam Ali. With him he lived and in him he remained fully absorbed. Imam Ali (as) was the light of his heart and the rejoicing of his soul; and he was not willing to lose this rejoicing even to gain all the wealth of the whole world.

One day Imam Ali (as) said to Maytham *"After my death you will be hanged. A spear will be thrust into your body. On the third day your beard will be stained with the blood of your nose and mouth. You will be hanged beside the house of Amr ibn Hurayth along with nine others. The gallows on which you will be hanged will be the shortest. Come along I'll show you the date-palm from the branches of which you will be ultimately hanged."* And then he showed Maytham the tree.

Years passed and Imam Ali (as) was martyred. The Umayyads gained power over the people. Maytham went out from time to time to look at the tree; offered his prayers and spoke to it thus *"Tree, may Allah bless you! I have been created for you and you are growing for me."*

In the year of his martyrdom Maytham had the honor of visiting Ka'bah, the House of Allah. There, he met Umme Salama, the Mother of the Faithful. *"I've often heard your name*

---

[154] Maytham At-Tammar by Kamal Syyed

from the Holy Prophet (s). He recommended you to Ali," she said.

Maytham asked about Imam Hussain (as) and learnt that he had left the city. *"Convey my regards to him"*, he said, *"and tell him that it will not be long before he and I see each other in the presence of our Lord."*

Umme Salama ordered perfume to be brought. She applied it to the beard of Maytham. Then she said to him. *"Before long your beard will be painted with your own blood"* (because of your love for the Prophet and his progeny).

Maytham then went to Kufa, where Ibn Ziyad's agents arrested him. When he was produced before Ibn Ziyad, the following dialogue took place between them:

Ibn Ziyad: *"Where is your Allah?"*

Maytham: *"He is lying in wait for the oppressors, and you are one of them."*

Ibn Ziyad: *"What did your master Ali say about me and you?"*

Maytham: *"He said that you will hang me along with nine others, and my gollows will be shorter than those of others."*

Ibn Ziyad: *"I would like to go against what your master said and kill you in some other way."*

Maytham: *"How can you? He learnt that from the Prophet and the Prophet learnt it from Allah. Can you go against Allah? I even know the place of my martyrdom. I also know that I am the first Muslim in whose mouth a bridlebit will be laid."*

Ubaydullah ibn Ziyad was enraged. He ordered that for the time being Maytham might be taken back to prison. It was in this very prison that Maytham gave Mukhtar Thaqafi the good news of his release and said: *"In revenging for the Doyen of the Martyrs you will kill Ibn Ziyad."* And so it was.

At last, Maytham was taken to the place where he was to make supreme sacrifice; to the place of his spiritual rise; the place from which he was to soar to the greatest heights of human spirituality. He was hanged beside the house of Amr ibn Hurayth from the tree that he already knew. The people gathered round him, and on the gallows, he found a good opportunity to tell them of the virtues of Imam Ali (as). He spoke and moved the hearts of the people. He made them acquainted with the truth.

Ibn Ziyad was informed that Maytham was defaming him whereupon he ordered him to be gagged so that he might not utter a word further. As Imam Ali (as) had foretold, a spear was thrust into Maytham's body. *"Allahu Akbar"*, he cried. At the end of the third day the blood from his mouth and nose flowed down and coloured his beard. May peace of Allah be upon him![155]

Another account of the Maytham at-Tammar

It was dawn. As usual, Maytham went to the date-palm trunk. He splashed it with water. The good ground sent out a sweet smell. Maytham said two rakat's. Then he put his back against the date-palm trunk. Maytham had visited the date palm for more than twenty years. It had not been a mere dry trunk. It had been a tall date palm before twenty years.

Days, months, and years passed. Maytham said two Raka'as near the date palm. Then he addressed it: *"Allah has created you for me. And He has created me for you. Maytham liked that date palm. He watered it when it was green."*

One day, he came to the date palm. He found it a dry trunk. He cut the top of the trunk. That tall date palm became a mere short trunk. Still Maytham went on visiting that dry trunk.

---

[155] Master & Mastership by Allama Murtaza Mutahhari

What was the relationship between him and that date palm?

Amru bin Huraith was a leader from Kufa. Maytham said to him: *"I'll be your neighbour. Treat me kindly."*

Amru said: *"Do you want to buy bin Masoud's house or bin al-Hakim's?"* Maytham kept silent.

Amru bin Harith was puzzled. He wondered: What does Maytham mean? Days and years passed. Unjust rulers succeeded each other over Kufa. They treated its people rudely. Ziyad bin Abeeh became a ruler over Kufa. He began killing Imam Ali's companions. He carried out Mu'awiya orders. Mu'awiya was full of spite. He ordered people to abuse Imam Ali.

The ruler appointed a man to look after the market. The man was unjust. The people complained of his bad treatment. The people were afraid of the man. Thus, they went to Maytham. They asked Maytham to go with them to the prince. They said to him: Maytham, come with us to the prince. Maytham went with them. He met the prince and told him about the rude treatment in the market. A policeman in the palace was displeased with Maytham's words. He said to the prince: *"Your Highness, the Prince, do you know this man?"*

The prince said: *"No! He's a liar! The supporter of a liar!"*

The policeman meant that Maytham was one of Imam Ali's companions.

Maytham said: *"Surely, I'm truthful! I'm the supporter of a truthful man. Really, he's Amirul Mu'mineen! (the Commander of the Faithful)"*

Habeeb bin Mudhahir was a good companion. After our Master Muhammad's demise, Habeeb had a close relationship with Imam Ali. One day, Maytham was riding a horse. Habeeb bin Mudhahir was riding a horse, too. They met each other before Bani Asad. They had a short talk. Bani Asad listened to their talk. Habeeb said with a smile: *"I predict that a bald man with a big belly will sell melons at Dar al-Rizk. The man will be killed for the love of his Prophet's family."*

Maytham said: *"I know that a red man with two plaits would appear. The man will support the son of the daughter of his Prophet (s). The man will be beheaded. His head will be carried through the streets of Kufa."*

The two friends saw each other off. Meanwhile, Bani Asad said: *"They are liars."* In the meantime, Rasheed al-Hajry passed by Bani Asad, He asked them about Habeeb and Maytham. Bani Asad said: *"They've just gone away."* Then Bani Asad told Rasheed about Habeeb's and Maytham's predictions.

Rasheed said with smile: *"May Allah have mercy on Maytham, He's forgotten to say: The person who brings the head will be given an extra hundred dirhams."* Rasheed went away while Bani Asad were astonished at his words. Then they said: *"Rasheed is a liar; too!"*

Days passed by then in Muharram, 61 A.H., Bani Asad saw Habeeb's head. It was tied to a long spear. They saw Ibn Ziyad's policemen carrying the head and walking through the streets of Kufa.

Mu'awiya bin Abu Sufyan died. His son Yazeed succeeded him. Yazeed was a young man aged 30. He drank alcohol. He amused himself with dogs and monkeys.

So, Imam Hussain (as) refused to pay Yazeed homage. Meanwhile, the Kufans were tired of Mu'awiya's persecution. Thus, they sent Imam Hussain (as) many letters. In their letters, they asked the Imam to come to save them from the Umayyad persecution.

The spies told Yazeed about the situation in Kufa. Yazeed had a spiteful Christian doctor called Sergon. He asked the advice of the doctor. Sergon advised him to appoint Ubaidullah bin Ziyad a ruler over Kufa.

Many companions of Imam Ali (as) supported Imam Hussain (as). Many Muslims supported him, too. Ubaidullah bin Ziyad arrived in Kufa, He began arresting and imprisoning Imam Hussain (as)'s supporters. Maytham, Mukhtar al-Thaqafi, Abdullah bin al-Harith were in the same prison.

Imam Hussain (as) died a martyr for Islam. The prisoners felt pain for him. Mukhtar said to his two friends: *"Be ready to meet Allah! After Imam Hussain's killing, Ubaidullah bin Ziyad will kill the Imam's supporters!"*

Abdullah bin al-Harith said: *"Yes, he will kill us sooner or later!"*

Maytham said: *"No, he won't kill you. My dear Imam Ali has told me that you (Mukhtar) will get revenge of Imam Hussain's killers. And you will kick Ubaidullah's head with your foot."* Then Maytham said to Abdullah bin al-Harith: *"You'll rule Basrah."*

Maytham deeply believed in Allah. He was not afraid of the unjust. People were afraid of Ibn Ziyad. They shook with fear when they saw him. But Maytham did not pay attention to him. He knew that Ubaidullah's death was certain. He knew that the unjust would not stay alive forever.

Mu'awiya and his son Yazeed prevented people from loving Imam Ali. The police arrested and killed the Imam's companions. Imam Ali (as) had told his companions about the Umayyad police. One day he said to Maytham: *"The Umayyad will order you to disown me. Will you do that?"*

Maytham said: *"No, I won't!"* Maytham thought that to disown Imam Ali meant to disown Islam. And to disown Islam meant to disown Allah.

The Imam said: *"Surely, you'll be killed!"*

Maytham said: *"I'll be patient! Death is little for Allah!"*

The Imam said: *"You'll be with me in Paradise."*

Ubaidullah bin Ziyad ordered the police to bring Maytham. He said to him: *"I've heard that you're a companion of Ali's!"*

Maytham said: *"Yes."*

Ubaidullah bin Ziyad said to Maytham: *"Will you disown him?"*

Maytham said: *"No, I won't!"*

Ubaidullah bin Ziyad said: *"Surely, I'll kill you!"*

Maytham said: *"By Allah, Imam Ali has told me that you will kill me! He has told me that you will cut my hands, legs, and tongue!"*

Ibn Ziyad stormily said: *"Your Imam is a liar!"*

Maytham jeered at that foolish person (Ubaidullah). Ibn Ziyad ordered the police to tie Maytham to the date-palm trunk near the house of Amru bin Huraith. Besides, he ordered them to cut off his hands and legs. Maytham was tied to the date palm trunk.

Amru bin Huraith saw him. Amru remembered Maytham's words: *"I'll be your neighbour. Treat me kindly."* So, Amru bin Huraith ordered one of his daughters to sweep the ground around the date-palm trunk. He also ordered her to splash it with water.

A person looked at Maytham and said: *"Disown Ali to save your soul!"*

Maytham said with a smile: *"By Allah, this date palm has*

been created for me! And I've been created for it!"

Thus, people knew the secret of Maytham's visit to the date palm throughout the long years.

Maytham addressed the people: *"People, if you want to hear some information about Ali bin Abi Talib, then come to me."*

The people crowded around Maytham. He began teaching them various kinds of knowledge. The spies told Ubaidullah bin Ziyad about Maytham's words. Ibn Ziyad ordered a policeman to cut off Maytham's tongue.

Maytham said: *"Amirul Mu'mineen has told me about that."*

The policeman cut off his Maytham's tongue. Another policeman stabbed him with a sword. Thus, this warriors's life was put out like a candle!

Maytham did a lot of good for people. The people loved him very much. They wanted to take Maytham's body to bury it. But the police strictly prevented them from approaching it. One night, seven dates-sellers came. They saw the policemen burning a fire. Two of them sawed the trunk. The seven dates-sellers carried Maytham's body outside Kufa. They buried it at a known place. Then they came back home.

Six years passed and Mukhtar announced his revolution in Kufa. His army met Ubaidullah's on al-Khazir Riverbank. Ibrahim al-Ashtar could behead Ubaidullah bin Ziyad. Some fighters brought Mukhtar the head of Ubaidullah. He stood up and kicked Ubaidullah's head. He remembered Maytham's words in prison; *"Mukhtar, you'll get out of prison. You'll get revenge on Imam Hussain's killers."*

Days passed and Imam Hussain's killers perished. People have cursed them throughout history. Today, when a visitor leaves the Holy City of Najaf and goes to see Kufa, on the way he sees a beautiful dome. That dome decorates Maytham's shrine.[156]

---

[156] Maytham At-Tammar by Kamal Syyed

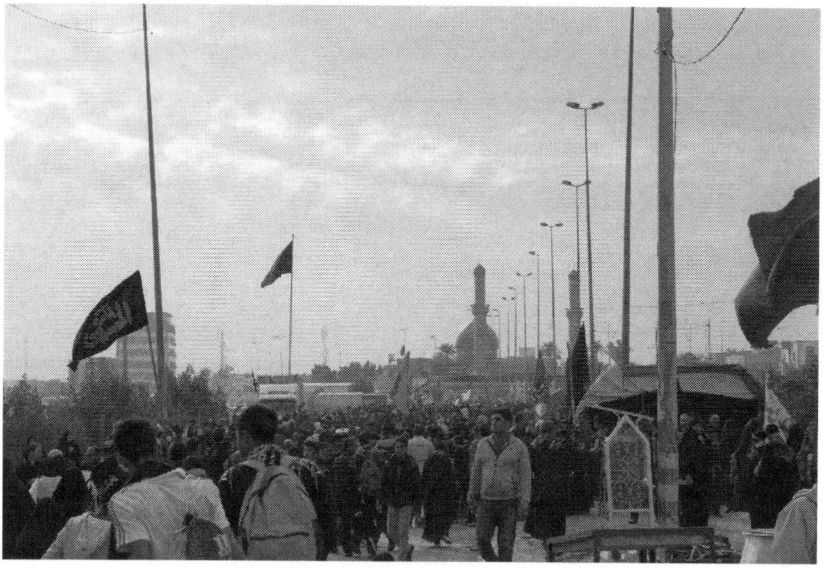

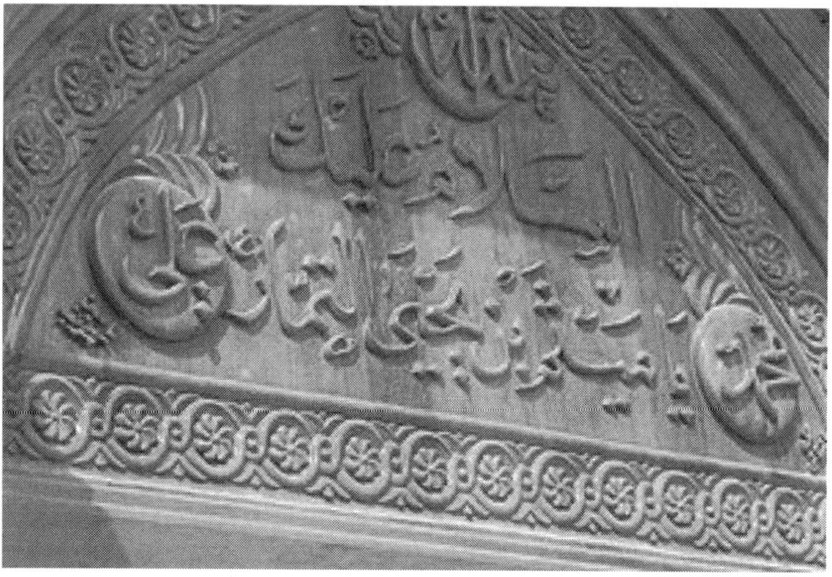

Martyrdom of Hujr ibn Adi, His Son and Companions

Hujr ibn 'Adi, who had been among the Holy Prophet's companions, did later align himself with 'Ali's group of devout Shi'a Muslims. He belonged to the tribe of Kinda, a southern tribe in Hijaz, who had migrated to Iraq in 17 A.H. This tribe was involved in Iraqi events as participants in Siffin and later in Mukhtar's uprising.

A crowd from among them was at odds with Hussain Ibn 'Ali (as) in Karbala. During Siffin he played a role as a commander in 'Ali's army, yet when many abandoned Imam, up to the very last moment he stayed beside him. Hujr could be found amid the most pious disciples of Allah's Apostle (s). Hukaym Niyshaburi called him the monk of Prophet's disciples.

After 'Ali's martyrdom, he was amongt the ones

stimulating the nation to swear allegiance to Hassan Ibn 'Ali (as). In the process of compromising, Hujr seemed discontented, but Imam elaborated that he had to consent merely due to protecting the lives of individuals like him. Nontheless later Mu'awiya by no means remained faithful to his pledge and martyred both Hujr and his followers.

During the governorship of Mughira over Kufa that lasted until the beginning of 50's (A.H.), despite relative freedom, insults were still hurled at Imam 'Ali (as) in the mosque. The leadership of 'Ali's Shi'ia Muslims was laid with the characters such as Hujr ibn 'Adi and 'Amr ibn Hamiq Khuza'i.

Hujr was among those who frequently objected to Mughira accustomed to insult Imam 'Ali (as). When Mughira was paved the way to send a caravan carrying some properties to Mu'awiya who was in need, Hujr intercepted the caravan and declared that as long as he has not granted the rights of the rightful, on no accounts would he allow these properties to be conveyed. At Mu'awiya's behest, Mughira had commanded them to take part in the congregational prayer at the mosque.

Once Hujr was urged by Mughira to go up the pulpit and curse Imam 'Ali (as) he went up and said, *"Mughira propels me to curse 'Ali (as), curse him you all."*

Immediately, the congregation perceived that his intention had been Mughira himself. Mughira, however, had already declared that he never intended to be the first one murdering the celebrity of Kufa and as a result contribute to Mu'awiya's grandeur in this world and his own abjectness in the Hereafter. This statement was the response to those objecting why he did not arrest or harass Hujr.

Following the demise of Mughira and Ziyad's governorship over Kufa, the status quo altered perceptibly. Ziyad, from the very first night of his governorship, did commence his rigors. His exceptional sermon for threatening Kufa people has been recorded as a typical Arab sermon in historical sources at that juncture. Well acquainted with Hujr Ibn 'Adi, he warned him stating, *"You and I have been in the same situation that you know yourself (concerning 'Ali's amity) but today everything has converted. Hold your tongue and stay at your home. My throne can be yours too. I will doubtlessly meet all your demands provided that you get along with me although you are rash."* Seemingly, Hujr who was convinced went away.

Once again, the status quo changed. It is said that one-time Hujr interrupted Ziyad's lengthy remarks as the time of prayer was elasping, yelling out, *"Al-Salat!"* (prayer).

It is also narrated that he along with other Shi'a Muslims had been convening meetings after Ziyad's departure to Basra. Ziyad's substitute, 'Amr Ibn Hurayth, wrote to Ziyad that if he desired to maintain Kufa, he should return without delay.

In this respect, Hujr was not merely solitary, but also, he was under any circumstances accompanied by a number of Shi'a Muslims. Quotedly, when Hujr protested against Mughira in the mosque, more than one-third of the audience validated his remarks.

As written by Abu l-Faraj, in the absence of Ziyad, being in Basra, Hujr together with his companions occupied one-third or half of the mosque and began denouncing and vilifying Mu'awiya. Ziyad himself had denounced the nobles of Kufa that: *"You are on my side whereas your brothers, offspring and tribes are on Hujr's side."*

After a while, a multitude of those on Hujr's side dispersed since the chiefs of tribes had menaced the members of the tribes. Therefore, there was no more companions who remained with Hujr.

When a group was sent to arrest him, he addressed his friends as saying, *"Since you are by no means able to defy them, there is no way for any struggle."* Eventually, Hujr conceded to surrender provided that for judgement he should be taken to meet

Mu'awiya. Having accepted the condition, Ziyad was making an attempt on the other hand to expose him to murder. By the same token, he compelled four characters having been appointed as the chiefs of the tribes in Kufa to make an affidavit against Hujr. It was stipulated in the affidavit that Hujr had formed some assemblies wherein Mu'awiya had been cursed.

His belief was that no one merited the caliphate save those from Talib's lineage. As stated by them having caused chaos within the town, he had expelled 'Amr Ibn Hurayth, the governor; furthermore, he had not only saluted 'Ali, but expressed his disgust for his foes and those having combated him.

Ziyad who had on no accounts approved the aforesaid affidavit ordered Abu Burda, son of Abu Musa Ash'ari, to prepare a more pungent one. What he wrote as a result was, *"Hujr has declined to comply with the caliph and seceded from "Jama'a". He has cursed the caliph and summoned all to a battle and sedition. Having congregated the people around himself, he has urged them to breach their pledges. He dethroned Mu'awiya, Amir al-Mu'minin, from the caliphate and blasphemed against Allah in addition."*

This time Hujr was labeled a blasphemer. Abu Burda who was one of the eminent Sunni traditionists bore the witness of it. Ziyad persuaded others to sign it too. Among the signatories were Ishaq and Moses, sons of Talha, Mundhir, Zubayr's son, 'Umar, son of Sa'd ibn Abi Waqqas and 'Umara, son of 'Uqba Ibn Abi Mu'ayt.

As narrated by historians, while Hujr was being arrested, he yelled out, *"I am still faithful to my allegiance."* He was absolutely right because he never ever intended to revolt against Mu'awiya. What he insisted on was about 'Ali (as) not to be insulted. And it was precisely what had been stipulated in Mu'awiya's commitment and conceded by him.

Fascinatingly, it was specified in the affidavit that Hujr

believed that caliphate was well deserved to only those from Talib's lineage. It was the manifestation of Hujr's pure Shi'a belief. The belief of such Shi'a Muslims is that Imamate does solely belong to Prophet's household (Ahl ul Bayt).

In a poem quoted from Hujr we read, *"Ali was a friend of the Prophet's (s) and he was gratified with his successorship."*

Hujr described 'Ali as Prophet's friend and successor. At that time many were of this belief in Iraq. When Abu l-Aswad Du'Ali was sneered due to his in-depth enthusiasm for 'Ali, he stated in a poem, *"I adore Muhammad (S), 'Abbas, Hamza and the successor ('Ali)"*

He did introduce 'Ali (as) as the Holy Prophet's successor manifesting his successorship. Corresponding to it is Malik's statement regarding 'Ali, *"The successor of the successors and the inheritor of all Prophets' body of knowledge is he."* This description was also what Imam al-Baqir's Shi'a Muslims like Jabir Ibn Yazid Ju'fi uttered about 'Ali (as). Further instances have been presented earlier in discussion of Shi'ism at Imam 'Ali's time.

Ultimately, Hujr along with his fourteen companions, known as the heads of Hujr's followers, were sent to Damascus. A few of them were interceded for and forgiven by Mu'awiya in Damascus. Although Hujr also was interceded for, Mu'awiya did in no way accept. Reportedly, Mu'awiya was at first ambivalent and on this account, he had already written to Ziyad that he believed that Hujr should never be murdered but Ziyad had replied that liberating him would result in corruption of Iraq, and he could allow Hujr to return to Iraq on the condition that he did not require Kufa. Mu'awiya eventually decided to assassinate Hujr; not withstanding, since he was terrified to meet him face to face, he commanded to detain them in Marj 'Adhra' a few farsangs far away from Damascus.

Later he read out the affidavit of dwellers of Kufa to those of Damascus and appealed to them to voice their opinions!

It was utterly evident that what they could ever say when the disciples' descendants were of that opinion!

Mu'awiya deployed a number to Marj 'Adhra' to carry out what they were supposed to. They were at first duty-bound to propose them that if they expressed their loathing for 'Ali (as), the verdict would be declared null and void. Under no circumstances did Hujr and his companions agree. And it might have been owing to this fact that Imam 'Ali (as) had asserted that after him if they were impelled to insult him, they should abide by but never ever express loathing for him.

Subsequently digging their own graves, Hujr and his companions spent dusk to dawn in worshiping. Eight out of them were set free but six of them announced their readiness for martyrdom.

The next morning, they were again requested to express their idea about 'Uthman, *"The foremost one who did injustice was 'Uthman,"* they retorted. They were asked whether they would pronounce disgust for 'Ali. They responded, *"No, never, we do all love him and hate those who hate him."*

Then they prepared themselves for being martyred. Hujr who was prominent among the devout of Iraq said a very-long-two-Rak'at prayer and stated, *"As yet, I have never performed a prayer shorter than this and I yearned to prolong it if you did not accuse me of being scared of death."*

Six of them were martyred. Karim Ibn 'Afif Khath'ami and 'Abd al-Rahman Ibn Hassan al-'Anzi were both taken to meet Mu'awiya. Karim was interceded for, but when it was 'Abd al-Rahman's turn, Mu'awiya questioned him about 'Ali (as).

"You had better not enquire any question," he responded.

When Mu'awiya insisted, he declared, *"I do attest that he was among the ones bearing Allah invariably in mind, enjoining good, establishing justice and being magnanimous."*

And when he was asked about 'Uthman, he replied, *"He was the first one who opened the door of injustice and closed the doors of justice."*

Mu'awiya sent him to Iraq and instructed Ziyad to kill him brutally. Then, he was buried alive at Ziyad's behest.[157]

References in relation to the killing of Hujr bin Adi can be located in the Sunni texts.[158]

We read in *Al Isaba*: *After the battle of Qudsiya Hujr ibn Adi participated in Jamal and Sifeen, alongside Ali and was amongst his Shi'a. He was killed upon the orders of Mu'awiya in a village called Marj Adhra near Damascus. At the time of his execution he requested: 'Do not remove these chains after I am killed, nor clean the blood. We will meet again with Mu'awiya and I shall petition my case against him'.*

We read in *Al Bidaya*: *When the time of death approached Mu'awiya, he said to himself thrice: 'Hujr bin Adi! The day of answering for your murder is very lengthy.'*

We read in *Tarikh ibn Asakir*: *"'Aisha said: 'Mu'awiya you killed Hujr and his associates, By Allah! The Prophet told me 'In the ditch of Adra seven men will be killed, due to this all the skies and Allah will be upset."*

---

[157] History of The Caliphs From the Death of the Messenger (S), to the Decline of the 'Umayyad Dynasty 11-132 AH by Rasul Ja'fariyan

[158] Al Bidaya wa al Nihaya, Volume 8 page 53 Dhikr 51 Hijri, Tarikh Kamil, Volume 3 page 249 Dhikr 51 Hijri, Tarikh ibn Asakir, Volume 12 page 227 Dhikr Hujr ibn Adi, Tarikh ibn Khaldun, Volume 3 page 13 Dhikr 51 Hijri, al Isaba, Volume 1 page 313 Dhikr Hujr ibn Adi, Asad'ul Ghaba, Volume 1 page 244 Dhikr Hujr ibn Adi, Shadharat ul Dhahab, Volume 1 page 57 Dhikr 51 Hijri, Tabaqat al Kubra, Volume 6 page 217 Dhikr Hujr ibn Adi, Mustadrak al Hakim, Volume 3 page 468-470 Dhikr Hujr ibn Adi, Akhbar al Tawaal, page 186 Dhikr Hujr ibn Adi, Tarikh Abu'l Fida, page 166 Dhikr 51 Hijri, Muruj al Dhahab, Volume 3 page 12 Dhikr 53 Hijri, Tarikh Yaqubi, Volume 2 page 219

We read in *Asad'ul Ghaba*: "*Hujr and his associates were arrested and taken to a ditch in Adhra which was near Damascus. Mu'awiya ordered that Hujr and his associates be executed in this ditch*"

Hujr bin Adi was a pious lover of Ali (as). Mu'awiya made his bastard brother the Governor of Kufa, he would disgrace the family of the Prophet (s) whilst standing on the pulpit, Hujr as a true lover of 'Ali (as) was unable to tolerate such insults. He would praise 'Ali (as) and object to such insults. Ibn Ziyad through his usual deception fabricated allegations to Mu'awiya who ordered that they be apprehended and sent to him.

On route to Damascus Mu'awiya ordered their execution. This is a fact that the Nawasib cannot escape, a fact that has even been vouched for by the Salafi scholar Hassan bin Farhan al-Maliki who on page 170 of his book *'Qeraah fi Kutub al-Aqaed'* said: *"The Bani Umayya killed and humiliated the lovers of Ahl ul bayt, and ruthlessly killed Hujr bin Adi during Mu'awyia's reign on account of his criticism of their act of cursing Ali from the pulpits."*

It is also said that when the time came when they were about to murder Hujr they asked him according to the customs if there was one last request that they could grant him. Hujr asked them if they could kill his son in front of him before they killed him. The executioner asked what was the reason for this? Hujr said that he would like to see that his son would die with the love of Ali (as) in his heart and that he was afraid that if he himself was killed first then his son might leave on account of fear and go over to the side of Mu'awiya and denounce Ali. These cruel heartless people then murdered Hujr's son in front of him and then proceeded to murder Hujr next.

May Allah bless Hujr ibn Adi, his son and his faithful companions!

Martyrdom of Qambar the servant of Ali

Qambar was also one of those brave men who secured a high position through the influence of the spiritual power of the Prophet Muhammad (s) and Imam Ali. He was not afraid of telling the truth and following the right path. Though from the viewpoint of the worldly people he was apparently no more than a servant, he spiritually secured such a high position that he became a confidant of Imam Ali.

The powerful and piercing words with which this man of iron will replied to Hajjaj binYusuf, the bloodthirsty sadist, are well-known. Once Hajjaj said: *"Qambar! What were your duties when you were in the service of Ali?"*

Qambar: *"I used to bring him water for ablution."*

Hajjaj: *"On finishing ablution, what did he use to say?"*

Qambar: *"He used to recite this verse of the Qur'an: "When they forgot Our admonition, We opened to them the gates of everything they desired; but just as they were rejoicing in what they were given, We seized them unawares with the result that they were left confused. Thus, the last remnant of the people who did wrong was cut off. Praise be to Allah, the Lord of the worlds." (Surah al-An'am, 6:44—45)*

Hajjaj: *"I think that he applied this verse to us."*

"Yes," said Qambar boldly.

Hajjaj: *"If I put you to death, what will you do?"*

Qambar: *"I shall be lucky, and you will be unlucky."*

Hajjaj: *"Confess that you no longer acknowledge Ali to be your master."*

Qambar: *"If I renounce his way, can you show me a*

better way?"

Hajjaj did not answer this question and said: *"In any case I am going to put you to death. Now tell me how you would like to be killed?"*

Qambar: *"I leave that choice to you."*

Hajjaj: *"Why?"*

Qambar: *"The way you will kill me, the same way I'll kill you in the next world. Ali, my master told me that I'd be beheaded unjustly."*

So, Hajjaj ordered him to be beheaded.

Indeed, if a man obeys Allah, the Holy Prophet (s) and his Ahl al-Bayt, he can have spiritual and esoteric guidance even today and can tread the path of perfection and proximity. For him then, there shall be no fear nor grief for because he will be a Muslim perfectly spiritual and divine.

The Holy Qur'an declares: *"As for those who say that our Lord is Allah and then they remain firm in their faith, the angels will descend on them saying: Neither be afraid nor be grieved." (Surah al-Fussilat, 41: 30)*[159]

---

[159] Master & Mastership by Allama Murtaza Mutahhari

Martyrdom of Amr bin Humaq

Amr bin Humaq, (as has been related earlier that he was present with Hujr bin Adi in the Mosque) accompanied by Rufa'ah bin Shaddad fled from Kufa and reached Madaen and from there, went to Mosul. They took shelter in a huge mountain therein. When this news reached Ubaydullah bin Balta'ah Hamadani, the governor of Mosul, he proceeded with the horsemen and a group of the people of the town towards them.

Amr, who was suffering from dropsy, did not have the courage to confront them. But Rufa'ah, who was a strong youth, mounted his horse and told Amr that he would defend him. Amr replied, *"What is the use? Save yourself and go away."*

Rufa'ah attacked them and they gave way, while his horse fled away from their midst. The horsemen chased him but he wounded them with his arrows, hence they returned.

They arrested Amr bin Humaq and asked him as to who he was? He replied, *"I am the one whom if you release, it will be better for you, and if you kill me, you will be in great loss"*, but he did not disclose his identity.

They took him to the ruler of Mosul, who was Abdul Rahman bin Usman Saqafi, the nephew of Mu'awiya, and renowned as Ibne Ummul Hakam. He wrote to Mu'awiya regarding him. Mu'awiya replied that, *"He is the one who has acknowledged having inflicted Uthman with nine wounds of a spear, then haven't you punished him? He should be inflicted with nine wounds of the spear."* They brought him out and inflicted nine wounds of spears and Amr succumbed to the first or the second stroke of the spear, later he was beheaded, and his head was despatched to Mu'awiya. His being the first head in Islam, which was sent from one place to another.

The Author says that this is what has been narrated by the

non-Shi'ah books of Islamic history (simply to justify his murder by Mu'awiya and alleging him to be the murderor of Caliph Uthman). As regards the Shi'ah reports, it is related from Shaikh Kashshi, that once the Prophet Mohammad (s) sent a group of people with the orders that, *"At such and such time of the night you shall loose your way, then go towards the left and you shall meet a man, who will be having a herd of Sheep. You ask him the way, but he shall not show you the way until you eat with him. Then he will sacrifice a sheep and prepare food for you and eat alongwith you, then he will show you the way. You convey my greetings to him and inform him about my appearance in Madina."*

They left, and as predicted lost their way. One of them said, *"Did not the Prophet tell us to go to the left side?"* They went towards the left and met the man, regarding whom the Prophet (s) had prophesied and asked him the way. The man being none other than Amr bin Humaq, who asked them, *"Has the Prophet appeared in Madina?"*

They replied in the affirmative and he accompanied them. He went to the presence of the Prophet (s) and remained there until Allah willed, then the Prophet (s) told him, *"Return to the place where you have come from, when the Commander of the faithful Ali becomes in charge of Kufa, go to him."*

Amr returned until the time Imam Ali (as) became the Caliph in Kufa, and he came to him and resided there. Imam Ali (as) asked him, *"Do you have a house here?"*, to which he replied in the affirmative.

The Imam continued, *"Then sell your house and buy one in the midst of (the people of the clan of) Azd. For tomorrow when I am gone from among your midst and some people will be in your pursuit, the people of the clan of Azd will defend you till you leave Kufa and find yourself in the fort of Mosul. You will pass by a paralytic man, you will sit down besides him and ask for water. He will give you water and then inquire about you, you then relate your condition to him and invite him towards Islam. He will accept Islam, and then place your hands upon his thighs and Allah will cure him of his disease. Then arise and walk till you pass by a blind man seated on the way. You ask for water and he will give it to you. And then he will inquire about you, you then relate your condition to him and invite him towards Islam. He will accept Islam, and then you place your hands upon his eyes and Allah the Honourable, the Glorified, will grant him sight. He too will accompany you, and verily these men will be the ones to bury you. Then some riders will pursue you and when you reach such and such place near a fort, they shall come to you. Then you dismount from your horse and enter the cave. Verily the worst men from among the men and jinn will unite to kill you."*

Whatever Imam Ali (as) had predicted occurred, and Amr did exactly what he was told to do. When they reached the fort, Amr told those two men to go on top and inform him what they saw.

They went on top and said that they saw some riders coming towards them. Hearing this Amr dismounted from his horse and entered the cave, while his horse fled away. When he entered the cave a black serpent, who had taken shelter therein, bit him. When the riders reached near they saw his horse running and concluded that Amr should be somewhere near. They started searching for him and found him inside the cave. And wherever they touched his body, the flesh thereat came out (due to the lethal poison). Then they beheaded him and took his head to Mu'awiya, who ordered it to be placed on the lance, this being the first head in Islam, which was placed on the lance.

As with Zahir, who was martyred with
Imam Husain (as) in Karbala, was the retainer of Amr bin Humaq, he was the same person who had buried him. It is related in Qamqaam, that Amr bin Humaq was from the progeny of

Kahin bin Habeeb bin Amr bin Qayn bin Zarrah bin Amr Rabi'ah Khuza'i.

He came to the presence of Prophet Mohammad (s) after the Peace Treaty of Hudaybiyah. While some are of the opinion that he accepted Islam in the year of the farewell Pilgrimage (*Hajjatul Wida*), but the first report seems to be more reliable. He remained in the presence of the Prophet and memorized numerous traditions.

The author of the book *Qamqam* relates from Amr bin Humaq that he quenched the thirst of the Prophet (s) who prayed for him thus: *"O Lord! Grant him a youthful life."* Thus, he remained alive for eighty years but none of the hair of his beard turned white.

He was included among the Shi'ah of Imam Ali (as) and fought the battles of Jamal, Siffeen and Naharwan alongwith him. Besides he was among those who stood up to support Hujr bin Adi and was among his companions.

He left Iraq in fear of Ziyad and took refuge in the cave in Mosul. The governor of Mosul sent his soldiers to arrest him. When they entered the cave, they found him to be dead because a snake bit him. His grave is renowned in Mosul, and is a place for pilgrimage, and he holds a great position. A dome is erected upon his grave. Abu Abdullah Sa'eed bin Hamadan, the cousin of Saifud Dawla and Nasirud Dawla, started its renovation in the month of Sha'ban 336 A.H. There ensued clashes between the Shi'ah and the Sunni because of the building of his shrine. Shaikh Kashshi relates that he was among the disciples of Imam Ali (as) and among the foremost who turned towards him.

In the book *Ikhtisas* it has been enumerated, regarding the preceding and close companions of Imam Ali (as), that Ja'far bin Husain relates from Mohammad bin Ja'far Mu'addab that he said, *"Imam Ali's four pillars from among the companions of the Holy*

Prophet (s) are Salman, Miqdad, Abu Zarr and Ammar. And among the Tabe'een are Owais bin Anees Qarnee, who will intercede (in Qiyamah) for the people equal to the tribes of Rabi'ah and Muzar, and Amr bin Humaq. Ja'far bin Husain says that Amr bin Humaq enjoyed the same status near Imam Ali (as) as Salman had near the Holy Prophet (s). Then there are Rushayd al Hajari, Maytham at- Tammaar, Kumayl bin Ziyad Nakha'i, Qambar the freed retainer of Imam Ali (as), Mohammad bin Abu Bakr, Muzre' the freed retainer of Imam Ali (as), and Abdullah bin Yahya regarding whom on the day of Jamal, Imam said, "O son of Yahya! I give glad tidings that you and your father are among the Shartatul Khamees.[160] Allah has chosen you on the empyrean."

Thus, those referred to as Shartatul Khamees are those warriors (of the army) between whom and Imam Ali (as) a covenant (*Shart*) was entered.[161]

Then there are Janad bin Zuhayr Amiri, while all the progeny of Amir were the Shi'ah of Imam Ali (a.s), Habeeb bin Muzhaahir Asadi, Al-Harth bin Abdullah Aa'awar Hamadani, Malik bin Hurayth Ashtar, Alam Azdi, Abu Abdullah Jadali, Juwayrah bin Musahhir Abadi.

In the same book it is related that Amr bin Humaq told Imam Ali (as) that, *"I have not come to you in pursuit of wealth or prestige of this world, but have come to you for you are the cousin of the Prophet and best among all men and the husband of Fatima, the mistress of women, and the father of the Prophet's*

---

[160] It is narrated that it was asked to Asbagh bin Nabatah Majashe'i as to why Imam Ali (a.s) had referred to him and other men like him as Shartatul Khamees, to which he replied that, "It is so because we had covenanted with him, that we would fight on his side until we attain victory or are killed. Then he too covenanted and stood surety that he would send us to Paradise in reward of this struggle." An army is also referred to as Khamees because it is comprised of five sections: Muqaddamah (Front Wing), Qalb (Central Wing), Maymanah (Right Wing), Maysarah (Left Wing), and Saqqah (Rear Wing).

[161] Muntahal Amal

progeny, and your share is more than any other Emigrant (Muhajir) or Helper (Ansar). By Allah! If you command me to shift the mountains from their place and pull out the water from the deep seas, I shall obey you until death overtakes me. I will always strike your enemies with the sword in my hand and shall assist your friends and may Allah elevate your position and grant you victory. Even then I do not believe that I may have accomplished what is due towards you."

Imam Ali (as) prayed for him thus: *"O Allah! Illuminate his heart and guide him towards the Right Path. I wish there were a hundred similar to you among my Shi'ah."*

In the same book it is related that at the beginning of Islam, Amr bin Humaq was a keeper of Camels of his tribe. His tribe was under the pledge with Prophet Mohammad (s). Once some of the Prophet's companions passed by him, whom the Prophet (s) had sent to propagate. They had asked the Prophet (s) that they did not have the provisions for their journey nor knew the way. The Prophet replied that, *"On the way you shall meet a handsome man who will feed you, quench your thirst and guide you to the path, and he shall be of the people of Paradise."*

They reached Amr, who fed them with Camel meat and milk, and his coming to the presence of the Prophet (s) and accepting Islam until the caliphate reached Mu'awiya. Then he remained aloof from the people in Zoor in Mosul.

Mu'awiya wrote to him: *"Now then! Allah extinguished the fire of battle and cooled down the mischief, and Allah bestowed success to the pious. You are not distant nor more guilty than your friends, they have bowed down their heads in front of my command and have hastened to assist me in my task. But you still remain withdrawn, thus come to assist me in my task so that your past sins may be forgiven by it and your good deeds which have worned out may ripen. Perhaps I may not be as bad as my predecessors. If you are self-respecting, abstentiuos, obedient and well-behaved, then enter the security of Allah and the Prophet of Allah in my refuge. Cleanse your heart of envy and your soul from rancour. And Allah is a sufficient witness."*

Amr refused to go to Mu'awiya, hence he sent someone who killed him and brought his head to Mu'awiya. They sent his head to his wife, who kept it in her lap, and said, *"For a long time you had kept him away from me, and now you have killed him and have brought him to me as a gift. How fair is this gift which is my pleasure and who also liked me. O messenger! Take my message to Mu'awiya and tell him that Allah will surely take revenge for his blood, and very soon His wrath and woe will hasten. You have committed a grievous crime and killed a devout and pious person. O Messenger! Convey to Mu'awiya, whatever I have said."*

The messenger conveyed her message to Mu'awiya, hence Mu'awiya called the woman to him and inquired of her, *"Did you utter these words?"* She replied that, *"Yes, I have said them, and I do not regret nor am sorry for it."*

Mu'awiya told her to go away from his town, to which she replied that, *"I will surely do so, for your town is not my native place and I consider it to be a prison, which has no place in my heart. Much time has passed when I have not slept herein, while my tears are (constantly) flowing. My debt has increased here, and I have not found anything here which would illuminate my eyes."*

Abdullah bin Abi Sarh Kalbi told Mu'awiya, *"O commander of the faithful! She is a hypocrite woman, let her follow her husband."*

When the woman heard this, she looked towards him and said, *"O you ulcer of a frog! Haven't you killed the one who clothed you with blessings and bestowed a cloak upon you? Indeed you have abandoned the Religion and verily a hypocrite is the one who pursuits unjustly and claims to be one of the servants of Allah, and Allah has condemned his infidelity in the Qur'an."*

Hearing this Mu'awiya ordered his porter to throw her out. She said, *"Astonishment at the son of Hind, who has signalled by his finger and has (tried to) stop me from using a harsh tongue, by Allah! I shall split open his belly with my harsh speech sharp as iron, if not I be Amenah, the daughter of Rasheed."*

Imam Husain (as) in his letter to Mu'awiya wrote: *"Are you not the murderer of Amr bin Humaq, the companion of the Prophet (s), and a devout man, whose body had become slender and whose colour had turned pale due to excessive worship? With what face did you give him (the promise of) security, and promised him in the name of Allah, if similarly it would have been given to a bird, it would have come down from the mountain in your lap. Then you confronted Allah and deemed the promise to be low?"*[162]

---

[162] Nafasul Mahmoom by Sheikh Abbas al-Qummi

Mass Murder & Torturing the Shia of Ali

Mu'awiya sent another circular letter saying: "If any person is suspected of being a supporter of Ahlul Bayt he should be subjected to torture and his house should be demolished". This order was implemented so strictly that as written by Ibn Abil Hadid, the Shi'ah took refuge in the houses of their relatives and friends. Even then they were afraid of their servants and servant-girls lest they should divulge the secret, because if anyone was not on good terms with another, he reported to the authorities that such and such person was a supporter of Ahlul Bayt. The people were, therefore, arrested on mere accusation and suspicion and were tormented and made homeless. This persecution was more severe in Iraq during the rule of Ziyad bin Sumayya as compared with other places. Despite Imam Ali's brilliant past record and the honor enjoyed by him in Islam it was made necessary that, in all the Islamic countries and the areas, which formed part of the territories of Islam, he should be abused and cursed in the sermons of Friday prayers and at other times, and Mu'awiya and Yazid should be honored and praised.

---

[163] The Shrine of the 11th Imam Hassan al-Askari (as) in Samarra, Iraq after the 2006 bombing. It has now been rebuilt, al-hamdu lillah.

Mu'awiya wrote officially to Ziyad bin Sumayya, the Governor of Iraq, that the evidence given in any matter by a person, who was known to be a Shi'ah, should not be accepted, and those, who provided him shelter should also not be treated to be honorable.

Hujr bin Adi, Rashid Hujari and their eleven companions were subjected to the severest persecution and torture, so much so that Mu'awiya killed six of them who were at that time the best persons. There were many, whose hands and feet were amputated, and pins reddened in fire were thrust into their eyes, and some others were buried alive.

The evil propaganda of Mu'awiya and his agents in Syria and other Islamic territories misled the people. Whosoever uttered a word against Mu'awiya was treated to be a murderer of Uthman and shedding his blood was considered lawful. Credulous persons, who are numerous in all ages, and are easily impressed by evil propaganda, came to believe that Uthman's blood was shed without any justification, and those, who were satisfied with this act deserved to be punished.

This was how Mu'awiya and his agents poisoned the public mind. The Khawarij, too, who were inimical towards both Mu'awiya and Imam Ali (as) kept quiet regarding Mu'awiya on account of fear, but abused the Commander of the Faithful openly and treated him to be an infidel. This thing in itself rendered great help to Mu'awiya and created a grudge in the hearts of the people against Imam Ali (as) and his followers, so much so that when on the day of Āshura Imam Hussain (as) mentioned the reason for his coming towards Kufa and then asked his opponents as to why they had gathered to kill him they replied: *"It is due to the grudge, which we have against your father."*[164]

Imam Ali (as) spoke about the Umayyad's in a sermon

---

[164] A Probe into the History of Ashura by Dr. Ibrahim Ayati

from Nahjul Balagha: *"By Allah, they would continue like this till there would be left no unlawful act before Allah but they would make it lawful and no pledge but they would break it, and till there would remain no house of bricks or of woolen tents but their oppression would enter it. Their bad dealings would make them wretched, till two groups of crying complainants would rise, one would cry for his religion and the other for this world and the help of one of you to one of them would be like the help of a servant to his master, namely when he is present he obeys him, but when the master is away he backbites him. The highest among you in distress would be he who bear best belief about Allah. If Allah grants you safety accept it, and if you are put in trouble endure it, because surely (good) result is for the God-fearing."*[165]

In 659 Mu'awiya stepped up his war of nerves against Ali (as) and sent several contingents into Jazirah and Hijaz to terrify people and to destroy their morale. His policy at first was to strike a spark of terror and then to let the fire do the rest but his captains soon changed it into a scene of violence and death. In Jazirah, Ne'man bin Bashir attacked Ain-at-Tamar with 2,000 men; Sufyan bin Auf attacked Anbar and Madaen with 6,000 soldiers; Abdullah bin Masadah Fizari attacked Tima with a force of 1,700; and Zahhak bin Qays and his followers laid waste the township of Waqsa. They killed all those men, women, and children whom they suspected to be friendly to Ali, and they plundered the public treasury wherever they found one.[166]

The acquisition of Egypt immeasurably strengthened Mu'awiya's hands. He then sent units of his army into Hijaz, Jazirah and Iraq. They went around plundering, spreading terror, and killing. Mu'awiya attacked the banks of the Tigris in person

---

[165] Nahjul Balagha sermon 98

[166] Dr. Hamid-ud-Din

and seized the public treasury in Jazirah.[167]

Mu'awiya and his generals had adopted a policy of waging irregular warfare against the successor of the Prophet of Islam and the sovereign of all Muslims. To them irregular warfare meant unconventional warfare; limited conventional military actions, and unlimited terrorism. They plunged the Dar-ul-Islam into a trauma from which it has never recovered.

In 660, Mu'awiya sent Bisr bin Artat with 3,000 soldiers to Hijaz and Yemen on a rampage of pillaging, destroying, burning and killing. In Yemen, Bisr killed with his own hands, the infant twins of Obaidullah ibn Abbas who was the governor of that province. When he returned to Syria, gorged on innocent blood, tens of thousands of Muslims had been killed.

One of the governors of Ali (as) in a frontier district, was Kumayl ibn Ziyad. He sought his master's permission to raid Syria. Such raids into Syria, he said, would compel Mu'awiya to halt his own raids into Hijaz and Iraq. But his application drew forth a characteristic reply from Ali (as) who wrote to him: *"I hardly expected you to suggest that we raid the towns and villages in Syria. It is true that the Syrians are our enemies, but they are also human beings, and what's more, they are Muslims. If we send raiding parties into Syria, it is most probable that the victims of our punitive action will not be the Syrian marauders who violate our borders but the Syrian civil population - the non-combatant folks. Is it therefore right and fair to plunder and to kill them for the crimes they did not commit? No. They will not pay the penalty for the crimes of their leaders. The best thing for us to do, therefore, is to strengthen our own defenses against the enemy, and to rout him before he can do any harm to our people."*

The dominant logic of "mirror image" of matching terror with terror did not appeal to Ali; he considered is basically

---
[167] History of Islam, Lahore, Pakistan, p. 204, 1971

fallacious. Though Ali (as) drove the intruders out of his dominions, law and order had broken down. The Syrian's began to violate the frontier with growing frequency. Bisr bin Artat defeated the small garrison defending the strategic town of Anbar and occupied it. He then put the whole population to the sword as was customary with him.

Ali (as) called upon the Iraqi's to stand up in defense of their homes against the Syrian's but found them unresponsive. In winter they said that it was too cold to go on a campaign, and in summer they said that it was too hot. Many Iraqi leaders were still working for Muwaiya in return for his gifts and promises, and they spread disaffection in the country. Mu'awiya also worked hard to undermine the allegiance to Ali (as) of the Iraqi army. For him, conflict was not limited to the operation of armies, but was carried on behind the front by his agents and partisans, by subversion and sabotage, and by propaganda and indoctrination.

Since there was no punitive action against them, the Syrian marauders were emboldened to penetrate deeper and deeper into Iraq.

Ali (as) made many attempts to shake the Iraqi's out of their lethargy but they acted as if the Syrian raids were not hurting them. Their head-in-the-sand attitude so exasperated him that he told them that if they did not obey his orders, and take up arms to defend their borders, he would abandon them in Kufa, and with the handful of loyal followers he still had with him, would go and try to stop the enemy, regardless of the consequences.

This threat appears to have worked. The Iraqi's suddenly realized that if Ali (as) abandoned them, they would be left leaderless. They, therefore, assured him that they would obey him - in peace and in war.

Ali (as) immediately set to work to reorganize the army, and to mobilize fresh troops. He summoned Abdullah ibn Abbas from Basra, and he ordered other leaders and their troops to assemble in the camp at Nukhayla near Kufa.

Ali (as) had plunged into work to make up for time already lost through the earlier tardiness of the Iraqis in obeying his orders. But this new spurt of energy alarmed his enemies, and they plunged into intrigue to forestall him.

Ali (as) had completed his preparations for an invasion of Syria but just when he was giving finishing touches to his logistical plans, he was assassinated in the Great Mosque of Kufa at the dawn of Ramadan 19 of 40 A.H. (January 27, 661).[168]

We also condemn Abu Huraira for his collusion with Busr Ibn Artat in the massacre of thousands of Muslims. It has been reported by the Sunni historians, including Tabari, Ibn Athir, Ibn Abi'l-Hadid, Allama Samhudi, Ibn Khaldun, Ibn Khallikan, and others that Mu'awiya Ibn Abu Sufyan sent the cruel Busr Ibn Artat with 4,000 Syrian soldiers to Yemen via Medina to crush the people of Yemen and the Shias of Ali. The assailants murdered thousands of Muslims in Medina, Mecca, Ta'if, Tabala' (a city of Tihama), Najran, Safa, and its suburbs. They did not spare the young or old of the Bani Hashim or the Shias of Ali. They even murdered the two small sons of the Holy Prophet's cousin, Ubaidullah Bin Abbas, the governor of Yemen, who had been appointed by Ali. It is said that more than 30,000 Muslims were killed on the order of this tyrant. The Bani Umayya and their followers committed these insane atrocities. The Sunni's beloved Abu Huraira witnessed this slaughter and was not only silent but actively supported it. Innocent people, like Jabir bin Abdullah Ansari, and Abu Ayyub Ansari sought refuge. Even the house of Abu Ayyub Ansari, who was one of the Prophet's chief companions, was set on fire. When this army turned towards Mecca, Abu Huraira remained in Medina.

Now I ask you to tell us, in the name of Allah, whether

---

[168] The Restatement of the History of Islam and Muslims by Sayed Razwy

this deceitful man who had been in the company of the Holy Prophet (s) for three years, and who narrated more than 5,000 hadith from the Prophet (s), had not heard those famous hadith regarding Medina. The ulema of both the sects[169] have quoted from the Holy Prophet (s), who said repeatedly: *"He who threatens the people of Medina with oppression will be threatened by Allah and will be cursed by Allah, by His angels, and by humanity. Allah will not accept anything from him. May he be cursed who threatens the people of Medina. If anyone harms the people of Medina, Allah will melt him like lead in fire."*

So why did Abu Huraira join the army which devastated Medina? Why did he fabricate hadith in opposition to the rightful successor to the Prophet? And why did he incite people to revile the man about whom the Prophet (s) had said: *"To abuse him is to abuse me"?* You decide whether a man who fabricated hadith in the name of the Prophet (s) was not cursed.

Many notable ulema[170] have written that Mu'awiya ordered Busr to attack San'a, Yemen from Medina and Mecca. He gave a similar order to Zuhak Bin Qais Al-Fahri and others. Abu'l-Faraj reports it in these words: *"Whoever from the companions and Shia of Ali is found should be killed; even women and children should not be spared."*

With these strict orders, they set out with a force of 3,000 and attacked Medina, San'a', Yemen, Ta'if, and Najran. When they reached Yemen, the governor, Ubaidullah Ibn Abbas, was out of the city. They entered his house and slaughtered his two sons Sulayman and Dawud in the lap of their mother.

---

[169] like Allama Samhudi in Ta'rikhu'l-Medina, Ahmad Bin Hanbal in Musnad, Sibt Ibn Jauzi in Tadhkira, page 163

[170] Abu'l-Faraj Ispahani and Allama Samhudi in Ta'rikhu'l-Medina, Ibn Khallikan, Ibn Asakir and Tabari in their histories; Ibn Abi'l-Hadid in Sharh-e-Nahju'l-Balagha, vol.I, and many others of notable ulema

Ibn Abi'l-Hadid writes in his *Sharh-e-Nahju'l-Balagha*, vol.I, p.121, that in this raid 30,000 people were killed, excluding those who were burnt alive.

Allah says: *"And whoever kills a believer intentionally, his punishment is Hell; he shall abide in it, and Allah will send His wrath on him and curse him and prepare for him a painful chastisement."*[171]

This Holy verse explicitly says that if a man kills a single believer intentionally, he deserves Allah's curse, and his abode is in Hell. Wasn't Mu'awiya associated with the murder of believers? Did he not order the killing of Hajar Ibn Adi and his seven companions? Did he not order that Abdu'r-Rahman Bin Hassan Al-Ghanzi be buried alive?

Many Sunni scholars[172] have reported that Hajar Bin Adi was one of the eminent companions who, along with seven companions was brutally murdered by Mu'awiya. Their crime was refusing to curse Ali.

Imam Hassan (as) was the elder grandson of the Holy Prophet (s). Was he not included in *Ashab-e-Kisa* (people of the mantle)? Was he not one of the two leaders of the youths of Paradise and a believer of exalted rank? According to the reports[173], Mu'awiya sent poison to Asma' Ju'da and promised her that if she killed Hassan Ibn Ali (as), he would give her 100,000 dirhams and would marry her to his son Yazid. After the martyrdom of Imam Hassan (as), he gave her 100,000 dirhams but refused to marry her to Yazid. Would you hesitate to call Mu'awiya accursed? Is it not a fact that in the Battle of Siffin the

---

[171] Quran 4:93

[172] Ibn Asakir and Yaqub Bin Sufyan in their Histories; Baihaqi in his *Dala'il*; Ibn Abdu'l-Bar in *Isti'ab*; and Ibn Athir in *Kamil*

[173] of Mas'udi, Ibn Abdu'l-Bar, Abu'l-Faraj Ispahani, Tabaqa of Muhammad Bin Sa'd, Tadhkira of Sibt Ibn Jauzi, and other accredited ulema of the Sunnis.

great companion of the Holy Prophet (s), Ammar Yasir, was martyred by Mu'awiya's order? All the prominent ulema say with one accord that the Holy Prophet (s) said to Ammar Yasir: *"It will not be long before you will be killed by a rebellious and misguided group."*

Have you any doubt that thousands of devout believers were killed by Mu'awiya's subordinates? Wasn't the pure and valiant warrior, Malik Ashtar, poisoned by Mu'awiya's order? Can you deny that Mu'awiya's chief officials, Amr bin al-Aas and Mu'awiya Bin Khadij, brutally martyred the Commander of the Faithful's governor, the pious Muhammad Bin Abi Bakr? Not content with that, they put his body into the carcass of a donkey and set it on fire.

If I were to give you the details about the believers killed by Mu'awiya and his officials, it would require not one night, but several. Do you gentlemen still doubt that Mu'awiya deserves to be cursed?![174]

Slaying Shi'a Muslims had begun since Imam 'Ali's term. After Imam's forces dispersed and there was no security found but in Iraq, Mu'awiya deployed his troops along with some envoys to various areas among whom were Busr Ibn Artat, Sufyan Ibn 'Awf Ghamidi and Dhahhak Ibn Qays. Their responsibility in cities was to trace and, "Kill any Shi'a they noticed at Mu'awiya's behest."

Busr set out to Medina where he killed many of 'Ali's disciples and enthusiasts and demolished their houses as well. He then went to Mecca and Sarat respectively and slayed any Shi'a Muslim he discovered. Ultimately, he left there for Najran and martyred 'Abd Allah Ibn 'Abd al-Muddan as well as his son. Earlier we presented a profile of his crimes.

Among areas that Busr passed en route and plundered

---

[174] Peshawar Nights by Sultanul Waizin Shirazi

was an area the residents of which were from the tribe of Hamdan, 'Ali's Shi'a Muslims. Ambushing them, Busr killed numerous men and captured a number of women and children. For the ever-first time Muslim women and children were captured. These measures were once again adopted later in Karbala. About Busr, Mas'udi has written that he slayed a number from the tribes of Khuza'a and Hamdan together with a group known as al-Abna' (from Persian race) in Yemen. He killed anyone of whose attachment to 'Ali he heard.

Setting out to Anbar, 'Awf Ibn Sufyan martyred Ibn Hassan al-Bakri in addition to Shi'as men and women.

After Hassan Ibn 'Ali (as) had to compromise with Mu'awiya, one of the menaces the Imam felt was the security of 'Ali's Shi'a Muslims. Hence it was stipulated within the contract that 'Ali's disciples should be all endowed with security. Although Mu'awiya had conceded it, immediately on the same day he announced that he would disregard the entire commitments.

Mu'awiya's Governor of Kufa, Ziyad's main mission was to suppress the Shi'a Muslims of Kufa throughout Iraq.

"He was always seeking after Shi'a Muslims and anywhere tracing he slayed them," Ibn A'tham said.

The first measure taken by Ziyad was cutting off the hands of those (nearly eighty) who were not convinced to swear allegiance to him. Ziyad's harsh treatment in Basra, with a group of the Kharijites in addition to Shi'a Muslims, was proverbial. He had declared a kind of martial law in Basra. At nights, following the night prayer, the opportunity people had for staying outdoors was as long as reciting the Sura (chapter) of The Cow. During the curfew, Ziyad's soldiers slayed anyone they traced. Historians have introduced Ziyad as the ever-first one who drew his sword to people, arrested them by accusing them and chastized them with suspicion.

Among the Shi'a Muslims martyred by Ziyad were Muslim Ibn Zaymur and 'Abd Allah Ibn Nuja who were both from the tribe of Had'ram. In a letter to Mu'awiya succeeding Hujr's martyrdom, Imam Hussain (as) had commemorated their martyrdom too. He cut off the limbs of people and blinded them. Mu'awiya himself murdered a great number as well.

Elsewhere it has been written that Mu'awiya had issued the verdict of executing a group of Shi'a Muslims. Ziyad assembled Shi'a Muslims in a mosque in order to make them express loathing for 'Ali. He also searched for Shi'a Muslims in Basra to kill.

In a letter Imam Hassan (as) objected to Mu'awiya in this regard. Treating the same way, Samura Ibn Jundab, a substitute for him in Basra, had allegedly augmented the number of orphans in Basra and massacred nearly 8,000 people until Ziyad objected.

Although the accuracy of the above-mentioned figures is not definite, it manifests a profile of their atrocities. Ziyad's treatment towards 'Ali's friends was unjust, in a real sense exactly the same as that of 'Abd Allah Ibn 'Amir, Mu'awiya's another governor. Nu'man Ibn Bashir, ex-governor of this area, on account of his acute rancor to dwellers of Kufa did not even want to obey Mu'awiya's order to increase their provisions from Bayt al-Mal (public treasury).

Under the guise of a peace-seeking character, Mu'awiya had commanded Ziyad to decimate anyone at 'Ali's religion. *"Kill anyone amongst you who is from 'Ali's Shi'a Muslims or accused of his amity",* he wrote to his agents, *"and for it find evidence even hidden under the rocks even though it was solely an assumption. Exclude the name of the one for whose amity to 'Ali you found any proof from Bayt al-Mal and discontinue his provision."* He then wrote in conclusion, *"Kill anyone from among yourselves who is accused of having devotion to 'Ali and demolish his house as well."*

Ibn Abi l-Hadid has also written that as far as Ziyad was well acquainted with Shi'a Muslims, *"He massacred them all anywhere whom he noticed, intimidated them, cut off their limbs, blinded them, hung them from tree branches and banished them."*[175]

---

[175] History of The Caliphs From the Death of the Messenger (S), to the Decline of the 'Umayyad Dynasty 11-132 AH by Rasul Ja'fariyan

Martyrdom of Imam Hassan (as) & His Burial Met with Arrows

While he was still only viceroy of Syria Mu'awiya created a strong material base for himself, his kin and his military following, becoming a very big landlord by large-scale seizure of land. The Umayyad Caliph Mu'awiya rested on far stronger economic foundations and possessed more trustworthy armed forces than his political opponents. He had become the all-powerful permanent viceroy of the rich and civilized Syria as early as the days of Omar and having spent more than twenty years in this important post, became the recognized leader of Arab tribal aristocracy in Syria.[176]

It was in this manner that Mu'awiya, the political phoenix of the Arabs, rose from the ashes of a failed effort to restore a pagan past, to become, first the arch-rival of Ali ibn Abi Talib,

---

[176] *Arabs, Islam and the Arab Caliphate in the Early Middle Ages, 1969*

the successor of the Prophet (s), and then to become the successor himself!

Mu'awiya was a man of many innovations. He changed khilafat into monarchy, and openly boasted: "I am the first of the Arab kings." Monarchy, of course, must be hereditary, and it had to be hereditary in his family. He, therefore, made Yazid, his son, his successor. Even those Muslim's who either condoned or connived at his crimes, winced when he struck this blow for his family.

The designation by Mu'awiya of his son, Yazid, as khalifa, was a flagrant breach of the pledge he had given to Hassan ibn Ali (as) not to appoint his own successor. But Mu'awiya was not the man to be inhibited by any pledge or code of ethics. Ethics in his hands became the first casualty.

Mu'awiya, however, was aware that Muslims would not willingly accept Yazid as their khalifa. He, therefore, silenced opposition with gold and silver or with bluff and threats. But if these weapons failed, then he employed a subtle, secret, and fail-safe weapon – poison. He was a "pioneer" in Muslim history in the art of silencing his critics and opponents forever through poison. Anticipating opposition from Hassan (as) to Yazid's succession, he engineered his death. The historian, Masoodi, writes: *"Mu'awiya sent word to Jo'dah bint Ash'ath, the wife of Hassan, that if she would kill her husband, he would pay her 100,000 dirhams, and would marry his son, Yazid, to her."*

Mu'awiya awakened in Jo'dah the ambition to become a queen, and when he sent the poison to her, as it was arranged between them, she administered it to her husband, and he died from it. Mu'awiya rewarded her by paying 100,000 dirhams but backed out of his promise to marry her to Yazid by saying: *"I love my son."*[177]

---

[177] The Restatement of the History of Islam and Muslims by Sayed Razwy

Many scholars of the Sunni sect[178] have reported that Asma Ju'da, by order and promise of Mu'awiya, gave poison to Abu Muhammad Hassan Ibn Ali (as). Ibn Abdu'l-Bar and Muhammad Bin Jarir Tabari have also reported that when Mu'awiya was informed of the demise of the Imam, he shouted the *takbir*.

'Aisha's Preventing the Burial of Imam Hassan, the Grandson of the Prophet (s)

Some members of 'Aisha's own family wished she had never led armies and fought battles. On one occasion, she sent a

---

[178] Abu'l-Faraj Ispahani in his Maqatilu't-Talibin, Ibn Abdu'l-Bar in his Isti'ab, Mas'udi in his Isbatu'l-Wasiyya, and many other ulema

messenger to her nephew, Ibn Abil-Ateeq, asking him to send his mule to her for riding. When her nephew received the message, he said to the messenger: *"Tell the mother of believers that by God, we have not washed the stains of the bloodshed in the battle of the camel yet. Does she now want to start a battle of the mule?"*[179]

Ibn Abil Ateeq's remark was prompted in jest. But in 669 the day actually came when 'Aisha rode a mule in another "campaign." When the coffin of Imam Hassan (as) was brought to the mausoleum of his grandfather, Muhammad Mustafa, for burial, Marwan bin al-Hakam and other members of the Banu Ummaya appeared on the scene, in battledores. They were going to prevent the Banu Hashim from burying Imam Hassan (as) beside his grandfather. The Umayyads were not alone; 'Aisha came with them, riding a mule!

'Aisha may have lost the battle in Basra but she "won" the "battle" in Medina. Hassan (as) could not be buried with his grandfather because of her and Umayyad opposition, and he was buried in the cemetery of Jannat-ul-Baqi. [180]

We have discussed how she vexed the Holy Prophet (s) and how she subsequently went into battle mounted on a camel to fight against his successor. But later, this time mounted on a mule she stopped the corpse of the elder grandson of the Holy Prophet (s) from moving ahead for burial near the Holy Prophet (s). The sunni eminent ulema and historians[181], have written that

---

[179] *Baladhuri in Ansab al-Ashraf, vol. I, page 431*

[180] The Restatement of the History of Islam and Muslims by Sayed Razwy

[181] Including Yusuf Sibt Ibn Jauzi in his Tadhkira Khawasu'l-Umma, p.122; Allama Mas'udi, author of Muruju'z-Dhahab, in Isbatu'l-Wasiyya, p.136; Ibn Abi'l-Hadid in Sharh-e-Nahju'l-Balagha, vol. IV, p.18, reporting from Abu'l-Faraj and Yahya Bin Hassan, author of Kitabu'n-Nasab; Muhammad Khwawind Shah in his Rauzatu's-Safa, and many others.

when the corpse of Imam Hassan (as) was being transported to Medina, 'Aisha, mounted on a mule and accompanied by a group of the Bani Umayya and their servants, stopped the group with Imam Hassan's body. They said that they would not let Imam Hassan (as) be buried by the side of the Holy Prophet (s).

According to the report of Mas'udi, Ibn Abbas said: *"It is strange of you, 'Aisha! Was not the Day of Jamal, that is, your entering the battlefield mounted on a camel, sufficient for you? Now should the people also keep in memory the Day of Baghl (mule)? Mounted on a mule, you have stopped the bier of the son of the Holy Prophet (s). One day mounted on a camel, another mounted on a mule, you have torn asunder the modesty of the Holy Prophet (s). Are you determined to destroy the Light of Allah? But surely Allah perfects His light however unpleasant it is to the polytheists; verily, we are Allah's and to Him shall we return."*

Some people have written that Ibn Abbas said to her: *"One time you mounted a camel and one time a mule. If you live longer, you will also mount an elephant (that is you will fight against Allah)! Though out of one-eighth you have one-ninth share, yet you took possession of the whole."*

The Bani Hashim drew their swords and intended to drive them away. But Imam Hussain (as) intervened and said that his brother had told him that he did not want a drop of blood to be spilled because of his funeral procession. Accordingly, the body was taken back from there and buried in Baqi' (a cemetery in Medina)[182]

---

[182] Peshawar Nights by Sultanul Waizin Shirazi

Martyrdom of Zaid ibn Ali and His Son Yahya ibn Zaid

The Zaidi's follow Zaid Bin Ali Bin Hussain. They consider the 4th Imam Zainu'l-Abidin's son, Zaid, to be his successor. At present these people are found in large numbers in Yemen and its surroundings. They believe that of the descendants of Ali (as) and Fatima (as), he is the Imam who is learned, pious, and brave. He draws the sword and rises against the enemy.

During the time of the oppressive Umayyad Caliph, Hisham bin Abdu'l-Malik, Zaid rose against those in authority and courted martyrdom and was therefore acknowledged as Imam by the Zaidi's.

The fact is that Zaid possessed a far higher position than that which the Zaidi's claim for him. He was a great Sayyid of the Hashimi dynasty, and was known for his piety, wisdom, prayers, and bravery. He passed many sleepless nights in prayer and fasted frequently. The Prophet (s) prophesied his martyrdom, as narrated by Imam Hussain (as): *"The Holy Prophet put his sacred hand on my back and said: 'O Hussain, it will not be long until a man will be born among your descendants. He will be called Zaid; he will be killed as a martyr. On the day of resurrection, he and his companions will enter heaven, setting their feet on the necks of the people.'"*

Zaid himself never claimed to be an Imam. It is sheer slander for people to say that he did. In fact, he recognized Muhammad Baqir as the Imam and pledged his full obedience to him. It was only after Muhammad Baqir's demise that unknowing people adopted the doctrine that "he is not the Imam who remains sitting at home and hides himself from the people; the Imam is one who is a descendant of Fatima (as), an Alim, and who draws the sword and rises against the enemy and invites people to his side."

Historians of both Shias and Sunnis recorded that when Hisham bin Abdu'l-Malik became the caliph, he committed many atrocities. Regarding the Bani Hashim, he was particularly cruel.

At last, Zaid bin Ali, the son of Imam Zainu'l-Abidin (as) and well known as a great scholar and a pious theologian, went to see the caliph to seek redress for the grievances of the Bani Hashim. But as soon as Zaid arrived, the caliph, instead of greeting him as a direct descendant of the Holy Prophet (s), abused him with such abominable language that I cannot repeat it. Because of this disgraceful treatment, Zaid left Syria for Kufa, where he raised an army against the Bani Umayyad. The governor of Kufa, Yusuf bins Umar Thaqafi, came out with a huge army to face him. Zaid recited the following war poem: *"Disgraceful life and honorable death: both are bitter morsels, but if one of them must be chosen, my choice is honorable death."*

Although he fought bravely, Zaid was killed in the battle. His son, Yahya, took his body from the field and buried him away from the city near the riverbank, causing the water to flow over it. However, the grave was discovered, and under Yusuf's orders, the body was exhumed, Zaid's head was cut off and sent to Hisham in Syria. In the month of Safar, 121 A.H., Hisham had the sacred body of this descendant of the Prophet (s) placed on the gallows entirely naked. For four years the sacred body remained on the gallows. Thereafter, when Walid Bin Yazid bin Abdu'l-Malik bin Marwan became caliph in 126 A.H., he ordered that the skeleton be taken down from the gallows, burnt, and the ashes scattered to the wind.

This accursed man committed a similar atrocity to the body of Yahya bin Zaid of Gurgan. This noble man also opposed the oppression of the Bani Umayya. He too was martyred on the battlefield. His head was sent to Syria and, as in the case of his revered father, his body was hung on the gallows - for six years.

Friend and foe alike wept at the sight. Waliu'd-din Abu Muslim Khorasani, who had risen against the Bani Umayya on behalf of Bani Abbas, took his body down and buried it in Gurgan, where it is a place of pilgrimage.[183]

---

[183] Peshawar Nights by Sultanul Waizin Shirazi

Martyrdom of Muslim ibn Aqil, His Sons and Hanee ibn Orwah

Pin-drop silence prevailed in the mosque at Kufa where a large congregation had gathered to offer evening prayers. Outside the mosque the town crier was reading out the proclamation. Every one of the congregation was straining his ears to listen to every word with rapt attention.

At the top of his voice the town-crier was shouting: *"Be it known to the people of Kufa that Obeidullah, son of Ziad, has assumed the governorship of Kufa under the orders of the Khalif Yazid ibn Mu'awiya. He has noted with perturbation that the people of Kufa have extended their welcome to Muslim, son of Aqil, who has come from Medina as an emissary of Hussain, son of Ali, who has declined to owe allegiance to the Khalif. It is hereby proclaimed for the information of all the citizens of Kufa that any person found associating with Muslim, son of Aqil, will be considered a rebel against the Khalif and, by way of punishment, he will be hanged, drawn, and quartered, his entire family will be put to the sword and his property confiscated. In case of those who have hither to extend their welcome to him, if they now repent and desist from doing so, amnesty will be given."*

With bated breath everyone listened to the proclamation. It was this same Muslim, son of Aqil, who was to lead the prayers that evening, and as the proclamation ended, he arose to fulfill his duty. A few exchanged enquiring glances with their friends. Some others whispered some words to their neighbours. At this moment the call for prayers was given and Muslim silently rose to lead the congregational prayers.

When Muslim completed the prayers and turned back, he found the mosque empty, except for one person only Hanee Ibne Orwah at whose house Muslim was staying as a guest. The two looked at each other. No words were needed to tell Muslim why the people of Kufa had deserted him. The people of Kufa, who had so persistently asked Hussain (as) to come over to them and take up the responsibilities of their spiritual amelioration, had on hearing the proclamation, got scared out of their wits. These were the people who had in the past betrayed Muslim's Uncle Ali, the Commander of the Faithful, and shown cowardice in times of trouble and tribulations. These were the people who had deserted Muslim's cousin, Hassan (as), son of Ali (as), in his hour of need.

Muslim stood for a while motionless. His face was full of anguish. He was not dismayed at the fate that awaited him, because a fighting death was the heritage of his family. He was only disconsolate at the thought that he had reposed confidence in these people's sincerity and written to his cousin, Hussain (as), to come over to Kufa as their moral, mental, and spiritual preceptor, to save them from sinking into the depths of moral degradation. How he wished he had not been hasty about judging these people.

A moment's reflection was sufficient to make up his

mind. At least there was one man with him who could be relied upon. If he could only send a message to Hussain (as) through Hanee Ibne Orwah about the treachery of the people of Kufa!

With these thoughts Muslim turned towards Hanee. Before he could give expression to his thoughts, Hanee Ibne Orwah anticipated his words. In low whispers he said: *"Muslim, my respected guest, I know what is uppermost in your mind. If God enable me to leave this cursed town in time, I shall rush post-haste to warn our master and Imam to turn back."*

He hung his head down and, in a tone which was hardly audible, added, as if muttering to himself: *"Muslim, my duty towards you as your host demands that I should remain here to protect you and shed the last drop of my blood in your defence. But I know that you would like me to attend to the higher duty that we both owe to our master, Hussain ibn Ali. There is hardly time to be lost and so I bid you farewell. May Almighty God protect you and your innocent sons from the fury of these treacherous fiends."*

Hanee Ibne Orwah rushed out of the Mosque. He knew that he had to act quickly, if at all he was to succeed in his mission. Before leaving Kufa he had to do something for the safety of the two young sons of Muslim who had not yet reached their teens. He was quickly revolving in his mind how he could hide these innocent boys and where. He could not think of anybody known to him who could be trusted to give shelter to them. He hardly had any time at his disposal to make arrangements because his paramount obligation was to convey Muslim's message to Imam Hussain (as). His quick-working mind decided that the children of Muslim must be warned to get out of the house where they were no longer safe and leave the rest to God.

On reaching his house, Hanee asked his wife to whisk the children out of the house by the back door for their safety. He asked his servant to harness his horse as quickly as he could.

Hardly Muhammad and Ibrahim, the young sons of Muslim, had been put on the road to face the world and its turmoils in a strange and unfriendly city, the house of Hanee was surrounded by armed troopers sent by Obeidullah. Hanee realized that the hope he had cherished to leave the town and carry the message of Muslim to Hussain (as) was completely frustrated. He unsheathed his sword and fell upon the hirelings of Obeidullah with the intention of selling his life as dearly as he could. The odds against him were too heavy. He was soon overpowered and chained and marched off to the court of the Governor.

After Hanee's departure from the Mosque, Muslim reflected for a while. At first his mind was put at ease by Hanee's assurance that he would carry the warning to Hussain (as) about the happenings in Kufa. But on second thoughts he realized that there was every possibility of Hanee being captured before he could leave the town. What if that happened? He had fullest confidence in Hanee's sincerity, but how could he be so sure that Hanee would be able to make good his escape from Kufa? Although Muslim was fully alive to the lot that would befall his innocent sons on their capture, he realized that the right course for him was to find some other person whom he could trust to carry the message to the Imam. Kneeling in prayer he muttered: *"Merciful Allah, spare me for a while so that I can send the warning to my Imam."*

He came out of the mosque slowly. He did not know which way to turn he only knew that the whole town had turned hostile to him. As soon as he stepped out of the mosque, he saw groups of people collected here and there and engaged in animated conversation. On seeing him coming out they scattered and walked away as if they had never known him. Muslim realized that they were, one and all, mortally afraid of the reprisals that would befall them if they stood by him. Now he saw how difficult it was for him to find a single person who could fulfill his purpose; where to look for him, where to find him?

With a heavy heart Muslim was now trudging the narrow by-lanes of Kufa. The sun was fast descending and the dark narrow lanes of Kufa becoming darker every moment. Making a hood of his gown, to cover his head to avoid identification, Muslim was walking on and on, almost aimlessly ambling. The deserted cobbled pavements were echoing his footsteps. The only other sound to be heard was of the horses' hoofs as the soldiers were patrolling the streets and searching for him in all nooks and corners. Whilst walking aimlessly he was furiously thinking how to find someone who could carry his message to Hussain (as).

Soon darkness descended on the whole town. As curfew had been imposed by the orders of the Governor, not a soul was venturing out. It became evident to Muslim that, if he walked on there was every possibility of his being arrested by the patrolmen and, if that happened, his last hope of finding a messenger would vanish. The events of the day had made him tired in body and soul.

He sat on the doorstep of a house, hesitating whether to knock at the door and ask for water. Whilst he was still wavering, he heard the opening of the door against which he was leaning. An old lady stood there with a flickering candle in her hands. From her enquiring eyes he could understand that she was wondering why he was seated there. Muslim turned to her and requested a glass of water. She asked him to wait for a minute and, going into the house, returned with a tumbler of water. Muslim drank it to the last drop and thanked the lady profusely. He again sat down on the doorstep. The old lady looked at him for a while and then asked him: *"My son, why do you not return to your house? Do you realize how your wife and children must be worrying about you by your remaining away from the house in such troubled atmosphere? Don't you have a house with wife and children?"*

A lump came into Muslim's throat with the recollection of his family and home. Controlling his emotions and checking the tears which were gushing from his eyes he said: *"Good lady, I have a house, but in a distant land. My wife and young daughters are at home and my sons are in Kufa but perhaps they will wait for me forever."* After a brief pause, he added: *"In this unfriendly town I have no home and nobody to whom I can turn for shelter."*

These words of despondency moved the lady. Sympathetically she said: *"From where do you come and why are you here in these troubled times?"*

Muslim murmured in reply: *"I am from the city of the Prophet. I came on the invitation of the people of Kufa as their guest. Though thousands welcomed me on my arrival, there is now not a soul who will admit me into his house."*

The venerable old lady was taken aback by this reply. She raised the candle she was carrying to bring it nearer Muslim's face. With an exclamation of recognition, she bent down on her knees and said: *"My God, you are Muslim, the emissary of my Imam, my beloved Hussain, who is hunted by Obeidullah's soldiers. How did I not recognize you at the first glance when your words, your accent, your demeanor, all had the stamp of people of the Prophet's House?"* Sobbing bitterly and overcome by contrition she added, *"How will I face my Lady Fatima on the day of reckoning when she will ask me: "Taha, my Hussain's emissary came to you, friendless and shelterless, but you callously and relentlessly turned him out!" What reply will I give to her? The least that I can do for you is to give you shelter in my house till an opportunity arises for you to make good your escape from this cursed city whose people are steeped in treachery."*

Muslim felt reluctant to accept her offer for fear that the god-fearing old lady might be victimized for giving him protection. But on second thoughts he decided to stay in her house with the hope that, if he could avoid arrest for some time, he might be able to find someone to carry his message to Hussain (as).

Taha asked Muslim to remain in the attic of the house. She gave him whatever food there was in the house, but he could hardly partake of anything. How can a person in his predicament relish food? He decided to pass the night in prayers as he had a premonition that this would be his last night.

Before retiring into the attic, Muslim told Taha about his desire to send a message to the Imam not to come to Kufa in view of what had transpired. She assured him that when her son, who was in the Government armed forces, returned from his beat, she would take him in her confidence and enlist his support in finding some reliable person for this mission.

Hardly a few hours had passed when Taha's son returned home. He looked tired and worn out. When Taha enquired from him the reason for his coming home so late, he told her that, along with other soldiers he was patrolling the streets in search of Muslim. She was aghast at the thought that her son, of all people, should be in the party searching for Muslim, when she herself was so devoted to the House of the Prophet (s). She strongly protested to her son at the role he was playing. That cunning man turned round and assured his mother that, though he had in the course of his duty to pretend as if he was searching for Muslim, in reality he was as much devoted to Muslim, and the House of the Prophet (s), as she was. His disingenuous assurances carried conviction to the simple old lady and, after making him swear by his faith; she took her son into confidence and told him everything about the happenings of that evening.

The crafty son of Taha was inwardly elated at the thought that he would be able to collect the prize placed on Muslim's head. His first thought was to behead Muslim achieved in his sleep but, coward that he was, he got scared at the fate that would befall him if Muslim would wake up before he accomplished his purpose. He thought furiously for a few moments and then decided to go and inform Obeidullah Ibn

Ziyad that he had Muslim in his house, and he could be easily captured. His warped mind quickly invented an excuse for going out in the dead of night, without arousing the suspicions of his noble mother. He told her that, as in his presence, Hanee Ibn Orwah, at whose house Muslim and his two sons had been staying, had been beheaded and as the two young boys were roaming the streets of Kufa, he thought it his bounden duty to search for them and bring them home so that the father and sons could be reunited. He told Taha that he would also see one of his trusted friends and through him arrange to convey Muslim's message to the Imam for which he was so anxious. Taha was taken in by the guiles of her perfidious son. She felt elated that her son was so keen to do the good work that he could not wait till daybreak.

The avaricious son of Taha hastened to the Governor's house and lost no time in getting himself admitted to his presence. In fact, Obeidullah was awake waiting for the news of Muslim's arrest as he was mighty afraid that, if Muslim remained at large, he might succeed in rallying round him a few persons who could offer very stiff opposition to his forces and even upset his ugly plans. He felt relieved and overjoyed at the tidings brought to him by Taha's treacherous son. He immediately ordered one of the commanders of his forces to get together a well-equipped contingent for Muslim's arrest.

Accompanied by mounted soldiers, the traitor returned to his house for Muslim's arrest. Muslim was at that time engaged in prayers. When he heard the beating of several horses' hoofs on the paved roads, he understood that the soldiers had come for his arrest. He snatched his sword which was lying by his side and rushed out. Taha stood at the threshold of her house flabbergasted to see that her son had brought the soldiers for the arrest of her revered guest. She fell on Muslim's feet and cried: *"Muslim, my prince, how can I explain to you that I have not betrayed you but my cursed son, whom I trusted and never suspected of such blatant treachery, has ruined me. I shall not let them cross my threshold except over my dead body."*

Muslim did not require to be told that Taha's averments were sincere. He gently told her, *"My benefactor, I know that you have been very kind and considerate to me and the thought of betraying me cannot even cross your noble and pious mind. I do not in the least blame you for the treachery of your son. As your guest, who has partaken of your hospitality, I cannot allow you to be killed by these merciless brutes and let your house be reduced to a shambles. Let me go out of the house and sell my life as dearly as I can."*

Muslim gently pushed aside Taha from the threshold and walked out sword in hand. By this time the soldiers had reached the house. They were taken by surprise at seeing Muslim emerging from the door like an enraged lion. The lane was so narrow that two horses could not come up abreast. This gave Muslim the best opportunity for single combat. Though he was on foot and the soldier opposite to him was mounted, he possessed the prowess which was the heritage of Ali's family. One after the other the soldiers were tasting the sword of this warrior and falling down from their horses. In the process they were getting crushed and trampled under the hoofs of horses of their own men.

The leader of the band of soldiers, who had discreetly kept himself behind his men, sent word for more men. Though more and more soldiers were pouring in, the topography of the scene of this street battle was such that they could not attack en masse. Heads of enemy soldiers were falling like nine-pins. Hours passed but still Muslim was fighting his defensive battle most courageously.

When Obeidullah Ibne Ziad's couriers, who were bringing to him the news of the fight, informed him that Muslim was giving a fight the like of which had not been seen since the days of Ali, the Khalif, he got infuriated. He tauntingly asked his generals how many thousands of warriors they needed to capture one solitary person. One of them angrily retorted to him that he was forgetting that the person to be captured was not an ordinary home-keeping youth or shopkeeper but a renowned warrior of the House of Ali. He even suggested that if Obeidullah had no confidence in the generals, he could himself demonstrate his skill with the sword by offering combat to Muslim. This suggestion scared the wits out of Obeidullah. He, of all people, knew what it meant to cross swords with Ali's nephew. Swallowing the taunt, he replied: *"My good general, I fully know what it means to fight with a person so desperate who finds himself at bay. Instead of letting our men die by his sword in such large numbers, why cannot some one adopt some stratagem to make him leave his vantage position so that it may be easier to attack him from all sides?"*

This suggestion appealed very much to the cowardly soldiers of Kufa. After some consultations amongst themselves, they decided to send soldiers to the top of the roof of an adjoining building and from there to hurl stones, burning embers and missiles at Muslim. It did not take them long to carry out their strategy. With showers of arrows, stones, fire and missiles, Muslim was so much wounded that he decided to give up his vantage position. He charged on the soldiers in front of him and they fell back. He went forward, wielding his sword, and in the process, sending those who were within its reach to the perdition and doom that they merited.

Once again hasty counsels were held among the captains of the army. Someone suggested that, since Muslim was now desperately moving forward, a trench could be dug on the road and covered up with straw so that it was completely camouflaged. The idea was to trap Muslim as he marched forward. It was realized that, without such subterfuge, Muslim could not be killed or captured without sacrificing the cream of the army.

The treacherous ruse proposed by Obeidullah's mercenaries worked as planned. While rushing on and wielding his sword dexterously, Muslim fell into the trench. Now those who were avoiding coming within the reach of his sword swooped down on him. With gushing blood Muslim could not regain his feet. He toppled over and lay unconscious in the trench. It was now a matter of minutes to capture him and soon he was chained and bound.

When Muslim regained consciousness, he found himself a captive. His wounds had accentuated his thirst. The dawn was now breaking and the call for prayers was raised in the mosques of Kufa. Muslim requested his captors to give him some water to drink and for ablution. Instead of acceding to his request, they mocked and jeered at him. Muslim was extremely surprised and pained to see that the people of Kufa, who were claiming to be the followers of the Prophet (s), were flouting the injunctions of Islam for kindness to all in a helpless predicament. Little did Muslim know that these same people would behave with utter callousness and beastliness towards Hussain (as) and his children in the near future.

Before being marched off to the Court of Obeidullah, Muslim was paraded through the streets of Kufa with heavy chains on his hands and feet. The people of Kufa, who only a few days before were vying with one another just to have a glimpse of him, were now watching him from their windows with perfect equanimity, as if he was an utter stranger to them. Some devils amongst them were hard-hearted enough to pelt stones at him.

When Muslim was presented before Obeidullah he stood erect with dignity. The Governor asked him whether he knew the fate that awaited him and his master Hussain Ibn Ali. With utter disdain Muslim replied: *"O mercenary of Yazid, I do not care what you do to me, but I do not like to hear your cursed tongue mentioning Hussain's name."*

Obeidullah Ibne Ziyad felt crest fallen at this bold rebuke of Muslim. With intention of creating an impression of his magnanimity on the people who were gathered in his court, he said to Muslim, *"According to the age-old Arab custom I want you to mention your last desire before you are beheaded so that I may fulfill it."*

A glint of hope came into Muslim's eyes. Could he take this man at his word and ask him to send the message that he wanted to be conveyed to his master? Like a drowning man who catches at a straw, Muslim decided that, if at all, this was his only chance. He immediately replied: *"Obeidullah, if you are true to your word, fulfill my last wish and send a message to my master Imam Hussain, asking him to go back to Medina and abandon the idea of his visit to Kufa."*

Obeidullah had never expected this request from Muslim. He had thought that perhaps Muslim might request him to spare the lives of his two young sons when they were captured, as they were sure to be. For a while he was nonplussed; he was at a loss what to say. He knew that he could not fulfill this wish of Muslim without incurring the displeasure of Yazid; but to decline this request would betray him in his true color. His crooked mind did not take long to find a solution to this problem. He beckoned to his executioners to take Muslim to the top of the Government House and to behead him. He immediately dismissed his court and hurried back to his apartment.

When the sword of the executioner was swaying over Muslim's head his last thoughts were with his master, Hussain (as), whom he had loved and cherished more than anything in life. His only regret was that till the end he could not do what he wanted most, to warn Hussain (as) against the treachery of the people of Kufa. As the sword fell on his neck, he silently muttered a prayer to God to so ordain that Hussain (as) might come to know of the happenings in Kufa. This was the last prayer of the brave warrior who stood steadfast in death as in life.

Merciful God did not allow Muslim's last prayer to go in vain. He who listens to the prayers emanating from the hearts of sincere devotees like Muslim, enabled one witness to the ghastly enactments of that day, who had some sparks of faith in him, to go riding out of Kufa at the earliest opportunity. He reached the camp of Imam Hussain (as) a few days after Muslim's martyrdom. He conveyed the sad tidings to Hussain (as) who wept bitterly as if his heart would rend. He called the young daughter of Muslim, who was travelling with him, and told her that henceforth she should regard him as her guardian. He gave one pair of earrings to her and one to Sakina. When the messenger asked him whether he was turning back and returning to Medina in view of what had happened to Muslim, he replied: *"I am going forward to meet my destiny; to fulfill the purpose of my life. My death is beckoning to me and so there is no question of my retracing my steps."*[184]

Muslim ibn 'Aqil had taken two of his sons to Kufa with him. The older son was called Muhammad and the younger Ibrahim. Both were under the age of ten years. When Muslim ibn 'Aqil realized how dangerous a threat Ibn Ziyad was, he called for Qadi Shurayh and handed over his two sons to him. Qadi Shurayh kept the two boys in his house until the martyrdom of Muslim ibn 'Aqil.

After the death of Muslim ibn 'Aqil, Ibn Ziyad issued a warning saying that anyone who was aware of the whereabouts of the sons of Muslim ibn 'Aqil and did not inform him would be put to death. On hearing this, Qadi Shurayh went to the sons of Muslim ibn 'Aqil. He showed them affection and kindness as he shed tears. The boys asked him, *"Why are you weeping?"*

Shurayh replied, *"Your father has been mercilessly killed."*

The children cried in grief, *"O father! O exile!"*

After Shurayh had consoled them, he informed them of Ibn Ziyad's threats against them. Hearing this, the children

---

[184] *Tears and Tributes* by Zakir

stopped crying out of terror. Seeing this Shurayh said, *"Do not be frightened. You are the apples of my eye. I will not allow any harm to come to you. I have arranged for you to be in the care of a trustworthy person who will see to it that you are taken back to Medina."*

Shurayh called for his son Asad and gave him the following instructions, *"News has come to me that a caravan is preparing to depart for Medina. Take these children and hand them over to the trustworthy person who will see to it that they reach Medina safely."*

Shurayh kissed the two boys and gave them each 50 dinars. Then he bade them farewell and handed them over to his son Asad. In the darkness of the night, Asad carried the two boys in his arms until he was a few kilometers outside Kufa in order to meet with the caravan. However, the caravan had set off before they arrived. The dark shapes of the rear of the caravan were barely visible in the distance. Asad bid the two orphans of Muslim ibn 'Aqil farewell and told to run after the caravan until they caught up with it. Under no circumstances were they to stop before they had reached it.

In the darkness of the night the two orphans started running through the desert towards the caravan. However, tiredness overcame them, and they paused for a while. It was at this moment that an inhabitant from Kufa happened to be passing. He saw the two boys and recognized them as being the orphans of Muslim ibn 'Aqil. He seized them and brought them to Ibn Ziyad.

Ibn Ziyad summoned the jailor and handed the two orphans over to him. The jailor was a person by the name of Mashkur and he was among the lovers of the Household of the Prophet (s). When Mashkur learned of the identity of the two boys, he treated them with great kindness and affection and brought them food and water. Finally in the middle of the night, Mashkur decided to free the two boys. He gave them his ring and instructed them to go to Qadisiyyah where they would find his brother. He told them to give the ring to his brother who would then assist them to get to Medina. When news of Mashkur's freeing of the boys was given to Ibn Ziyad, he ordered him to be given fifty lashes. Mashkur died as the sentence was being carried out.

On the same night Ibrahim and Muhammad, the sons of Muslim ibn 'Aqil, left Kufa and started their journey towards Qadisiyyah. They walked all night. However, due to the darkness and the fact that they did not know the way, they found themselves still on the outskirts of Kufa in the morning. The frightened boys saw a palm-grove and went to it. There they hid themselves on top of a date palm.

An Ethiopian maid came to the palm-grove to drink some water from a pond underneath the tree in which the children were hiding. As she knelt by the pond, she saw the reflection of the two children in the water. The maid quickly looked up at the tree and saw the young boys concealed in it. She treated them with kindness and gentleness and took them to her mistress, who was the wife of Harith ibn 'Urwah. As soon as this woman saw them, she put her arms around them and asked them who they were. They replied, *"We are from the family of the Prophet and are the sons of Muslim ibn 'Aqil."*

When she learned of their true identities, she showed them greater affection and embraced her maid in joy. However, she warned her to not to inform her husband Harith about the boys because she knew of his evil disposition.

After the boys had eaten and gone to bed, Harith returned home in a state of rage. When Harith's wife asked him of the reason for his anger, he replied that that he had been in search of the two sons of Muslim ibn 'Aqil who had been freed by Mashkur the jailor. He said that it had been announced in the palace of Ibn Ziyad that the one who captured the boys would be rewarded handsomely. However, despite a lengthy search during which his horse had died of exhaustion and in which he himself had become tired, he had been unable to find them. At this Harith's wife said, *"May sorrow be your lot! Fear God and the day on which Muhammad the Messenger of Allah will be your opponent. Do not harm those children."* Harith replied, *"Silence! O woman! If I were to find them, I should be rewarded by vast amounts of gold and silver from Ibn Ziyad. Get up and prepare my supper."*

After eating his supper Harith went to his bed. Muhammad and Ibrahim were asleep in one of the rooms. Suddenly Muhammad the elder brother of the two woke up from his sleep. He had had a dream that had disturbed him. He said to Ibrahim, *"Wake up! O brother! I have just had a dream and I am afraid that that we will soon be killed. I saw the Prophet with Imam Ali, al-Hassan, al-Hussain and Lady Fatima sitting in Paradise with our father. The Prophet looked at us and wept. Then he turned to our father and said, 'O Muslim! How could you leave your sons among the enemies?' At this our father said that they would be united with us tomorrow."*

Ibrahim replied, *"I have had the same dream."* The children embraced each other in the darkness of the night, frightened and not knowing what was to become of them.

Harith was woken from his sleep by the sound of the children's voices. Holding a candle, he came inside the room and saw the two frightened children sitting in a corner of the room clinging to each other. He asked, *"Who are you?"*

They answered, *"We are your guests, the family of the Prophet. We are the sons of Muslim ibn 'Aqil."* Harith shouted angrily, *"I have destroyed myself and my horse in searching for you while you were sitting inside my own house?"*

Harith began to slap the children viciously. Then he tied their hands and feet and pushed them into a corner of the room. Harith's wife came to him and kissed his hands and feet begging him to not to harm the children as they were orphans and from the family of the Prophet (s) and their guests. However, the hard-hearted man was without any compassion and paid no heed to her pleas. Thus, the boys were left in that state until the morning.

In the morning Harith, with his sword in his hand and accompanied by his son and his servant, took the two sons of Muslim ibn 'Aqil to the banks of the Euphrates. Harith's wife was crying and pleading with him as she followed them. However, whenever she got near to them, Harith would push her away with his sword. At the Euphrates Harith gave his sword to his servant and ordered him to behead the two boys. The servant refused to carry out his orders and Harith killed him. After this Harith handed the sword to his son and told him to behead the two children. At this his son replied, *"I seek refuge with Allah! Never will I commit such a crime and I will not allow you to kill them."*

Harith's wife cried out, *"What crime have these children committed? Take them alive to the governor."*

Harith answered, *"I have no option but to kill them, I have no guarantee that members of the Shi'ah will not rescue them from me while I make my way to the governor."*

At this Harith took hold of his sword with an intention of killing his own son. His wife screamed and begged for mercy but to no avail. Harith took his son's life. Then he turned to the children who were crying and shaking with fear at what they had witnessed. The children begged for some time for them to offer their final prayers, but Harith did not grant them their wish. Harith grabbed hold of Muhammad, but Ibrahim threw himself on Muhammad in an attempt to save him. Muhammad did the same to save the life of his younger brother. Impatiently Harith struck his sword at Muhammad beheading him. Ibrahim grabbed the head of his brother in his lap. As he wept over his brother, Harith struck at Ibrahim neck beheading the orphan.

Harith threw the headless bodies of the orphans of Muslim ibn 'Aqil in the river and placed their heads on a stake and set off to the palace of Ibn Ziyad.

The heads of the orphans of Muslim ibn 'Aqil were brought and placed in front of Ibn Ziyad. The latter asked, *"Whose heads are these?"*

Harith replied, *"These are the heads of your enemies whom I caught and beheaded in return for the reward that you promised."*

Ibn Ziyad asked, *"Which of my enemies?"*

Harith answered, *"The sons of Muslim ibn 'Aqil."*

Ibn Ziyad asked for the heads to be washed and brought on a tray. Then he gazed at them and said to Harith, *"May sorrow be your reward! What wrong did these children do to you?"*

Ibn Ziyad called for his personal jester Muqatil who was a devoted lover of the Holy Family and to deny the murderer death at the hands of soldiers said, *"This accursed man has killed these children without my permission. Take him to the banks of the Euphrates where he murdered the children and execute him as you will."*

Muqatil grabbed Harith by the shoulders and marched him through the streets of Kufa bare-footed and bare-headed as he showed the heads of the orphans to the onlookers shouting, *"O people! This is the murderer of the two orphans of Muslim ibn 'Aqil."*

The people wept at the sight of the orphan's heads and cursed Harith. As Muqatil proceeded to the river, the people gathered with him to witness Harith's execution. When they arrived at the place where the children were killed, they found the dead bodies of Harith's son and his servant and his bruised wife crying over her son. The people were extremely disturbed at the scene.

Harith asked Muqatil to release him for the sum of ten thousand dinars. To this Muqatil replied, *"By Allah! If all the wealth of the entire world were yours and you offered it to me, I would not accept. I desire to attain the Paradise of Allah by executing you."*

His head was brought to Ibn Ziyad, it was placed on a lance and children threw stones and arrows at it and said, *"This is the murderer of the progeny of the Prophet"*[185]

---

[185] The Tragedy of the Two Young Sons of Muslim Ibn Aqil, Nafasul Mahmoom, Shaikh Sadooq has related this in his Ama-li

Tragedy of Karbala

'If our Shia truly knew what happened in Karbala, they would die from the grief'

Imam Al-Baqir (as)

  Upon Mu'awiya's death, Yazid, 30 years old, managed to impose himself on the people and become the Khalifa. At first people refused to accept him as a representative of the Prophet (s) and Islamic Ummah, but Yazid approached people in mosques for their favors. Like his father Mu'awiya, Yazid used all possible means like bribery, coercion, pressure, threats, and force to receive the people's acceptance of him as the legitimate ruler. Many people were worried, threats to their lives and livelihood were too menacing, so they grudgingly and reluctantly gave in. Imam Hussain (as) and his family (who practiced Islam in its true sense), did not give in. As the true representative of Prophet Muhammad (s), Al-Hussain (as) flatly refused accepting Yazid either as a Khalifa or a leader of Islam. Despite Yazid's intimidating military power the Imam stood firm in his resolve and chose to challenge Benu Umayya's authorities.

  Yazid commissioned Waleed Ibn Ut'ba, his Governor over Medina, to ask for Imam Hussain's allegiance of loyalty or else upon refusal, his head. Waleed invited Al-Hussain (as) to a meeting for the purpose. Imam Hussain (as) did not give his word at the meeting and decided to leave Medina along with his family to proceed to Mecca. When Al-Hussain (as) reached Mecca, he received 12,000 letters from Kufa urging him to go to Kufa to be their leader, and be the Khalifa. Imam sent an emissary, his cousin Muslim Ibn Aqeel, to Kufa to ascertain first-hand information about the situation in Iraq. In the meantime, Yazid spread a network of informants and secret agents in Mecca to assassinate the Imam during pilgrimage. Imam learned about the spies, and carefully evaluated the situation in Mecca. Imam Hussain (as) knew that Yazid son of Mu'awiya had no regard for Islamic values and teachings, that he would do anything to enforce his tyrannical rule. Imam Hussain (as) also knew that giving allegiance of loyalty to an imposter like Yazid would certainly place Islam in great jeopardy. Therefore, he decided to leave Mecca for Kufa to prepare for a confrontation with Yazid and his forces.

Many friends and relatives urged Imam Hussain (as) not to go to Kufa, but he insisted on going. Imam Hussain (as), along with family, friends, and companions began the journey toward Kufa (1,100 miles) in a long caravan in the blistering heat of summer.

Imam Hussain (as) received the first letter from his emissary Muslim Ibn Aqeel with good news. The letter indicated that the people were more than ready to welcome the Imam in Kufa and were looking forward to his leadership. Imam Hussain (as) decided to send another emissary to Kufa with a message. The caravan kept proceeding toward Kufa. Many days passed but the Imam did not receive any more responses from Muslim Ibn Aqeel.

In Kufa Muslim Bin Aqeel with the help of Mukhtar Al-Thaqafi and Hanee Ibn Urwah continued to hold secret meetings with the supporters of the Imam. Within a short time, the gatherings started to gain momentum. Yazid through his spies and informants learned about Muslim's successes in Kufa. He appointed the tyrant Ubaidullah Ibn Ziyad to replace al-Nu'man Ibn al-Basheer as Governor of Kufa.

Meanwhile, as Al-Hussain's caravan got closer to its destination (Kufa), coming to a place called Zubalah, Imam Hussain (as) unexpectedly received shocking news. The shocking news was about Muslim Ibn Aqeel and the person who provided him shelter, Hani Ibn Urwah, both of whom were arrested and beheaded by the Governor Ibn Ziyad. Mukhtar was also arrested and imprisoned and tortured by Ibn Ziyad.

Imam Hussain (as) gathered his companions and disclosed to them about the bad news, and said, *"Our Shi'a have deserted us, those of you who prefer to leave us may do so freely and without guilt."*

Becoming scared, some companions left the caravan. Imam Hussain (as) continued with the journey along with close companions and family members until he was face to face with 1,000 horsemen led by Hurr al-Riyahi representing the enemy. The enemy army blocked the camps of Imam Hussain (as) from advancing. Tension started to rise between the two. The Imam addressed the enemy explaining to them his motives for going to Kufa, that it was in response to the invitation of the people. He even showed them a bagful of letters he received from Kufa. Hurr said that he and his men were not the writers of those letters. Imam told them that if they did not like him to advance with the journey, he was prepared to return to Hijaz.

Hurr replied, *"We are commissioned to follow you until we take you to Governor Ibn Ziyad, and suggested to the Imam to go towards a station which is neither Kufa nor Medina."*

Imam Hussain (as) found the proposal fair and turned the caravan away from Kufa. Hurr and his army marched parallel to the Imam. The two sides reached a village called Nainawa where Ibn Ziyad's messenger (Yazid's governor over Kufa) delivered a message to Hur. The message read, *" ...force Hussain (as) to a halt. But let him stop in an open space, without vegetation or water."*

Hurr conveyed the contents of the letter to Imam Hussain (as). The Imam, his family and companions defiantly resumed their journey and reached a place where another enemy force blocked their move and forced them to stop. When Imam Hussain (as) learned that the place was called Karbala, he felt he reached the destination and ordered his camp to be setup. That day was 2nd of Muharram, Hijri 61.

Upon learning that his army had succeeded to lay a siege around the Imam's camp, Governor Ibn Ziyad sent additional military units to Karbala and appointed Umar Ibn Sa'ad in charge. Imam Hussain (as) opened a dialogue with Umar Ibn Sa'ad and convinced him to lift the siege so that the Imam with his family and companions could leave Iraq. Umar Ibn Sa'ad liked the Imam's proposal and sent a message to Governor Ibn Ziyad notifying him about the results of the talks with Imam Hussain (as). Ibn Ziyad also found the Imam's proposal acceptable. However before agreeing to it officially, Shimr Bin Dhil-Jawshan, opposed it strongly. As a result, Ziyad wrote a letter to Umar Ibn Sa'ad commanding him to either go to war with Imam Hussain (as) or be relieved of his duties as commander of the army and Shimr would not only replace him but dispatch Ibn Sa'ad's head to Kufa.

Umar Ibn bin Sa'ad got the letter. After pondering over the consequences, he decided to fight Imam Hussain (as). On the 7th day of Muharram, he moved his troops closer to the camp and began to surround the Hussaini camp. Ibn Sa'ad laid a blockade around the camp to cut it off from access to the river Euphrates, to deprive it of water in a move to force them to surrender.

Two days later, (on the 9th of Muharram), the enemy's military forces closed in on the camp of Imam Hussain (as). Imam asked his brother, Abbas, to talk to Ibn Sa'ad and request a delay of the aggression by one night. Umar Ibn Sa'ad agreed to the demand. He ordered his troops to delay the aggression till next morning. Imam Hussain (as) and his pious companions spent that night in prayers. During the night the Imam told the companions, *"....the enemy is interested in none but me, me alone. I'll be most delighted to permit each and every one of you to go back, and I urge you to do so...."*

All companions screamed in response, *"By Allah, never, never! We will either live with you or die together with you."*

Finally, the Day of Ashura dawned upon the soil of Karbala. It was the day when Jihad would be in full bloom, blood would be shed, 72 innocent lives would be sacrificed, and a decisive battle would be won to save Islam and the Ummah.

It had been a few days since the enemy cut off the water supply. Children were crying for water, the women were desperate for water, Zainul-Abideen, the son of Imam Hussain (as) was sick with fever. The suffering from the thirst was too painful to bear. And despite this, not a single person in the camp made any complaints or even questioned the mission of Imam Hussain (as). Each member supported the Imam wholeheartedly and enthusiastically.

Next morning Imam Hussain (as) went out of the camp and saw Umar Ibn Sa'ad mobilizing his troops to start the hostility. He stared at the intimidating army, and as large as it was Imam Hussain (as) showed no signs of compromise. Imam Hussain (as) raised his hands in prayer: *"O Allah! It is Thee in whom I trust amid all grief. You are my hope amid all violence. Thou are my refuge and provision in everything that happens to me. How many grievances weaken the heart leaving me with no means to handle them, during which friend deserts me, and enemy rejoices in it. I lay it before Thee and complain of it to Thee, because of my desire in Thee, Thee alone. You relieve me of it and remove it from me. Thou are the Master of all Grace, the Essence of Goodness, and the Ultimate Resort of all Desire."*

Hurr ibn Yazid ar-Riyahi

Before the actual engagement was to take place Hurr, the previous commander of the enemy force, felt his conscience violently stirring, he was in turmoil. Upon realizing the gravity of the situation, he suddenly broke away from Umar Ibn Sa'ad's camp (along with two others). They rushed toward Imam Hussain (as) to join his camp. Hurr's heart was jumping with joy, his mind relieved of an agonizing tension. Hur's defection worried Umar Ibn Sa'ad very much, lest others do the same and defect. So, Umar Ibn Sa'ad threw an arrow in the air to indicate the start of the battle. This was the outset of a catastrophe and a tragic event that Mu'awiya had once conceived to happen.[186]

Hurr ibn Yazid ar-Riyahi was the one responsible for trapping Imam Hussain and his family in the land of Karbala, forbidding them from proceeding to Kufa or to return to Madina. Even though Imam Hussain offered Hurr's soldiers' water and even water to their animals, here it was that now on the Day of Ashura Imam Hussain and his family had been without water for 3 days. All that could be heard were the cries of the thirsty children *al-'Atash al-Atash*! The thirst is killing us!

Imam Hussain (as) came to deliver a speech to the enemy calling them to fear Allah and condemning them for what they were doing to the children of Rasulullah[187]. Hurr stood in a difficult spot. He was having a mental tug of war.

Should he remain in the army of Yazid and kill Imam Hussain to receive countless rewards from Yazid or should he abandon this wretched army and join the grandson of the Prophet protecting him till his death? It was a choice between Heaven and Hell.

---

[186] Karbala Chain of Events by Ramzan Shabir

[187] The Messenger of Allah (s)

One of the soldiers of Ibn Ziyad saw Hurr and said to him: *"By Allah, I have never seen you like this before! If I was asked who was the bravest man from amongst the people of Kufa, I wouldn't hesitate to mention you. What is this I see in you today?"*

Hurr's conscience called him to recognize his Imam. Hurr replied to him: *"By Allah I find myself between Heaven and Hell and I will not prefer anything to Paradise even if I am cut into pieces and burnt!"*

He went and tried to dissuade Ibn Sa'ad from fighting the Imam, but he saw they were intent on killing him. So, he knew what he must do: go and join the army of Imam Hussain and protect him till his last breath.

With that he set off on his horse and rushed to join the Imam while he was immersed in shame and regret.

When he reached the Imam (as), he said in a loud voice, *"O my Lord I am turning towards you while I have terrified Your saints and the son of Your Prophet. O' Aba Abdillah[188], I have repented, would I be forgiven?"*

He dismounted his horse while his tears were glistening on his face. He stood before the Holy Imam and said, *"May I be your ransom, son of the Apostle of God?"* he said, *"I was your companion who stopped you from returning. I accompanied you along the road and made you stop in this place. But I did not think that the people would refuse to respond to what you have offered them and that they would ever come to this. By God, if I had I known that they would finish up by doing what I am seeing them do to you, I would not have committed what I have committed against you. I repent to God for what I have done. Will you accept my repentance?"*

---

[188] Imam Hussain (as)

Imam was glad he was joining him, and he forgave him saying, *"Yes, Allah has accepted your repentance and forgiven you."*

At that time Hurr related to the Imam a dream he had seen, *"Last night I saw my father in dream that he was asking me: What are you doing these days, and where are you?*

I replied: I was in pursuit of Hussain. He told me: Woe be on you, what has happened to you. Are you pursuing Hussain, the son of Allah's Messenger (S)'?

Hurr said: *"Yaa Hussain, I request you to grant me the permission to fight so that I may be the first to be killed in your service just as I was the first one to attack you?"*

Hurr asked the Imam's permission to give a speech to the people of Kufa and counsel them. Perhaps some of them would turn back from their wrong way towards the path of truth. The Imam gave him the permission and Hurr called out in a loud voice:

"O people of Kufah! May your mothers lose you and weep over you! You invited him and then cut him off; surrounded him from all sides and forbid him from going to the vast land of Allah, so that he and his family find security. And he became like a prisoner in your hands, he can't help or harm himself.

And you prevented him and his women and children and companions from the running waters of Furat, who the Jews, Christians and Zoroastrians drink from it, and the pigs and dogs of the woods enter it! And here they are, dying from thirst. What a terrible way for you to repay Muhammad in his progeny, may Allah not quench your thirst on the Day of Thirst."

This speech affected 30 soldiers from the army of Ibn Saad and they joined the Imam's camp and before leaving they said to the people of Kufa, *"The son of Allah's Messenger (S) presented three proposals but you did not accept anyone of them."* They fought bravely on the side of the Holy Imam till they were martyred in his service.

On the Day of Ashura upon seeing the death of Habib ibn Mazahir, Hurr saw that the death of Habib deeply affected Imam Hussain (as). The Imam stood beside body of Habib sighing in sorrow and grief and said, *"Allah shall be pleased with me and those friends of mine who render help."*

At that moment, the great warrior, Hurr bin Yazid Riyahi, knew what he must do to gain the pleasure of Allah and that was to help Imam Hussain (as). He went out to the battlefield and went to welcome death smiling in joy of having helped the grandson of Rasulullah (S).

Hurr fought while Zuhair bin Qain accompanied him. When one of them was surrounded by the crowds of soldiers the other would rush to his aid and rescue him.

Then while fighting, Ayyub bin Mashruh aimed an arrow at Hurr's horse and maimed it. The horse stampeded out of control, but Hurr jumped from it like a lion without encountering any harm. He began to fight on foot courageously till many men from the side of the enemy surrounded him.

Then the soldiers preceded to attack him with swords and spears and he fell down drenched in his own blood. The companions of the Imam rushed towards him and carried him to the Imam's tent and placed him on the ground. The Imam stepped forward and cleaned the blood from Hurr's face and mourned for him with the following lines: *"Hurr, you are 'free' like your mother named you. You are free in this world and the Hereafter."*[189]

Imam Hussain's supporters insisted on being the first to fight. Therefore, they took the brunt of the enemy attack. The battle was ferocious. Within a short time, the Imam's supporters slay a large number of the enemy fighters, they were on the offensive and the enemy on the defensive. This caused apprehension and confusion in the enemy military, the 72 of Hussain's against the 5,000 of the enemy (some say 30,000) being on the defensive. So worried and nervous, the enemy commander-in-chief ordered his army not only to set fire to the Imam's tents (which were occupied mostly by frightened females and children), but at the same time reinforced his fighters with more troops.

The heroes began to fall, they were men of valor welcoming martyrdom, they fell one after another, for the enemy was overwhelming in number. By noon time the Imam stopped the fight to perform the Salat. By this time those left were mainly his family and a few supporters. They performed the Salat together. Two supporters were guarding the performers of Salat. The enemy was standing still, watching!! When Salat was

---

[189] Recalling the Sacrifices of Karbala by Sheikh Mateen Charbonneau

finished one of the guards fell dead; there were 17 arrows in his back. [190] Instead of dodging the arrows like most people would these brave souls were jumping in front of the arrows to catch them with their bodies. This was to protect Imam Hussain (as) and his Shia who were praying so that they did not get hit by arrows while they were calling upon Allah.

Wahab ibn Abudullah Qalbi

This is the story of a young bride and a young bridegroom who were at Karbala'. They had been married only two months. The bridegroom was his mother's only child.

After his marriage the mother decided to go for Hajj and take the son and his bride. They left Kufa for Mecca in the month of Shawwaal.

---

[190] Karbala Chain of Events by Ramzan Shabir

On their way back, they found Kufa sealed off. At the border the mother asked why Kufa had been placed under such a strict blockade. She was told that a rebel group was camped at Karbala' and that Kufa was sealed off to protect the city and its inhabitants from an attack by the rebels. She asked who the rebels were. She was told the leader was Hussain Ibn Ali Ibn Abu Taalib.

On hearing the name, the lady almost fainted. This lady was the widow Abdullah Qalbi and her son, the newlywed bridegroom, was Wahab Bin Abdullah Qalbi. His father was a companion of Ali. In 40 Hijrah when Abdullah Qalbi's wife was pregnant she became very ill. Abdullah Qalbi went to Ali (as) and said, "My wife and I have been childless for so long. Now that she is expecting a baby, she is so ill that I may lose her. Please Mawla, pray for her." Ali (as) prayed, and Abdullah Qalbi's wife recovered. Same year Ali (as) was martyred. A few months later Wahab was born. Two years later his father died. The widow had brought up her son with great love.

Now she heard the son of Ali (as) being accused of wanting to attack Kufa and kill the people there. She refused to believe it. She said to her son, *"Wahab, I must go and find out what is happening."*

Wahab said, *"Mother, I too would like to come."* The three arrived in Karbala' on the 7th Muharram.[191]

On learning the true situation Wahab decided to stay on with Imam Hussain (as) and fight for him. When he told his mother of his decision, she said, *"I am the proudest mother in Iraq."*

Wahab bin Abdullah bin Habbab Kalbi came out into the battlefield. His mother too was accompanying him on that day, who told him, "Arise O son! And defend the grandson of the

---

[191] The Journey of Tears by Bashir Hassanali Rahim

Prophet of Allah (s)."

Wahab replied, *"Verily I shall not act miserly."* Thus he came out into the battlefield while saying: *"If you do not know me, I am from Bani Kalb, very soon you will see me and my sword, and will behold my attack and influence in battle, I will seek my revenge after the revenge of my companions, and I will ward off grief and affliction before my grief, to fight me in the battlefield is not a joke."*

He attacked the Kufan army and killed a group among them one after the other. Then he returned to his mother and wife and stood facing them and said, *"O mother! Are you pleased now"*?

She replied, *"I shall not be pleased until you attain martyrdom in the presence of Imam Hussain (as)."*

Then his wife said, *"I request you in the name of Allah not to bereave me."*

Hearing this his mother said, *"O dear son! Do not accept what she says, go and fight in the way of the grandson of the Prophet (s), so that he may intercede for you on the day of Qiyamah (resurrection)."*

Wahab returned back saying: *"I swear to you O Umme Wahab, to strike them with spears and sword, similar to the swordsmanship of a youth who believes in the Almighty, so as to give a taste of the bitter battle to this nation, I am valorous and a youth possessing a clear-cut sword, I am not fearful during battle, Allah, the Wise, is sufficient for me."*

Then he laid siege until he had killed nineteen horsemen and twelve-foot soldiers. Both his hands were severed, seeing this his mother lifted a peg of the tent and ran towards him saying, *"May my parents be your ransom! Strive in the way of the Household of the Prophet (s)."*

Wahab proceeded further to return her back to the tents, when she caught hold of his shirt and said, *"I shall not return back until I am killed along with you."*

When Imam Hussain (as) saw this, he said, *"May Allah reward you favorably due to the right of my family! Return back to the ladies, may Allah have mercy upon you."*

Hearing this the woman returned and Wahab fought until he was martyred.

The wife of Wahab came and sat at his head and started wiping the blood from the face of her husband. When Shimr saw her, he commanded his retainer to strike her with his club. He did so and she was the first woman to attain martyrdom in the ranks of Imam Hussain (as) (May Allah's Mercy and Blessings be upon her).

It is stated in *Rawzatul Wa'ezeen* and *Amali* of Shaikh Sadooq, that formerly Wahab and his mother were Christians, and they had accepted Islam at the hands of Imam Hussain (as). They accompanied the Imam to Karbala, and on the Day of Ashura Wahab mounted his horse, while a peg of the tent was in his hands. He fought until he had killed seven or eight men among the enemies. Then he was arrested and taken to Umar bin Sa'ad, who ordered him to be beheaded.

Allamah Majlisi says that he saw in a narration that Wahab was formerly a Christian, then he along with his mother accepted Islam at the hands of Imam Hussain (as). When he entered the battlefield, he put to sword twenty-four foot soldiers and twelve horsemen. Then he was arrested and brought to Umar bin Sa'ad who told him, *"What a marvelous valor you possess."*

Then he ordered him to be beheaded. He was beheaded and his head was thrown towards the tents of Imam Hussain (as). His mother lifted his head up and kissed it, then she threw it towards the army of Umar bin Sa'ad, which hit a man and killed him. Then she lifted up a peg of the tents and killed two others until Imam Hussain (as) saw her and said, *"O mother of Wahab! Return. You and your son will be along with the Prophet (s), while Jihad is lifted off from the women."*

Hearing this she returned back saying, *"O Lord! Do not disappoint me."*

Imam told her, *"May your Lord not disappoint you, O mother of Wahab"*![192]

On the Day of Ashura, Wahab fought for Imam Hussain (as). When he was killed the mother and the bride were standing at the gate of the camp. Their faces were radiant with pride. Umar Sa'ad ordered Wahab's head to be cut off from the body. He threw the head at Wahab's mother. She picked it up, kissed it and threw it back at Umar Sa'ad saying, *"What we have sacrificed for our Imam and for Islam we do not take back. I am sorry I have one son only. If I had twenty, they all would have fought Yazid today."*

Then she went into the camp and took the young bride in her arms. Just then, the tent's curtain lifted, and Bibi Zainab (as) came in. She embraced them both and offered her condolences saying: *"May Allah grant you patience to bear Wahab's loss!!*[193]

John bin Huwai the Freed Servant of Abu Dharr

Among those who were martyred at Karbala' were sixteen servants or freed servants. Most of them were from Abyssinia, the present-day Ethiopia. Some of them belonged to Imam Hussain's family and others to the companions of Imam who remained with him.

---

[192] Nafasul Mahmoom by Sheikh Abbas Qummi

[193] The Journey of Tears by Bashir Hassanali Rahim

On the night before Ashura, the Imam and the companions freed all their servants and urged them to go away and seek their safety, but these sixteen would not leave. Amongst them was an Abyssinian called John bin Huwai.

Ali (as) had given John to Abu Dharr Ghiffari, Abu Dharr freed him, but John stayed on with Abu Dharr as a companion. When Abu Dharr was exiled from Madina John went back to Ali (as) who invited him to stay on as his companion. In the company of Ali (as) he learnt the tafseer of Quraan and the traditions of the Holy Prophet (s). He also knew the Holy Quraan by heart. When Ali (as) was martyred John stayed with Imam Hassan (as) and after Imam Hassan (as) he moved in with Imam Hussain (as). When Imam Hussain (as) left Madina John insisted on accompanying him.

At Karbala' John could always be seen at the side of Imam Hussain (as). He was an old man, dark with grey curly hair. Because of his profound knowledge and pleasant manners he was greatly respected by all.

John spent the whole night of Ashura sharpening his sword. On the following day he helped in repelling the first two attacks from Yazid's army. At midday, after the Zuhr prayers, John came to the Imam, and stood silently with his arms folded. It was his habit never to speak in the presence of the Imam until spoken to.

Imam Hussain (as) looked at John and said, *"John, I know you have come for my permission to go to the battlefield. You have been a good and trusted friend. I will not deny you martyrdom for Islam. Go, Allah be with you!"*

John smiled happily. He faced the enemy and recited a poem that said *"I am a soul willing to die for Allah and have a sword thirsty of the blood of the enemies of Allah. Before I die, I shall fight the enemies of Allah with my sword and my tongue, and thus shall I serve the grand-son of the Holy Prophet (s)."*

John fought courageously, all the time reciting the poem. He received several mortal blows, but his recitation of the poem continued. John fell from his horse; he still continued to fight with his tongue by reciting the poem. And then a few horsemen moved to where he lay. John, the Abyssinian, was silenced.

Habib ibn Mazaahir

Another who died upon the love of Ahl ul Bayt (as) was the dear friend of Imam Hussain: Habib ibn Mazahir.

Habib Ibn Mazaahir didn't know the whereabouts of Imam Hussain until the letter from Hussain arrived at his home. At that time, he was having breakfast with his wife and his young son. Habib read the letter from Hussain. He kissed it and tears began to flow from his eyes.

His wife asked him what's wrong?

Habib said: *"I have received a letter from my master, hussain. He has asked me to join him in Karbala. Yazid's soldiers have surrounded him and are after his life."*

Habib's wife said: *"Habib! Your childhood friend has called you. Your master needs your help. What are you waiting for? Go habib, before it's too late!"*

Habib was worried as to how to escape from Kufa without being seen. He instructed his servant to take his horse to a farm outside the city and wait for him there. The servant took Habib's horse to a farm outside the city and preceded to wait for him.

Habib was delayed and the servant started talking to the horse: *"O' horse! Our master hussain is in trouble. He needs help. He has asked habib to join him, yet habib is late. O' horse! If he does not manage to escape from kufa, i will ride on you and go to hussain's help."*

At 'Asr time, most of the men were in mosque, so Habib managed to sneak out and reach the farm where his horse was waiting. He quickly mounted his horse and said to his servant: "Go, my friend, go! I am freeing you from my services."

His servant replied: "Master! You are not being fair. I have served you faithfully for years. now, I have a chance to serve the son of Sayyida Fatima, and you are asking me to go?! Why are you denying me a place in heaven'?!"

Habib was taken aback by the words of his servant. He was pleased to hear that he had recognized the difference between truth and falsehood. He wanted to sacrifice his life for truth. Habib asked his servant to mount his horse. Together they galloped towards Karbala.

Habib reached Karbala late in the evening where Imam Hussain greeted him with great affection. Sayeda Zaynab heard that Habib had come. She asked her maid, Fizza, to convey her greetings to Habib.

When Habib heard that Bibi Zaynab had sent greetings to him, he screamed out in grief! He threw his turban down to the ground. He slapped his face. Tears rolled down his cheeks as he spoke: *"What a sad day! What has happened to the household of Sayyida Fatima? The master of the women of the worlds! Yazid! You tyrant! What have you done to the household of Sayyida Fatima?"*

The first days and nights of Muharram passed by, and Ashura came. At dawn, Ali Akbar came and gave Adhan for the last time. Yazid's soldiers blew the trumpets to start the battle. One-by-one, Hussain's companions went to the battlefield and gave their lives for Islam. Between Zuhr and Asr time, Habib Ibn Mazaahir came to Hussain (as).

He said: *"My master, Hussain, allow me to go to the battlefield. Let me sacrifice my life for islam."*

The Imam replied: *"Habib, my childhood friend. Stay with me. You give comfort to me, my friend."*

Habib persisted with his request *"Please let me go."* Eventually, Hussain gave his permission. Hussain helped his friend, Habib, onto the horse.

Habib lbn Mazaahir rode into the battlefield. He fought bravely but was finally over-powered. He fell to the ground. As Habib ibn Mazaahir fell to the ground, an enemy soldier came over and cut off his head. All the martyrs of Karbala had their heads cut off, but Habib's was the first to be cut off by the enemy. Habib's head was not mounted on the spear like that of the other martyrs. Habib's head was tied to a horse and pulled on the ground of Karbala!

Later, in Shaam, Habib's head was tied to a horse's neck. A young boy, called Qasim, followed the horse wherever it went. One day, the man riding the horse asked the young boy Qasim: *"Why are you following me around? What do you want?"*

Qasim just looked at the head hanging from the horse's neck. The man asked again: *"Why are you staring at the head?"*

The boy replied: *"This head is the head of my father, Habib ibn Mazaahir; please give it to me so that I can bury my father's head."*

Habib's head seemed to look at his son and say: *"My son qasim, you are thinking of burying my head? What about the head of hussain on top of the spear?!"*[194]

Ali Akbar

Ali Akbar went over to his father to ask his permission to go out into that gory arena from which no person from his camp had returned. Hussain (as) looked at his face; it would be more

---

[194] Recalling the Sacrifices of Karbala by Sheikh Mateen Charbonneau

correct to say that for a couple of minutes his stare was fixed on that face which he loved so much; which reminded him every time of his grandfather whom he resembled every inch. He tried to say something, but his voice failed him. With considerable effort he whispered with downcast eyes: *"Akbar, I wish you had become a father; then you would have known what I am experiencing at this moment. My son how can a father ask his son to go, when he knows that the parting would be forever! But Akbar, the call of duty makes me helpless in this matter. Go to your mother, and to your aunt Zainab (as) who has brought you up from childhood and loved you and cared for you more than for her own sons and seek their permission."*

Ali Akbar entered the tent of his aunt Zainab (as). He found her and his mother Umme Laila gazing vacantly towards the battlefield and listening intently to the battle cries of the enemy hordes. Their instinct made them aware that, now that all the devoted followers of Hussain (as) had laid down their dear lives defending him and them, the turn of his sons, and brothers and nephews had come. It was now only a question of time. It was only a question who would go first from amongst them.

The light footsteps of Ali Akbar roused both of them from their reverie. Both of them fixed their gaze on him without uttering a word. Zainab (as) broke the silence with an exclamation: *"O' God, can it be true that Akbar has come to bid me and his mother the last farewell Akbar do not say that you are ready for the last journey. So long as my sons Aun and Muhammad are there, it is impossible for me to let you go."*

Akbar knew what love and affection his aunt Zainab (as) had for him. He was conscious of the pangs of sorrow she was experiencing at that moment. Her affection for him transcended everything except her love for Hussain (as). He looked at her face, and at his mother's who was rendered speechless by her surging feelings of anguish. He knew not how to tell them that he had prepared himself for the journey to Heaven that lay ahead. He summoned to his aid his most coaxing manners that had always made his mother and Zainab (as) accede to his requests and said: *"My aunt, for all my father's kinsmen the inevitable hour has come. I implore you, by the love you bear for your brother, to let me go so that it may not be said that he spared me till all his brothers and nephews were killed. Abbas, my uncle, is Commander of our army. The others are all younger than me. When death is a certainty, let me die first so that I can quench my thirst at the heavenly spring of Kausar at the hands of my grandfather."*

The earnestness of Akbar's tone convinced Zainab (as) and his mother that he was determined to go. It seemed to be his last wish to lay down his life before all his kinsmen. Since on no other occasion they had denied him his wishes, it seemed so difficult to say no to his last desire. With a gasp Zainab (as) could only say, *"Akbar, my child, if the call of death has come to you, go."*

His mother could only say: *"May God be with you, my son. With you I am losing all I had and cared for in this world. Your father has told me what destiny has in store for me. After you, for me pleasure and pain will have no difference."* With these words she fell unconscious in Ali Akbar's arms.

The battle cry from the enemy's ranks was becoming louder and louder. Ali Akbar knew that he had to go out quickly lest the enemy, seeing that their challenges for combat were remaining unanswered, got emboldened to make a concerted attack on his father's camp. Even such a thought was unbearable for him. So long as he was alive, how could he permit the onslaught of Yazid's forces on his camp where helpless women and defenseless children were lying huddled together? He gently put his mother in his aunt Zainab's arms saying: *"Zainab, my aunt, I am leaving my mother to your care. I know, from your childhood, your mother Bibi Fatima (as) has prepared you for the soul-stirring events of today and what is to come hereafter. My mother will not be able to bear the blows and calamities that are to befall her, unless you lend her your courage. I implore you by the infinite love you bear for me to show the fortitude that you are capable of, so that your patience may sustain my mother when she sees my dead body brought into the camp's morgue. I entrust her to your care because there will be none to solace her and look after her in the years of dismay and despondency that lie ahead of her."*

Ali Akbar embraced his loving aunt Zainab (as) with tender love and affection for the last time. she exclaimed: *"Akbar, go. My child, I entrust you to God, to ease your last moments I promise you that, so long as I live, I shall look after Umme Laila with the affection of a mother."*

With a heavy heart Ali Akbar returned to his father. There was no need for him to say that he had bid farewell to his mother and aunt Zainab (as), for the sorrow depicted on his face spoke volumes to Hussain (as). Silently he rose and put the Prophet's turban on Akbar's head, tied the scabbard on his waist and imprinted a kiss on his forehead. In a failing, faltering voice he muttered: *"Go Akbar, God is there to help you."*

Treading heavily Akbar came out of the tent with Hussain (as) following closely behind him. He was about to mount his horse when he felt somebody tugging at his robe. He could hardly see because his eyes were almost blinded with tears. He heard the voice of his young sister Sakina supplicating him not to leave her: *"O my brother,"* she was saying, *"do not go to the battle ground from which nobody has returned alive since this morning."*

Softly Akbar lifted her, gently and affectionately kissed her on her face and put her down. His grief was too deep for words. Hussain (as) understood the depth of Akbar's feelings and picked up Sakina to console her.

The scene of Ali Akbar's march towards the battlefield was such as would defy description. The cries of ladies and children of Hussain's camp were rising above the din of battle cries and beating of enemy drums. It was appearing as if a dead body of an only son, dead in the prime of youth, was being taken out of a house for the last rites.

Ali Akbar was now facing the enemy hordes. He was addressing the forces of Umar ibn Saad with an eloquence that he had inherited from his grandfather and the Prophet (s). He was telling them that Hussain (as), his father, had done them no harm and had devoted his life to the cause of Islam. He was explaining to them that by shedding the blood of Hussain (as) and his kinsmen they would be incurring the wrath of God and displeasure of the Prophet (s) who had loved Hussain (as) more than any other person. He was exhorting them not to smear their hands with the blood of a person so Holy, so God-fearing and so righteous. His words cast a spell on the army of the opponents. The older ones from amongst them were blinking their eyes in amazement and wondering whether the Prophet (s) had descended from the Heavens to warn them against the shedding of Hussain's blood. What a resemblance there was with the Prophet (s), in face, features and even mannerism! Even the voice was of Muhammad! But on second thoughts, they realized that this was Ali Akbar, the 18-year-old son of Hussain (as), about whose close resemblance with the Prophet (s) people were talking so much.

Seeing the effect that Ali Akbar's address had produced on his soldiers, Umar ibn Saad exhorted them to challenge him to single combat. A few of them, coveting the honor and rewards they would get if they overpowered and killed this brave son of Hussain (as), emaciated by three days of hunger and thirst, came forward to challenge him. One by one he met them in battle, gave them a taste of his skill and prowess in fighting and flung them from their horseback to meet the doom they so much deserved. Now it was his turn to challenge the warriors of Yazid to come forward. Seeing that in spite of his handicaps, he was capable of displaying valor and battle craft for which his grandfather Ali had acquired name and fame and which had struck terror into the hearts of enemies of Islam none dared to come forward.

Ali Akbar had received several gaping wounds in the course of his victorious single combats. He was fast losing blood and the effect of his thirst was getting accentuated with every second that was passing. He realized that the treacherous enemies would attack him en masse. He had left his mother in a dazed condition. An irresistible urge to see his dear ones for the last time seized him and he turned his horse towards his camp.

He found his father standing at the doorstep of the tent and his mother and aunt standing inside the tent. Hussain (as) had been watching the battles of this thirsty youth and the two ladies were watching his face: they knew that if any calamity befell Ali Akbar, Hussain's expression would indicate it. Whilst watching Hussain's face, they were both praying offering silent prayers: *"O Allah, Who brought back Ismail to Hajra; O Allah, Who granted the prayers of the mother Musa and restored her son to her; O Allah, Who reunited Yakoob with his son Yusuf in response to the aged father's supplications, grant us our one wish to see Ali Akbar for once."*

Was it the effect of these prayers that brought back Ali Akbar to the camp? Ali Akbar was now facing his aged father and his loving mother and Zainab (as). With an exclamation of joy and relief they clung to him. Hussain (as) lovingly embraced his son saying: *"Bravo, my son. The gallantry you how displayed today reminded me of the battles of my revered father, Ali. The only difference was that, during his fights, my father Ali had not to battle against hunger and thirst as you had to."*

Ali Akbar with his head bent replied: *"Father, thirst is killing me because my wounds have added to its effect. It is usual to ask for rewards from parents for celebrating victories in single combats and I would have asked for a cup of refreshing water from you. But alas! I know that you have not even a drop of water with which you can quench the thirst of the young children. Father, knowing this, I shall not embarrass you by asking for water. I have come only to see you and my dear ones for the last time."*

Ali Akbar met each and every one of his family. The second parting was sad as the first one, perhaps sadder. Without being told, everyone realized that this was the last time they were beholding Akbar. Fizza, the faithful maid of Fatima (as) and Zainab (as), was as disconsolate with grief as Zainab (as) and Umme Laila. Hussain (as) followed Ali Akbar out of the tent. As he rode away, Hussain (as) walked behind him with a brisk pace for some distance, as a man follows his sacrificial lamb in Mina. When Akbar disappeared from his sight, he turned heavenwards and, with his hands raised, he prayed: *"O Allah, Thou art my Witness that on this day I have sent away for sacrifice one whom I loved and cherished most, to defend the cause of righteousness and truth."*

He sat on the ground as if trying to listen expectantly to some call from the battlefield. It was not very long before he received a wailing call, a call from Ali Akbar, a call of anguish and pain: *"Father, Akbar has fallen with a mortal wound in his chest. Father, come to me for I have not long to live. If you cannot reach me, I convey my last salutations to you and my dear ones."*

Though Hussain (as) was anticipating such a call, what a ghastly effect it had on him! He rose from the ground and fell; he rose again and fell again. With one hand on his heart he struggled to his feet. Torrential tears were flooding his eyes. He rushed in the direction from which the cry had come. It seemed as Hussain's strength had ebbed away on hearing that fateful cry of his dearest son, for he was falling at every few steps. He was sobbing: *"Akbar, give me another shout so that I can follow its direction. Akbar, my sight is gone with the shock I have received and there is nobody to guide me to where you lie."*

Abbas came rushing to the aid of his master. Holding his hand he led him on to the place from where Akbar's dying cry had come. Now Hussain (as) was stumbling his way onwards resting his hands on Abbas' shoulders. The distance seemed interminable but at last Hussain (as) and Abbas reached the place where Akbar was lying in a pool of his own blood. Ah, that tragic sight! May no father have occasion to see his young son in such a condition. With one hand on his chest covering a deep wound from which blood was gushing out, with his face writhing with pain, Akbar was lying on the ground prostrate and unconscious. With the agony he was enduring on account of the wound and the thirst that he was suffering, he was digging his feet into the sand. With a cry of anguish Hussain (as) fell on the body of Akbar: *"My son, tell me where you are hurt; tell me who has wounded you in the chest. Why don't you say something? My Akbar, I have come in response to your call. Say one word to me, Akbar."*

Seeing that Akbar was lying there without any response to his entreaties, Hussain (as) turned to Abbas and said: *"Abbas, why don't you tell Akbar to say something to me? My dutiful son, who used to get up on seeing me, is lying on the ground pressed by the hand of death."*

Hussain (as) once again flung himself on the body of Akbar. His breathing was now heavier, a gurgling sound was coming from his throat. It seemed that his young life was engaged in an uneven struggle with death. Hussain (as) put his head on Akbar's chest. He lifted it and put his own cheeks against Akbar's and wailed: *"Akbar, for once open your eyes and smile, as you were always smiling to gladden my heart."*

Though Akbar did not open his eyes, a faint smile appeared on his lips as if he had listened to his father's request. With the sweet smile still playing on his lips, he heaved a gasp and with that his soul departed. The cheeks of the father were still touching the cheeks of the son, in death as so many times in life.

On seeing his son, his beloved son, breathe his last in his own hands, Hussain's condition became such as no words can describe. For quite some time he remained there weeping as only an aged father who has lost a son, in his prime of youth, in such tragic circumstances, can weep. Abbas sat there by his side shedding tears. What words of consolation could he offer when the tragedy was of such a magnitude? All words of solace and comfort would sound hollow and be in vain when a father, an aged father, gives vent to his pent-up emotions. After a time, Abbas reverentially touched Hussain (as) on his shoulders and reminded him that, since he had rushed out of the camp, Zainab (as) and the other ladies of his house were waiting for him, tormented by anxiety, demented by the thoughts of the tragedy that had befallen them. Only mention of this was enough for Hussain (as). He knew that, as the head of the family, it was his duty to rally by the side of the grief-stricken mother, his grief-stricken sister Zainab (as), and the children for whom this bereavement was the greatest calamity.

Hussain (as) slowly rose from the ground and tried to pick up the dead body of Akbar but he himself fell on the ground. Abbas, seeing this, bent over him and said: *"My master, Abbas is still alive by your side. How can I leave you carry the body of Akbar and remain a silent spectator? Let me carry his body to the camp."*

No Abbas, replied to Hussain (as), *"Let me do this as a last token of my love. To hold him by my heart, even in his death, gives me some comfort, the only comfort that is now left to me."*

Saying this, he made all the efforts that he was capable of and, assisted by Abbas, he lifted the body of Akbar. Clasping it close to his bosom, he started the long walk to his camp. How he reached is difficult to say. It would not be too much to imagine that his grandfather Muhammad, his father Ali, his brother Hassan (as) and perhaps his mother Fatima (as) had descended from heaven to help him in this task.

Hussain (as) reached the camp and laid down Akbar's body on the ground. He called Umme Laila and Zainab (as) and Kulsum, Sakina and Rokayya, Fizza and the other ladies of the house to see the face of Akbar for the last time. The loving mother came, the loving aunts came, the children came, and surrounded the body of Ali Akbar. They looked at Akbar's face and then at Hussain's. They knew that their weeping would add to Hussain's grief that was already brimful. Ali Akbar's mother went up to her husband and with stifled sobs and bent head, she said to him: *"My master, I am proud of Akbar for dying such a noble death. He has laid down his life in the noblest cause and this thought will sustain me through the rest of my life. I implore you to pray for me, to pray for all of us, that Almighty Allah may grant us patience and solace."*

Saying this she turned to the dead body of her son lying on the ground and put her face on his. Zainab (as) and Kulsum, Sakina and Rokayya had all flung themselves on Akbar's body. The tears that were flowing from their eyes were sufficient to wash away the clotted blood from the wounds of Akbar.

Hussain (as) sat for a few minutes near the dead body of his son; the son whom he had lost in such tragic circumstances; the son who had died craving for a drop of water to quench his thirst. He felt dazed with grief. Qasim, the son of his brother, who had come to seek his permission to go to the battlefield, awakened him from his stupor. He rose from the ground, wiped the tears from his aged eyes and muttered: *"Verily from God we come, and unto Him is our return."*

The Youths of Karbala Qasim, Aun and Muhammad

Next to the battlefield went the sons of Imam Al-Hassan (as) and Zainab (as). They were all in their teens, but each stood bravely, believing in the mission, facing a formidable enemy, and showed no less enthusiasm in their quest to embrace the martyrdom.

'The days of our youth are the days of our glory'. What hopes and feelings surge in young hearts during this time of life!

How every nerve and tendon quivers with the joy of living! But there are some youths to whom the cup of life is dealt in another measure. There are some budding flowers that are destined to be swept away by the hot desert winds before they have the opportunity to bloom. Such was the destiny of Hussain's three nephews who were gathered outside the tents on the eve of that eventful day of Muharram.

Qasim, Aun and Muhammad were gathered to discuss the part they would play on the following day in defense of their uncle. There was grim determination writ large on their young faces. They were watching the progress of the moon as it was marching slowly through that cloudless sky, anxiously waiting for the morrow to unfold its event. Each one of them had the desire to go first into the battlefield to shed his blood. Even the few words they exchanged amongst themselves pertained to their anxiety lest their uncle Hussain (as) might hold them back. They were discussing among themselves how to secure the permission of the Imam to march off into the battlefield.

Their talks were interrupted by someone coming and informing Qasim that his mother Umme Farwa wanted him to see her. He hurried to the tent. As soon as he entered it, his mother put her arms round him and said: *"Qasim my son, do you know why I called you? I want to remind you about your duty towards your uncle, Hussain (as). I want to tell you something about the unparalleled love and affection Hassan (as) your father had for Hussain (as). The two of them were so much devoted to each other that they were always thinking and acting in unison. The other instantaneously felt the slightest pain suffered by one as if they were twins from the same embryo. With the unique love your father had for Hussain (as), I can well imagine how he, if alive, would have felt today! He would have been the first to sacrifice his life for his beloved younger brother."*

She stopped for a few seconds and then, in a soft tone, as if reminiscing, added: *"I am sure he wanted you to deputize for* him on this day. My child, when he passed away, you were too young to understand life. On his death-bed his last words to me were: "Umme Farwa, I entrust you and my children to God and Hussain (as). When Qasim grows up, you tell him that my dying desire was that he should stand by Hussain (as) through thick and thin. I can see the clouds of treachery gathering against Hussain (as). A day may come when he may need the unflinching devotion and sacrifice of his near and dear ones. Though I will not live to see that day, as my last wish I want you to prepare Qasim for it from his childhood." Her voice choked with emotion, as she continued: "My Qasim, since that day your father breathed his last, Hussain (as) has looked after you as his own son. Nay, he has treated you on all occasions better than his own sons. You know how he has fulfilled your every wish so that you may not miss the love and affection of your father. Now it is your turn to show that you can repay, to some extent, your debt of gratitude by laying down your life for him before any of his sons, brothers and kinsmen. Now is your chance to reciprocate his love and affection, by demonstrating to the enemies that you are a scion of the House of Ali and can wield the sword in defense of truth."

Qasim listened to his mother with his head bowed in respect. He felt very much relieved by what his mother had said to him because he had felt very apprehensive as to how she would react when he approached her for her permission to go for the fight. He knew how his mother was attached to him after his father's death. He was well aware how restless she used to become, if she would not see him even for a few hours. He had thought that the very idea of her son marching out into the battlefield would make her demented. He felt as if his mother had taken a load off his head. He affectionately hugged her and said: "My dearest mother, I know not how I can thank you for what you have said to me just now. You know my filial affection for my uncle Hussain (as). From my childhood I have not known what a father's love means but I know this for certain that even my father, if alive, would not have been so kind, so considerate, so affectionate to me as my uncle Hussain (as) has been to me.

He has not allowed me to feel even for a moment that I am an orphan. Thanks to him, in our house my every wish has been a command. How is it possible for me, the son of Hassan (as), to be oblivious of my obligations to him? For me death would be far better than life without him and my dear uncle Abbas, and my cousins Ali Akbar, Muhammad and others."

Umme Farwa felt elated at the brave reply of her brave son. A painful thought passed her mind, the thought that this dear child who was so devoted to her and in whom she had reposed all her hopes, would perish on the fields of Karbala. With great efforts she controlled herself.

On the departure of Qasim, Aun and Muhammad waited for some time for him to return. Then both returned to their tent to console their mother, Zainab (as), whose grief and sorrow defied description. As they entered the tent, they saw her sitting on the ground with a candle in her hand looking intently at Ali Akbar, their cousin, whom she had brought up as her own son and for whom her love and affection was without a parallel. When she saw both entering the tent, she beckoned to them to come and sit near Ali Akbar. Both did so according to her bidding. She turned towards them and said in a low tone: *"My children, do you know what tomorrow has in store for us? It will be a day of trial; it will be a day when the blood of our family will flow like water; it will be a day on which all the vendetta nurtured by the enemies of the Prophet's house for all these years will be spilled out. I want both of you, my beloved sons, to defend your uncle Hussain (as) and his children at the cost of your lives."* After a pause she added: *"When I was leaving Mecca, your father Abdullah asked me to take both of you with me so that, if an occasion arose you, Aun, could be the deputy of your father in seeking martyrdom, and you, Muhammad, could be my offering in the cause of Islam."*

Hearing their mother talk in this vein touched both to the quick. How could they tell their mother Zainab (as) that they were fully prepared for the doom that awaited them; that they were both coveting martyrdom in defense of the cause of Islam and its inviolable principles for which Hussain (as) stood up so boldly and firmly in the face of odds! Aun was the first to speak. His voice was quivering with emotion when he said: *"Mother, we both feel so elated to know that we have your permission to fight in defense of our uncle and his family. God willing, we both will show the army of Umar ibn Saad that we are the grandsons of Jaafar-e-Tayyar whose prowess in battle had become legendary. We shall offer such fight tomorrow that, whenever you will remember us and mourn for us, your grief will be mingled with pride that we lived up to the reputation of our family."*

Hardly had Aun concluded when Muhammad, the younger one, burst out saying, *"My loving mother, do not think that we need any exhortation to fight valiantly tomorrow. I am itching to go out in defense of my uncle. From my childhood I have been hearing about the valor of my maternal grandfather Ali, and paternal grandfather Jaafar-e-Tayyar. It is not for nothing that we both have learnt the art of single combat from our uncle Abbas. You may rest assured that, so long as we breathe, we shall not let the least harm come to our uncle Hussain (as) or to any of his children."*

With this reply of the brave youngsters Zainab (as) felt reassured. It was not that she, for a moment, doubted their devotion or sense of duty. It was not that she considered it necessary to instill any courage in them, for she knew that both were brave and noble sons of a brave and noble father. Her love for her brave sons was surging within her. She was feeling as if her heart was getting squeezed when she was conjuring up the vision of these youths dying as martyrs.

Ali Akbar who was listening quietly to the talk between the mother and the two sons, looked at the face of the mother and then at the sons. With a faint smile playing on his lips, he said: *"We of the Prophet's family will go out to meet death as is our wont. In what order it will be, it is for God to determine."*

When he said this, perhaps he had the conviction that Hussain (as) would never allow his nephews to die so long as he, Ali Akbar, was there. How rightly he had surmised, the events of Ashura would show!

Like all passing things that night also passed away to become a chapter of history. The day dawned and with it began the gory events that make mankind, who have the vestiges of humanity, tremble with rage and grief. As Ali Akbar had surmised that night, when the turn of members of the family came, Hussain (as) came over to him and, with his hand on his heart, said to him: *"My son, go forward to fulfill your appointed task."*

As much as Zainab (as) and Umme Farwa protested that, so long as their sons lived, they could not think of Ali Akbar laying down his life, much as Abbas pleaded to let him be the first among the Hashimites to die fighting, Hussain (as) insisted that he would send Ali Akbar as his own representative to be the first among his kinsmen. Ali Akbar went to the battlefield never to return from it.

Zainab (as) was disconsolate on Ali Akbar's death. Now Aun and Muhammad were hovering round Hussain (as) with entreaties to let them go.

Qasim was no less vehement in his supplication for the Imam's permission to die on the battlefield. To Qasim's repeated requests his uncle's reply was: *"My dear child, how can I permit you to go when I know for certain that death awaits those who venture out. Your father, my beloved Hassan (as), had entrusted you to my care on his deathbed. My heart trembles at the very thought of sending you into the jaws of death."*

This reply of Hussain (as) broke Qasim's heart. He thought that his uncle would not under any circumstances allow him to share the fate of the other martyrs. With tears in his eyes he stood there, not knowing what to do to secure Hussain's permission.

At that moment Zainab (as) came over to her brother. With folded hands she said to Hussain (as), *"My dearest brother, in my whole life I have never asked you for a favor. Now, for the first time, I am requesting you to grant me one wish; let my sons follow in the footsteps of Ali Akbar."*

Hussain (as) looked at Zainab (as) and then at her sons. With his head bent, he replied; *"Zainab; my dearest sister, I find it impossible to deny your first and last request, though my granting it makes my heart sink within me."*

Turning to Aun and Muhammad he said: *"My dear children, go forward and fulfill your heart's desire to die like heroes. I shall soon be joining you on your journey to eternity."*

At this reply the two young heroes felt delighted in the midst of unbounded sorrows. They fell at their mother's feet and asked her for her blessings. Zainab's grief at the parting with these beloved children found its way through her tears which were now pouring from her eyes in torrents. She felt an urge to clasp her young sons to her bosom before they marched out on their last journey; but for fear that such display of emotion might unnerve them, she held back. She could not say anything to them in farewell. With suppressed sobs she whispered to them: *"My beloved ones, may God be with you and may He grant you quick relief from the agonies that you are to endure. It is Zainab's lot to endure ignominies with no brothers, no nephews, no sons to console her. My last request to you is to fight bravely and to die bravely so that, in the midst of my unbearable sufferings in captivity, I may at least have one remembrance to console me: your bravery in the face of overwhelming odds."*

She mutely watched her sons mounting their horses assisted by Hussain (as). Her lips were moving in silent prayers; her eyes were following the horses as they galloped out into the arena. When they both got out of sight, with a sigh she sat on the sand near her tent as if lost in a reverie.

When Qasim saw that Aun and Muhammad had been

granted permission to march out on the entreaties of their mother, he rushed to his mother's tent. Almost sobbing with disappointment, he told Umme Farwa that Aun and Muhammad had secured the Imam's permission on the intercession of their mother, but he had nobody to plead on his behalf with his uncle. In utter despondency he said; *"If I am not destined to be a martyr on this day, life has no charm left for me. Am I destined to be a captive and led through the streets to a prison cell?"*

Upon seeing Qasim so bitter and dejected Umme Farwa burst into tears of grief. Controlling herself she began to think what to do to get Hussain's permission for him. Her first reaction was to go over to the Imam and to implore him as his brother's widow and seek permission for Qasim. However, in a flash she remembered her husband's words to her shortly before his death. He had told her that for Qasim a time might come when he would find himself in the trough of despair and despondency and feel dejected and depressed beyond description. He had told her that, when this happened, she should deliver to him an envelope wherein he had kept a letter especially for this occasion. This she had carefully preserved and kept with her as her most cherished thing in a box. Fortunately for her, she had brought the box with her. She hastened to fetch the letter and handing over the envelope to Qasim she said: *"Qasim, your present plight brought back to me your father's words that a day like this would come for you and when this happened, I should deliver the letter to you."*

With rekindled hopes and expectation Qasim took the envelope from his mother's hand and opened it. In it he found two letters one addressed to himself and the other addressed to Hussain (as). He anxiously opened the letter meant for him and read it aloud for his mother's benefit. Hassan (as) had written in it: *"My child, when this letter reaches you, I will be no more. When you read it, you will find yourself torn with a conflict between your desire to do your duty and fulfill your obligations and demonstrate your love and esteem for your uncle, and his love and affection for you compelling him to hold you back. My*

Qasim, I have provided for this event by arming you with a letter for my dearest brother Hussain (as). You may deliver the letter to Hussain (as) so that he may grant you your heart's desire. There is much that I could say for this occasion but when you read this, you will find that time separating us is not long. So, hurry along, my child, as I am waiting for you with open arms to welcome you."

When he had completed reading the letter Qasim felt choked with emotion. His mother also stood speechless with feelings surging in her heart. Both were thinking in unison how loving and thoughtful it was of Hassan (as) to provide a solution for their dilemma. Qasim reverentially bowed over the letter and kissed it. The tears rolling from his eyes fell on the writing but, instead of smearing the lettering, they lent glitter to it.

Umme Farwa was the first to get out of the reverie. She broke the silence and said: *"My dearest Qasim, now that your father has come to your rescue even in death, take his letter to your uncle Hussain (as). I have no doubt that now he will not be able to refuse you his permission for laying down your life."*

Qasim could now hardly contain himself. He rushed towards the tent of Imam Hussain (as) with the letter in his hands. He found Hussain (as) standing outside Zainab's tent looking intently towards the battlefield. Abbas was by his side and Zainab (as) was standing near the door holding up the curtain and looking at the faces of Hussain (as) and Abbas Qasim knew that they were all watching the combats of Aun and Muhammad. How could he disturb his uncle at such a time? He stood quietly by the side of Hussain (as) and Abbas and gazed in the direction of the army pitted against his two young cousins. He could see from clouds of dust rising in the far distance that one of them had gone ahead of the other. Not so far away he could see the younger one, Muhammad, battling against a number of enemy soldiers clustered round him.

Hardly a few minutes had passed in watching the battle,

when they saw Aun falling from his horse and giving a cry to his uncle to come to him and carry his body. Hussain (as), who had already borne the afflictions of his companions' death and the loss of his dearest son, Ali Akbar, seemed to wince as if he had received a stab in his chest. He turned to Zainab (as) to see her reaction on hearing her son's last cry. Abbas and Qasim rushed to her side to hold her. As if this blow was not enough, Muhammad also fell from his horse mortally wounded and similarly shouted to Hussain (as) to come to him. Abbas and Qasim knew that for Hussain (as) to reach his dying nephews, one after the other, was too trying even for a person of his mettle who had right through the morning performed this task himself. Abbas wanted to accompany Hussain (as) and assist him in bringing the dead brothers to the camp, leaving Qasim to attend to Zainab (as) who had collapsed with grief and sorrow on hearing the parting cry of Muhammad. But Hussain (as) beckoned to him to remain with Zainab (as). Qasim tried to follow him, but Hussain (as) asked him also to remain near Zainab (as) and console her.

Hussain (as) first reached the place where Muhammad was lying mortally wounded. He bent over his body to find that, on account of loss of blood, his young life was ebbing fast. The child was gasping heavily. His throat was so parched that even with great efforts he was not able to speak clearly. Hussain (as) put his ear near Muhammad's mouth. In a faint, faltering voice the young lad said: *"My last salutations to you, uncle. Tell my mother that I have lived up to her expectations and am dying bravely as she and my father wanted me. Give my last salaams to her and console her as much as you can."*

The efforts made by the child in saying these words appeared to exhaust him. He added after a few seconds: *"I heard the cry of Aun before I fell. Now that I am beyond any help, Uncle please go over to him and see if you can do something for him before it is too late."*

Hardly had he said these words when his life became extinct. Hussain (as) was beside himself with grief. But he could not remain there long as he had to go over to Aun. He rushed in the direction where Aun had fallen. On reaching his body he found that he had breathed his last. He picked up his lifeless body and pressed it to his heart.

With a heavy tread, with tears flowing in torrents, the aged uncle began his march towards the camp with the body of his nephew in his arms. Abbas came rushing from the camp towards him and said, *"Let me carry Aun's body to the morgue and you take Muhammad's body. My master, Abbas is still alive to share your burden and grief."* Quietly Hussain (as) handed over Aun's body to Abbas and went over to pick up Muhammad's body. The two brothers, one old and one young, were each carrying the body of a young nephew. The sight was such as to evoke sorrow and grief in the hearts of the most hard-hearted persons.

On reaching their camp Hussain (as) and Abbas laid the bodies of Aun and Muhammad on the ground. Zainab (as) who was waiting for them came over and fell on the two bodies of her sons. *"My sons, my sons,"* she cried, *"What mother is there to*

send her beloved ones to meet death as I have sent mine?" Her face was bathed in tears. With sobs she was saying: *"My darlings, you have gone from this world with your thirst unquenched. Your grandfather Ali will be there to quench your thirst in heaven. My beloved sons, for Zainab there is still a long, weary, unending future to face without you two to lighten the burden with your brave talk."* Overpowered by her grief and emotions she fell unconscious on the dead bodies.

Hussain (as), Abbas, Qasim and the ladies who were all standing and crying by her side, gently picked up Zainab (as) and took her to her tent. They all knew that in such a great tragedy as had befallen her; all words of consolation would only be in vain.

As was the practice of Yazid's army, they started beating the drums on the slaughter of the two nephews of Hussain (as), to herald their victory. When the beating of drums stopped, they raised the usual cry challenging the young defenders of Hussain (as) to come out into the field to face death. Now Qasim came over to Hussain (as), who was standing near Zainab's prostrate form with his head bent. Qasim could not muster sufficient strength to say what he had come to convey to the Imam. He quietly handed over the letter of his father for Hussain (as) that he had found in the envelope given to him by his mother. Hussain (as) glanced at the handwriting on the letter and at once recognized it as his late lamented brother's. With surprise he opened the letter and as he eagerly read it, he could not control himself and burst into a cry of grief. In the letter it was written: *"My beloved Hussain (as), when this letter will be read by you, you will be surrounded by sorrows on all sides, with dead bodies of your near and dear ones strewn round you. I will not be there to lay down my life for you, Hussain (as), but I am leaving behind my Qasim to be my deputy on this day. Hussain (as), I beseech you not to reject my offering. In the name of love that you bear for me, I implore you to let Qasim go forth and die in your defense. Dearest brother, in spirit I am with you, watching your heroic sacrifices and sharing your woes and affliction."*

Hassan's letter brought back to Hussain (as) the memories of his dear brother to whom he was devoted, and he wept copiously recollecting his love and affection. What unique love Hassan (as) had for him that, though dead, he had left his deputy in Qasim for this day!

With effort Hussain (as) controlled himself turned to Qasim saying: *"Dear child, your father's wishes, which I regard as commands for me, leave me no other alternative. March on Qasim, as your father wished you to do. If it is so ordained that I may bear the wound of your martyrdom, I shall bow to the Will of God."*

Qasim bowed reverentially and hurried to his mother Umme Farwa who was sitting dazed with grief on receiving the sad news of Aun and Muhammad's martyrdom. As Qasim entered her tent, she raised her head and looked at him expectantly. She could see from the look of satisfaction he had on his face that he had received Hussain's permission for which he had been begging so long. An exchange of looks between the mother and son confirmed to Umme Farwa that she was right. Slowly she rose and said to Qasim: *"My beloved son, all these years I have been waiting for the day when you would become a bridegroom, and dressed as a groom, come to receive my blessings. It seems that fate has decreed otherwise. Qasim, I have preserved the dress your father wore on the day of his marriage with me. I had hoped that, on your wedding day, I would ask you to wear it. Now that you are going to the land of no return, my wish is that you put on that dress so that my desire to see you dressed as a groom may be fulfilled."* After a pause she continued in a reflective tone: *"It is the custom for grooms to apply henna on their hands- Though I have none with me, I know that you will not need it. Your hands will be dyed with your own blood."*

With these words she kissed her son's cheeks and embraced him. It was a long embrace, the embrace of a mother who knew that she was seeing her young darling for the last time in this world. Holding him tightly in her arms she was looking longingly at his face, as if she wanted to let his image sink into her mind's eye forever. All partings are sad but where the parting is forever, and in such circumstances, what words can describe it?

> *My son Qasim,*
> - a day will come when my brother Hussain will be facing an enemy army of tens of thousands. That will be the day when Islam will need to be saved by sacrifice.
>
> YOU MUST REPRESENT ME ON THAT DAY.

The mother and son tore themselves from each other lest their surging love and attachment might make their parting impossible. Umme Farwa brought out the wedding garments of Hassan (as) for Qasim to wear. Dressed in these clothes Qasim was looking the very image of Hassan (as). The son, followed by the mother, went over to Zainab's tent to bid her good-bye. Zainab (as) had not completely recovered from her swoon: In her dazed mind she thought for a moment that Hassan (as) had descended from heaven to defend his brother. It was just a flitting thought that passed away like lightning. She realized that it was Qasim who had come to pay his last respects She looked at him and then at this mother who was following him. She understood with what efforts Umme Farwa was controlling her feelings. Much as her own heart was bursting with grief at this parting with her beloved brother's son, she knew that it was essential for her to control herself for the sake of Umme Farwa. With one hand on her head and the other on her heart, she came forward to bid adieu to Qasim. With hot tears rolling down her cheeks she kissed Qasim on his forehead saying: *"Qasim, my dear child, your aged aunt had hoped that you, my dear ones, would carry my funeral bier. But it is written in Zainab's fate that she should see the young lives of her dearest ones extinguished before her. It has fallen to my lot to see you all dead before me and to carry your memories for the rest of my dreary, unending days. March on my child with the name of God."*

Qasim came to Hussain (as) and reverentially kissed his hands. Seeing Qasim so vividly resembling Hassan (as), his dear, departed brother, Hussain (as) wept bitterly. He kissed Qasim on his cheeks and held the horse for him to mount. Abbas came forward to do this service, but Hussain (as) would not let him do so. *"This is the last occasion for me to give a send-off to my Qasim and let me do this for him."* He turned to Qasim and said: *"Qasim, I shall not be long in joining you."*

Reaching the battle arena, Qasim addressed the enemy with an eloquence that reminded many of the sermons of his grandfather Ali. With gaping mouths, they were transfixed to the ground at his words of admonition on the betrayal of the Imam. Umar Ibne Saad ordered his men to challenge him to single combat, fearing that this youth's eloquence might rouse the vestiges of goodness in some of his men. Qasim fought battles with several of them and threw them from their horses as if he were a seasoned warrior and not a youth of 14, with three day's thirst and hunger. Such was his skill with the sword and horsemanship that Hussain (as), who was watching his nephew's fight from a hillock near his camp, burst into spontaneous acclamation. Now no warrior from the enemy ranks was coming forward to meet the challenge of this brave son of Hassan (as). He was now repeatedly challenging the soldiers of Umar ibn Saad to come forward and match their skill and swordsmanship against him in single combat. Umar ibn Saad, seeing that none of his warriors was prepared for this, ordered his soldiers to attack Qasim together. It was now a fight between one and thousands, if such a thing can at all be called a fight. How long could Qasim ward off the attacks of swords, spears, daggers, and arrows coming at him from all directions? He was wounded from head to foot. When he saw that he could no longer remain in the saddle, he gave a cry offering his last salutation to his uncle Hussain (as).

Hussain (as), who was watching from a distance the dastardly attack of the multitude of soldiers on his helpless Qasim, heard this cry full of agony and pain. He felt as if he had himself received all the wounds inflicted on Qasim. He unsheathed his sword, and like an enraged lion, he rushed towards the battlefield. With sword in one hand, he galloped his horse cutting through the enemy hordes. Such was the fury of his charge that the enemy were reminded of the charges of Ali, his father, in the battle of Siffin, when the dexterous Lion of God had singly scattered the enemy, running through them like a knife through butter, and killing hundreds with the powerful sweeps of his sword, while the remainder of the arrant towards ran helter-skelter to save their contemptible lives. The stampede of Yazid's soldiers was such that the body of Qasim was trampled under the feet of hundreds of minions who were a disgrace of their calling. When the battlefield was cleared of the cowards and Hussain (as) reached the body of Qasim, he found that it was torn to pieces. What feelings this gruesome sight evoked in Hussain's heart can better be imagined than described. Hussain (as) stumbled down from his horse and fell to the ground exclaiming: *"My God, what have these cowards done to my Qasim?"*

For some time, he wept with such agony that his body convulsed. After a while he took off his robe and started picking up pieces of Qasim's body. One by one he put them all in his robe and, lifting the bundle, put it on his aged shoulders and mounted the horse. As he did so, he muttered: *"My Qasim, your mother had sent you out dressed as a groom. Now you are returning to your mother with your body cut to pieces."*

As he was riding back towards his camp, Hussain (as) was disconsolately exclaiming: *"My God, has there been an instance where an uncle had to carry his own nephew's body in such a state?"*

On reaching the camp Hussain (as) put down the body on the ground. He called Abbas and asked him to bring Umme Farwa and his sisters Zainab (as) and Kulsum to the morgue. He besought Fizza, his mother's devoted maid, to console Umme Farwa and Zainab (as), for he knew that the condition of Qasim's body might give them such a shock as would kill them.

Qasim's mother came with Zainab (as) on one side and Umme Kulsum on the other. Fizza went over to the ladies and said: "I beseech you, in the name of my lady Fatima (as), to muster all the strength and courage you can to see Qasim's mortal remains. They may be torn and cut to pieces but remember his soul is now with my lady and Hassan (as), who must have welcomed him with open arms." Saying this, she opened the robe and unfolded the body. Zainab (as) held her aching heart, Kulsum held her reeling head and Umme Farwa fell with a shriek and fainted.

What pen can narrate the grief of a mother who has lost her only son? What words can describe the agony of a mother's loving heart on seeing her son in such a state? The land of Karbala was echoing the cries of the ladies and the wailing of the children on Qasim's death. Can anyone attempt to depict Hussain's plight at that time? Resting his head on Abbas's shoulders, Hussain (as) was saying: *"My God, my God, if my enemies wanted to kill me, they could do so; but what have my dear ones done that they slay them so mercilessly?"*

Hussain (as) stood there for some time as if in a trance. Abbas who softly said to him *"My master, now let me go, as others have done, brought him back to the reality of the situation. I am now the commander of soldiers who are no more."* Hussain (as) for a moment did not reply. Then he equally softly said: *"Verily we come from God and unto Him we shall return."*

Abu Fadl Abbas ibn Ali

The shifting sand dunes of Karbala were smeared with blood. Near one of the wash dunes lay the prostrate figure of a youth with blood gushing out from innumerable wounds. The crimson life-tide was ebbing fast. Even so, it seemed as if he was anxiously expecting somebody to come to him, to be near him before he breathed his last. Through his starched throat he was feebly calling somebody. Yes, Abbas was anxiously expecting his master to come to him before he parted with his life, as he had come to the side of all his devoted friends who had laid down their dear lives for him and in espousing his cause.

It is said that before a man's death all the past events of

his life pass before his mind's eye in a flashback. In his last moments Abbas was experiencing this. He was seeing himself as a child in Medina following Hussain (as) with a devotion that was considered unique even for a brother. He was seeing the events of that hot and sultry day in Kufa when his illustrious father Ali was addressing a congregation in the mosque and he, as a child, with his characteristic devotion, was looking at the face of his beloved brother watching him intently so that he could attend to his wishes on an instant command. Seeing from the parched lips of Hussain (as) that he was feeling extremely thirsty, how he had darted out from the mosque and returned with a tumbler full of cool, refreshing water and in the hurry to carry the water as quickly as possible to quench the consuming thirst of his dearest brother, how he had spilled water on his own clothes. He was recalling how this incident had made his illustrious father stop amid his speech, with tears rolling down his cheeks at the sight of his young son all wet with water. He was remembering his father's reply to the queries from his faithful followers as to what had brought tears in his eyes, that Abbas who had wetted his body with water in the process of quenching Hussain's thirst would in the not too distant future wet his body with his own blood in attempting to quench the thirst of his young children. He was vividly seeing the scene on the 21st Ramadhan, way back in 40 Hijra, when his father mortally wounded, was lying on his death-bed and entrusting his children and dependents to the care of his eldest brother, Hassan (as) - all except him. Seeing that his father had commended all but him to the care of Hassan (as) - how he, a child of 12, had burst out into uncontrollable tears. His father, on hearing him sobbing, had called him to his side and given his hand in Hussain's hand with the words: *"Hussain (as), this child I am entrusting to you. He will represent me on the day of your supreme sacrifice and lay down his life in defending you and your dear ones, much as I would have done if alive on that day."*

How his father had turned to him and affectionately told him: *"Abbas, my child, I know your unbounded love for Hussain (as). Though you are too young to be told about it when that day dawns, consider no sacrifice too great for Hussain (as) and his children."*

He saw before his mind's eye that parting with his aged mother Fatima (as) in Medina. How she had affectionately embraced him and reminded him of the dying desire of his father to lay down his life in the defense of Hussain (as) and his dear ones.

A faint smile of satisfaction flickered for a brief moment on his parched lips a smile of satisfaction that he had fulfilled his father's wish; that he had performed his duty for which he was brought up. It just flitted for a moment and vanished as other scenes came before his mind's eye. He was reliving the events of the night before. He was seeing Shimr stealthily coming to him; and talking to him about his ties of relationship; about the protection he had been promised for Abbas by the Commander of Yazid's forces, only if he would leave Hussain (as) and go over to Yazid's camp; about the promises of riches and rewards that he would get; how he had spurned the suggestion of Shimr with the utmost disdain to the chagrin of that servile minion who had sold his soul for a mess of pottage. How he had scared away that coward by his scathing rage saying: *"You worshipper of Mammon, do not think that Abbas will be lured by your tempting offer of power and pelf. If I die in defending my master, Hussain (as), I shall consider myself the luckiest person. O' coward, remember that valiant die but once. Nobody is born to live eternally. By betraying my master, you have betrayed the Prophet (s), whose religion you profess to follow. On the Day of Judgment, you will be doomed to eternal perdition. I am ashamed to own any relationship with you. Had it not been for the fact that you have come here unarmed, I would have given you the chastisement you deserve for your impudence in asking me to become a turncoat."*

How that wretch had scampered from there seeing him roaring like an enraged lion. The thought of that unpleasant interlude contracted his brows. Or was it the excruciating pain he was suffering on account of the deep gashes he had all over his body?

Yet another scene passed before Abbas's eyes - Sakina leading 42 children, each with a dry water bag. The children were shouting as if in chorus: *"Thirst, consuming thirst, is killing us!"*

Sakina coming to him and putting her dry water bag at his feet and saying to him: *"O uncle, I know you will do something to get water for us. Even if you can bring one bag full of water, we can wet our parched throats."*

He could see that thirst, aggravated by the scorching heat of the desert, was squeezing their young lives out of them. The sight of these youngsters had moved him more than any other soul-stirring events of that faithful day. How he had picked up the water bag with assurance to Sakina that he would go and bring water - God Willing.

How he had taken Hussain's permission and marched out of the camp with a sword in one hand, the flag in the other, and the bag on his shoulder, with the children following him in a group up to the outer perimeter of the camp. How Hussain had repeatedly requested him to avoid fighting as much as possible and confine himself to the task of bringing water!

His thoughts switched over to the events that had preceded his fall from the horse. With the object of procuring water for his dear little Sakina, he had charged on the enemy who held the riverbanks. He had run through the enemy ranks like a knife through butter. Again, this surging onslaught the cowards could not stand and had run helter-skelter shouting for protection. For a moment it seemed as if Ali, the Lion of God, had descended from heaven. In no time Abbas was near the rivulet. He had jumped down from the horse and bent to fill the waterbag. When it was filled to the brim, he had taken some water in his cupped hand to drink and satisfy his killing thirst. But, on second thoughts, he had thrown the water away. How could he drink water when Sakina and the children were still withering without it? How could he be so callous as to forget that his master Hussain (as) had not had a drop of water since the last three days. He had turned to his horse that had been let loose so that it could satisfy its thirst. The animal had been intently looking at its master as if to say: *"I too am aware that, so long as our master and his children remain without water, our thirst cannot be quenched."*

With the water bag filled he had jumped into the saddle with one thought uppermost in his mind, to get the water to the anxiously waiting children as quickly as possible. Seeing him galloping towards the camp of Hussain (as), the enemy had turned. Somebody had shouted from the enemy ranks that if Hussain (as) and his people got water, it would be difficult to fight them on the battlefield. Though it was an uneven fight, he fought them with valor that was so characteristic of his fathers. Though he was thirsty and hungry he charged on them and scattered them. The mercenaries of Yazid were running like lambs in a fold when charged by a lion. Seeing that a frontal assault on a man so brave was not possible, they had resorted to a barrage of arrows. When arrows were coming from all sides, Abbas had only one thought in his mind, how to protect the waterbag rather than his life. Seeing that Abbas was preoccupied with this thought, one treacherous foe, hiding behind a sand dune, had rushed out and dealt a blow on his right hand and cut it off. In a flash Abbas had transferred his sword to his left hand and the standard he was bearing he had hugged to his chest. Now that the Lion of Ali was crippled, the foes had found courage to surround him. A blow from an enemy's sword severed his left arm. The odds were now mounting against him. He held the bag with his teeth and protected the flag with his chest pressed on the horse's back. Now the paramount thought in his mind was to reach the camp somehow or the other. A silent prayer had escaped his lips: *"Merciful Allah, spare me long enough to fulfill my mission."*

But that was not to be. An arrow had pierced the water bag and water had started gushing out of it. Was it water that was flowing out of that bag or the hopes of Abbas? All his efforts had been in vain. After all Sakina's thirst would remain unsatisfied and all her hopes would be frustrated. The enemies who had made bold to surround him, now seeing his helpless condition, were now gathering thick round him. One of them came near him and struck mortal blow with an iron mace. He reeled over and fell from the horse. He tossed on the burning sand with excruciating pain. He felt that life was fast ebbing out but his wish to see his master had remained unfulfilled. With one last effort, with all the strength that was left in him, he shouted: *"O' my master, do come to me before I die."*

As it in answer to his prayers he felt some footsteps near him, yes, his instinct told him that it was his lord. An arrow had blinded his one eye and the other filled with blood and so he could not see. But he felt his master kneeling down beside him, lifting his head and taking it into his lap. Not a word was said for a few seconds because both were choked with emotion. At last he heard Hussain's voice, a half-sob, half-muffled cry: *"Abbas, my brother, what have they done to you?"*

If Abbas could see, would he have recognized his master? With back bent and beard turned white and hoary, on hearing the parting cry of his beloved brother, Hussain's plight was such that nobody could have recognized him - such was his transformation. Abbas was now feeling the loving touch of his master's hand. With effort he muttered: *"You have come at last, my Master. I thought I was not destined to have a last farewell with you but, thank God, you are here."*

With these words he put his head on the sand. Tenderly

Hussain (as) lifted his head and again put it on his lap, inquiring why he had removed it from there.

"*My Master,*" replied Abbas, "*the thought that when you will be breathing your last, nobody will be there to put your head in a lap and to comfort you, makes me feel that it would be better if my head lies on the sand when I die, just as yours would be. Besides, I am your servant and you are my master. It is too much for me to put my head on your lap.*"

Hussain (as) burst into uncontrollable tears. The sight of his brother, whose name was to become a byword for devotion and unflinching faithfulness, laying down his dear life in his arms, was heart-rending.

Abbas was heard to whisper softly: "*My master, I have some last wishes to express. When I was born, I had my first look at your face and it is my last desire that when I die, my gaze may be on it, too. My one eye is pierced by an arrow and the other is filled with blood. If you will clear the blood from my one eye, I'll be able to see you and fulfill my last dying desire. My second wish is that when I die you may not carry my body to the camp. I had promised to bring water to Sakina and, since I have failed in my attempt to bring her water, I cannot face her even in death. Besides, I know that the blows that you have received since morning have all but crushed you and carrying my body to the camp will be heart breaking work for you. And my third wish is that Sakina may not be brought here to see my plight. I know with what love and affection she was devoted to me. The sight of my dead body lying here will kill her.*"

Hussain (as) sobbingly promised him that he would carry out his last wishes added: "*Abbas, I too have a wish to be fulfilled. Since childhood you have always called me master. For once at least call me brother with your dying breath.*"

The blood was cleared from the eye one brother looked at the other with a longing lingering look. Abbas was heard to whisper: "*My brother, my brother.*"

And with these words he surrendered his soul to his Maker: Hussain (as) fell unconscious on the dead body of Abbas with a cry: *"O Abbas, who is left to protect me and Sakina after you?"*

The flow of Furat became dark as winter and a murmur arose from the flowing water as if to protest against the killing of a thirsty water bearer on its banks.[195]

---

[195] The Journey of Tears by Bashir Hassanali Rahim

The 6 month old Infant Son of Hussain (as), Ali Asghar

By the afternoon 70 brave persons had sacrificed their lives in Karbala to save Islam. All had fought under nerve racking conditions, severe thirst, dehydration, exhaustion, and agonizing feeling of what would happen to the family of the Prophet (s) afterwards. Hussain (as) endured all that and more, for he saw his entire beloved ones brutally cut to pieces, including children.[196]

---

[196] Karbala Chain of Events by Ramzan Shabir

By the afternoon his brave companions had sacrificed their lives in Karbala to save Islam. All had fought under nerve racking conditions, severe thirst, dehydration, exhaustion, and agonizing feeling of what would happen to the family of the Prophet (s) afterwards.

Husain endured all that and more, for he saw his entire beloved ones brutally cut to pieces, including the children.

Remaining the only one, Imam Husain was to face the enemy head on. Precisely at that moment Imam Husain heard his baby crying incessantly, agonizing because of the thirst. Imam Husain's love for his family was without end, especially for a suffering baby.

Parents think of your children right now and how it pains you to see them cry for the slightest thing. Now imagine the pain of Imam Hussain seeing his infant son the grandson of Rasulullah without milk for 3 days.

The voice of lamenting of the ladies arose and Imam came to the door of the tent and called for Zaynab (as) saying, *"Give me my infant child so that I may bid him farewell"*.

Zaynab brought him his son, Abdullah, whose mother was Rabab. He sat him on his lap, kissing him and saying,

بُعداً لِهَؤُلاءِ القَومِ إذا كانَ جَدُّ لَكَ المُصطَفى خَصمُهُم

"Distanced are these people (from the Mercy of Allah), when your grandfather, Al-Mustafa, will be their enemy."

He held the six months old baby, his youngest son Ali Asghar in his arms, and appealed to the enemy fighters for some water for the baby. Imam wanted to awaken their conscience and stir their human feelings but the stonehearted enemy.

He then carried him and brought him to the enemies asking them for water. Instead of giving water, Harmalah ibn Kahil Al-Asadi shot at arrow at the child, which pierced his neck. It not only pieced his neck but it severed his head![197] He was martyred while in the arms of his father. Imam Husain was shocked. He felt an unbearable wave of pain. The sight of the limp baby in his arms was agonizingly painful.

Imam Husain (as) filled his hand with the blood of the baby and threw it to the skies, and not a single drop of it came back, and he said,

"What eases what I have experienced is that he is cared for by Allah. O Allah! Do not let the one who killed him go unpunished as you did not leave the one who killed the baby camel of Saleh go unpunished. O my Lord! If you kept victory away from us, then make it for what is better to come for us, and seek revenge to us from the oppressors. Make what is happening to us now a reward for us in the future. O Allah! You are the Witness of people who killed the one who most resembles your Messenger Muhammad (s)."

He then heard a voice saying,

دَعهُ يا حُسين، فَإنَّ لَهُ مُرضِعاً في الجَنَّة

"Let him go, O Husain! Indeed, there is a nursing mother for him in Paradise."

Imām Abū Ja`far al-Bāqir has said, *"Not a drop of it fell."*

---

[197] Nafasaul Mahmoom by Sheikh Abbas Qummi

Imam Mahdi may Allāh hasten his reappearance, says,

السّلامُ عَلى عَبدُ اللهِ الرَضيع

"Peace be unto Abdullāh, the slaughtered infant, the one shot with an arrow, the one whose blood was shed in a most cruel manner and whose blood ascended to the heavens, the one slaughtered with an arrow in his father's lap! The curse of Allāh be upon the person who shot him, Harmalah ibn Kahil al-Asadi, and upon his people."

He came back to the tent of Zaynab (as) carrying his slain baby. He did not take him back to his mother, for surely it would have been unbearable for her to see her son slain in such manner. Zaynab (as) came out of her tent, and saw the young boy slain from one end of his neck to the other, and the arrow is in his throat, with the blood all over his chest.

Imam Husain (as) then dismounted from his horse and dug a grave for the baby with the end of his sword, and buried him, covered in his blood, and prayed over him.[198] [199] [200]

Imam Hussain (as)

Our Imam is all alone! He looks around him. There lie Habeeb ibn Mazahir, Muslim ibn Awsaja, Zuhair ibn Qain and all his friends and companions. There lie Awn and Muhammad. He looks at Qasim's trampled remains. He looks at Ali Akbar, his beloved son, with that dreadful wound on his chest. He looks towards Furaat. Gently he whispers, *"Abbas, Abbas, I am alone, So very alone!"*

Slowly Imam Hussain (as) moves towards the tent of Imam Zain ul 'Abideen. Zain ul 'Abideen is lying unconscious on his bed. Lovingly Imam shakes his son by the shoulder. The sick Imam opens his eyes, *'Father, Father, why are you alone? Where is my uncle Abbas? Where is Ali Akbar? Where is Qasim? Where are all your companions?'* Imam Hussain (as) says, *'Son, no man, save you and I, is left alive. All of them have died for*

---

[198] It is also narrated that he kept him with those killed from his family members.
[199] Maqtal of Abu Zahra al-Ka'bi

[200] Recalling the Sacrifices of Karbala by Sheikh Mateen Charbonneau

Islam.'

Imam Zain ul 'Abideen tries to get up. 'Where are you going, my son?' asks Imam Hussain (as). *'To fight Yazid's army!'* replies the young man. *'No, my son, you are too ill for Jihad. I have come to say good-bye. Look after the ladies and the children. And, my son, when you get to Madina, gives my love to Fatima Sughra. Tell her that I always remembered her and that in these last moments of my life, I wish I could give her a hug before I get killed. And, my son, give salaams to our friends and tell them to think of me when they drink water!'*

Imam Hussain (as) then stands in the centre of the camp and cries out, "*O Zainab, O Kulthoom, O Sakina, O Ruqayya, O Rubaab, O Fizza my greetings to you! Farewell to you all!*" The ladies and children weep and wail as they say farewell to Imam.

Imam walks towards his horse. There is no one to help him mount. Bibi Zainab (as) steps forward. She holds the reins as Imam mounts the horse. The horse moves a few steps and then it stops. Imam Hussain (as) urges the horse to move, but it stands still looking towards its hind legs. Imam turns his head. He sees Sakina clinging to the horse's leg, pleading, *'O horse, do not take my father away from me. Do not let them make me an orphan!'*

Imam dismounts. He says, *'Sakina, you are the great grand daughter of the Holy Prophet (s)! I love you so much that if you tell me not to go, I will not. But then Islam will be destroyed. How will you or I be able to face the Holy Prophet (s) on the Day of Judgment?'* Fighting back her tears the four-year-old Sakina[201] can only

---

[201] Who was otherwise known as Ruqayya

manage to say, *'Bismillah, father!'* The four-year-old holds the reins as her father mounts for a certain death!!

Hussain (as) rides on. He stands on a hill and cries out, *"Who is there who will come to my help?"*

Of course, our Imam is not expecting any of the enemy soldiers to come to his help! To whom is he addressing this plea for help? Our Imam is addressing the plea to all the Muslims, in every age and everywhere, young, and old, men and women, grown ups and children urging us all to always fight the way of Yazid and refuse to disobey the commands of Allah. Every little effort we make to preserve and act according to our Islamic conscience is a response to our Imam's call with Labbaika Yaa Hussain! Labbaika Yaa Hussain![202]

Imam rides towards the enemy. There is a shower of arrows! Imam ignores the arrows and rides on. He wants to make one last effort to preach true Islam to the enemies of Islam. He stops and turns towards the enemy and begins to speak: *"O those of you who do not know me, know that I am the grandson of the Holy Prophet (s). I am on the path of truth. Yazid personifies falsehood and corruption. He wants to lead you away from Islam. Do not follow him. Do not kill the grandson of Allah's messenger. Allah will never forgive you! Remember that when you see a ruler who does what has been forbidden by Allah and His Messenger, who indulges in sins, who oppresses the people he rules, and you do nothing to stop such a ruler, before Allah you are as guilty as he is. You know my ancestry. My parents did not raise me to submit myself to an evil tyrant. I am your Imam. You have surrendered the freedom of your mind to the evil ways of Yazid. If you do not care for Islam, do, at least, care for the freedom of your spirit!!"*

Umar Sa'ad cries out, *"Do not fall victims to Hussain's oratory! Kill him!"*

---

[202] We are at your service O' Hussain!

From all directions the soldiers advance towards Imam Hussain (as) with their naked swords! Imam says: *"You are determined to fight me then fight you I shall! I do not fear death. Death to me is sweeter than dishonor. Now I shall let you witness the valor of the son of Ali ibn Abu Taalib!"*

Imam Hussain (as) takes out his sword and begins to fight. Thirsty, tired, wounded, grieving, our Imam fights as no one had ever seen any one fight! Wherever he turns to, the soldiers flee as rabbits do at the sight of a lion! Umar Sa'ad sends all his best warriors against Imam. They all perish. No one dares come near our Imam! Imam stands on his stirrups. Casts his eyes to where Abbas lies, and murmurs, *"Abbas did you see the battle of your brother, the thirsty, the broken hearted brother?"*

And then Jibra'eel appears and says, *'O Hussain, Allah is pleased with your bravery. The moment has now arrived for you to save Islam with your life!"*

Hussain (as) looks at the sky! Yes, it is the time of Asr! Hussain (as) returns the sword into the sheath. Lowers himself on the horseback. Whispers to the horse *"Take me to where my mother Fatima is waiting for me! But O' my faithful horse, go past where my Akbar is lying so that I may see my beloved son just one more time before I die."*

Seeing that Imam has sheathed his sword the enemy came from all sides some threw stones at him, some hit him with swords. Arrows are shot at him! Suddenly the horse stops! *"My son, my son!"* cries out the soul of Fatima Zahra. Imam Hussain (as) falls from the horse! But his body does not touch the ground. It is resting on the blades of the arrows. He performs his Asr prayers lying on this prayer mat of arrows! Now he goes in to his last sajdah (prostration) and says: *"O Allah! All praise is to You and You alone!"*

Someone is moving towards where our Imam is in sajdah on the arrows. He is holding a dagger in his hand. The earth trembles! The sun goes into eclipse! Jibraeel cries out: *"Oh*

Hussain has been killed, Hussain has been killed!!!!"

Sakina falls on to the ground unconscious! Bibi Zainab (as) runs to the tent of our fourth Imam. *"Oh Son! What has happened?"* Imam Zain ul 'Abideen staggers towards the curtain of his tent. Lifts it up and pointing his finger at a head mounted on a lance. He cries out in a trembling voice: *"Assalaamu 'alaika, Yaa Aba 'Abdillah!!!"*[203]

Shimr whose mother was a disbeliever, came forward and severed Imam Hussain's noble head from the body, the noble head kissed often by the Prophet (s)! The narrations say that Imam Hussain (as) was beheaded while he was patient. When you slaughter an animal, you give it water before and you cut the neck from the front so that the vein is cut and the death is fast. Imam Hussain (as) was not given any water nor was his head cut like this. He was beheaded from the back of the neck so that he had to feel every bit of pain and suffering before the knife reached the front! Shimr and others had the audacity to carry it on the tip of a spear to Yazid, 600 miles away!

Umar Ibn Sa'ad ordered the horsemen to trample upon the supine bodies of Imam Hussain (as) and all others killed, to disfigure them even further, as if the wounds, the bloodied bodies, and the headless forms were not enough.

For three days the exposed bodies of the martyrs were left lying in the desert of Karbala. Afterwards, the people of the tribe of Bani-Asad, who were not far away from the battlefield, helped bury them.[204]

إِنَّا مُرْسِلُواْ ٱلنَّاقَةِ فِتْنَةً لَّهُمْ فَٱرْتَقِبْهُمْ وَٱصْطَبِرْ (٢٧) وَنَبِّئْهُمْ أَنَّ ٱلْمَآءَ قِسْمَةٌۢ بَيْنَهُمْۖ كُلُّ شِرْبٍ مُّحْتَضَرٌ (٢٨) فَنَادَوْاْ صَاحِبَهُمْ فَتَعَاطَىٰ فَعَقَرَ (٢٩) فَكَيْفَ كَانَ عَذَابِى وَنُذُرِ

---

[203] The Journey of Tears by Bashir Hassanali Rahim

[204] Karbala Chain of Events by Ramzan Shabir

(٣٠) إِنَّا أَرْسَلْنَا عَلَيْهِمْ صَيْحَةً وَاحِدَةً فَكَانُوا كَهَشِيمِ ٱلْمُحْتَظِرِ (٣١) وَلَقَدْ يَسَّرْنَا ٱلْقُرْءَانَ لِلذِّكْرِ فَهَلْ مِن مُّدَّكِرٍ (٣٢)

> "For We will send the she camel by way of trial for them, So watch them (O Saleh) and possess thyself in patience! And tell them that the water is to be divided between them: each one's right to drink being brought forward (by suitable turns). But they called to their companion, and he took a sword in hand, and hamstrung (her). Ah! How (terrible) was My Penalty and My Warning! For We sent against them a single Mighty Blast, and they became like the dry stubble used by one who pens cattle. And We have indeed made the Qur'an easy to understand and remember: then is there any that will receive admonition?"[205]

If Allah destroyed the people of Prophet Saleh for killing a she camel of a Prophet can you imagine the fate of those who killed the grandson of their Prophet![206]

Umar Ibn Sa'ad and his forces (representing Benu Umayya) then took the women and children as prisoners in shackles, put them on camels, and proceeded in a caravan from Karbala to Kufa. At the forefront of the procession were the heads of Imam Hussain (as) and his followers on the tip of spears. The scene was both grotesque and pathetic. This was the leftover of the beloved family of Prophet Muhammad (s), in such a deplorable unimaginable condition, all caused by people who called themselves Muslims!

Karbala is the cruelest tragedy humanity has ever seen. Yet, the startling (though appalling) events in Karbala proved like a powerful volcano that shook the very foundation of Muslims, it stirred their consciousness, ignorant or learned alike. For sincere Muslims, Karbala turned into a triumph. The tragic

---

[205] Quran 54:27-32

[206] Note from compiler.

event became the very beacon of light to always remind Muslims to practice Islam honestly and sincerely, to do what is right irrespective of consequences, and fear no one except Allah (swt).

On the other hand, Yazid never achieved what he and his father had planned to achieve, for within three years, Allah's wrath fell upon him, causing him to die at the age of 33 years. And within a few decades the rule of Benu Umayya crumbled and came to an end. The tragedy of Karbala taught humanity a lesson that standing for the truth and fighting unto death is more honorable and valuable than submitting to the wrongful, especially when the survival of Islam is at stake.[207]

---

[207] Karbala Chain of Events by Ramzan Shabir

The Fate of the Women of Ahl ul Bayt after Karbala

It was after 'Asr (afternoon) on the Day of Ashura. Imam Hussain (as) lay dead. The earth had trembled! The Furaat[208] had broken its banks! From the camp of the family of the Holy Prophet (s) such lamentation arose as had never been heard before! Yazid's army had brutally murdered our Imam, his sons, his brothers, his nephews, his companions. No one was spared. Amongst the male adults there remained only our fourth Imam, Imam Zain ul 'Abideen, who lay unconscious in his tent with his young son Muhammad (al-Baqir) hovering around him, weeping.

One would think that even the devil himself would halt in exhaustion after so much evil. But that was not to be! Umar Sa'ad received a letter from ibn Ziyad. The governor of Kufa instructed that they should not be satisfied with the death of Hussain (as). His body must be subjected to the ultimate insult of

---

[208] Euphrates River

being trampled by the hooves of horses. And this was done to the grandson of the Holy Prophet (s)!

As the sun was setting in the horizon, the soldiers rushed to Imam Hussain's camp in search of booty. They looted every tent. Sakina's earrings were pulled off her ears, splitting her ear lobes. When the little girl pleaded for her veil to be left untouched, she was slapped.

Surely, they would stop now. But they did not. They set fire to all the tents. Humayd Ibn Muslim describes how he saw a little girl with her dress on fire, her ears bleeding, running from the scene of carnage. He says: *"I ran after her. I took her by hand. Put out the fire in her dress. I wiped the blood off her ears. She looked at me and said, "You seem like a kind person, are you a Muslim?" I told her I was. She thought a while and then said, "Can you please show me the way to Najaf?" I asked, "Why do you want to go to Najaf at this hour and in this state?" She said, "I want to go and complain to my grandfather Ali ibn Abi Talib about how they killed my father." Realizing that she was Hussain's daughter, I took her back to her aunt Zainab."*

As the night descended, Bibi Zainab (as) gathered all the ladies and children, in to one small space in between the gutted tents. Imam Zain-ul 'Abideen lay on the ground surrounded by these widows and orphans. There was no fire, no light. Only the moon cast its dull light.

Umar Sa'ad asked Hurr's widow to take some food and

water to the ladies and the children. As she neared to where they were resting, Bibi Zainab (as) recognized her. She stood up, went towards Hurr's widow and offered her condolences for the death of Hurr. This gesture on the part of Bibi Zainab (as), who had suffered so much, lost so many, and carrying so much grief in her heart, is a lesson in Islamic akhlaq that the world should never be allowed to forget.

Bibi Zainab (as) took the jug of water. She went to Sakina[209] who had fallen into a fretful sleep. Gently she stroked the girl's disheveled hair. Sakina opened her eyes. Bibi Zainab (as) said, *"Here is some water, Sakina. Please drink a little. You have been thirsty for so long!"*

On hearing the word 'water' Sakina cried out hopefully, *"Has my uncle Abbas come back?!"*

When she was told that Hurr's widow had brought the water, she got up, went to Hurr's widow, thanked her and then asked Bibi Zainab (as): *"Have you all drank water?"*

Bibi Zainab (as) shook her head. Sakina asked, *"Why then do you ask me to drink water?"*

Bibi Zainab (as) said, *"Because, my dear, you are the youngest."*

Sakina replied, *"No! no! Asghar is the youngest!"* Sakina took the jug of water, ran towards where Asghar lay buried, crying *"Yaa Asghar! Yaa Asghar!"*

This was how the homeless spent their night in Karbala'. This was Shami Ghareeban (Farsi)[210], the night of the homeless. They had lost everything. Their men had died. Their children had been killed. In this desolate desert our fourth Imam, the women

---

[209] Who was otherwise known as Ruqayya

[210] *Lailatul Wahshah* in Arabic

and the remaining children are huddled where only a few hours before had stood their camp. Abbas, Qasim and Ali Akbar had taken turns to guard the camp. Now Bibi Zainab (as) and Bibi Kulthoom lay awake to make sure that Imam Zain ul 'Abideen and the children were not attacked.

Suddenly, Bibi Zainab (as) notices that Sakina has disappeared. She is alarmed. She looks around but Hussain's darling daughter is not to be seen. Bibi Zainab (as) slowly walks to the battlefield. She comes to where Abbas lay. *"Abbas! Abbas! My dear brother, have you seen Sakina?"* There is silence! She makes her way to where Hussain's headless body lay. There, hugging her father, she finds Sakina, deep in sleep!!

Dawn breaks out on the desolate sands of Karbala'. What was the battlefield yesterday is a stretch of desert covered with the bodies of the slain. In the corner where there had stood Imam Hussain's camp the mourning widows and orphans have completed their morning prayers.

Imam Zain ul 'Abideen is in sijdah glorifying Allah. Umar Sa'ad walks over with a few soldiers and orders the women and the children to be tied with ropes as captives. There is a renewed wailing. Our fourth Imam consoles them. He himself is put under heavy chains. Yazid's soldiers spend the day burying their dead. The bodies of the grandson of the Prophet of Islam (s) and the other martyrs are left unattended. Imam Zain ul 'Abideen (as) pleads to be allowed to bury but all his pleas go unheeded.[211]

The soldiers had gathered all the bodies but noticed that one body remained missing. The body of a small infant child. They could not find the body of Ali Asghar. Where had he gone? They realized that Imam Hussain (as) must have buried him in a shallow grave somewhere around the camp, so they started stabbing the ground with their spears in order to find the body of the young baby who they had killed.

They stabbed the land of Karbala, and the spear pierced the chest of Ali Asghar! They pulled the small body out of the ground and cast him aside with the other headless ones from among the Bani Hashim[212]. Ali Asghar shared the pain of his elder brother Ali Akbar as they were now both laying on the plains of Karbala pierced by the spears of the enemy soldiers.

The army of Yazid went on to loot the tents and the women of their belongings. Now a man comes to the body of Imam Hussain and notices a ring on the Imam's hand. He tries to remove it, but he can't. So, this man proceeds to take out his knife and cut off the finger of the grandson of *Rasulullah*![213]

Another night in Karbala' followed by another dawn! The prisoners remain tied. Our Imam suffers the discomfort of the chain. His wrists and ankles are bruised. On the morning of the 12th Muharram the enemy brings unsaddled camels upon which the women and children are made to mount. A huge procession is being prepared.

At the head of the procession is Umar Sa'ad followed by the officers. Then a few foot soldiers carrying lances upon which are mounted the heads of the martyrs. In their midst is our fourth

---

[211] The Journey of Tears by Bashir Hassanali Rahim

[212] Tribe of the Holy Prophet (s)

[213] Recalling the Sacrifices of Karbala by Sheikh Mateen Charbonneau

Imam, chained and shackled, then the camels carrying the women and children as prisoners. Shimr and the rest of the infantry bring up the rear. The journey to Kufa begins.

Yes, the tale of Karbala' is a tale of five sad journeys! Now begins the third journey of tears. We look at the travellers. Some of those who had set out on that first journey, from Mecca to Madina, can be seen but the rest can not. No! They also can be seen if we look around! They are lying slaughtered on the sands of Karbala'.

Who is the hero and who is the heroine of this third journey? We see the hero, handcuffed, chained, exhausted with the long illness and the great suffering, our Fourth Imam, Zain ul 'Abideen. And the heroine? Yes, we see the lady. Her face full of pain and yet reflecting courage and the strength of her spirit! She knows that for the sake of Sakina and the other ladies she can not possibly give in to her grief and sorrow. Yes, it is Bibi Zainab (as)!

Umar Sa'ad cruelty is not exhausted. He decides to lead the procession past where the bodies of the martyrs lie. As the camel carrying Bibi Zainab (as) goes past the body of Imam Hussain (as) she can no longer contain her pain and anguish, and turning her face to Madina she cries out: *"Ya Muhammad, the angels in heaven send their blessings upon you! Look here lies your beloved Hussain (as), so humiliated and disgraced, covered with blood and cut into pieces. Here are we your daughters' taken captives by Yazid!"*

Imam Zain ul 'Abideen walks over to Bibi Zainab (as). *"Dear Aunt, have patience. Your sacrifices for Islam have only just begun."*

Ibn Ziyad, the Governor of Kufa, had declared a holiday. The city was decorated with flags and pennants. People had been told that the rebels who wanted to attack their city and murder them had been defeated at Karbala' and that their women were being brought into the city as prisoners. Those who believed this, and many did, came out to line the city streets through which the procession was to pass so that they might mock and jeer at the prisoners. Big crowds had gathered everywhere. There was a holiday mood. The procession slowly entered the city and began to move towards the Governor's palace. People jeered and shouted at the prisoners. There were a few, however, who guessed the truth. When they saw Imam Hussain's head and saw the misery and grief of the widows and orphans, they began to shed tears. The majority were ignorant. They believed, or found it convenient to believe, the lies which Umar Sa'ad had told them.[214]

The Sunni's till this present day and time celebrate on the Day of Ashura, the 10th of Muharram. I don't know how anybody can celebrate on Ashura day?! This is the day when the grandson of the Prophet (s) was martyred along with his 6 month old baby, his sons, nephews, and close friends. 72 people who didn't eat or drink for 3 days against 100,000 troops of Yazid's so called Muslims. Their heads were cut off and put on sticks to be at the front of the caravan of Hussain's women and children who were made to march across the hot desert from Karbala, Iraq to Damascus, Syria as prisoners bound and shackled. Remembering such tragic events how can one begin to even celebrate anything?! The big question is would you think that the Prophet (s) would have celebrated on Ashura day knowing his grandson would be killed on that day?!

It is reported from Jabir Abdullah Ansari that the angel Gabriel brought some clay/soil to the Prophet (s) and told him this was from the land where Imam Hussain (as) would be killed and told him the events which were to happen where upon the Prophet (s) wept and was very sad. He gave this clay to one of his wives Umm Salma and told her to keep this in a safe place and when she sees this clay turn into blood she will know that Imam Hussain (as) was martyred. This prophecy came true on

---

[214] The Journey of Tears by Bashir Hassanali Rahim

the 10th of Muharram. The rulers of the time wanted to get the people to celebrate this day making it a holiday with fasting and big iftar (dinner) after to make you forget about the tragic events of the 10th of Muharram. They want to replace the events of the day with something else to distract you from what they did to the grandson of the Prophet (s). Wake up and remember true Islam as taught by our Imam Hussain (as), not the "Islam" of the rulers who killed him and celebrated his death as a victory to their regime. We should mourn the loss of our Imam and remember the sacrifices that Ahl ul Bayt made for saving Islam.

As the procession neared the palace, the crowds thickened. Most of the people who gathered around the Governor's palace were those who worked for Yazid or supported him. The jeering and insults grew louder. The face of Bibi Zainab (as) was red with anger. She stood up on the camel, looked at the crowd and in a loud and clear voice said: *"Praise be to Allah and blessings upon my grandfather Muhammad, His beloved Prophet (s)!! Woe unto you, O people of Kufa! Do you know whom you have killed? Do you know what pledge you have broken? Do you know whose blood you have shed? Do you know whose honor you have defiled?"*

There was a stunned silence then a gentle sound of people crying! There was a blind old man in the crowd. He had been a companion of Ali (as). When he heard Bibi Zainab's voice, he cried out, *"By Allah, if I had not known that he had died, I could have sworn that what I just heard was the voice of my master Ali ibn Abu Taalib."*

Imam Zain ul 'Abideen went up to him and said, *"Oh Shaikh! This is not Ali but his daughter Zainab binti Ali! She is the daughter of Fatima, the beloved daughter of the Holy Prophet (s)."* The sound of weeping from the crowd grew louder. But as Bibi Zainab (as) continued. Immediately there was a hushed silence: *"And well may you weep, O people of Kufa! The crime which you committed against your Prophet (s) was so great that the skies shook, the earth trembled, and mountains crumbled down! You have killed your Imam, and by doing so lost your shelter against hardship, evil and kufr (disbelief)! His blood stains your souls. Nothing can protect you from the anger of Allah for having killed the son of the last of His Prophets!"*

People could no longer control their wailing. Umar Sa'ad was frightened and quickly led the prisoners into the palace. The prisoners were brought before ibn Ziyad. Shaikh al-Mufid reports that ibn Ziyad sat on his throne and in front of him was the head of Imam Hussain (as). He frequently poked the face with his cane. An old companion of the Holy Prophet (s), Zayd bin Arqam, was in the court and when he witnessed this indignity being inflicted on the head of Imam he cried out, *"Take your cane away from those lips! By Allah I have seen the lips of the Apostle of Allah on those lips!"*

Ibn Ziyad was livid with rage. He retorted, *"O old man! How dare you interrupt our celebrations of the victory of our Imam, Yazid ibn Mu'awiya. Because of your age I spare your life. Leave my court immediately."*

Ibn Ziyad then pointed at Imam Zain ul 'Abideen and asked: *"Who is this young man?"*

"He is Ali ibnal Hussain," replied Umar Sa'ad.

"Why is he alive?" asked ibn Ziyad. and added, *"Kill him straight away!"*

Bibi Zainab (as) rushed forward and planted herself in front of Imam Zain ul 'Abideen. *"You will have to kill me first!"* She said looking at ibn Ziyad with such defiance, determination, and anger that ibn Ziyad got up and walked away ordering that the prisoners be locked up.

Bibi Zainab's speeches had stirred Kufa. The people of Kufa were filled with remorse. There was unrest in the city. In the marketplace they were whispering: *'What have we done? How could we invite the Prophet's grandson and then desert him to be mercilessly butchered at Karbala'? How can we permit the Holy Prophet's grand daughters be paraded in the streets like servants? What have we done?'*

Ibn Ziyad feared that the people of Kufa might rise against him. He ordered that the prison be strictly guarded. No one was allowed to visit them. Only the most trusted guards were allowed in or around the prison. In the mean time messengers ran between Kufa and Damascus. Although at first Yazid had ordered that the captives be detained at Kufa until he had completed all the arrangements for their entry into Shaam (Damascus), because of the mood in Kufa, Ibn Ziyad was anxious to have the prisoners out of Kufa as soon as possible. It was agreed that they be taken to Shaam.

Once again, the prisoners were assembled, and a procession left Kufa. But this time the departure was kept secret from the people of Kufa and took place at night.

So, began the fourth journey of tears! It was a long and difficult journey.

Who was the hero and who was the heroine of this journey through the Iraqi and the Syrian deserts? Was it Bibi Rubaab, who from her unsaddled camel kept on staring at Ali Asghar's cradle loaded on another camel carrying the goods looted from Hussain's camp during the Shami Ghareeban? Was it Sakina who now sat mournfully on her mother's lap staring at the 'alam of Abbas and her mashk still tied to the 'alam, and who kept whispering: *"I am not thirsty, Uncle, I am not thirsty!"* Was the hero Imam Zain ul 'Abideen who was made to walk all the way, the hot chains eating into his flesh?

Sometimes our Fourth Imam would faint. His captors however knew no pity. They would flog him if he slowed down or fainted. On these occasions Bibi Zainab (as) would intervene to stop the Imam from being flogged to death.

This was the journey of which the hero was the valor of

Ali (as) which ruled the heart of Imam Zain ul 'Abideen (as) and the heroine was the sabr (patience) of Fatima Zahra (as) which inspired Bibi Zainab (as).

The journey from Kufa to Shaam was a long one. It took over twenty days. The women and the children were exhausted. Their suffering was great! Quite often the children would faint under the scorching desert heat and fall off the camels.

The mothers would scream. Imam Zain ul 'Abideen (as) and Bibi Zainab (as) would go looking for the children. Sometimes they would find them by the roadside barely alive and there were occasions when they were discovered too late. Our fourth Imam would dig a grave to bury the dead child. A historian revisiting this route a few years later discovered a large number of small graves on the wayside!

Some Zakir's relate the following story: *"Once Bibi Zainab (as) looked at the camel on which Sakina was riding. Sakina was not there! She looked at all the other camels; Sakina was nowhere to be seen. She panicked. Where could Imam Hussain's darling daughter be? She asked Shimr to untie her to that she could go and look for Sakina. At first Shimr responded with his whip. Unmindful of her own pain she kept on begging.*

Shimr untied her with the warning that if she did not return soon, he would flog Imam Zain ul 'Abideen to death. Bibi Zainab (as) ran in the direction from which they had travelled. Some distance away she saw an elderly lady holding Sakina affectionately, kissing her cheeks and wiping away her tears. She could hear Sakina telling the lady how her uncle Abbas had gone to fetch her water and how he had never returned. When Sakina saw her aunt, she explained that she had fallen off the camel but the kind lady had looked after her. Bibi Zainab (as) turned to the lady and said, "May Allah reward you for your kindness to this orphan!" The lady replied, "Zainab, my dear, how can you thank your own mother? Do you not recognize me?" As the lady lifted her face, Bibi Zainab saw that it was Fatima Zahra!![215]

---

[215] The Journey of Tears by Bashir Hassanali Rahim

The Christian Monk

One night they rested in the mountaintop of a hermitage of a monk who had devoted his life to prayers and meditation. Shimr gave the heads of the martyrs to him for safe keeping. Just one look at the face of Imam Hussain (as) convinced the hermit that it was the head of a saint. He took it with him and kept it near his bed and then retired to sleep.

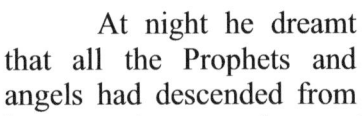

At night he dreamt that all the Prophets and angels had descended from heaven to keep watch over the head. He woke up from his sleep startled and baffled as to what he should do. He decided to ask the leader of the guards about the identity of the people whom they had beheaded and whose family they had taken prisoners.

Rushing out of the monastery he woke up Shimr and demanded to know who the martyrs were. When Shimr told him that the army of Yazid had killed the grandson of the Prophet Muhammad (s) who had defied the authority of the ruler Yazid ibn Mu'awiya and refused to acknowledge his spiritual superiority and they were carrying the heads of all the people who had been killed in Karbala, the hermit was shocked beyond words.

Recovering himself he said: *"You cursed people! Do you realize that you have committed the most heinous crime by beheading your own Prophet's grandson who undoubtedly was a great saint! Fie upon you coward that not satisfied with what you have done that you are so brutally treating his innocent ladies and children and subjecting them to such atrocities!"* [216]

He asked to kiss the head, but they refused till he paid them some money. He declared the testimony of faith and embraced Islam through the blessing of the one who was just beheaded for supporting the divine call.[217]

These words of the hermit enraged Shimr who had even otherwise lost his temper with him for waking him up from sleep in the dead of night. With one sweep of his sword, he chopped off the hermit's head. This brute had little regard for the Prophet's injections and orders granting the fullest protection to those who had retired from the world and dedicated their lives to prayers and penance. When the life of the Prophet's own grandson was not spared by this brute what regard could he be expected to have for the commands of the Prophet (s)?[218]

When they left that place they looked at the money the monk had given them and saw this verse inscribed on it *"And those who oppressed shall come to find how evil their end shall be."*[219]

When the caravan reached the outskirts of Damascus Omar Sa'ad sent a message to Yazid that they had arrived. Yazid ordered that the caravan remain where it was until the morning. He wanted the people of Shaam to line the streets to look at the captives and witness his victory. In the meantime, the streets through which the captives were to be marched were being decorated with flags and pennants.

---

[216] Tears and Tributes by Zakir

[217] Karbala and Beyond by Yasin Al-Jibouri

[218] Tears and Tributes by Zakir

[219] Karbala and Beyond by Yasin Al-Jibouri

Bibi Zainab (as) had conquered Kufa. Now Shaam had come and was waiting for her!

The Court of Yazid

When at long last the caravan reached the outskirts of Damascus, Umar Sa'ad received a message that the prisoners were not to be brought into the capital until Yazid had completed all the preparations.

Yazid invited all the ambassadors, foreign dignitaries, and leading citizens to his court. People were ordered to line up the streets. Musicians were asked to play music and dancers were told to dance in the streets. Such were the festivities organized by the Khalifah for the entry of the grandson and the grand daughters of the Holy Prophet of Islam (s) into what had become the metropolis of the Islamic Empire!!

Surrounded by the dancers, the musicians, and the jeering crowds of the citizens of Damascus the prisoners were led toward the palace of Yazid. The ladies had been forced to travel from Karbala' to Kufa, and Kufa to Shaam with their arms tied with a single rope. If any one of them stumbled, she was whipped. Never in the history of Islam had prisoners been treated with disrespect, let alone the cruelty meted out to the members of the Holy Prophet's household and now this ultimate insult of being led into the court of Yazid like a herd of cattle!

Bibi Zainab (as) seemed to be drawing strength from some divine source. She wiped away her tears. Imam Zain ul 'Abideen straightened himself. Exuding dignity and confidence, he maintained his position behind the bearer of the lance upon which was mounted his father's head. Such was the jostle of the multitude thronging the streets that it took them more than twelve hours to traverse the short distance between the city gates and the palace.

They entered the palace and were made to stand in front of Yazid. The tyrant was dressed in his best finery. Umar ibn

Sa'ad formally presented Imam Hussain's head to him. Yazid, with a cup of wine in one hand, ceremoniously accepted the ultimate symbol of his victory and commanded Umar Sa'ad to call out the names of the prisoners.

And then, in his drunken arrogance, Yazid recited a few couplets which enshrine a diabolical confession, a confession that explains the history of the division in Islam and the motives not only his but of his father and grandfather in accepting Islam! He said: *"If my venerable ancestors who fell at Badr fighting Muhammad had witnessed how the supporters of Muhammad's faith were thrown into confusion with thrusts given with my spears, they would be blessing me today. The Banu Hashim played a trick to win power. There was never any revelation to them nor did they receive any revelation. Today the souls of my ancestors and friends killed by Muhammad at Badr will rest in peace!"*

The foundation of the Umayyad dynasty was vengeance against Islam, a blood thirsty continuation of Uhud where Yazid's grand-mother had been only partially successful in her determination to have Ali and Hamza killed in retaliation for the deaths of her father and brother at Badr!! Yazid never believed in Islam, and yet the system forced upon the people after the death of the Holy Prophet (s) had resulted in this worst of all the hypocrites becoming the Khalifah of the Holy Prophet (s) and the Ameer-ul-Mu'mineen of the ummah!!

Yazid looked at the prisoners lined up in front of him. He said: *"It has pleased Allah to grant us victory! Look how He has caused the death of Hussain (as) and humiliated his family!"* He then recited an ayah of the Holy Quraan which means 'Allah grants honor to whom He pleases and brings disgrace upon whom He pleases.'

There were over seven hundred dignitaries sitting in the Court. They smiled and nodded approvingly. Bibi Zainab (as) could stand it no more! She was filled with wrath. How dare this unclean man say such things? How dare he with his najis tongue recite from Holy Quraan? How dare he make mockery of the family of the Holy Prophet (s)? In a loud and clear voice Bibi Zainab (as) said: *"O Yazid! Do you think that it is Allah who has caused you to commit all these foul deeds? Do you blame the Rahman and the Rahim for the oppression we have suffered? Do you blame Allah for the death of the beloved grandson of his most beloved Prophet (s)? How dare you make these false accusations against the Almighty? No, Yazid, it was not Allah! It is you, with your insatiable ambition and greed for wealth and power, who are the only cause of the suffering inflicted not only upon the household of the Holy Prophet (s) but on Islam itself!*

Do not forget what Allah has said in the Holy Book: "Let not the unbelievers take it that the respite we give them would do them any good. We allow them time in order that they might continue to indulge in sin to their hearts' content. Indeed, a humiliating punishment has been kept ready for them.

Do you think that by killing the grandson of the Holy Prophet (s) and bringing us to your palace as prisoners, you have scored a victory against Islam? No, Yazid, No! Hussain (as) with his blood has made sure that tyrants like you will not be able to use Islam as a toy to carry out their evil designs. The victory is not yours. The victory is of Hussain (as)! The victory is of Islam!"

Yazid was stunned! The people present there could not but be moved by what this courageous lady had to say. This lady, who had seen and experienced great suffering, dared today defy the very man who had inflicted those sufferings. Who was she? They asked one another. When they learnt that she was the granddaughter of the Holy Prophet (s), their hearts began to fill with admiration!

In an effort to save the situation Yazid turned towards Imam Zain ul 'Abideen and said: *"Well you can tell us who has been victorious?"*

The Imam looked at him and replied: *"Yazid, final victory can only belong to those on the right path. Let us look at you and look at Hussain. My father, whom you got killed so mercilessly, was the grandson of the Holy Prophet who had said that "Hussain is from me, and I am from Hussain." He was born a Muslim and all his life he upheld the laws and principles of Islam. You are the grandson of Abu Sufiyan and Hinda, who most of their lives fought Islam and the Holy Prophet!"*

Yazid was now greatly embarrassed. To silence the Imam, he asked his muezzin to recite the adhaan. When the Muezzin cried out *'Ash-hadu anna Muhammadar-Rasuul'ul-lah'* (I testify that Muhammad is the messenger of Allah) Imam Zain ul 'Abideen, addressing Yazid, said, *"Yazid speak the truth! Was Muhammad my grandfather or your grandfather!"*

Yazid ordered the prisoners to be moved to a prison. This was not a prison. It was a dungeon! Only a part of it had any sort of ceiling. The rest was open to the sky. An iron grill surrounded the place so that no one could get in or out.

Bibi Zainab (as) reports that the place was so cold at nights that no one could have proper sleep. During the day, it got hot like an oven. It is here that our fourth Imam, still under chains, the ladies and the children spent many days of great agony and discomfort.

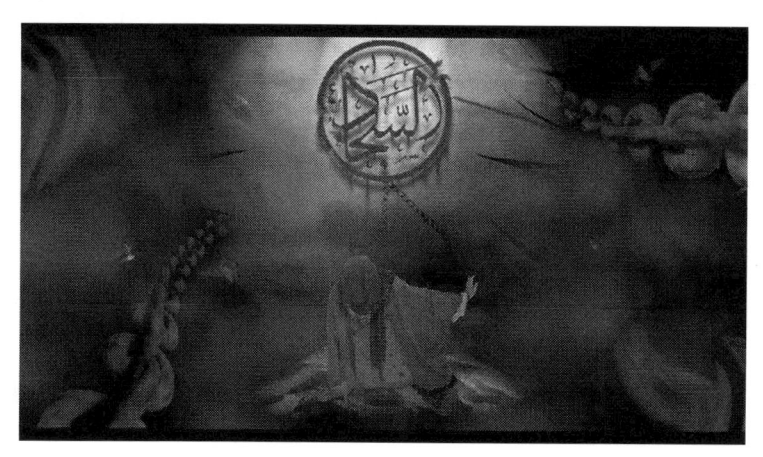

Bibi Sakina

Bibi Sakina was the youngest daughter of Imam Hussain (as) (who was otherwise known as Ruqayya). She was a vivacious child, full of love and happiness. Everyone loved Sakina. She was also a very religious girl. She enjoyed reading the Holy Quraan and never missed her prayers. From the age of two she took great care to make sure that her head and face were properly covered when in public.

Sakina was Imam Hussain's most beloved child. Our Imam was often heard to say, *"A house without Sakina would not be worth living in!"* She always had a sweet and cheerful smile and a very friendly nature. Other children sought her company as much as the grown-ups did. She was very generous and always shared whatever she had with others.

There was a special bond between Abbas and Sakina. He loved her more than he did his own children. If Sakina requested for anything, Abbas would not rest until he satisfied her request. There was nothing that Abbas would not do to make Sakina happy.

During the journey from Madina to Mecca and then Mecca to Karbala', Abbas was often seen riding up to where Sakina sat to make sure that she had everything she wanted. Sakina loved her uncle just as much. While in Madina she would, several times a day, visit the house in which Abbas lived with his family and his mother, Ummul Baneen.

Like any other four old when Sakina went to bed at night she wanted to spend some time with her father. Imam Hussain (as) would tell her stories of the Prophets (as) and of the battles fought by her grandfather Ali (as). She would rest her head on her father's chest and Hussain (as) would not move from her until she fell asleep. When from the second of Muharram the armies of Yazid began to gather at Karbala', Hussain (as) said to his sister Zainab (as), *"The time has come for you to get Sakina used to going to sleep without my being there!"* Sakina would follow her father at night and Hussain (as) had to gently take her to Zainab (as) or Rubaab.

At Karbala' when from the seventh Muharram water became scarce Sakina shared whatever little water she had with other children. When soon there was no water at all, the thirsty children would look at Sakina hopefully, and because she could not help them, she would have tears in her eyes. Sakina's lips were parched with thirst.

On the Ashura day, she gave her Mashk to Abbas. He went to get water for her. The children gathered round Sakina with their little cups, knowing that as soon as Abbas brought any water, Sakina would first make sure that they had some before taking any herself. When Sakina saw Imam Hussain (as) bringing the blood drenched 'alam she knew that her uncle Abbas had been killed. From that day on Sakina never complained of thirst.

Then came the time when the earth shook, and Sakina became an orphan! But even then, she always thought of the others first. She would console her mother on the death of Ali Asghar (as) and when she saw any other lady or child weeping Sakina would put her little arms around her.

Yes, Sakina never again asked anyone for water. Bibi Zainab (as) would persuade her to take a few sips, but she herself would never ask for water or complain of thirst!!!!

From the time when Imam Hussain (as) fell in the battlefield, Sakina forgot to smile! Kufa saw her as a somber little girl lost in thought. Quite often she would sit up at night. When asked if she wanted anything, she would say, *"I just heard a baby cry? Is it Asghar? He must be calling out for me!"*

Knowing that her weeping upset her mother, Sakina would cry silently and quickly wipe away her tears! In the prison in Shaam she would stare at the flock of birds flying to their nests at sunset and innocently ask Bibi Zainab (as), *"Will Sakina be going home like those birds flying to their homes?"*[220]

In the dead of the night Sakina got up with a shriek! She burst into torrents of tears. Her weeping and wailing aroused everybody. Zainab (as) rushed to her side and tried to console her. *"My beloved child,"* she said, *"How often have I told you that the last wish of your father was that you should endure all the sufferings that are inflicted on you with complete resignation to the will of Allah?"*

The child tried to control herself and replied: *"Dear aunt, I know that, but in my dream I saw my father. He came to me and said 'O' Sakina you have suffered enough. My darling, the days of your suffering are over. Now I have come to fetch you. Come with me!' O' sister of my beloved father! I narrated to him in my dream all the sufferings I have endured since he did not come back from the battlefield. I told him how I had gone in the dark night in search of him. What a dream it was and what a disappointment it is for me to know that in reality I shall be away from my beloved father!"*

Saying this she burst into uncontrollable lamentation. Such was the grief of the child that all the ladies lost control over their emotions and their wailing echoed through the prison walls.

Yazid in his palace adjoining the prison was pacing the floor. He heard the bemoaning and lamentations and sent for his servants to enquire about the cause. Soon they hurried back to report what happened. When Yazid was told that Sakina had seen her father in her dream and was disconsolate, he asked his men to put the head of Hussain (as) on a silver tray, cover it with a silk cloth and take it to the prison.

This was done and the prison door was opened. Yazid's men entered with the covered tray, and they placed it before Sakina. The child cried out: *"I am not hungry and I do not want*

---

[220] The Journey of Tears by Bashir Hassanali Rahim

food. I only want to see my father. Why has he left me after promising me that he would not leave me for long?"

One of Yazid's attendants removed the cloth from the tray and Sakina beheld the face of her father, the face she had kissed a million times. It was the same dear, dear face though the beard was smeared with blood. With a cry she flung herself on the tray and snatched the head from it, hugging it to her heart. In indescribable grief she bent down over the head putting her small cheeks against the cheeks of her father as she used to do when he was alive. Within a few moments her sobs stopped and so did her heartbeats.

When Zainab (as) saw the child lying motionless on the head of her father she went over to her and whispered with tears in her eyes: *"O' Sakina how long will you lie on your fathers head?"* She touched her hand only to find that life was extinct, to find that Sakina had gone with her father never to return to this world where she had known nothing but tortures and torments since her becoming an orphan. She realized that her beloved father Hussain (as) had kept his promise given to the child in her dream not to leave her in the cell.[221]

How was Sakina buried? Zainab (as) held the still child as Imam Zain ul 'Abideen dug a grave in the cell. As the grave was being filled up after the burial the mother let out a scream! How could anyone console Bibi Rubaab? What could they say? They huddled around her, and the prison walls began to shake with the cry: *"Yaa Sakina, Yaa mazloomah (O' Oppressed One)!!" Bibi Rubaab put her cheek on Sakina's grave and cried out: "Speak to me, Sakina! Only a word, my child! Speak to me!!"*

The tragedy of Karbala' had begun to arouse great sympathy for the Ahl ul Bait in Hejaz (Arabia) and Iraq. Even in

---

[221] Tears and Tributes by Zakir

Damascus some people began to ask whether it was necessary to inflict so much suffering on the members of the family of the Holy Prophet (s).

When the charming little Sakina died and the people of Damascus came to learn about the death of the little girl whom they had seen and come to admire, they began to talk openly about Yazid's cruelty. Yazid feared that the people might rise against him. He was now anxious to get rid of the prisoners.

He called Imam Zain ul 'Abideen and told him that he was prepared to free them and compensate them for the death of the martyrs. He also asked the fourth Imam whether they wanted to remain in Damascus or return to Madina. Imam Zain ul 'Abideen replied that he would consult his aunt Zainab (as).

When Imam spoke to Bibi Zainab (as) she was grief stricken at the audacity of Yazid in offering compensation. She said, *"Tell Yazid to talk of compensation with the Holy Prophet (s). We would certainly return to Madina. But first Yazid should provide a house so that we may hold mourning ceremonies for the martyrs in Damascus. We shall then go to Madina via Karbala' to visit the graves of the martyrs."*

Imam Zain ul 'Abideen conveyed the message to Yazid who after some hesitation agreed. In asking for a house to mourn the martyrs in Damascus Bibi Zainab (as) scored a major victory over Yazid. When this house was made available the ladies held Aza' al-Hussain (as) for seven days in the very city which was the capital of Yazid who had murdered Imam Hussain (as).

The women of Damascus poured in to offer their condolences and Bibi Zainab (as) and the other ladies would tell them of how the martyrs had been killed, how they had been denied water, how young children had been crying *al-'Atash* (I'm Thirsty), how Imam had taken Ali Asghar and pleaded for a few drops of water and how the baby had been slain. These tales so moved the ladies of Damascus that they would break into sobs and begin wailing and beating their chests.

Thus, in the very house of the murderer Bibi Zainab (as) laid the foundation of *Aza' al-Hussain*[222]. This is so much like the story of Musa (as). Firaun orders all the male children of Banu Israel to be put to death. Allah's miracle is that his Prophet finds refuge in the palace of the very Firaun who had plotted to kill him!

These *majalis*[223] have continued to this day. Every Muharram Shia all over the world gather together to mourn the tragedy that took place more that 1,350 years ago. These *majalis* have a great meaning for us. Firstly, they mean that we love our Imam and grieve for the suffering to which he was subjected.

Secondly, they mean that year after year we protest against all that Yazid stood for. We make a solemn promise to Allah never to follow Yazid's footsteps. In whatever country we may be, we have to remember that taking alcohol or any kind of drugs, is Yazid's way. To keep ourselves ignorant of Quraan or Islamic way of life is Yazid's way. To oppress anyone, is Yazid's way. To indulge in any un-Islamic activity, is Yazid's way. We can not truly mourn Hussain (as) and then continue to follow Yazid in our actions!![224]

---

[222] Mourning of Imam Hussain

[223] Gatherings

[224] The Journey of Tears by Bashir Hassanali Rahim

Benefits of Ziyarat Imam Hussain (as)

Hussain's place of martyrdom has been the visiting place for the lovers of Ahl ul Bayt who struggle to reach there enduring all the hardships and barriers placed before them. They come to his shrine to show their love and respect, honor his sacrifice, renew their covenant, pledge themselves to his goals, and follow the Prophet's advice about him.

The following is an interesting tradition from the Prophet (s) narrated by Ibn Abbas. He said: *"I came to the Messenger of Allah and saw al-Hassan (as) on his shoulder and al-Hussain (as) on his thigh; the Prophet (s) was kissing them saying, "O Allah befriend him who befriends them and be hostile to him who is hostile to them." Then he said, "O Ibn Abbas! It is as if I see the beard of my son al-Hussain (as) dyed with his blood, calling people but is not being answered, asking for help but is not being helped." I asked, "Who will do this?" He replied, "The wicked of my nation. May Allah deny them my intercession!" He then continued, "O Ibn Abbas! He who visits him while recognizing his rights, Allah shall write for him the reward of 1000 Hajj and 1000 Umra. Behold! He who visits him has indeed visited me, and he who visits me, it is as if he has visited Allah. And the right of the visitor of Allah over Him is that He shall not punish him by Fire. Behold! Answering (of supplications) is guaranteed under the dome of his grave, cure is placed in the soil of his place (of martyrdom), and the (succeeding) Imams are from his progeny... O Ibn Abbas! Their Wilaya (divine guardianship) is my Wilaya, which is the Wilaya of Allah. Fighting them is fighting me, which is fighting Allah. Making peace with them is making peace with me, which is making peace with Allah. He then recited: 'Their intention is to put out the light of Allah with their mouths; but Allah will complete His light, even though the disbelievers may detest.' (61:8)"*

The Ahl ul Bayt (as) put great emphasis on Ziyarat of the Chief of the Martyrs and urged their followers to it. In this manner, they kept alive the two important principles of faith, which are to love the friends of Allah and to disassociate from their enemies.

What follows is a brief presentation of the importance and benefits of visiting Imam al-Hussain (as) while recognizing him as an Imam whose obedience is obligatory, as mentioned in the traditions. Visiting Imam al-Hussain (as) is the sign of love for Ahl ul Bayt. Whoever loves Ahl ul Bayt should aspire to visit the grave of al-Hussain (as). One who does not visit Imam al-Hussain (as), is deficient in faith, and if he ever enters Paradise, his rank will be below the rank of believers in Paradise.

1.

2. When Allah intends goodness for a servant, He places love of al-Hussain (as) and love of visiting him in his heart.

3- According to several traditions, Ziyarat of Imam al-Hussain (as) is the best deed.

4- If a wretched person performs the Ziyarat of Imam al-Hussain (as), felicity shall be written for him, and he shall be continuously immersed in the blessings of Allah.

5- He who wishes to look towards Allah on the Day of Judgment, be relieved from the agony of death, and pass the stops of the Day of Judgment with ease should go for visitation of the grave of the Chief of Martyrs frequently.

6- The Messenger of Allah will embrace the visitors of Imam al-Hussain (as) on the Day of Judgment.

7- By performing the Ziyarat of the Chief of the Martyrs, one has made/observed a relationship with the Messenger of Allah and the guiding Imams. The requests of the pilgrim at his grave are fulfilled, his supplications are answered, sooner or later, and what the pilgrim had left behind is protected.

8- On the Day of Judgment, the visitors of Imam al-Hussain (as) will be seated on tables of light, because of what Allah will grant them in terms of endless dignity and honor. There will be no one on the Day of Judgment except that he would wish to have been a pilgrim to the grave of Imam al-Hussain (as). They shall be around heavenly tables with the Prophet (s), Lady Fatima (as), and the Imams while people are held in reckoning.

9- On the Day of Judgment, the Leader of the Faithful will command the bridge (al-Sirat) over Hell to yield to the visitors of Imam al-Hussain (as) and will command the fire (surrounding it) to hold back its scorching heat before them until they pass it with an Angel accompanying them.

10- If people know what Allah has placed in the visitation of the grave of Imam al-Hussain (as) in terms of excellence, they would die out of eagerness, and their breath would stop with a sigh.

11- The Messenger of Allah, Lady Fatima, and the Imams pray to Allah for forgiveness of the visitors of Imam al-Hussain (as).

12- The Angels pray to Allah for their forgiveness, welcome their arrival, accompany them in their departure, visit their sick, attend their funeral prayers whenever they die, continue to pray for them after their death, and open for them a gate to Paradise in their graves.

13- Allah has appointed 70,000 Angels around the blessed grave of the Chief of the Martyrs, who stay there until the Day of Judgment and perform prayers; each of their prayers is equal to 1000 prayers of human beings. The rewards and merits of these prayers are offered to the visitors of Imam al-Hussain (as).

14- The Angels cover the pilgrims with their wings in such a way that they feel the blessings of their presence.

15- For each day that a pilgrim resides in that sacred place, the reward of 1,000 months (of worship) is written for him.

16- If the pilgrim is killed by a transgressor on his way to Ziyarat of Imam al-Hussain (as), for the first drop of his blood, all his mistakes shall be forgiven. The Angels shall wash his character, cleansing and purifying it of the impurities merged in it from the characteristics of the people of disbelief, until it becomes pure like the purity of the immaculate Prophets, and they shall cleanse his heart and broaden his chest. He shall be rewarded with the right to intercede for his family and 1,000 of his friends. His grave shall be widened and illuminated. The Angels shall bring gifts for him from Paradise. On the Day of Judgment, the first people to embrace him shall be the Messenger of Allah and his successors.

17- If the pilgrim is detained on his way to Ziyarat of Imam al-Hussain (as), for each day of his captivity and distress, he shall have certain happiness (in this world and after his death) until the Day of Judgment. For any pain that his body receives, one million good deeds are written for him and one million evil deeds are removed from his record. On the Day of Judgment, He shall be able to speak with the Messenger of Allah until he is discharged from reckoning. The carriers of the throne shall embrace him and shall tell him, *"Ask for what you wish."* On the other hand, the person that has harmed him shall be taken to Hell without questioning and reckoning, and Allah's requital and His punishment for him shall be shown to whom he had harmed.

18- A pilgrim who goes to Ziyarat of Imam al-Hussain (as) in a state of fear and insecurity, he or she shall receive security on the day of great terror and shall be under the shadow of the throne on that day. He shall return from the Ziyarat forgiven and covered with mercy. The Angels shall greet him, and the Messenger of Allah

(s) shall receive him and shall pray for him.

19- If a person comes to Ziyarat of the Chief of the Martyrs by ship, and the ship sinks and he is drowned, a caller will call from the heaven, giving him glad tidings of Paradise.

20- For a single penny that the one gives as charity during the Ziyarat journey or pays to accommodate the journey of a visitor of Imam al-Hussain (as), Allah shall grant him 10,000 bounties. As per another Hadith, Allah shall write for him good deeds to the extent of the mount of Uhud and shall reimburse the money he has spent many fold.

21- For each footstep of one who goes to Ziyarat of Imam al-Hussain (as) on foot, Allah, the mighty and the majestic, writes a good deed for him and removes a sin from his record. When he reaches the sanctified place, Allah will write him amongst the prosperous.

22- He who ritually rinses his body (Ghusl) in the Euphrates (al-Furat) intending the Ziyarat of the Chief of the Martyrs, will be free of sins like the day he was born.

23- He who sets out for the Ziyarat of Imam al-Hussain (as) leaves behind his sins on the door of his house like a person who crosses abridge. He returns to his family while all his burdens and faults have been wiped out from his record. His sustenance increases, and Allah suffices him from what he is concerned about the affairs of his worldly life. No distressed one goes there, except that Allah returns him delighted.

24- When the pilgrim intends to leave the sacred place of Imamal-Hussain (as), a heavenly caller will call, and were it possible for the pilgrim to hear his voice, he would stay beside the grave of the Imam forever. The caller states, *"Blessedness (Tuba) is for you O servant! Indeed, you profited, are saved (from Hell), and are forgiven for the past (sins). Thus, resume (good) deeds."*

25- Numerous traditions confirm that he who visits the grave of al-Hussain (as) believing that he is an Imam assigned by Allah and that his obedience is obligatory, Allah shall forgive his past and future sins. In one of many traditions that convey this, Imam al-Sadiq swore by the name of Allah three times when stating this fact.

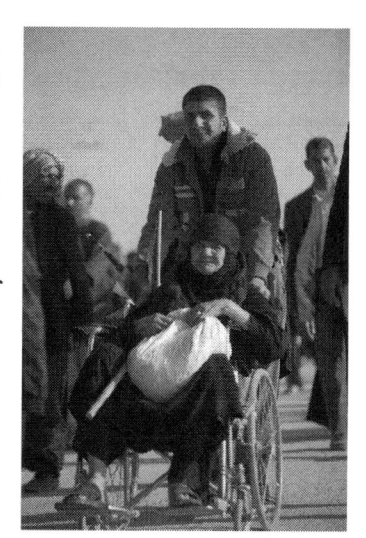

26- He who wishes to personally own a palace in Paradise should visit the grave of Imam al-Hussain (as). He who dies while he has not visited Imam al-Hussain (as) (due to negligence) is not a true Shia, and even if he is admitted to Paradise due to his love for the Ahl ul Bait, he will dwell there as a guest of the people of Paradise.

27- Visiting the grave of the Chief of the Martyrs will increase one's sustenance, prolongs one's life, and repels the cannons of evil. On the other hand, avoiding it will decrease one's natural lifetime and (spiritual) sustenance.

28- On the Day of Judgment, the visitor of Imam al-Hussain (as) will be allowed to intercede for 100 people of his choice even if for all of whom Hell had been necessitated, except for a Nasibi (one who hates the Ahl ul Bayt) because no one can intercede for a Nasibi.

29- Any number of pilgrimages to the House of Allah in Mecca, with all its due importance, cannot replace the Ziyarat of Imam al-Hussain (as). One who performs the pilgrimage to Mecca yearly yet does not visit al-Hussain (as), has indeed neglected one of the rights of Allah and

His Messenger, because performing it is a duty for every capable believing man and woman.

The excellence of the reward of the Ziyarat of Imam al-Hussain (as) is so much so that even some of the lovers of Ahl ul Bayt (as) who lived during their lifetime could not digest the traditions in this regard. Dharih al-Muharibi narrated: I said to Imam al-Sadiq (as), *"When I narrate to my folks and family some of the rewards of the pilgrimage to the grave of al-Hussain (as), they deny my narrations, and say that I am associating lies to Ja'far ibn Muhammad."* The Imam replied, *"O Dharih! Let people believe what they want. By Allah! Allah recounts His glory (to the Angels) for having servants who are visitors of al-Hussain (as). When a new pilgrim arrives, the favored Angels and the carriers of the throne receive him. Allah tells them, 'Don't you see the pilgrims of the grave of al-Hussain (as) who have come to him eagerly, and in love for him and for Fatima, the daughter of Allah's Messenger? By My might, majesty, and glory, I shall certainly make incumbent My honor for them, and shall surely enter them to My Paradise that I have prepared for*

My friends, Prophets, and Messengers. O My Angels! These are the visitors of al-Hussain (as), the beloved of Muhammad, My Messenger, and Muhammad is My beloved. Whoever loves Me, should love My beloved, and whoever loves My beloved, should love whom he loves. He who hates My beloved, has hated Me, and he who hates Me, it is My right to make him suffer with My severest torment, burn him with the heat of My fire, make Hell his abode, and torment him with a punishment that I have not punished anyone within the worlds.'"

When a faithful individual is reminded of the Prophet (s) and Ahl ul Bayt (as) and the troubles, they confronted and endured his heartbreaks and his tears flow.

A tearful eye is a blessing from Allah bestowed upon his servants and draws near even greater blessings. As one avoids sins, clears his heart from the love of worldly pleasures, implores Allah for help, turns to His chosen ones, he will have a more humble, responsive, and pure heart, as well as more tearful eyes. Although emotions such as liking, loving, and shedding tears depend on the state of one's heart, one should try to increase his love of what Allah loves even if his heart does not initially respond, by avoiding what Allah has prohibited and acting upon what He has ordered. One such order is to remember the tragedies that Ahl ul Bayt faced until one enters a sorrowful state and is induced to crying. According to the traditions, trying to cry for Imam al-Hussain (as) is rewarded even if one cannot bring himself to shed a tear. Putting oneself in the state of crying, in the meetings held in memory of the Chief of the Martyrs, may also affect others and make them cry.

The traditions concerning the rewards and benefits of remembering Ahl ul Bayt and their hardships and the shedding of tears for them, especially concerning Imam al-Hussain (as), are numerous and enlightening. Here, for the sake of brevity, only a few traditions will be quoted. For more comprehensive presentation, the readers may refer to the excellent book written by a great traditionist of the latter era, Sheikh Abbas al-Qummi, called, *"The Breath of the Grieved" (Nafasul Mahmum)*, which has also been translated into English.

Shedding tears for Imam al-Hussain (as) is considered a natural outcome of faith.

Ibn Sinan narrated: Imam al-Sadiq (as) said, *"The Prophet looked at al-Hussain (as) Ibn Ali as he was approaching. He sat him in his lap and said, 'Verily, for the martyrdom of al-Hussain (as) there shall be a heat in the hearts of the believers that shall never subside.'"* Then, the Imam continued, *"He (i.e., al-Hussain) is the martyr of tears."* I asked, *"What is the meaning of the martyr of tears, O son of the Messenger of Allah?"* He replied, *"No faithful remembers him except that he weeps."*

Rayyan Ibn Shabib narrated: Imam al-Ridha (as) said, *"O Son of Shabib! Muharram is a month in which even the people of the former age of ignorance forbade oppression and bloodshed due to its sanctity. However, this nation did not honor the sanctity of this month nor did they honor the sanctity of their Prophet. In this month, they killed the Prophet's progeny, enservantd his women, and plundered his belongings. May Allah never forgive them for these crimes.*

O Son of Shabib! If you wish to cry for anything or anyone, cry for al-Hussain Ibn Ali for he was slaughtered like a sheep. Eighteen members from his family who were unparalleled on earth were also killed along with him. Certainly, the seven heavens and earths cried because of the murder of al-Hussain (as). Four thousand Angels descended on earth to aid him, but (when they were allowed to reach there) they found him martyred. So, they remained at his grave, disheveled and dusty, and will remain there until the rising of al-Qa'im (Imam al-Mahdi), whereupon they will aid him. Their slogan will be, 'Vengeance for the blood of al-Hussain.'

O Son of Shabib! My father related to me from his father, who related from his grandfather that when my grandfather

Imam al-Hussain was martyred, the sky rained blood and red sands.

O Son of Shabib! When you weep over the afflictions of al-Hussain so that tears flow from your eyes onto your cheeks Allah will forgive all your sins, big or small, few or numerous.

O Son of Shabib! If you wish to meet Allah, the mighty and the majestic, free of sin, then perform the Ziyarat of al-Hussain.

O Son of Shabib! If it pleases you to abide in the palaces of Paradise in company of the Prophet and his family, then invoke Allah's curse upon the murderers of Imam al-Hussain.

O Son of Shabib! If you wish to earn the reward of those who were martyred with al-Hussain, then whenever you remember him, say, 'If only I had been with them so that I would have attained the great felicity.'

O Son of Shabib! If you desire to be with us in the highest degree of Paradise, then grieve in our sorrows and rejoice in our happiness. Remain attached to our love, for even if a person loves a stone, Allah shall resurrect him with it on the Day of Judgment."

Masma' Ibn Abd al-Malik narrated: Imam al-Sadiq asked me, "Do you remind yourself about what happened to al-Hussain?"

I answered, "Yes."

He asked, "Do you become grieved?"

I answered, "Yes, by Allah! And I shed tears so much so that my family members notice its effect on my face and I abstain from food in such situation."

He said, "May Allah have mercy on your tears. Truly, you are counted among the people who are concerned about us, *who rejoice in our happiness and grieve in our grief. Indeed, at the time of your death you will see the presence of my ancestors who will give you glad tidings and will give their recommendations to the Angel of death about you. He will thus become more compassionate and merciful towards you than a tenderhearted mother is to her child... None (among the believers) sympathetically weeps for us and for what befell us but that Allah bestows upon him His mercy, even before his tears flow from his eyes. (It is so rewarding that) if a drop from the tears that flows on his cheeks drops over Hell, it will extinguish its heat completely ..."*

Imam al-Sadiq (as) said: *"Anyone (of the believers) who recites poetry about al-Hussain (as) and cries and makes another one cry, Paradise will be written for both of them. Anyone (of the believers) in whose presence al-Hussain (as) is mentioned, and tears come to his eyes even to the extent of a wing of a fly, his reward is with Allah, and Allah will not be pleased with anything less than Paradise for him."*

Between the Two Holy Shrines - Karbala, Iraq

Imam Mahdi (atf) said: *"I pray for any believer who remembers the sufferings of my martyred grandfather, al-Hussain (as), and then prays for my relief (al-Faraj)"*[225]

---

[225] Ziyarat Nahiya Muqaddasa by Dr. Vahid Majd

Miscellaneous

There are many instances of the Shia being oppressed during the time of each of our respected Imam's. To write about all the noble souls who sacrificed their lives for the love of the Ahl ul Bayt would take numerous volumes of books. Saying that, I would just like to mention a few that came to mind in my conclusion of this book.

The Imprisonment of the Man from Damascus & Miracle of Imam Jawad

Ali ibn Khalid was a Zaydi, and as such he did not acknowledge the Imam's who came after Imam Ali Zayn al-Abidin, the fourth Imam. (37—95 A.H.) He lived in the time of Imam Muhammad Taqi al-Jawad, the ninth Imam (as). (195—220 A.H.) He says: *"I was in the city of Samarrah, when I was told that a man from Damascus who claimed to be a Prophet had been brought there and put in prison. Ali ibn Khalid went to see him and asked him what was the matter with him?"*

He said: *"I was in Syria where I was busy in worship at the site supposed to be the resting place of the Holy head of Imam Hussain (as), the Doyen of the Martyrs. One night I found all of a sudden, a man standing before me. He asked me to get up. I rose unconsciously and went a short distance with him when I found myself in the Masjid of Kufa. He asked me if I knew that masjid. I said that I did and that it was the Masjid of Kufa. He offered his prayers. I too offered my prayers along with him. Then we set out again. We had not gone far, when I noticed that we were in the Masjid al-Nabi. There he invoked blessings on the Holy Prophet (s), and then we both offered our prayers.*

Thereafter, we left that place too and set out again. A

moment later I found myself in Mecca. There we circumambulated the Ka'bah, and then left the Masjid al-Haram.

After walking a few steps, I found myself at my original place in Damascus. Then all of a sudden that man disappeared from my sight as if he was a slight draught of breeze that swept my face and vanished.

A year had passed since this incident when I met that man again. He took me on the same journey and we visited once again all the Holy places that we had visited the first time. When he wanted to leave me, I said to him: 'I beseech you in the name of Him who has given you such a wonderful power to be so kind as to let me know your name'. He said 'I am Muhammad ibn Ali ibn Musa ibn Ja'far'. He was the ninth Imam.

Now I proceeded to tell this extraordinary event to everyone whom I met, till the news reached Muhammad ibn Abd al-Malik al-Zayyat. He ordered my arrest and accused me of posing as a Prophet. Now, as you see, I am in prison".

Ali ibn Khalid says further: "*I said to him: Would you like me to write to Muhammad ibn Abd al-Malik about your case?*"

"You may", he said: I wrote, but in my reply he wrote back: "Tell him to ask the person who took him in one night from Damascus to Kufa and then to Mecca and Medina and then brought him back to Damascus to get him released from this prison also".

I was distressed by this reply. Next morning, I went to the prison to convey the reply to that man. There I saw a large number of soldiers and a big crowd of other people coming and going around the prison. I asked the people what had happened? They told me that the prisoner who claimed to be a Prophet had escaped from the prison and it was not known how he had escaped whether he had gone into the ground or had flown to the sky like a bird.

Ali ibn Khalid says: *"After seeing this incident I gave up my Zaydite creed and became a Twelver Shi'ah, believing in the Imamate of Imam Jawad, the ninth Imam in the line of Ali ibn Abi Talib.*[226]

The Murder of Nisa'i the Famous Sunni Author of one the Sahih Sitta

Another instance of persecution was Abdu'r-Rahman Ahmad Ibn Ali Nisa'i's murder. He was a dignified man and is regarded as one of the authors of Sahih Sitta (Six Authentic Books of the Sunni sect). He belonged to the high-ranking ulema of the Sunni's in the 3rd century A.H. When he reached Damascus in 303 A.H., he saw that, because of the Bani Umayya, the residents of that place openly abused the name of Amiru'l- Mu'minin Ali Bin Abi Talib after every ritual prayer, particularly in the address of congregational prayers. He was much grieved to see this, and he decided to collect all the hadith of the Holy Prophet (s) in praise of Amiru'l-Mu'minin (as) with the chain of their sources, all of which he remembered. Accordingly, he wrote a book, *Khasa'isu'l-Alawi*, in support of the exalted position and virtues of Ali. He used to read to the people from the pulpit the hadith from his book the praises of the Imam.

One day when he was narrating the high merits of Ali (as), a rowdy group of fanatics dragged him from the pulpit and beat him. They punched his testicles and catching hold of his penis dragged him out of the mosque and threw him into the street. As a result of these injuries he died after a few days. His body was taken to Mecca where he was laid to rest. These events

---

[226] Master and Mastership by Allama Murtaza Mutahhari

are the consequence of enmity and ignorance.[227]

THE 6TH IMAM, ABU ABDILLAH JA'FAR B. MUHAMMAD (AS) SAID:

"A PERSON WHO SIGHS IN GRIEF OVER THE WRONGS METED OUT TO US, THAT SIGH IS EXTOLMENT OF ALLAH, AND HIS ANXIETY ABOUT US IS AN ACT OF WORSHIP, AND TO CONCEAL OUR SECRETS IS A STRUGGLE IN THE WAY OF ALLAH".

THEN ABU ABDILLAH (AS) SAID:

"THIS TRADITION OUGHT TO BE WRITTEN IN GOLD."[228]

---

[227] Peshawar Nights by Sultanul Waizin Shirazi

[228] Al-Amali by Sheikh al-Mufid

Printed in Great Britain
by Amazon

325acb3d-4454-4aac-84ce-ea93d244be34R01